REPORT

OF THE

CHICAGO RELIEF AND AID SOCIETY

OF

DISBURSEMENT OF CONTRIBUTIONS

FOR THE

SUFFERERS BY THE CHICAGO FIRE.

PRINTED FOR THE
CHICAGO RELIEF AND AID SOCIETY,
At the Riverside Press.
1874.

RIVERSIDE, CAMBRIDGE:
STEREOTYPED AND PRINTED BY
H. O. HOUGHTON AND COMPANY.

OFFICERS

OF THE

CHICAGO RELIEF AND AID SOCIETY.

PRESIDENT.
HENRY W. KING.

CHAIRMAN EXECUTIVE COMMITTEE.
WIRT DEXTER.

TREASURER.
GEORGE M. PULLMAN.

BOARD OF DIRECTORS.

HENRY W. KING, PRESIDENT.

WIRT DEXTER.
GEO. M. PULLMAN.
R. LAIRD COLLIER.
T. M. AVERY.
N. K. FAIRBANK.
MARSHALL FIELD.
J. McGREGOR ADAMS.
J. MASON LOOMIS.
C. H. S. MIXER.
B. G. CAULFIELD.
E. C. LARNED.
C. G. HAMMOND.
H. A. JOHNSON.
T. W. HARVEY.
N. S. BOUTON.
E. B. McCAGG.
MURRY NELSON.
J. T. RYERSON.
JULIUS ROSENTHAL.
A. B. MEEKER.
ABIJAH KEITH.

JOSEPH MEDILL, MAYOR (*ex-officio*).

EXECUTIVE COMMITTEE.

WIRT DEXTER, CHAIRMAN.

C. G. HAMMOND.
HENRY W. KING.
T. M. AVERY.
T. W. HARVEY.
N. K. FAIRBANK.
JULIUS ROSENTHAL.
H. A. JOHNSON.
R. LAIRD COLLIER.
N. S. BOUTON.
J. McGREGOR ADAMS.

CHARLES L. ALLEN, SECRETARY.

C. G. TRUSDELL, GENERAL SUPERINTENDENT.

PREFACE.

THE Chicago Relief and Aid Society having been constituted the almoner of the great Fund contributed to alleviate the sufferings of the people rendered homeless and destitute by the disastrous fire which laid waste the fairest sections of our city, is led by sacred considerations to make a full, and we hope, useful report of the manner in which this trust has been discharged.

Those who bore large share in these contributions have frequently and urgently expressed the wish that such a report might in due time be published, and that in view of the possibility of a similar calamity befalling other parts of the world, the experiences and agencies found valuable and efficient by this Society should be embodied in some permanent form.

The sympathy of mankind, and its fruit of charity, were not wholly unlooked for in the time of our unprecedented need, yet so instant and world-wide were these, that they came as a revelation of neighborly helpfulness, causing surprise not only to the stricken thousands who were the grateful recipients, but to all mankind.

To indicate in some measure this sympathy and charity, letters and telegrams of earliest dates are here embodied, representative in their character, received from all sections of our own and distant lands, and from all classes of persons, alike the humblest and most distinguished.

It is impossible in the nature of the case to account for all the merchandise, provisions, and other supplies sent within the few days immediately succeeding the fire, and which were doubtless received and efficiently disbursed, but without permanent, and in most cases without any account having been taken of their source or distribution.

It is quite possible also that many letters and telegrams did not reach the proper authorities or the persons for whom intended, by reason of the derangement of the postal and telegraph service.

It is not possible in this report to account for moneys or merchandise sent to other charitable societies, or to individuals, and concerning which this Society has no knowledge. It is believed, however, that these first contributions, of which no account can ever be rendered, reached the objects and wrought the great and immediate good intended.

In the survey of such various materials at command, and wholly without precedent in their use, we confess to the great distrust with which we undertake the performance of this task. We can only assure the philanthropic world of the purpose of this Society to express the gratitude of the community which it represents; to render in some measure a service to civilization, as well as to perform an obvious duty.

CONTENTS.

CHAPTER V.

CHAPTER VI.

CHAPTER VII.

CHAPTER VIII.

CHAPTER IX.

CHAPTER X.

CHAPTER XI.

CHAPTER XII.

CHAPTER XIII.

CHAPTER XIV.

CHAPTER XV.

CHAPTER XVI.

CHAPTER XVII.

REPORT

OF THE

CHICAGO RELIEF AND AID SOCIETY.

CHAPTER I.

TOPOGRAPHY OF CHICAGO.

THE conflagration of Chicago, October the 8th and 9th, 1871, in the amount of property destroyed, and the number of people rendered homeless and dependent, is without parallel in the history of ancient or modern times. In order to show how it was possible that such a fire could occur, it is deemed necessary to give some account of the topography and physical conditions of the city, and so much of its history as will indicate its rapid growth and hasty construction.

Chicago, the chief city of Illinois and of the Northwestern States, is situated on Lake Michigan, at the mouth of the Chicago River, eighteen miles north of the extreme southerly point of the lake, and has an elevation of six hundred feet above the ocean. On the west of the city is a wide expanse of prairie, on the south and north is timber, making the precise point of Chicago an opening or sort of funnel through which the adverse winds of prairie and lake sweep over the city. The Chicago River affords the only good harbor on the west side of the lake near its southern extremity, and to this fact is due the natural fitness of this site for a mart of commerce, and primarily its chief importance. The city is located on both sides of this river; a sluggish stream originally of the nature of a lagoon, and which at a point three-quarters of a mile from its mouth is formed by the junction of two branches, one flowing from the northwest, and the other from the southwest.

The city is thus divided into three natural parts. The South Side, as it is called, includes the territory east of the South Branch and south of the main river. The North Side embraces the area east of the North Branch and north of the river. The West Side is that part of the city west of the two branches.

The United States Government established a military post at this point in 1804, which was destroyed in 1812. It was rebuilt in 1816, and continued to be garrisoned till 1837. During these years Fort Dearborn served as a resting-place for emigrants passing to the west, and a hamlet slowly clustered about it, which took the name of Chicago.

In 1831 Cook County was organized, and in 1832 the total tax list of the county was returned by the sheriff at \$148$\frac{23}{100}$.

In the spring of 1833 Congress made an appropriation of \$30,000, for improving the harbor; a post-office was established; and in the month of August of the same year Chicago was incorporated as a town.

The following are the statistics of the corporation for this year: —

Area of the town, about	560 acres.
Number of inhabitants	550
Number of voters	29
Number of buildings	175
Valuation of property	\$60,000.00
Valuation of taxable property	\$19,560.00
First year's taxes	\$48.90

In 1834 the poll list had increased to one hundred and eleven, and a loan for sixty dollars was negotiated for the opening and improvement of streets.

The construction of the Illinois and Michigan Canal, which was begun in 1836 and completed in 1848, and by which the chain of the great northern lakes was united to the waters of the Mississippi River, made Chicago the *entrepôt* of this water traffic, and constituted the first memorable impulse in the growth of the city.

The first charter of the City of Chicago was passed by the Legislature, and approved March 4, 1837, and the first election was held under this charter on the first of May following.

The first census was taken in the following July, and the population was shown to be four thousand one hundred and seventy-nine souls. In this year the city contained four warehouses, three hundred and ninety-eight dwellings, twenty-nine drug stores, nineteen provision stores, ten taverns, twenty-six groceries, five churches.

In 1839 three thousand cattle were driven in from the prairies, slaughtered, packed, and shipped, and thus began one of the chief branches of business here largely controlled, and one which has contributed to the rapid increase of the city's population and wealth.

In the same year the first shipment of wheat, amounting to one thousand six hundred and seventy-six bushels, was sent from this port, which is now the world's chief market for bread-stuffs and provisions.

The following table shows the increase of population from the time Chicago was incorporated as a city in 1837 to 1871.

POPULATION.

Year.	Population.	Year.	Population.
1837	4,179	1854	65,872
1838	4,000	1855	80,023
1839	4,200	1856	86,000
1840	4,470	1857	93,000
1841	5,500	1858	Not taken.
1842	6,590	1859	90,000
1843	7,580	1860	109,263
1844	8,000	1861	120,000
1845	12,088	1862	137,030
1846	14,169	1863	150,000
1847	16,859	1864	161,288
1848	20,023	1865	187,446
1849	23,047	1866	200,000
1850	28,269	1867	220,000
1851	34,000	1868	242,383
1852	38,734	1870	298,977
1853	60,662	1871	334,270

During these years of rapid growth and prosperity, the history of the city becomes so complex that it is unnecessary, for our purposes, to trace it further, except in the most comprehensive form.

The method of communication between the three sections of the city up to a recent time had been a system of bridges upon turn-tables or pivots, thrown across the river at intervals of two blocks, the average width of which is about two hundred feet. Vessels are usually towed up and down the river by steam-tugs, and these bridges were necessarily an impediment to navigation, and not less serious impediment to vehicles and pedestrians. Therefore some different method of communication became a necessity.

And in 1869 a tunnel was built at Washington Street, arched for two hundred and ninety feet, by which an uninterrupted communication was established between the South and West divisions; the tunnel having a double roadway for vehicles, and a twelve feet passage for pedestrians. In September, 1871, a tunnel of much better construction was completed, under the line of Lasalle Street, establishing similar communication between the North and South sides of the city.

The streets of Chicago were laid out on a liberal plan and at right angles, with sidewalks ten feet wide, and usually with grass plats, and shrubbery separating these from the ample space remaining for vehicles in the centre.

In the year 1870 the city occupied a space of six miles long and about three miles wide; houses dotted the lake shore, however, from its southern boundary to Hyde Park, and from its northern boundary to Lake View, in all a distance of more than ten miles.

To some extent Chicago had begun to tear away the buildings at first constructed for the homes of the people and the demands of traffic, and which were, for the most part, small, unsightly, and insecurely built. Other structures of enduring material, convenience of arrangement, grandness of proportion, and architectural ornamentation, were being rapidly erected in their stead.

But side by side with these were the wooden and inflammable buildings which at first sprang up by the necessities of the case, and gave to the city a unique and in some instances an almost grotesque appearance. Within the limits of the burnt district alone there were nearly thirty miles of pine sidewalks.

The most massive buildings, though constructed mainly

of imperishable materials, as it was supposed, had joists, partitions, floorings, cornices, door and window frames of wood, and only the smallest number of the largest warehouses had iron shutters. The river winding through the entire length of the city, and through the very heart of it, was lined with immense lumber yards, coal yards, planing mills, sash factories, and various other combustible materials.

The commerce of the city had been necessarily occupied, as it seemed, in providing only for its instant and temporary demands. And the public authorities had fallen in with what seemed to be the necessities of the case, and provided mainly for these commercial interests rather than for the permanent security of the homes and property of the people. Thus the topographical and physical conditions of the city, together with the character of its structures and improvements, rendered it peculiarly exposed to an overwhelming catastrophe.

During the days when Chicago was being wasted by the flames, the devouring elements were making similar havoc in other parts of the country. In the lumber regions of Wisconsin, Michigan, and Minnesota, the fires were laying bare thousands of acres of timber land, and destroying every organic substance on a vast range of improved land in these States. Fires were occurring at the same time in the Rocky Mountain region, California, Nevada, Kansas, Missouri, Indiana, Pennsylvania, and New York. Over the whole region of the Northwest the autumn had been without rains, and indeed, for twenty-four months, the country had not been visited by the usual drenching storms, and the earth, the trees, and the dwellings were baked to a crisp.

These features grouped together, but in brief outline, may indicate the conditions which made possible the conflagration which swept out of existence the accumulations of years, and rendered homeless thousands of people. A complete theory of the fire is not intended to be sought, but must be left among the desiderata in speculative and scientific research.

CHAPTER II.

AN ACCOUNT OF THE FIRE.

THE imagination is the only faculty of the human mind equal to any comprehension of the appalling night when Chicago was in flames.

During the continuance of the fire, a driving gale of wind was surging up from the southwest, and the increasing magnitude of the conflagration, from hour to hour, caused a mingled sense of terror and despair.

From the pine tenements of its origin, the fire swept into the central quarter of the city, compactly built, mostly of brick, stone, and iron; and thence, into the heart of that section containing the most palatial residences, and onward until it laid waste one entire section of the city.

As the fire raged, the number of homeless people became greater and greater, and possessed by fright many were inapt in expedients of self-preservation.

Many sought temporary abodes for themselves and their effects, in the hospitable homes of their near neighbors. But the hope of security here was soon surrendered, and those who had been but mere spectators of their neighbors' calamities, were now panic-stricken householders, engaged in taking care of themselves, their families, and their property, until thousands together were fleeing west, north, and south, in consternation and frequently in despair of saving life.

And thus the streets were filled with an indescribable mass of fugitives, forcing their way through the stifling clouds of dust, smoke, and cinders, and the confusion and utter chaos of the night — a night lurid with flames, the reflection of which, in itself, gave to the countenances of these fleeing thousands an awe-stricken and almost unearthly aspect. The hissing and crackling of the flames, and the deafening roar of the gale, the pelting cinders and brands, and the crumbling of material, gave tragic coloring to the scene, and leaves the night memorable in the minds of those who witnessed it, as a picture of appalling horror, distinct in its outlines, weird in its dark shadings, but utterly incapable of verbal representation.

LOSSES BY THE FIRE.

In the West Division, where the fire originated, the number of acres burned over was one hundred and ninety-four. There were five hundred buildings, mostly of an inferior class, destroyed, which were inhabited by about two thousand five hundred persons.

The burned area in the South Division comprised four hundred and sixty acres. This district, though comparatively small in extent, was the business centre of the city. It contained a great majority of those structures which were costly and magnificent, and were filled with the merchandise which made the city the great emporium of the Northwest. All the wholesale stores of considerable magnitude, the daily and weekly newspaper offices, the principal hotels, the public halls and places of amusement, the great railroad depots, and a large number of the most splendid residences, and in short, the great bulk of the wealth, and the chief interests of the city, were located in this district. In this division alone there were three thousand six hundred and fifty buildings destroyed, which included one thousand six hundred stores, twenty-eight hotels, sixty manufacturing establishments, principally of clothing, boots and shoes, and jewelry, and the homes of about twenty-two thousand people.

In the North Division, not less than one thousand four hundred and seventy acres were swept by the flames, destroying thirteen thousand three hundred buildings, the homes of seventy-five thousand people, about six hundred stores, and one hundred manufacturing establishments.

The total area burned over in the city, including streets, was two thousand one hundred and twenty-four acres, or nearly three and one-third square miles. This area contained about seventy-three miles of streets, eighteen thousand buildings, and the homes of one hundred thousand people.

The following statistics of the destruction of property, and the actual losses by the fire, seem to be approximately reliable.

BUILDINGS.

Eighty business blocks, enumerated	$8,515,000	
Railroad depots, warehouses, and Board of Trade	2,700,000	
Hotels	3,100,000	
Theatres, etc.	865,000	
Daily newspapers (offices and buildings)	888,000	
One hundred other business buildings	1,008,420	
Other taxable buildings	28,880,000	
Churches and contents	2,989,000	
Public schools and contents	249,780	
Other public buildings, not taxed	2,121,800	
Other public property (streets, etc.)	1,763,000	
		$53,000,000

PRODUCE, ETC.

Flour, 15,000 barrels	$97,500	
Grain	1,245,000	
Provisions (4,400,000 lbs)	340,000	
Lumber	1,040,000	
Coal	600,000	
Other produce	1,940,000	
		$5,262,500

BUSINESS — WHOLESALE AND RETAIL.

Dry goods	$13,500,000	
Drugs	1,000,000	
Boots, shoes, leather, etc.	5,175,000	
Hardware, iron, and other metals	4,510,000	
Groceries and teas	4,120,000	
Wholesale clothing	3,650,000	
Jewelry, etc.	1,300,000	
Musical Instruments, etc.	900,000	
Books on sale	1,145,000	
Millinery	1,610,000	
Hats, caps, and furs	1,060,000	
Wholesale paper stock	700,000	
Shipping and dredges	800,000	
Manufactures (stock, machinery, and product)	13,255,000	
Other stocks, and business furniture	25,975,000	
		$78,700,000

PERSONAL EFFECTS.

Household property	$41,000,000	
Manuscript work (records, etc.)	10,000,000	
Libraries, public and private	2,010,000	
Money lost (Custom House $2,130,000)	5,700,000	
		$58,710,000

GENERAL SUMMARY.

Improvements (buildings, etc.)	$53,000,000	
Produce, etc.	5,262,000	
Manufactures	13,255,000	
Other business property	65,445,000	
Personal effects	58,710,000	
Miscellaneous	378,000	
		$196,000,000

In the first table the contents of churches and schools and of newspaper offices are included in the footing of $53,000,000. Placing these where they belong, we shall have the following distribution of loss: —

On Buildings, etc.	$52,000,000	
On Business Property (besides buildings)	85,000,000	
On Personal Effects	59,000,000	
		$196,000,000
On this there was a salvage in foundations and available material for rebuilding of about		4,000,000
Making the actual loss		$192,000,000

The value of property in the city, real and personal, taxed and untaxed, was estimated at $575,000,000, of which, according to the above figures, the loss by the fire was thirty-three per cent. of the whole.

MUNICIPAL LOSSES.

The destruction of city property as estimated by the different Boards, is as follows: —

IN CARE OF BOARD OF PUBLIC WORKS.

City Hall, including furniture	$470,000	
Bridges burned	71,000	
Damage to street pavements	270,000	
Damage to sidewalks and crossings, payable out of general fund	70,000	
Damage to water-works	35,000	
Damage to lamp posts	15,000	
Damage to fire hydrants, reservoirs, sewers, water service, etc.	60,000	
		$1,085,000

FIRE DEPARTMENT LOSS.

Buildings, worth	$60,000	
Furniture	7,500	
Damage to engines	8,200	
Damage to hose	10,000	
Damage to fire-alarm telegraph	45,000	
		$130,700

POLICE DEPARTMENT LOSS.

Buildings, worth .	$53,600	
Furniture, fixtures, etc.	32,500	
		$86,100

Board of Education loss, buildings, furniture, etc., worth	$251,000
Board of Health lost property worth . .	$15,000
Add Sidewalks	$941,380
Total Municipal Losses	$2,509,180

CHAPTER III.

ACTION OF THE CITY AUTHORITIES.

TOWARD nightfall, on Monday, the flames had accomplished their work of destruction. The homeless people of the South Side were for the most part received into the abodes of their more fortunate neighbors, or taken to the hearts and hospitalities of those to whom a day before they were utter strangers, without formalities or ceremonies, for a kindred sorrow which had left no human interest untouched had done its work.

Those of the North Division had betaken themselves for the night to the sands of the lake shore, to Lincoln and other small parks, and the prairies. Comparatively few had found shelter for the night.

Those of the West Division who were left homeless were for the most part sheltered in the churches and school-houses, and on the prairies on the northwest of the city. Comparatively few of those who had fled before the flames, had tasted food since early Sunday evening, and hunger came to them to add its terrors to those of exposure, and in many instances apprehension of death.

And then came the greatest terror of all, the consciousness of the fact that families had been separated; husbands and wives, parents and children were missing. The flight had been so rapid, and in all directions the thoroughfares had been so obstructed, and in some cases utterly impassable, by the crowding of vehicles and masses of people, and the city itself a wave of fire; it is no marvel that under these circumstances, thousands for the time were lost sight of, and became lonely wanderers; and that hundreds perished in the flames.

The seeds of permanent or temporary disease sown, the bodily suffering and mental anguish endured, can never have statistical computation, or adequate description.

The bodies of the dead, not less than three hundred in number, who perished in the flames, were given interment at the county burying ground.

The city authorities were prompt in their endeavors to bring order out of the chaos which, in some measure, we have essayed to describe. The Mayor telegraphed to neighboring cities, first of all, for engines to help stay the ravages of the fire, and for bread to feed the homeless and destitute.

A council of city officers was held, who issued and signed the following, which was the first proclamation from the Mayor and Government: —

PROCLAMATION.

WHEREAS, In the providence of God, to whose will we humbly submit, a terrible calamity has befallen our city, which demands of us our best efforts for the preservation of order and the relief of suffering: —

Be it known, That the faith and credit of the city of Chicago are hereby pledged for the necessary expenses for the relief of the suffering.

Public order will be preserved. The police and special police now being appointed will be responsible for the maintenance of the peace and the protection of property.

All officers and men of the Fire Department and Health Department will act as special policemen without further notice.

The Mayor and Comptroller will give vouchers for all supplies furnished by the different relief committees.

The headquarters of the City Government will be at the Congregational Church, corner of West Washington and Ann Streets.

All persons are warned against any act tending to endanger property. Persons caught in any depredation will be immediately arrested.

With the help of God, order and peace and private property will be preserved.

The City Government and the committee of citizens pledge themselves to the community to protect them, and prepare the way for a restoration of public and private welfare.

It is believed the fire has spent its force, and all will soon be well.

R. B. MASON, *Mayor.*
GEORGE TAYLOR, *Comptroller.*
(By R. B. MASON.)
CHARLES C. P. HOLDEN, *President Common Council.*
T. B. BROWN, *President Board of Police.*

October 9, 1871, 3 P. M.

Promptly following the above proclamation, and growing out of the exigencies of the day, or the hour, as it came, others were issued; and no better account of the action of the municipal government can be given than that which is contained in these several official papers, and therefore, without comment, which would be needless, the text of these proclamations, which in some instances were only fly-sheets, is herein given.

BREAD ORDINANCE. — NOTICE.

CHICAGO, *October* 10, 1871.

The following ordinance was passed at a meeting of the Common Council of the City of Chicago, on the 10th day of October, A. D. 1871: —

An Ordinance.

Be it ordained by the Common Council of the City of Chicago: —

SECTION 1. That the price of bread in the City of Chicago for the next ten days is hereby fixed and established at *eight* (8) *cents per loaf* of twelve ounces, and at the same rate for all loaves of less or greater weight.

SECTION 2. Any person selling or attempting to sell any bread within the limits of the City of Chicago, within said ten days, at a greater price than is fixed in this ordinance, shall be liable to a penalty of ten (10) dollars for each and every offense, to be collected as other penalties for violation of City Ordinances.

SECTION 3. This Ordinance shall be in full force and effect from and after its passage.

Approved October 10*th*, 1871.

R. B. MASON, *Mayor.*

Attest:

C. T. HOTCHKISS, *City Clerk.*

MAYOR'S PROCLAMATION—ADVISORY AND PRECAUTIONARY.

1. All citizens are requested to exercise great caution in the use of fire in their dwellings, and not to use kerosene lights at present, as the city will be without a full supply of water for probably two or three days.

2. The following bridges are passable, to wit: All bridges (except Van Buren and Adams streets) from Lake Street south, and all bridges over the North Branch of the Chicago River.

3. All good citizens who are willing to serve are requested to report at the corner of Ann and Washington streets, to be sworn in as special policemen.

Citizens are requested to organize a police for each block in the city, and to send reports of such organization to the police headquarters, corner of Union and West Madison streets.

All persons needing food will be relieved by applying at the following places: —

At the corner of Ann and Washington; Illinois Central Railroad Round-house.

M. S. R. R. — Twenty-second Street Station.

C. B. & Q. R. R. — Canal Street Depot.

St. L. & A. R. R. — Near Sixteenth Street.

C. & N. W. R. R. — Corner of Kinzie and Canal streets.

All the public school-houses, and at nearly all the churches.

4. Citizens are requested to avoid passing through the burnt districts until the dangerous walls left standing can be leveled.

5. All saloons are ordered to be closed at 9 P. M. every day for one week, under a penalty of forfeiture of license.

6. The Common Council have this day by ordinance fixed the price of bread at eight (8) cents per loaf of twelve ounces, and at the same rate for loaves of a less or greater weight, and affixed a penalty of ten dollars for selling, or attempting to sell, bread at a greater rate within the next ten days.

7. Any hackman, expressman, drayman, or teamster charging more than the regular fare, will have his license revoked.

All citizens are requested to aid in preserving the peace, good order, and good name of our city.

R. B. MASON, *Mayor*.

October 10, 1871.

On the same date appeared the following: —

LET US ORGANIZE FOR SAFETY IN CHICAGO.

1. The Mayor's headquarters will be at the corner of Ann and Washington streets.

2. Police headquarters at the corner of Union and Madison streets.

3. Every special policeman will be subject to the orders of the sergeant for the district in which he performs duty. The sergeants of districts will be appointed by the police superintendent.

4. Five hundred citizens for each of the districts will be sworn in as special policemen.

5. The sergeant of each district will procure of police headquarters rations and supplies for special policemen in his district.

6. Orders to the police will be issued by the Superintendent of Police.

7. The military will coöperate with the police organization and the city government in the preservation of order.

8. The military are invested with full police power, and will be respected and obeyed in their efforts to preserve order.

R. B. Mason, *Mayor.*

Health Department, corner of Ann and Washington streets.

DISTRIBUTION OF RELIEF.

1. All supplies of provisions will be received and distributed by the Special Relief Committee, of which O. E. Moore is Chairman and C. T. Hotchkiss Secretary. Headquarters of Committee on Ann and West Washington streets.

2. All contributions of money will be delivered to the City Treasurer, David A. Gage, who will receipt and keep the same as a Special Relief Fund.

3. All moneys deposited at other places for the relief of the city will be drawn for only by the Mayor of this city.

4. No moneys will be paid out of the Special Relief Fund except upon the order of the Auditing Committee.

George Taylor, City Comptroller, Mancell Tallcott, Esq., of the West Division, and Brock McVickar, of the South Division, are hereby appointed such Auditing Committee.

5. Railroad passes from the city will be issued under direction of the Relief Committee, corner of Ann and West Washington streets, until further orders.

Given under my hand this 11th day of October, 1871.

R. B. Mason, *Mayor.*

LOCATION OF CITY OFFICES.

From and after the 12th day of October, 1871, the Mayor's Office, City Comptroller's, City Treasurer's, and other City Offices will be at the corner of Hubbard Court and Wabash Avenue.

The Department of the Board of Public Works and other departments of the City Government will be located in the immediate vicinity of the other City Offices.

Given under my hand this 11th day of October, 1871.

Attest: R. B. Mason, *Mayor.*

C. T. Hotchkiss, *City Clerk.*

MILITARY CORRESPONDENCE.

BY LIEUTENANT-GENERAL SHERIDAN.

Chicago, *October* 9.

To General Belknap, *Secretary of War:* —

The city of Chicago is almost utterly destroyed by fire. There is now reasonable hope of arresting it if the wind, which is yet blowing a gale, does not change. I ordered, on your authority, rations from St. Louis, tents from Jeffersonville, and two companies of infantry from Omaha. There will be many houseless people, much distress.

P. H. Sheridan, *Lieutenant-general.*

Chicago, *October* 9.

W. W. Belknap, *Secretary of War:* —

The fire here last night and to-day has destroyed almost all that was very valuable in this city. There is not a business house, bank, or hotel left. Most of the best part of the city is gone. Without exaggerating, all the valuable portion of the city is in ruins. I think not less than 100,000 people are houseless, and those who had the most wealth are now poor. It seems to me to be such a terrible misfortune that it may with propriety be considered a national calamity.

P. H. Sheridan, *Lieutenant-general.*

BY THE SECRETARY OF WAR.

Washington, *October* 10.

Lieutenant-general Sheridan, *Chicago:* —

I agree with you that the fire is a national calamity; the sufferers have the sincere sympathy of the nation. Officers at the depots at St. Louis, Jeffersonville, and elsewhere, have been ordered to forward supplies liberally and promptly.

Wm. W. Belknap, *Secretary of War.*

To the Mayor of Chicago: —

General Sheridan has been authorized to supply clothing, tools, and provisions from the depots at Jeffersonville and St. Louis to the extent and ability of the Department.

(Signed) William W. Belknap, *Secretary of War.*

TURNING AFFAIRS OVER TO GENERAL SHERIDAN

The preservation of the good order and peace of the city is hereby intrusted to Lieutenant-general Philip H. Sheridan, United States Army.

The police will act in conjunction with the Lieutenant-general in the preservation of the peace and quiet of the city, and the Superintendent of the Police will consult with him to that end. The intent being to preserve the peace of the city without interfering with the functions of the city government.

Given under my seal this October 11, A. D. 1871.

R. B. Mason, *Mayor.*

The following was issued by the Police Commissioners: —

Ordered, by the full Board of Police, that all powers granted to special police since Sunday, October 8th, be and hereby are revoked. The large military force now in the city under the command of Lieutenant-general Sheridan, coöperating with the regular police organization, is now deemed sufficient to maintain good order and quietude for the future.

T. B. Brown,
F. Gund,
Mark Sheridan, } *Commissioners.*

Headquarters Military Division of the Missouri,
Chicago, *October* 12, 1871.

To his Honor the Mayor: —

The preservation of peace and good order of the city having been intrusted to me by your Honor, I am happy to state that no case of outbreak or disorder has been reported. No authenticated attempt at incendiarism has reached me, and the people of the city are calm, quiet, and well-disposed.

The force at my disposal is ample to maintain order, should it be necessary, and protect the district devastated by fire. Still, I would suggest to citizens not to relax in their watchfulness until the smouldering fires of the burnt buildings are entirely extinguished.

P. H. Sheridan, *Lieutenant-general.*

HEADQUARTERS MILITARY DIVISION OF THE MISSOURI,
CHICAGO, *October* 17, 1871.

TO HIS HONOR MAYOR MASON, *Chicago, Illinois:* —

I respectfully report to your Honor the continued peace and quiet of the city. There has been no case of violence since the disaster of Sunday night and Monday morning. The reports in the public press of violence and disorder here are without the slightest foundation. There has not been a single case of arson, hanging, or shooting — not even a case of riot or street fight. I have seen no reason for the circulation of such reports. It gives me pleasure to bring to the notice of your Honor the cheerful spirit with which the population of this city have met their losses and suffering.

Very respectfully, your obedient servant,
P. H. SHERIDAN, *Lieutenant-general.*

DISMISSING CITY EMPLOYÉS.

To the Heads of all Departments of the City Government: —

The late fire has, of necessity, caused the suspension of public improvements, and of much work heretofore done in various departments of the city government. It therefore becomes necessary to discharge all employés of the city government whose services are not absolutely required. I respectfully request that you, in your several departments, immediately give notice of discharge to all such, with a view to the most rigid economy, which must now be observed in all departments.

R. B. MASON, *Mayor.*

[Not dated. Issued the 19th.]

FAST DAY RECOMMENDED.

In view of the recent appalling public calamity, the undersigned, Mayor of Chicago, hereby earnestly recommends that all the inhabitants of this city do observe Sunday, October 29, as a special day of humiliation and prayer; of humiliation for those past offenses against Almighty God, to which these severe afflictions were doubtless intended to lead our minds; of prayer for the relief and comfort of the suffering thousands in our midst; for the restoration of our material prosperity, especially for our lasting improvement as a people in reverence and obedience to God. Nor should we even, amidst our losses and sorrows, forget to render thanks to Him for the arrest of the devouring fires in time to save so many homes, and for the unexampled sympathy and aid which has flowed in upon us from every quarter of our land, and even from beyond the seas.

Given under my hand this 20th day of October, 1871.

R. B. MASON, *Mayor.*

DISCONTINUANCE OF MILITARY AID.

THE MAYOR TO GENERAL SHERIDAN.

LIEUTENANT-GENERAL P. H. SHERIDAN, *U. S. A.*: —

Permit me to tender you the thanks of the city of Chicago and its whole people for the very efficient aid which you have rendered, in protecting the lives and property of the citizens, and in the preservation of the general peace and good order of the community. I would like your opinion as to whether there is any longer a necessity for the continued aid of the military in that behalf. Very respectfully,

R. B. MASON, *Mayor*.

CHICAGO, *October* 22.

GENERAL SHERIDAN TO THE MAYOR.

CHICAGO, ILL., *October* 23.

TO HIS HONOR, R. B. MASON, *Mayor of Chicago*: —

SIR, — I have the honor to acknowledge the receipt of your kind note of the date of yesterday, and in reply I beg leave to report a good condition of affairs in the city. If your Honor deem it best, I will disband the volunteer organization of military on duty since the fire, and will consider myself relieved from the responsibility of your proclamation of the 11th instant. With my sincere thanks for your kindness and courtesy in my intercourse with you, I am respectfully your obedient servant,

P. H. SHERIDAN, *Lieutenant-general*.

THE MAYOR TO GENERAL SHERIDAN.

LIEUTENANT-GENERAL P. H. SHERIDAN, *U. S. A.*: —

Upon consultation with the Board of Police Commissioners, I am satisfied that the continuance of the efficient aid in the preservation of order in this city which has been rendered by the forces under your command in pursuance of my proclamation is no longer required. I will therefore fix the hour of 6 P. M. of this day as the hour at which the aid requested of you shall cease. Allow me again to tender you the assurance of my high appreciation of the great and efficient service which you have rendered in the preservation of order and the protection of property in this city, and to again thank you in the name of the city of Chicago and its citizens therefor. I am respectfully yours,

R. B. MASON, *Mayor*.

CHICAGO, *October* 23.

ORDERS OF DISBANDMENT.

HEADQUARTERS MIL. DIV. OF THE MISSOURI,
CHICAGO, ILL., *October* 24, 1871.

Special Orders No. 76.

1. The companies of the Fourth, Fifth, Sixth, Ninth, and Sixteenth United States Infantry, on duty in this city, are hereby relieved, and will proceed to their respective stations as follows: —

Companies F, H, and K, of the Fourth, and E, of the Sixteenth, to Louisville, Ky.

Companies A, H, and K, of the Fifth, to Fort Leavenworth.

Company I, of the Sixth, to Fort Hays.

Companies A and K, of the Ninth, to Omaha.

The Quartermaster's Department will furnish the necessary transportation.

By command of Lieutenant-general Sheridan.

JAMES B. FRY, *A. A. G.*

Official:

M. V. SHERIDAN, *Lt.-col. A. D. C.*

CHAPTER IV.

EXPRESSIONS OF SYMPATHY.

NO words suggested by the thoughts of the present time, although only comparatively distant from the date of the fire, could give an adequate impression of the sentiments of mankind as expressed in the telegrams and letters received within the days immediately succeeding that great calamity; and as embodied in the official action of Corporations, Commercial Associations, Municipal and State authorities, not only of our own but foreign lands. As it is the intent to make record of the surprising philanthropy of the whole world, which no event in its history had ever heretofore called forth, it is deemed the part of gratitude as well as historic integrity and accuracy, to record the words, and were it possible the very voice, which came in love and helpfulness to our city — a city prostrate and really crying for help. But not more urgent in its need, than the civilized world was quick to respond.

The heart of mankind was touched with a sense of brotherhood, so lyric that poets will sing of it; so unique that historians will record it; and so divine that philosophy will treasure it as the first memorable proof, that the race, of all lands and creeds, has advanced beyond the forms of civic and religious limitation, and henceforth, in its march toward a final and perfect civilization will unite its sentiments and endeavors wherever man is to be pitied, or his sufferings assuaged.

The telegrams and letters of earliest dates, representative in character and chosen from many hundreds containing similar expressions of condolence and assistance, are here embodied in the order of their reception.

TELEGRAMS.

PITTSBURG, PA., *October* 9, 1871.

MAYOR OF CHICAGO: —

We can reach you with our Fire Department in ten hours. Answer quick.

JARED M. BRUSH, *Mayor.*

PITTSBURG, PA., *October* 9, 1871.

MAYOR OF CHICAGO: —

Pittsburg Council have appropriated one hundred thousand dollars ($100,000). A large meeting of citizens is being now held and subscriptions being taken up. Will send funds to-morrow.

JARED M. BRUSH, *Mayor.*

MILWAUKEE, WIS., *October* 9, 1871.

R. B. MASON, *Mayor:* —

We send a car load of provisions by morning train. Will do all we can for you.

H. LUDINGTON, *Mayor.*

CLEVELAND, OHIO, *October* 9, 1871.

HON. R. B. MASON, *Mayor:* —

We send you on seven-twenty train two car loads provisions consisting of bread, crackers, dried beef, cheese, etc. A committee of citizens accompanies them. Will send more supplies to-morrow.

F. W. PELTON, *Mayor.*

CLEVELAND, OHIO, *October* 12, 1871.

HON. R. B. MASON: —

The Police force of Cleveland have placed in the hands of our committee two thousand dollars for the relief of the suffering Police of Chicago.

F. W. PELTON, *Mayor.*

BOSTON, MASS., *October* 9, 1871.

MAYOR OF CHICAGO: —

Boston sends her warmest sympathies to Chicago. Will do our utmost to aid you. What are your needs?

WILLIAM GASTON, *Mayor.*

4

BOSTON, MASS., *October* 10, 1871.

MAYOR OF CHICAGO:—

You are authorized to draw on Kidder, Peabody, & Co., of this city for the sum of one hundred thousand dollars for the relief of the sufferers by the late fire at Chicago. WILLIAM GASTON, *Mayor.*

BOSTON, MASS., *October* 11, 1871.

THE MAYOR OF CHICAGO:—

The undersigned committee of the citizens of Boston expect to reach Chicago Saturday morning to offer their services in coöperation with you for the relief of your suffering people.

WM. GRAY,
ALEXANDER H. RICE,
EBEN D. JORDAN.

BOSTON, MASS., *October* 12, 1871.

HON. R. B. MASON:—

Such as we had we sent you. Your loss is ours. We commend you to God in your great calamity. May He shelter your wives and little ones. WILLIAM CLAFLIN.

BROOKLYN, N. Y., *October* 9, 1871.

THE MAYOR OF CHICAGO:—

The Common Council of the city of Brooklyn have unanimously adopted resolutions expressing the deepest sympathy for the authorities and inhabitants of Chicago in their suffering, and are calling a public meeting immediately, to raise funds for their relief.

JACOB J. BERGEN, *President.*

BROOKLYN, N. Y., *October* 10, 1871.

THE MAYOR OF CHICAGO:—

The Common Council of the city of Brooklyn have this day appropriated the sum of one hundred thousand ($100,000) dollars in cash, or its equivalent in the necessaries of life for the relief of the sufferers of Chicago. Please confer with the Mayor of Brooklyn as to your immediate wants. J. J. BERGEN, *Prest. Board of Aldermen.*

PHILADELPHIA, PA., *October* 9, 1871.

HIS HONOR THE MAYOR OF CHICAGO:—

Our city is sad with the news of your terrible disaster. Our citizens sympathize with your people. Give me particulars.

DAN'L M. FOX, *Mayor of Philadelphia.*

PHILADELPHIA, PA., *October* 9, 1871.

MAYOR OF CHICAGO:—

The Commercial Exchange of Philadelphia having heard with unspeakable anguish of the terrible calamity that has been permitted to overtake your city, desire to express their sympathy by extending to it, in this hour of its deep distress, material aid in any manner you may indicate.

S. J. CONELY, *Prest. Com'l Exchange.*

PHILADELPHIA, PA., *October* 12, 1871.

HON. R. B. MASON, *Mayor:*—

Your dispatch this moment received, and the city of Philadelphia instantly responds by authorizing you to draw on A. J. Drexel, Treasurer of Executive Committee, at sight, for one hundred thousand dollars ($100,000), raised in one hour at a meeting of citizens held at the Mayor's office, and this is sent with the profound sympathy of our city and people.

Have your draft drawn or countersigned by treasurer of your duly authorized committee. Inform me also who is chairman of your committee.

We have appointed committees to canvass the city, and hope to have the pleasure of sending you a hundred thousand dollars more. Our people are alive to the distress prevailing in your community.

Very respectfully,

DAN'L M. FOX, *Mayor of Philadelphia.*

NEW YORK, *October* 9, 1871.

MAYOR OF CHICAGO:—

I have sent the following dispatch to our Mayor here:—

"To Hon. A. O. HALL, Mayor, New York:—

"I have a telegram purporting to come from the Mayor of Chicago, giving report of lamentable destruction of life and property in that city by fire. I take this early opportunity to notify you that I have a force at our depot, foot of 23d Street, New York, and will there receive and forward, free of charge, on fast train, through to Chicago, all contributions which the citizens of New York may contribute in aid of the sufferers. My messenger will come immediately and confer with you.

(Signed) JAY GOULD, *President.*"

Let our company know at once anything we can do for you.

JAY GOULD, *President Erie R. R.*

NEW YORK, *October* 9, 1871.

MAYOR OF CHICAGO:—

We are using every effort to raise supplies to send forward to you by fast train for the suffering of your city.

Have you any instructions to give us? Be sure and let me hear from you to-night.

JAMES FISK, JR.,
Vice-President Erie Railroad.

NEW YORK, *October* 10, 1871.

HON. R. B. MASON, *Mayor:* —

You may draw on me for fifty thousand dollars ($50,000) to be applied by yourself, in conjunction with my friends Messrs. Field & Leiter and Mr. John V. Farwell, of your place, in aid of the sufferers by the terrible calamity which has befallen your city, or, if preferred, I will purchase and send forward that amount in such articles of necessity as you may designate.

ALEXANDER T. STEWART.

NEW YORK, *October* 10, 1871.

THE MAYOR OF CHICAGO: —

On account of contribution New York Cotton Exchange you can draw, or we will remit, five thousand dollars ($5,000) in aid of sufferers. Answer.

M. B. FIELDING,
Chairman Relief Committee, 118 *Pearl Street.*

PRODUCE EXCHANGE, NEW YORK, *October* 10, 1871.

THE MAYOR OF CHICAGO: —

Ten thousand dollars now to your credit in this institution for benefit of suffering people in your city.

More coming in. Will you draw for it at sight?

ISAAC H. REID, *President.*
B. C. BOGERT, *Treasurer.*

NEW YORK, *October* 10, 1871.

HON. ROSWELL B. MASON, *Mayor Chicago:* —

In accordance with a cable telegram received from our London friends, Messrs. J. S. Morgan & Co., this morning, we telegraphed you as follows, viz.: "J. S. Morgan & Co., London, cable this morning as follows: 'Place five thousand dollars ($5,000) at disposition of citizens of Chicago as our contribution for relief of sufferers, with expressions of our warmest sympathies. Draw on us for the amount, advising us by mail.'"

We hereby confirm this telegram, and your draft on us as above shall have due honor.

Yours very truly,
DREXEL, MORGAN, & CO.

MANCHESTER, N. H., *October* 10, 1871.

THE MAYOR OF CHICAGO: —

Upon the recommendation of our citizens in mass meeting this evening, the City Council have unanimously appropriated the sum of fifteen thousand dollars ($15,000), in aid of the suffering citizens of Chicago, which awaits your order. Proffering the deepest sympathies of our whole population to the people of Chicago,

I remain, sincerely yours,

JAMES A. WESTON, *Mayor.*

NEW HAVEN, CONN., *October* 10, 1871.

HON. R. B. MASON:—

The city of New Haven, Conn., sympathizes with you in your sore affliction, and wishes to know how she can best serve you. Please reply soon as convenient.

H. G. LEWIS, *Mayor.*

ALBANY, N. Y., *October* 10, 1871.

MAYOR OF CHICAGO:—

You are hereby authorized to make draft on Edward Duncan, Treasurer, for ten thousand dollars ($10,000), for benefit of sufferers by the fire.

J. D. TOWNER,
President Board Lumber Dealers.

ALBANY, *October* 10, 1871.

HON. MR. MASON, *Mayor of Chicago:*—

You can draw on me for the sum of ten thousand dollars ($10,000), the first installment of the contribution of the citizens of Albany for the relief of the suffering people of Chicago.

GEO. H. THATCHER, *Mayor.*

BOSTON, MASS., *October* 10, 1871.

MAYOR OF CHICAGO:—

Our entire receipts of Friday night, thirteenth, will be forwarded to you, for the sufferers of your city. We trust that our example will be followed by the entire profession through the country.

Respectfully,

J. C. TROWBRIDGE & Co.
St. James Theatre.

BROOKLYN, N. Y., *October* 10, 1871.

THE MAYOR, *Chicago:*—

A meeting has been called to-day of the Mechanics' and Traders' Exchange of this city, for the purpose of extending their aid and sympathy to your citizens. You shall have our means.

Yours truly,

H. HARTEAU, *President.*

BALTIMORE, MD., *October* 10, 1871.

THE MAYOR OF CHICAGO: —

You may draw on me at sight at the National Bank of Baltimore, for two thousand and fifty dollars ($2,050), the offering of the Protestant Episcopal Church, in General Convention last night, for the houseless and homeless inhabitants of the city of Chicago, without distinction of race or sect.

WM. STEVENS PERRY, *Secretary.*

BUFFALO, N. Y., *October* 10, 1871.

HIS HONOR THE MAYOR OF CHICAGO: —

The Board of Directors of this company have voted the sufferers of your city two thousand dollars ($2,000). The money is at your disposal.

ALEX. MARTIN,
Secretary Buffalo German Insurance Company.

CHARLESTON, ILL., *October* 10, 1871.

MAYOR: —

The sympathies of Charleston go forth to night in shape of eatables and clothing enough to fill one or two cars. This is a small tribute, but we give it cheerfully, and more if needed.

J. W. OGDEN, *Mayor.*

ERIE, PA., *October* 10, 1871.

THE MAYOR OF CHICAGO: —

At a meeting of the citizens of the city of Erie it was resolved that the city authorities are required to raise and forward the authorities of Chicago fifteen thousand dollars ($15,000), in aid of the sufferers.

JAMES C. MARSHALL, *President.*
E. CAMPHAUSEN, *Acting Mayor.*

HAMILTON, ONTARIO, *October* 10, 1871.

MAYOR OF CHICAGO: —

The citizens of Hamilton send heartfelt expressions of sorrow to the citizens of Chicago in this their great calamity. Draw on me at sight for two thousand dollars as a first installment in aid of the sufferers.

D. B. CHISHOLM, *Mayor.*

ITHACA, N. Y., *October* 10, 1871.

THE MAYOR OF CHICAGO: —

We, the Baptist pastors of the State of New York, in pastoral conference assembled, before proceeding to the transaction of the business which has called us together, tender to our fellow citizens and fellow Christians in the city of Chicago, our heartfelt sympathies in the great calamity which has befallen them, and pledge ourselves to enlist our congregations, as far as possible, in relieving the distress occasioned by the recent conflagration in that city; by unanimous vote of the conference.

MONTREAL, CANADA, *October* 10, 1871.

THE MAYOR OF CHICAGO:—

To whom shall we remit funds to aid you? Members of Board of Trade and Corn Exchange have made a beginning by subscribing ten thousand dollars. Public meeting to-morrow.

JOHN YOUNG, *President Board of Trade.*

TROY, N. Y., *October* 10, 1871.

MAYOR OF CHICAGO:—

At a meeting of the Board of Trade held here to-night it is—

Resolved, That the citizens of Troy deeply sympathize with the people of Chicago in the terrible disaster which has befallen them.

Resolved, That a committee of sixteen be appointed by the chairman to collect money, food, and clothing to be forwarded to the proper authorities at Chicago for the relief of the destitute and suffering people of that city.

Resolved, That the Mayor of Chicago be authorized to draw on N. B. Squires, chairman of the Troy Relief Committee, for ten thousand dollars ($10,000). CHAS. EDDY, *President Board of Trade.*

SARATOGA, N. Y., *October* 10, 1871.

THE MAYOR OF CHICAGO:—

The citizens of Saratoga Springs send by express to-night one thousand dollars ($1,000) for the sufferers by the great fire. Further remittances will follow. JOHN C. HURLBERT, *Chairman Committee.*

SARATOGA, N. Y., *October* 10, 1871.

THE MAYOR OF CHICAGO:—

I send by mail to-day draft for one hundred dollars ($100) from C. E. Durkee Steam Fire Company No. Three (3) for sufferers.

C. E. DURKEE.

ROCHESTER, N. Y., *October* 10, 1871.

MAYOR OF CHICAGO:—

In what manner can Rochester best aid the sufferers of your unfortunate city? CHARLES M. BRIGGS,
Mayor of Rochester.

POUGHKEEPSIE, N. Y., *October* 10, 1871.

MAYOR OF CHICAGO:—

Four thousand dollars ($4,000) deposited in City National Bank subject to your direction. Draw on W. A. Fanning, Treasurer, or direct how to send. H. J. EASTMAN, *Mayor.*

POUGHKEEPSIE, N. Y., *October* 10, 1871.

MAYOR OF CHICAGO: —

Twenty-five hundred dollars ($2,500) just contributed by private citizens. Will be immediately expressed. Large sum to follow, and also bedding and clothing.

H. J. EASTMAN, *Mayor.*

The following telegram from His Excellency, the President, explains itself: —

EXECUTIVE MANSION, WASHINGTON,
October 11, 1871.

TO HON. SAMUEL HOOPER, *Boston, Mass.*: —

Would it not be well for the good people of Boston to dispense with the ceremony and expense of a public reception on the occasion of my visit to your city, and appropriate such portion of the fund set apart for that purpose, as is deemed advisable, for the relief of the sufferers by the Chicago disaster? I am sure such a course would please me.

U. S. GRANT.

BALTIMORE, MD., *October* 11, 1871.

MAYOR OF CHICAGO: —

The city of Baltimore extends partial relief to your suffering people.

Resolved, by the Mayor and City Council of Baltimore, that the sum of one hundred thousand dollars be, and the same is hereby appropriated for the relief of the sufferers in Chicago, and that the Mayor of Baltimore be authorized to telegraph the Mayor of Chicago this action on the part of the authorities without delay.

Telegraph me what you need most, how this amount can be best expended for the relief of the pressing necessities of your sufferers.

Respectfully, ROBERT T. BANKS, *Mayor.*

CHELSEA, MASS., *October* 11, 1871.

THE MAYOR OF CHICAGO: —

Shall we send you money or suppplies? If supplies, what and kind?

J. W. FLETCHER, *Mayor.*

GALVESTON, TEXAS, *October* 11, 1871.

PRESIDENT CHAMBER COMMERCE, OR MAYOR: —

Chamber of Commerce passed the following resolutions and appointed committee to raise funds, which is now at work.

Resolved, That we have heard with deep pain of the disastrous conflagration that has afflicted our sister city of Chicago, and we tender our fellow merchants and citizens of that city our heartfelt sympathies in their distress.

Resolved, That a committee of three be appointed to raise funds by subscription, and such other measures as they may deem practicable, for the relief of the sufferers by the great fire in Chicago.

The resolution was amended to read, "a committee of three be appointed with authority to add to their number persons not members of the Chamber," then passed unanimously.

J. S. THRASHER, *Chairman.*

LOCKPORT, N. Y., *October* 11, 1871.

MAYOR, CITY OF CHICAGO: —

A meeting was called last evening in this city to sympathize with you in affliction, and responded to with generosity. We now want to know what you most need, money, clothing, bedding, or food.

ORIGEN STORRS, *Mayor City Lockport.*

LYNN, MASS., *October* 11, 1871.

TO THE MAYOR OF CHICAGO: —

Lynn sends her sympathies to stricken Chicago, and casts in her mite for the relief of her citizens. I have authorized Messrs. Doggett, Bassett, & Hill to draw on me for five thousand dollars ($5,000), more to come.

EDWIN WALDEN, *Mayor.*

NEW YORK, *October* 11, 1871.

R. B. MASON, ESQ., *Mayor:* —

Draw at sight upon this company for the sum of one thousand dollars ($1,000), for relief of sufferers by the Chicago fire.

WM. M. ST. JOHN, *Secretary,*
Standard Fire Insurance Co.

NEW YORK, *October* 11, 1871.

THE HON. R. B. MASON, *Mayor:* —

The New York Gold Exchange have appropriated and subscribed about twelve thousand dollars ($12,000), for the relief of the sufferers.

In what manner shall the remittance be made?

R. L. EDWARDS, *Treasurer.*

NEW YORK, *October* 11, 1871.

MAYOR OF CHICAGO: —

Barings telegraph us as follows: "Subscriptions for Chicago sufferers opened in London by the Lord Mayor. We and others give one thousand pounds each."

DUNCAN, SHERMAN, & CO.

NEW YORK, *October* 11, 1871.

HON. R. B. MASON, *Mayor of Chicago:* —

Draw at sight on Knickerbocker Life Insurance Company for fifteen hundred dollars ($1,500). Distribute same among needy of your city to the best of your judgment.

ERASTUS LYMAN, *President.*

NEW YORK, *October* 11, 1871.

HON. R. B. MASON, *Mayor*:—

The managers in this city of the North British and Mercantile Insurance Company have received from J. W. Carter, Esq., chairman of the London Board, by cable the following instructions:—

"Subscribe five thousand dollars ($5,000), for the Chicago sufferers, settle all losses promptly. Draw at three days' sight." We hold the amount, five thousand dollars, subject to your sight draft.

WM. CONNER, *Associate Manager.*

POUGHKEEPSIE, N. Y., *October* 11, 1871.

MAYOR OF CHICAGO:—

Draw upon me through Chemical National Bank for one thousand dollars ($1,000), raised by town of Hyde Park, N. Y.

JAMES ROOSEVELT.

PITTSFIELD, MASS., *October* 11, 1871.

MAYOR CHICAGO:—

This town forwards this morning to you fifty-five hundred dollars ($5,500). We will forward clothing to-morrow. JOHN C. WEST,

Chairman Board of Selectmen.

PALMYRA, N. Y., *October* 11, 1871.

THE MAYOR OF CHICAGO:—

Draw for three hundred dollars ($300), contributed by citizens for relief of your sufferers. GEO. W. CUYLER,

President First National Bank.

SAN FRANCISCO, *October* 11, 1871.

R. B. MASON, MAYOR CHICAGO:—

San Francisco tenders her heartfelt sympathies for her sister city in distress, and is making every effort for the relief of the sufferers. In pursuance of the general sentiment I called a public meeting to-day of the leading citizens, which I am happy to say was largely attended, and twenty-five thousand dollars ($25,000) subscribed on the spot. We have organized committees, who are soliciting subscriptions from the citizens at large, and expect to raise one hundred thousand dollars. To whom shall we remit it? THOS. H. SELBY, *Mayor.*

SYRACUSE, N. Y., *October* 11, 1871.

MAYOR OF CHICAGO:—

The city of Syracuse has voted twenty-five thousand dollars ($25,000), for the relief of your suffering citizens.

Advise me who will draw for it, as the money is now subject to the draft of the proper parties. F. E. CARROLL, *Mayor.*

TOWANDA, PA., *October* 11, 1871.

MAYOR OF CHICAGO:—

Towanda Lodge, two hundred ninety, Knights of Pythias, sends fifty dollars ($50) relief suffering brothers. IRA B. HUMPHREY, *W. C.*

TORONTO, ONT., *October* 11, 1871.

HIS HONOR THE MAYOR OF CHICAGO:—

I have the honor to transmit the following resolution, which was this afternoon unanimously adopted by the council.

JOSEPH SHEARD, *Mayor of Toronto.*

Resolved, That this council, on behalf of the citizens of Toronto, desire to give expression to the profound sorrow with which they regard the fearful conflagration that has befallen the city of Chicago; that they deeply sympathize with the inhabitants of that city in the serious affliction that at this moment presses so heavily upon them; that they lament with heartfelt pain the direful calamity that has, within a few hours, swept away their property, their homes, and their means of subsistence, and carried off, by a terrible death, some of their fellow citizens; and in extending to them the hand of friendship in this their hour of trouble, his worship, the Mayor of this city, be and he is hereby authorized to telegraph the Mayor of Chicago to draw upon our City Chamberlain for the sum of ten thousand dollars ($10,000) gold, to assist in meeting their present necessities.

STEPHEN RADCLIFF, *Clerk of the Council.*

COUNCIL CHAMBER, *October* 11, 1871.

AMSTERDAM, N. Y., *October* 11, 1871.

MAYOR OF CHICAGO:—

Draw on me for eight hundred dollars ($800), through First National Bank of Amsterdam, contributed by our citizens to aid your sufferers.

MATHIAS VAN BROCKLER,
President Amsterdam Village.

WILMINGTON, ILL., *October* 11, 1871.

R. B. MASON, *Mayor of Chicago:*—

Our citizens want to render assistance. We can shelter families or furnish food. Notify us what is most needed.

WM. H. ODELL, *Mayor.*

ALBANY, N. Y., *October* 12, 1871.

R. B. MASON, *Mayor:*—

The employés of E. J. Larrabee & Co. send twenty-five hundred (2,500), loaves of aerated bread. Will reach Chicago Saturday morning at eight o'clock. E. J. LARRABEE & Co.

CANANDAIGUA, N. Y., *October* 12, 1871.

HON. R. B. MASON, *Mayor*:—

Our citizens have subscribed over twenty-five hundred dollars ($2,500), and the amount no doubt will be considerably increased, for the relief of Chicago sufferers. How and when shall it be forwarded?

THOS. S. BEALS.

CLEVELAND, OHIO, *October* 12, 1871.

ANSON STAGER:—

Titusville, Pa., sends funds and a car of cooked provisions. Will reach Chicago to-morrow morning.

J. BRIGGS.

EASTON, PA., *October* 12, 1871.

MAYOR OF CHICAGO:—

Edward H. Green, President of Town Council, holds subject to your order, two thousand dollars ($2,000), the municipal donation to Chicago sufferers. Advise him.

RICHARD O'BRIEN,
W. U. Telegraph Co.

ERIE, PA., *October* 12, 1871.

THE MAYOR OF CHICAGO:—

We ship you a quantity of provisions by train to-day, donated by the employés of the Phila. and Erie R. R. at Renovo, PA.,

WM. A. BALDWIN,
General Supt., P. & E. R. R.

HARTFORD, CONN., *October* 12, 1871.

MAYOR OF CHICAGO:—

Hartford this evening raised twenty-five thousand dollars ($25,000), for the benefit of the sufferers in Chicago. How and when will you have it?

CHARLES R. CHAPMAN,
Mayor of Hartford.

HAVERHILL, MASS., *October* 12, 1871.

TO THE MAYOR OF CHICAGO:—

You are authorized to draw at sight on the Treasurer of the City of Haverhill for ten thousand dollars ($10,000), as a donation from our city, to be applied to the relief of the sufferers by the late fire.

W. R. WHITTENER, *Mayor.*
D. B. TENNY, *Treasurer.*

JERSEY CITY, N. J., *October* 12, 1871.

TO HIS HONOR, MAYOR MASON:—

DEAR SIR,—As Treasurer of the Chicago relief fund of this City, I beg leave to inform you that I have this day deposited in the Second National Bank of this City the sum of thirty thousand dollars subject to your draft, as Treasurer of the Chicago relief fund of your city.

Very respectfully yours,
C. H. O'NEILL, *Mayor.*

KITTANNING, PA., *October* 12, 1871.

R. B. MASON, Esq., *Mayor*:—

Kittanning sends by express to-day eleven hundred and thirty-two dollars ($1,132). E. A. GOLDEN.

MORRISTOWN, NEW JERSEY, *October* 12, 1871.

MAYOR MASON:—

Our New Jersey people are sending you clothing in considerable quantities, and the money contributions will exceed any our State has ever before gathered. THEODORE W. RANDOLPH, *Governor.*

MONTREAL, CANADA, *October* 12, 1871.

MAYOR OF CHICAGO:—

A public meeting of our citizens was held here yesterday, when a resolution expressive of great sympathy for the disaster at Chicago was unanimously adopted. A large and influential committee was appointed to collect subscriptions, and they are now actively at work. Ten thousand dollars' worth of clothing, blankets, etc., will probably be forwarded to Chicago to-night by express passenger train. They are carried free by the railroads, and I understand the U. S. Government will let them pass customs free of duty. A special messenger will go with them and report himself to you on arrival.

Subscriptions from this city promise to be large, and we propose to use the money in sending you clothing, blankets, etc. I trust this will meet with your wishes. C. J. BRYDGES,

Chairman Executive Committee.

MIDDLETOWN, N. Y., *October* 12, 1871.

R. B. MASON, *Mayor City of Chicago*:—

We have collected twenty-five hundred dollars ($2,500) for the sufferers of your city.

How can we safely send it? Answer.

ELISHA P. WHEELER.

NEW YORK, *October* 12, 1871.

THE MAYOR OF THE CITY OF CHICAGO:—

Our directors have appropriated five hundred ($500) dollars to be used at your discretion, in aid of the sufferers by the late fire. Your draft for that amount will be duly honored. EDWARD V. LOEW,

President Manufacturers and Builders Fire Insurance Company.

NEW YORK, *October* 12, 1871.

THE MAYOR OF CHICAGO: —

Our directors have appropriated one thousand dollars ($1,000) to be used at your discretion in aid of the sufferers by the late fire. Your draft for that amount will be duly honored. W. T. HOOKEY,

President Guardian Mutual Life Insurance Co.

NEW YORK, *October* 12, 1871.

THE MAYOR OF CHICAGO: —

Cornucopia Lodge, No. 106, I. O. O. F., State of New York, donated two hundred dollars ($200) towards the relief of the sufferers of Chicago.

Draw on the Bowery National Bank of New York, for the above amount. SAM'L BARNETT, 183 E. Broadway.

NEW YORK, *October* 12, 1871.

THE MAYOR OF CHICAGO: —

Saron Lodge, No. 3, I. O. B. B., of New York, donates one hundred dollars ($100) towards the relief of the sufferers of Chicago.

Draw on the Bowery National Bank of New York, for the above amount. SAMUEL BARNETT, 183 E. Broadway.

NEW YORK, *October* 12, 1871.

R. B. MASON, *Mayor:* —

The Adams Express Company transmits to you to-day ten thousand dollars ($10,000), as its contribution toward the relief of the sufferers by the late fire in your city. W. B. DINSMORE, *President.*

NEW YORK, *October* 12, 1871.

THE MAYOR OF CHICAGO: —

I have been instructed by our London office to subscribe five thousand dollars ($5,000) to the Chicago relief fund. How shall I remit?

E. W. CROWELL,

Resident Manager Imperial Fire Insurance Co.

NEW YORK, *October* 12, 1871.

HON. R. B. MASON, *Mayor:* —

New York Life Insurance Company, 346 and 348 Broadway, New York. Draw on this company for five thousand dollars ($5,000), appropriated yesterday by its Board for the sufferers of your city.

MORRIS FRANKLIN, *President.*

QUEBEC, CANADA, *October* 12, 1871.

THE MAYOR OF CHICAGO: —

The British Government have sanctioned by cable telegram the free gift for sufferers from fire in Chicago, of about five hundred tents, seventeen marquees, and six thousand five hundred blankets, if these would be acceptable. Please telegraph me if offer is acceptable, and to whom to consign the same.

All are part worn, but they are all we have here.

COL. MARTINDALE.

RONDOUT, N. Y., *October* 12, 1871.

MAYOR OF CHICAGO: —

You can draw upon Rondout Relief Committee at once for two thousand dollars ($2,000); further subscriptions will be made.

THOMAS CORNELL.

SACRAMENTO, CAL., *October* 12, 1871.

Sacramento sympathizes with Chicago. We are collecting for sufferers. Will remit soon twenty to twenty-five thousand dollars. Central Pacific Railroad Company contribute ten thousand.

EDGAR MILLS.

ST. PAUL, MINN., *October* 12, 1871.

HON. MAYOR MASON: —

St. Paul gives twenty thousand dollars ($20,000), for sufferers by Chicago fire. Committee with money start for Chicago to-morrow morning.

WM. LEE, *Mayor.*

UTICA, N. Y., *October* 12, 1871.

THE CHIEF ENGINEER OF CHICAGO FIRE DEPARTMENT,
(Care of the Mayor):

Tiger Hose Company, No. (1) one, of this city, have given two hundred dollars ($200), for the relief of injured firemen and their families. Draft will follow.

M. C. COMSTOCK, *Mayor.*

YORK, PA., *October* 12, 1871.

MAYOR OF CHICAGO: —

Draw at sight for benefit of sufferers, five hundred dollars ($500), subscription of workmen and ourselves.

BELLMEYER & SMALLS.

BRIDGEPORT, CONN., *October* 13, 1871.

HON. R. B. MASON, *Mayor*: —

Remembering you and those you represent in their great necessity, the citizens of Bridgeport tender their sympathy, and have raised by voluntary contributions ten thousand dollars ($10,000), and the fund is still increasing. Please indicate how to send the amount, and how otherwise we may serve you.

E. B. GOODSELL, *Mayor.*

BINGHAMPTON, N. Y., *October* 13, 1871.

HON. R. B. MASON, *Mayor:* —

Our little city last night placed to the credit of the suffering people of Chicago five thousand dollars ($5,000.) You can at sight draw on me for that amount.

Private subscription goes rapidly on.

WALTON DWIGHT, *Mayor.*

FALL RIVER, MASS., *October* 13, 1871.

HON. R. B. MASON, *Mayor:* —

The City Council of Fall River have voted twenty thousand dollars ($20,000), for the relief of the sufferers by fire at Chicago, subject to your draft on the City Treasurer. SAM'L W. BROWN, *Mayor.*

NORWICH, CONN., *October* 13, 1871.

HON. R. B. MASON, *Mayor:* —

Norwich grieves at her sister's calamity. Many citizens have subscribed and placed in my hands ten thousand dollars ($10,000), for her relief. I hold the money subject to your order. Please say if I shall remit in currency, or by draft on New York.

JAS. LLOYD GREEN, *Mayor, Norwich.*

NEW YORK, *October* 13, 1871.

HON. R. B. MASON, *Mayor of Chicago:* —

We have just received a second telegram from J. S. Morgan, Esq., London, as follows: "Pay to the Mayor of Chicago the equivalent of one thousand guineas, accompanied by the following message from the Lord Mayor of London: 'The corporation of London, through the Lord Mayor, sends to the Mayor of Chicago their deep sympathy and a contribution of one thousand guineas.'" This amount we hold subject to your order. DREXEL, MORGAN, & CO.

NEW YORK, *October* 19, 1871.

R. B. MASON, *Mayor of Chicago:* —

We to-day received the following cable dispatch. "The Lord Mayor of London, on behalf and in the name of the Chicago Mansion House Relief Fund, has handed the American Committee a further sum of eight thousand (£8,000) pounds, for the sufferers." This is held by us subject to your order. DREXEL, MORGAN, & CO.

NEW YORK, *October* 13, 1871.

THE MAYOR OF CHICAGO: —

Your draft for two thousand dollars ($2,000), for benefit of sufferers by the fire, will be honored by this company.

JUSTUS LAWRENCE,
President Continental Life Insurance Co. of N. Y.

NEW YORK, *October* 13, 1871.

HIS HONOR, R. B. MASON, *Mayor of Chicago:* —

Miss Haines and M'lle. De Janon, with their teachers and pupils, send a ticket of deposit of the Metropolitan National Bank of New York, for three hundred and fifty-six dollars ($356), for the suffering children of Chicago, with their profoundest sympathy.

No. 10 GRAMMERCY PARK.

NEW YORK, *October* 13, 1871.

HON. R. B. MASON, *Mayor of Chicago:* —

The Managers in this city of the North British and Mercantile Insurance Company, have received from G. W. Carter, Esq., Chairman of the London Board, by cable, the following instructions for the Chicago sufferers: "Settle all losses promptly. Draw at three days sight. Subscribe at once five thousand dollars ($5,000) for the sufferers." We hold the amount subject to your sight draft.

WM. CONNER,
Associate Manager.

NEW YORK, *October* 13, 1871.

MAYOR OF CHICAGO: —

I have this moment received the following dispatch with a request to communicate the same to you. "The Mayor of Birmingham to Mayor of Chicago. Birmingham has already raised one thousand pounds (£1,000), for the sufferers by the Chicago fire."

CYRUS W. FIELD.

NEW YORK, *October* 13, 1871.

HON. R. B. MASON, *Mayor of Chicago:* —

The Merchants Insurance Company of New York City tender you a contribution of one thousand dollars ($1,000), towards the relief of the suffering in Chicago. Please specify in what manner we shall send it.

C. V. B. OSTRANDER, *President.*
J. L. DOUGLASS, *Secretary.*

SALT LAKE CITY, *October* 13, 1871.

MAYOR MASON: —

Mail you twelve thousand dollars ($12,000), in New York Exchange to-day for relief of sufferers. More will follow.

DANIEL H. WELLS, *Mayor.*

WORCESTER, MASS., *October* 13, 1871.

MAYOR OF CHICAGO: —

I send you this morning a car-load of clothing and provisions from our citizens for relief of suffering in your city, and hold subject to your order one thousand dollars ($1,000).

J. C. PLUMER, *Mayor.*

WILLIAMSBURG, N. Y., *October* 13, 1871.

TO HIS HONOR THE MAYOR: —

The B. E. D. butchers send you the sum of one hundred and sixty-five dollars and fifty cents ($165 $\frac{50}{100}$) which is at your disposal for the sufferers, and you will oblige by sending a receipt to the L. I. Anzeiger Office, in Williamsburg, New York.

A. GEISER, *President.*
I. ZIMMER, *Secretary.*
H. RUDES, *Treasurer.*

BROOKLYN, N. Y., *October* 14, 1871.

HON. R. B. MASON, *Mayor of Chicago*: —

Draw on me at sight for five thousand five hundred and fifty dollars ($5,550), contributed by officers and employés at this yard toward relief of suffering at your city.

J. C. ELDRIDGE, *Pay Director, U. S. Navy.*

NIAGARA FALLS, N. Y., *October* 14, 1871.

TO THE MAYOR OF THE CITY OF CHICAGO: —

The citizens of this village have collected the sum of seventeen hundred dollars ($1,700), and have deposited the same in the Banking House of W. K. Van Husen of this place to the credit of the Mayor of the city of Chicago, and subject to his sight draft. The money to be used in aid of your suffering people, whose losses and griefs in the destruction of your beautiful city we most deeply deplore.

D. R. JERAULD,
Chairman Forwarding Committee.

NEW YORK, *October* 14, 1871.

THE MAYOR OF CHICAGO: —

Monroe & Co. of Paris authorize us to pay you thirty thousand dollars ($30,000), a first subscription from Americans in Paris, for sufferers at Chicago. More to follow. How will you have it?

JOHN MONROE & CO.

SING SING, N. Y., *October* 14, 1871.

R. B. MASON, *Mayor of the City of Chicago*: —

Draw on me for one thousand dollars ($1,000) for the relief of the suffering in Chicago. Contribution of the people of Sing Sing.

ISAAC B. NOXON,
President of the Village of Sing Sing.

SAN FRANCISCO, CAL., *October* 15, 1871.

On behalf of Mrs. D. P. Bowers, Mr. F. S. Chanfrau, and Mr. I. C. McCullom, and every member of the California Theatre, I remit you gold draft on Lee & Waller, New York, for fourteen hundred and forty-two dollars ($1,442). JNO. McCULLOUGH, *Manager.*

NEW YORK, *October* 16, 1871.

HON. R. B. MASON, *Mayor*: —

We are instructed by telegram to pay you ten thousand dollars ($10,000), gold, from city of Oakland, California; will do so on confirmation of telegram. JOHN T. HILL, *Cashier.*

DUBLIN, IRELAND, *October* 16, 1871.

MAYOR OF CHICAGO: —

Will remit one thousand pounds to-morrow.

LORD MAYOR OF DUBLIN.

LONDON, *October* 16, 1871.

THE MAYOR OF CHICAGO: —

Proceeds of a benefit given here this day, two hundred and fifty pounds (£250), paid to General Schenck.

CHATTERTON, *Drury Lane Theatre.*

BERLIN, PRUSSIA, *October* 16, 1871.

MAYOR MASON, *Chicago*: —

Relief Committee formed here. Hardt & Company, New York, directed to pay your order fifteen thousand dollars ($15,000), first installment. Empress contributes thousand thalers. KREISMANN.

EASTON, PA., *October* 16, 1871.

R. B. MASON, *Mayor*: —

We send car load of clothing by special agent, care Joseph Stockton, agent, Empire Line, Chicago.

Mr. De Barr will report to you on arrival. Car goes through by special train. EDWARD H. GREENE, *President Town Council.*

KINGSBORO, N. Y., *October* 16, 1871.

HON. R. B. MASON, *Mayor*: —

Draw through National Fulton Co. Bank, Gloversville, one hundred seventy-five dollars ($175), collection from Presbyterian Church yesterday. GEO. HARKNESS, *Pastor.*

MANCHESTER, ENGLAND, *October* 16, 1871.

TO MAYOR OF CHICAGO: —

At public meeting held here much sympathy expressed, and five thousand pounds (£5,000) subscribed immediately. Remittance forthwith.

JOHN GRAVE, *Mayor of Manchester.*

ST. JOHNSBURY, VT., *October* 16, 1871.

TO MAYOR OF CHICAGO:—

The citizens of St. Johnsbury deeply sympathize with your people. A mass meeting will be held this Monday evening to raise money for the relief of your suffering citizens. Be of good cheer, the heart of the nation beats warmly toward you. HORACE FAIRBANKS.

SAUGERTIES, N. Y., *October* 16, 1871.

MAYOR OF CHICAGO:—

I hold subject to order of the Treasurer of your Relief Committee, two thousand dollars ($2,000), from citizens of Saugerties.

B. M. FRELIGH, *Cashier First National Bank.*

PORTLAND, OREGON, *October* 17, 1871.

HON. R. B. MASON, *Mayor*:—

Citizens of Portland express their sympathy with sufferers by fire in your city by collection of ten thousand dollars ($10,000), for their benefit. Committee still at work, and amount will be increased. Amount named is held by First National Bank of this city subject to order of Chicago Relief and Aid Society. PHILIP WASSERMAN, *Mayor.*

NEW YORK, *October* 17, 1871.

HON. R. B. MASON, *Mayor*:—

Six hundred and fifty dollars ($650), for relief of Chicago sufferers, contributed by employês in the office of the "American Agriculturist," and "Hearth and Home" by the proprietors, subject to your order whenever wanted. ORANGE JUDD & CO.

OSWEGO, N. Y., *October* 17, 1871.

R. B. MASON, *Mayor*:—

Our Board of Trade donation is expressed in currency to J. W. Preston, President of your Board of Trade. B. HAGAMAN, *President.*

NEW YORK, *October* 17, 1871.

HIS HONOR, MAYOR R. B. MASON:—

We send you to-day fifteen thousand dollars ($15,000) for account of Berlin, Prussia, Committee. HARDT & CO.

SCRANTON, PA., *October* 18, 1871.

MAYOR OF CHICAGO:—

I will deposit five hundred and ninety-eight dollars ($598) in the Scranton Savings Bank, subject to your order. Proceeds of concert at Klein's Opera House this evening for the Chicago sufferers.

JOS. WALKER, *Manager.*

HARRISBURG, PA., *October* 18, 1871.

R. B. MASON, MAYOR OF CHICAGO:—

The employés of the Susquehanna and Shamokin division and telegraph department of the Northern Central Railway, have contributed nine hundred dollars ($900), for the relief of the sufferers by the great fire in your city. You can draw upon me at sight for the amount named.

EDMUND L. DUBARRY,
Asst. Supt. Northern Central Railway.

BELFAST, IRELAND, *October* 18, 1871.

MAYOR, CHICAGO:—

Belfast sympathizes deeply. Enthusiastic town meeting. Three thousand pounds (£3,000) already subscribed. MAYOR, *Belfast.*

WATERFORD, IRELAND, *October* 18, 1871.

MAYOR OF CHICAGO:—

Draw one hundred and fifty pounds (£150) on my account.

MAYOR OF WATERFORD.

GLASGOW, *October* 19, 1871.

MAYOR, CHICAGO:—

Henderson Brothers will pay you five thousand pounds (£5,000) sterling to account of Glasgow subscription for relief of sufferers from Chicago fire. Accept the sympathy of the citizens of Glasgow.

THE CHIEF MAGISTRATE, *Glasgow.*

LIMERICK, IRELAND, *October* 19, 1871.

MAYOR, CHICAGO:—

You may draw on me for three hundred pounds (£300).

MAYOR, *Limerick.*

NEW YORK, *October* 19, 1871.

THE MAYOR:—

The proceeds of the benefit given by the Parepa Rosa Opera Company amounts to fourteen hundred dollars ($1,400). How shall I send it?

CARL ROSA.

HUDDERSFIELD, ENGLAND, *October* 20, 1871.

MAYOR OF CHICAGO:—

Huddersfield subscription one thousand (£1,000). How send, in money, blankets, or what description of goods?

MAYOR OF HUDDERSFIELD.

PERTH, SCOTLAND, *October* 20, 1871.

MAYOR, CHICAGO:—

Devastation fund, draw three hundred pounds (£300).

PROVOST OF PERTH.

ABERDEEN, SCOTLAND, *October* 20, 1871.

MAYOR, CHICAGO:—

Aberdeen holds public meeting to-morrow for sympathy and aid to Chicago. Please acknowledge. PROVOST OF ABERDEEN.

CHARLESTON, S. C., *October* 21, 1871.

HON. R. B. MASON, *Mayor:*—

We forward to-day by express eight hundred and twenty-one dollars and fifty cents (821\frac{50}{100}$), a contribution from sympathizing citizens of impoverished Charleston to the suffering people of Chicago. Please acknowledge receipt. RIORDAN, DAWSON, & Co.,

Prop'rs Charleston News.

LAWRENCE, MASS., *October* 21, 1871.

HON. R. B. MASON:—

Sir,— You are hereby authorized to draw on our city treasurer, R. H. Tewkesbury, for ten thousand dollars ($10,000), for the relief of your suffering people. S. B. W. DAVIS, *Mayor.*

NEWBURYPORT, MASS., *October* 21, 1871.

MAYOR OF CHICAGO:—

Draw upon me at sight for two thousand dollars ($2,000) on account of donations of citizens of Newburyport in aid of sufferers by Chicago fire.

ISAAC S. BORDMAN, *Treasurer Relief Committee.*

BERLIN, PRUSSIA, *October* 24, 1871.

TO MAYOR MASON, *Chicago:*—

Hardt & Co., New York, directed to pay you additional ten thousand dollars ($10,000), including Emperor and Crown Prince's liberal contributions; collections continued; acknowledge amounts received.

KREISMANN, *American Consul.*

DUNDEE, SCOTLAND, *October* 24, 1871.

MAYOR OF CHICAGO:—

Dundee sympathizes deeply with Chicago. Draw at sight on Barings, London, one thousand pounds (£1,000), first installment of offering.

PROVOST OF DUNDEE, *Scotland.*

NEW YORK, *October* 24, 1871.

R. B. MASON, *Mayor:*—

We are in receipt of the following dispatch from American Committee, London, "Bradford, Yorkshire, remits two thousand pounds (£2,000); Greenock eight hundred pounds (£800), for Chicago."

DREXEL, MORGAN, & Co.

BRISTOL, ENGLAND, *October* 24, 1871.

TO THE MAYOR OF CHICAGO: —

Have paid to your credit at Messrs. Baring Brothers, the sum of one thousand pounds (£1,000), first installment as a contribution to the Chicago Relief Fund.

The sufferers have our sincere sympathy.

THE MAYOR OF BRISTOL.

GALASHIELS, SCOTLAND, *November* 10, 1871.

TO MAYOR OF CHICAGO: —

The people of Galashiels tender their sincere sympathy to the inhabitants of Chicago, and request you to draw on me for one hundred and forty pounds sterling, which please accept in aid of sufferers.

ROBERT STEWART,
Town Clerk, Galashiels.

NEW YORK, *December* 22, 1871.

JOSEPH FRANK, 63 *Canal Street*: —

By cable this date from Paris, France, I am directed to pay thirty-five hundred dollars ($3,500), product of a fund there subscribed for the most needy of the sufferers by the late fire in your city. Please hand that sum at once to the Mayor for immediate distribution, as the Treasurer of the fund wishes it should reach these unfortunates for Christmas day. The funds are in my hands subject to your sight draft. Please have the Mayor acknowledge receipt by telegram directed Alexander Servant, Treasurer, to my care here, and I will transmit at once to him by cable.

HENRY L. HOGUET.

LETTERS.

MAYOR'S OFFICE, CITY HALL,
CLEVELAND, OHIO, *October* 9, 1871.

TO HIS HONOR THE MAYOR OF CHICAGO, ILL.: —

Dear Sir, — The bearers of this communication are Messrs. N. A. Payne, Col. Hayward, and others, gentlemen selected at a meeting of the citizens of Cleveland, held this afternoon to devise means to afford relief to the people of Chicago, who have been overtaken and made destitute by this awful calamity.

These gentlemen come to you with such provisions as we have been able to get together in the short time we have allowed ourselves before shipment.

Please accept them as the first installment of our offerings, to meet your immediate and more importunate wants, and be assured that your people have, in this their great extremity, the profound sympathy of this entire community, and shall have their material aid to the extent of their ability, and as promptly as possible.

Very truly, your obedient servant,
F. W. PELTON, *Mayor.*

MILWAUKEE, *October* 10, 1871.

TO THE MAYOR OF CHICAGO AND THE CITY OFFICERS: —

Mr. C. H. Larkin visits you as chairman of the committee appointed by the Chamber of Commerce to see that the donations of our city are delivered over to any committee or parties you may select to receive the same.

Any command you make upon us as a city shall be promptly responded to, or anything that may be desired of the citizens of our city I will see that it is attended to.

Yours with respect and sorrowful feeling for the sad calamity that has been cast upon your once beautiful city.

H. LUDINGTON, *Mayor of Milwaukee.*

YORK, PA., *October* 10, 1871.

MAYOR OF CHICAGO: —

Dear Sir, — At a meeting of the men in my employ held this day, it was resolved to give one day's wages to the sufferers of your city, and I telegraphed you to draw on me, at sight, for three hundred dollars ($300).

A public meeting of citizens will be held this evening, when further aid will be rendered.

Yours truly,
MICHAEL SCHALL.

OFFICE OF THE SANTA FE POST,
SANTA FE, N. M., *October* 1, 1871.

TO THE HON. THE MAYOR OF CHICAGO: —

Dear Sir, — Our citizens hear with deep and most heartfelt regret of the sad calamity which has befallen your great city. Though distant and unable to be of that service which we would render could we act in accord with the impulses of our hearts, we are none the less touched by the misfortunes of your citizens. Our aid is but a mite, still it is given in a spirit of most sincere condolence, and we trust Divine Providence will extend His beneficent protection over the sufferers and restore your city to its wonted greatness.

Inclosed is a check to your order for four hundred and twenty-four dollars ($424).

Respectfully your obedient servants,

M. KAYSER,
A. P. SULLIVAN, } *Committee.*

ROCHESTER, N. Y., *October* 10, 1871.

TO THE MAYOR OF CHICAGO, ILL.: —

Dear Sir, — The agents and employés of the Erie R. R. Company in this city being desirous of testifying our sympathy with the citizens of Chicago in their great calamity, beg your acceptance of the inclosed sum, seventy dollars and fifty cents ($$70\frac{50}{100}$), to be used for the relief of sufferers by the recent fire.

Hoping the same will be accepted in the spirit we send it, we remain.

Yours truly,

J. C. BUTTERFIELD, *Agent.*
E. G. BILLINGS, *Passenger Agent.*
B. F. HARRIS, *Freight Agent.*
AND OTHERS.

MARBLEHEAD, MASS., *October* 10, 1872.

Dear Sir, — We have this day forwarded three (3) boxes clothing, and one (1) box of boots and shoes, numbered from one to four.

We have a committee of fifteen gentlemen and thirty ladies, who are soliciting subscriptions of money and clothing. The latter will be packed and forwarded daily until we get through, and you will be advised of the money.

When we shall have finished our work the cases of clothing will be numbered and addressed to "Aid and Relief Society."

Yours for humanity, in behalf of committee,

M. U. MARTIN.

TO THE CHAIRMAN AID AND RELIEF SOCIETY.

WILLIAMSBURG, L. I., *October* 11, 1871.

TO HIS HONOR THE MAYOR OF CHICAGO: —

Dear Sir, — The German Singing Society, "Williamsburg Sangerbund," in consideration of the terrible accident which occurred in our sister city, passed in their meeting yesterday the resolution to assist our Chicago brothers as much as we are able to execute.

According to this we send you, by "money order," one hundred dollars ($100), whereof we hand to your honor the inclosed receipt.

Besides this we make up a collection among our members, the amount of which also shall be put to your disposal.

Yours respectfully, PETER S. VORGANG,
Secretary of the Williamsburg Sangerbund.

TROY, N. Y., *October* 11, 1871.

TO THE HON. THE MAYOR OF THE CITY OF CHICAGO: —

My dear Sir: — At a meeting of Apollo Lodge, No. 13, F. & A. M., held last evening, it was unanimously resolved that the sum of one hundred dollars ($100) be donated to the relief of the Chicago sufferers. Inclosed you will please find draft on New York payable to your order for the relief of the needy and destitute of your city. Please acknowledge receipt of same, and oblige Yours very truly,

ROBERT B. RANKIN,
Worthy Master Apollo Lodge, No. 13, *Troy, N. Y.*

SARATOGA SPRINGS, *October* 11, 1871.

TO THE MAYOR OF CHICAGO: —

Dear Sir, — At a special meeting of Walworth Hose Association of this village, held Tuesday evening October 10, 1871, it was unanimously resolved to appropriate one hundred and twenty-five dollars ($125) in aid of the sufferers of the Chicago fire.

I inclose draft on New York, No. 15031, for that amount. We extend our hearty sympathy to you in your great misfortune.

Yours, etc., A. W. SHEPHARD,
Treasurer Walworth Hose Association.

ROCHESTER, N. Y., *October* 11, 1871

TO THE MAYOR OF CHICAGO: —

Sir, — The "Protectives" of this city sent to your care last evening per express train one car load of "relief supplies" amounting in the aggregate to one thousand dollars ($1,000). Three hundred dollars ($300) of this amount was donated by the company; two hundred dollars ($200) was voluntarily handed us to disburse by the wel-known seedsman and florist, James Vick, and the balance was contributed by citizens. Hoping that it arrived in good condition,

I am truly yours, E. A. Taquiet, *Foreman.*

New York, *October* 11, 1871.

R. B. Mason, Esq., *Mayor of Chicago:* —

Dear Sir, — As a token of our sympathy with the unfortunates of your city in this terrible hour of suffering, you will please take notice that we have this day dispatched to you eleven boxes of cheese and two boxes smoked meats.

Though but a small offering, yet we trust that as it comes from the willing hearts of the Advance Guard of Washington Market, it may prove serviceable to alleviate the distress of a few of the many deserving ones. I have the honor to remain on behalf of the subscribers,

Yours respectfully,

James J. Condon.

New York, *October* 11, 1871.

Hon. R. B. Mason, *Mayor of Chicago, Ill:* —

Dear Sir, — Inclosed please find check for one hundred dollars and twenty-five cents ($\$100\frac{25}{100}$) in aid of sufferers in your city.

This contribution is made up by the hands in our factory; many of whom are boys and girls, who have given voluntarily and gladly all they could of their earnings for this object. Respectfully yours,

Fr. Beck & Co.

New York, *October* 11, 1871.

Hon. R. B. Mason, *Mayor of Chicago:* —

Sir, — I have this day forwarded to you for the sufferers of your city, by American Merchants' Union Express, fifteen thousand dollars ($15,000) as a part of the subscription by members of the New York Produce Exchange. Will forward again as soon as I can make collections.

I now have thirty thousand dollars ($30,000) subscribed.

Please acknowledge receipt of package.

B. C. Bogert, *Treasurer.*

New York, *October* 11, 1871.

To the Mayor of Chicago: —

Dear Sir, — The Ladies' Sewing Society of the Hebrew Orphan Asylum of New York forward to you the amount of three hundred dollars ($300) for distribution amongst the poor sufferers of your city Yours most respectfully,

Mrs. Th. Frankenheimer, *Secretary.*

MAYOR'S OFFICE, JERSEYVILLE, ILL., *October* 11, 1871.

MAYOR OF CHICAGO:—

Dear Sir,—The citizens of Jerseyville tender their sympathy to your people, and instruct me to state that the Council of this city have unanimously appropriated one thousand dollars ($1,000) to their relief. How and to whom shall it be sent, in money or provisions? please answer. Yours, ROBERT M. KNAPP, *Mayor.*

WILLIAMSBURG, N. Y., *October* 12, 1871.

TO THE MAYOR OF CHICAGO:—

Inclosed please find draft for one day's pay of each of our workmen, amounting to two hundred and twenty-five dollars ($225). We employ eighty-three men, and trust their efforts will result in good.

Since subscribed five dollars ($5), making $230. My own contribution will be forwarded at an early day, and it should amount to ten thousand dollars ($10,000) if judiciously handled. There is already a bid of eight thousand dollars for the goods. They consist of two presses at the American Institute fair, and the Crystal Palace. They were donated on Tuesday, to be sold to the highest bidder at the close of the fair. Yours truly, A. CAMPBELL.

WELLSVILE, N. Y., *October* 12, 1871.

TO THE MAYOR OF THE CITY OF CHICAGO:—

Dear Sir,—At a regular meeting of this Lodge, held last evening, among other business it was

Resolved,—That an order be drawn on the treasurer for the sum of fifty dollars ($50), and that the Noble Grand be instructed to send said amount to the Mayor of the city of Chicago, to be applied as he may deem best towards relieving the sufferers by the late fire in said city.

In compliance with the above, I inclose draft for fifty dollars ($50), and at your leisure would like an acknowledgment of receipt of same.

Very respectfully yours, in F., L., and T.,

J. NEWTON STODDARD, N. G.

TROY, N. Y., *October* 12, 1871.

TO THE CHIEF ENGINEER OF THE CHICAGO FIRE DEPARTMENT:—

Sir,—Please find herewith one hundred dollars ($100), as our mite towards the relief of firemen who may have been injured during the continuance of the late deplorable fire in your city. Wishing we could do more, I am sir, very respectfully yours,

HUGH B. STOUGHTON,

Treasurer Washington Volunteer Steamer Co., Troy, N. Y.

TROY ACADEMY, TROY, N. Y., *October* 12, 1871.

TO THE MAYOR OF CHICAGO:—

Dear Sir, — Inclosed please find a draft for thirty dollars ($30), the contribution of Troy Academy towards the relief of sufferers by the late fire in your city. Please acknowledge receipt. Yours truly,

T. NEWTON WILLSON, *Principal.*

ST. MARY'S, PA., *October* 12, 1871.

Dear Sir, — I send you herewith in currency, one hundred and fifty-seven dollars eighty-five cents (157\frac{85}{100}$), collected here to-day from the citizens as per accompanying list, for the relief of the sufferers by the recent terrible fire in your city.

I also send you by express a box of worn clothing, etc., contributed by a few of the citizens here. Hav'nt time to examine it before train leaves this morning; possibly some of it is hardly worth sending, but it has been gathered together hurriedly and will perhaps serve to give temporary relief. Another box will be sent to-morrow, and probably more money will be collected. Yours truly, J. S. BATES,

In behalf of the citizens of St. Mary's.

SCRANTON, PA., *October* 12, 1871.

TO THE HON. MAYOR OF CHICAGO:—

Dear Sir, — As substantial evidence of sympathy, our citizens have placed in my hands about fifteen hundred dollars ($1,500), and efforts are being made to-day to increase this amount Please inform me by return mail how you wish it sent.

I will report to you as fast as it is paid in, and you can draw, or I will remit as you may direct. Respectfully,

GEO. CORAY, *Treasurer.*

MAYOR'S OFFICE, PORTLAND, ME., *October* 12, 1871.

HIS HONOR THE MAYOR OF CHICAGO:—

Dear Sir, — The citizens of Portland, deeply sympathising with your terrible calamity (having experienced something of like kind themselves), are moving to give their feelings practical expression. We have subscribed thus far some sixteen thousand dollars ($16,000) upon which you may draw on Samuel E. Spring, Treasurer of Chicago Relief Fund, at sight, for ten thousand dollars ($10,000), as the first installment. As fast as the balance is paid in we will advise you.

It has been suggested by leading business men, and I have been requested to communicate the suggestion to you, that a certain class of goods can be obtained here at cost (transportation free), which your sufferers will need during the coming winter, and which are all manufactured in this State; such as shoes, stoves, and other articles. It is thought that these can be obtained here at nearly fifty per cent less than in the West, in the ordinary markets. We, however, leave that to your own better judgment. Please advise me and oblige.

Yours truly, BENJ. KINGSBURY, *Mayor.*

PEEKSKILL, N. Y., *October* 12, 1871.

R. B. MASON, *Mayor of Chicago:* —

Dear Sir, — Knowing that there must of necessity be very great suffering in your city for want of everything, I yesterday telegraphed James Fisk, Jr., to learn if you could make use of some stoves for cooking purposes, and on receipt of his reply that they would be very acceptable, the employés of the Peekskill Mutual Stove Works each send a cookstove, in all twenty-five (25), which we ship you to-day, and confidently hope they may be of service to some of the hundreds of homeless people, and only regret that our means would not allow a greater contribution. You will please notify us on receipt of the stoves, and oblige,

Very respectfully, your most obedient servants,

THE PEEKSKILL MUTUAL STOVE WORKS,

per JOHN WORTHINGTON, *Superintendent.*

PORT JERVIS, N. Y., *October* 12, 1871.

HON. R. B. MASON, *Mayor of City of Chicago:* —

Dear Sir, — It gives me pleasure to send you for the relief of the sufferers by the terrible fire in the Garden City, a draft payable to your order on the Hanover National Bank of the city of New York, for the sum of eight hundred and thirty-three dollars and five cents (\$833$\frac{5}{100}$).

Please accept it as a small expression of the sympathy of our citizens in behalf of suffering humanity. Very truly yours,

JOHN CONKLING, *Treasurer of Citizens' Fund.*

ONEIDA, MADISON CO., N. Y., *October* 12, 1871.

HON. R. B. MASON, *Mayor of Chicago:* —

Dear Sir, — I am instructed by the members of Protection Engine Company No. 2 of Oneida, to advise you that at a meeting of said company last evening, the sum of fifty dollars (\$50) was by an unanimous vote of said company appropriated for the relief of the sufferers by the late disastrous fire in your city.

You can draw on our foreman at sight for the sum, or at your request he will remit draft or currency by express.

With the expression of our deep sympathy for those afflicted by the appalling calamity, we are, very respectfully, your obedient servants,

B. N. DYER, *Foreman.*

OIL CITY, PA., *October* 12, 1871.

TO HIS HONOR THE MAYOR OF CHICAGO: —

Dear Sir, — Inclosed you will find the receipts for five (5) boxes shipped you this morning per Union Express. They contain assorted clothing, collected by the ladies of this city for the sufferers by the fire. The boxes are numbered respectively 1, 2, 3, 4, and 5, and the accompanying schedule will enable your committee on distributions to understand what each box contains and thereby save confusion. If convenient, please acknowledge their receipt.

With every sentiment of the profoundest sorrow for the great calamity that has befallen your people, and the liveliest sympathy with their distress, I have the distinction to be, dear sir, your very humble servant,

JAMES MCCARTHY, *for the ladies of Oil City.*

NEW YORK, *October* 12, 1871.

HON. R. B. MASON, *Mayor of Chicago, Ill.:* —

Dear Sir, — In accordance with your printed notice of October 11th, requesting that donations in money in behalf of the Chicago sufferers be sent, subject to your order, we inclose our check on the National City Bank, New York, for five hundred dollars ($500), and with assurances of heartfelt sympathy,

We are, very respectfully, your obedient servants.

THE STAMFORD MANUFACTURING CO.,

S. K. SATTERLEE, *Treasurer.*

NEW YORK, *October* 12, 1871.

TO HIS HONOR THE MAYOR OF CHICAGO: —

Sir, — Inclosed check for two hundred dollars ($200) has been handed us by the Free Masons of Germania Lodge No. 182, for transmission to you in help of your suffering city.

The members of the Lodge, as they informed me, have taken this amount from their reserved funds, and will besides, personally, do all in their power to give effective assistance to the poor sufferers.

Please have the receipt for this contribution made out to the Master of Germania Lodge No. 182, and to be transmitted to the undersigned.

Respectfully yours, G. SCHREITMILLER, *Cashier.*

NEW YORK MILLS, ONEIDA CO., N. Y., *October* 12, 1871.

TO HIS HONOR THE MAYOR OF CHICAGO: —

This box contains clothing, etc., contributed by the operatives of New York Mills "Upper Mill," to the sufferers of the great conflagration at Chicago.

Another box containing comfortables will be sent in a few days.

It would be gratifying to many who contributed, to learn of its receipt, and whether such articles are acceptable, and if comfortables are wanted.

Walcott and Campbell have donated two thousand dollars ($2,000) worth of cloth to be made into garments at Utica, which will soon be forwarded. Yours truly,

W. S. WALCOTT, *for the Committee.*

LIVONIA STATION, N. Y., *October* 12, 1871.

MAYOR OF CHICAGO, ILL.: —

Hon. Sir, — The citizens of this village (situated on the Erie Railroad, Livingston Co., N. Y.), have by this evening's express, forwarded to your address four (4) boxes clothing, etc., for the use of some of your suffering citizens with whom they heartily sympathize in their great trouble. We presume you have proper agents engaged in the distribution of what is furnished. Yours respectfully,

C. BOWEN,
GEO. DUNLAP,
R. MUSSON,
In behalf of the ladies who have collected the articles sent.

KOSCIUSKO LODGE NO. 86, I. O. O. F.,
KINGSTON, N. Y., *October* 12, 1871.

TO THE HON. MAYOR OF CHICAGO: —

Dear Sir, — I inclose a draft on New York for fifty dollars ($50) as an expression of sympathy of this Lodge for the sufferers by the terrible calamity that has just befallen your city. Yours truly,

C. S. CLAY, *P. S.*

KITTANNING, PA., *October* 12, 1871.

R. B. MASON, ESQ., *Mayor of Chicago:* —

Dear Sir, — Inclosed you will find the sum of eleven hundred and thirty-two dollars ($1,132), contributed by the citizens of this place towards the relief of the sufferers of your once great but now devastated city.

Do with this mite as you think best to alleviate the woes of your stricken people.

May the Father of mercies put it into the hearts of the whole American people to come speedily to your assistance.

I am truly yours,

EDWARD S. GOLDEN, *Chairman of Committee.*

JOHN P. BROWN, *Treasurer.*

EASTON, PA., October 12, 1871.

HON. R. B. MASON, *Mayor of Chicago :—*

Dear Sir,— Mr. Wm. H. McLaughlin of this place collected yesterday one hundred dollars ($100), in one dollar subscriptions, from citizens of this borough, and at his request I inclose draft on New York to your order for the amount, to be applied by you in relieving the necessities of your suffering people. Respectfully,

BEATES B. SWIFT.

COHOES, N. Y., October 12, 1871.

HON. R. B. MASON, *Mayor of Chicago :—*

Inclosed I send you my draft on New York for twenty-five hundred dollars ($2,500), at the request of Hon. C. H. Adams, Mayor of this city, it being the amount to date of cash contributions by the citizens of this place for the relief of the sufferers by the late fire in Chicago.

We shall send more.

Mayor Adams shipped by to-day's express twelve (12) cases of knit goods of the value of about three thousand dollars ($3,000), contributed by the manufacturers of Cohoes for your destitute citizens.

Please acknowledge the receipt of both cash and goods, and oblige,

Yours respectfully,

MURRY HUBBARD, *Cashier.*

UTICA, N. Y., October 13, 1871.

OFFICERS AND MEMBERS OF CHICAGO TYPOGRAPHICAL UNION, No. 16 :—

Greeting :— In accordance with resolutions adopted by Utica Typographical Union, No. 62, we have exerted ourselves and raised a sum of money among the printers and proprietors, active and retired, for those of you who have suffered losses by the recent terrible burning. We assure you that you have our sympathy as well as that of every citizen.

Hoping the accompanying sum will prove beneficial and acceptable,

We remain yours fraternally,

E. M. CHASE,
JOS. JOYCE,
D. B. ROBERTS. } *Committee on Relief, No.* 62.

TROY, N. Y., October 13, 1871.

TO THE MAYOR OF CHICAGO :—

We send to-day by express one box, marked No. 55, containing clothing and underwear. The latter made by the girls in our employ.

Yours respectfully,

SMITH, HOUSE, & CO.

TROY, N. Y., *October* 13, 1871.

THE HON. R. B. MASON, *Mayor*: —

Dear Sir, — I beg to hand you herewith my certified check, to your order, on our Merchants' and Mechanics' Bank for one hundred and fifty nine dollars ($159), contributed to your relief fund by the employés of the Schaghticoke Woolen Mills, near this city.

With assurances of profound sympathy,

I am yours very truly,

J. L. MANNING, *Treasurer*.

THORNDALE, CHESTER CO., PA., *October* 13, 1871.

J. T. RYERSON, *Iron Merchant, Chicago*: —

Respected Friend, — Inclosed please find our check on National Bank of Chester Valley, Coatesville, Pa., for sixty-one dollars twenty-five cents (61\frac{25}{100}$), being amount of money contributed by our men and ourselves, which we send to thee to apply in thy discretion for the relief of the suffering caused by the late disastrous fire in your city.

Please acknowledge receipt when convenient and oblige,

Thy friends,

WM. L. BAILEY & CO.

ST. MARY'S, PA., *October* 13, 1871.

TO THE MAYOR OF CHICAGO: —

Dear Sir, — I send you herewith, in currency, sixty-five dollars ($65), subscribed yesterday by the miners at the St. Mary's Mines, in this place, for the relief of the sufferers by your recent terrible fire.

Please acknowledge the receipt of this remittance, as we consider the subscription from this source quite creditable to them, and it will be satisfactory to them to have an acknowledgment from you. More will be raised here soon, and the matter will be brought before the church here on Sunday. Yours truly, J. L. BATES,

In behalf of the Miners of the St. Mary's Mines.

PALMYRA, N. Y., *October* 13, 1873.

HON. R. B. MASON, *Mayor of Chicago*: —

Dear Sir, — Inclosed please find seventy-eight dollars sixty cents, (78\frac{60}{100}$), contributed by the Wayne County Teachers' Institute for the relief of your city. Respectfully,

E. M. ALLEN, *School Commissioner*.

New York, *October* 13, 1871.

Hon. R. B. Mason, *Mayor of Chicago* :—

Dear Sir, — Please place in the hands of the Relief Committee of Chicago the sum of fifteen hundred dollars ($1,500), inclosed, being the first installment from the bank clerks of the city of New York, expressive of their sympathy with the suffering people of your city in their great affliction. Yours respectfully, J. C. Parson,

President Bank Clerks' Mutual Benefit Association.

New York, *October* 13, 1871.

Hon. R. B. Mason, *Mayor of Chicago* :—

Inclosed please find my check for two hundred and fifty-eight dollars and fifty cents (258\frac{50}{100}$), the amount of the first collection by the "New York Demokrat."

Will you be kind enough to remit your receipt?

This morning I have transmitted to your address three boxes of clothing collected by the officers for the sufferers. F. Schwedler.

New York, *October* 13, 1871.

Hon. and Dear Sir :—

Our appeal on Tuesday morning, was hardly needed, so touched was the public heart by the sad misfortune in your beautiful city. It met, however, a very quick response in every direction. Our own subscription of five hundred dollars ($500) has been the nucleus for about seven thousand dollars, of which nearly three thousand has been handed in and the remainder will follow next mail. I inclose, herewith, currency, three thousand dollars ($3,000), and will send this evening an additional amount, with the names of the donors. We shall keep the subscription open as long as any offerings are likely to be made.

Into what nearness of fellowship are we brought when one member suffers. Yours, in new bonds,

David M. Stone,

Hon. R. B. Mason, *Mayor.* *Editor of Journal of Commerce.*

New York, *November* 13, 1871.

Hon. R. B. Mason, *Chicago* :—

My dear Sir, — Messrs. I. N. Pattison and Charles A. Holmes, the managers of a concert given recently in the Y. M. C. A. Hall for the benefit of the sufferers by your terrible fire, have requested me to forward you the inclosed check for three hundred dollars ($300), that being the amount realized.

The only regret felt by all connected with the entertainment is that the amount to be sent is not ten times as large.

Please sign and return the acknowledgment sent herewith, that it may be published in our daily papers for the satisfaction of the artists interested. Yours truly, L. H. HOLMES.

GRAMMAR SCHOOL NO. 17, 47TH STREET, 22D WARD,
NEW YORK, *October* 13, 1871.

HON. R. B. MASON, *Mayor of Chicago*: —

Dear Sir, — The children of the Grammar and Primary Departments of the above named school, wishing to testify their sorrow and sympathy for the suffering children and people of your severely afflicted city, will send to-morrow by the Erie R. R. sixteen cases of various articles of clothing. Said children, together with their respective teachers, do also contribute five hundred and thirty-three dollars and forty-two cents ($\$533\frac{42}{100}$), to be distributed among the sufferers of your city in such manner as your judgment may direct; which sum will be deposited Monday, October 16, with Mr. Bernard Smyth, President of the Department of Public Instruction, corner of Grand and Elm streets, subject to your order, which will be duly honored for that amount.

Yours, respectfully,
AMELIA KIERSTED,
MARY MCCLOSKEY, *Principals*.

LATROBE, PA., *October* 13, 1871.

TO HON. R. B. MASON, *Mayor of Chicago*: —

Dear Sir, — We have this day shipped to your address four boxes of clothing for the sufferers by the late fire in your city, who we assure you have our heartfelt sympathies. Our town is small yet we want to do something. Part of clothing is not entirely new, but good and warm, and you will also find many new blankets, shawls, hosiery, etc. We trust to a class of your people they may be useful and kindly received. We hope to do something more. You will do us a favor by acknowledging the receipt of this, as our people will be thankful to know that you have received them and to know that they are useful and acceptable to the sufferers.

Very respectfully yours,
D. W. MCCONAUGHY,
L. A. HOKE, *Committee*.

HON. R. B. MASON, *Mayor of Chicago*: —

Dear Sir, — It affords me very great pleasure to convey to you an expression of the profound sympathy felt for the afflicted of your city, in the village of Jamestown, N. Y., where I reside.

I inclose as the cheerful contribution of a few of our people, thirteen hundred and fifty dollars ($1,350), which I beg you to apply as you may see fit to the relief of the suffering. Very truly yours,

R. E. Fenton.

October 13, 1871.

Jamaica, N. Y., *October* 13, 1871.

Hon. R. B. Mason, *Mayor of the City of Chicago*: —

Dear Sir, — The members of Jamaica Division, No. 166, S. of T., deeply sympathizing with the sufferers by the late terrible conflagration in your city, at their meeting held last evening contributed the inclosed sum of twelve dollars ($12), with the sincere hope that it may be the means of relieving some unfortunate but worthy citizen in that once prosperous city. Very truly yours,

Charles Welling, *Treasurer*.

Fall River, Mass., *October* 13, 1871.

To the Hon. R. B. Mason, *Mayor of Chicago*: —

Sir, — The scholars of the second class of the Morgan Street Grammar School, Fall River, Mass., as a slight expression of their sympathy for the suffering children of Chicago, herewith inclose a check for twenty-six dollars ($26), payable to yourself.

Very respectfully,

Julia A. Read, *Teacher*.

Buffalo, *October* 13, 1871.

David A. Gage, *Treasurer of Chicago*: —

I have the pleasure of inclosing herewith the sum of five hundred dollars ($500) for the relief of the sufferers by fire in your city. This sum is a contribution from Neptune Hose Company, No. Five (5) of this city. And the company request me to ask you to apply it, if possible, to the relief of our brother firemen.

Please acknowlege receipt of inclosure, and oblige,

Lewis M. Evans, *President*.

Albany, N. Y., *October* 13, 1871.

Chicago Relief and Aid Society: —

Gentlemen, — I inclose herewith the contribution of the pupils of the Albany Free Academy, in aid of the sufferers by the great fire.

It represents a vast amount of sympathy and self-denying labor on the part of our students. May I not ask as a special favor that you will send, instead of a formal receipt, such a letter as would interest our young ladies and gentlemen.

Please make such use of the money as is most necessary and appropriate. Very truly yours,

J. E. BRADLEY, *Principal.*

DALTON, MASS., *October* 13, 1871.

TO HON. R. B. MASON, *Mayor, City of Chicago*:—

The people of this town, through their Relief Committee, express their sympathy for the suffering of your city, and herewith inclose a draft on New York for three hundred and fifty dollars ($350), payable to your order, for the relief of those rendered most needy by the late terrible conflagration.

Please to indicate receipt of same, so that we may know it has gone through safely. Very respectfully,

WM. H. WHARFIELD,
Treasurer Dalton Relief Committee.

BARBERS AND HAIR DRESSERS ASSOCIATION, No. 1.
NEW YORK, *October* 14, 1871.

TO HIS HONOR, THE MAYOR OF CHICAGO:—

We send you one hundred dollars ($100) by the American Merchants' Union Express Company, to aid the sufferers of your city.

Please reply on receipt.

Respectfully yours,

JOHN P. SCHENCK, *Treasurer*, 91 *Hudson St.*

NEW YORK, *October* 14, 1871.

TO THE HON. MAYOR OF CHICAGO:—

Dear Sir,—My two little girls, five and six years of age, are anxious to give the contents of their money-boxes to the suffering children of your city. Such was their own proposition, and although the amount is trifling, it is an offering from innocent and sympathizing little ones.

NEW YORK, *October* 14, 1871.

TO HIS HONOR, THE MAYOR OF CHICAGO:—

The accompanying amount of six hundred and one dollars and sixty-five cents ($\$601\frac{65}{100}$), is the proceeds of a hurriedly gotten up benefit for the sufferers of your city, and believing that a dollar now is worth more than many will be weeks hence, send it by first dispatch, at the same time hoping it may prove the benefit intended, and afford as much relief as it gives the donor pleasure in sending.

With heartfelt sympathy, I remain truly yours,

DAN RICE.

NEW YORK, *October* 14, 1871.

HON. R. B. MASON, *Mayor of Chicago:* —

Sir, — The officers of the Navy attached to this yard, the civil officers of the several departments and the employés under them, and the officers, crew, and marines of the U. S. receiving ship *Vermont* deeply sympathising with their suffering fellow citizens of Chicago in their present calamities, have contributed each one day's pay for their relief, and I have the pleasure hereby to authorize you to draw on me at sight for the sum of five thousand five hundred and fifty dollars ($5,550), the aggregate amount of the contributions.

Very respectfully, your obedient servant,

J. C. ELDREDGE, *Pay Director U. S. Navy.*

NEW YORK, *October* 14, 1871.

HON. R. B. MASON, *Mayor, Chicago:* —

Dear Sir, — We send you herewith, by Adams' Express, in U. S. currency, two thousand and forty-five dollars and seventy-seven cents ($2,045$\frac{77}{100}$), subscriptions received at this office; and five hundred dollars ($500), our own contribution, for the sufferers from the Chicago fire. Please acknowledge receipt.

Very respectfully,

JOHN IRELAND, *Cashier N. Y. Times.*

SYRACUSE, N. Y., *October* 14, 1871.

TO THE HONORABLE THE MAYOR OF CHICAGO: —

Sir, — At a meeting of the Mutual Benefit Society of the employés of the N. Y. C. & H. R. Railroad, at Syracuse, it was voted, that two hundred dollars ($200), be contributed to the relief fund for the sufferers of the late conflagration, with a request that it be used for the poor and needy.

W. H. DOANE,
STEPHEN GRANT,
A. P. TYLER. } *Committee.*

MAYOR'S OFFICE, CITY HALL,
MEMPHIS, TENN., *October* 14, 1871.

HON. R. B. MASON, *Mayor, Chicago, Ill.:* —

Dear Sir, — After my most sincere sympathy for the suffering citizens of your once magnificent but now almost desolated city, I have the pleasure to say to you that by order of the General Council of the city of Memphis, the sum of five thousand dollars ($5,000) has been appropriated by the Council out of the general fund of the city, for the relief of the sufferers by the recent terrible calamity to your unfortunate city and that the same is subject to your draft on me at three days' sight, at such time and in such sums as you may desire to draw. Regretting that the financial condition of our city would not admit of a much larger donation, I am most respectfully yours,

JOHN JOHNSON, *Mayor.*

U. S. NAVY YARD, BOSTON, *October* 14, 1871.

My Dear Sir, — I wish to confirm my telegram of this date, requesting you to draw on me for three thousand six hundred and fifty-eighty dollars and eighty-four cents ($3,658$\frac{84}{100}$), the amount of one days' pay subscribed by each of the military and civil officers and employés of this Navy Yard, for the relief of the sufferers from the disastrous fire in your city.

At the same time accept from us the assurances of our deep and heartfelt sympathy. Very respectfully,

CHAS. STEEDMAN,
Rear Admiral Commandant.

ABERDEEN, SCOTLAND, *October* 16, 1871.

THE WORSHIPFUL THE MAYOR OF CHICAGO: —

Sir, — The news of the sad disaster that has fallen on your city has produced a deep feeling of sympathy among all classes, and as a practical expression of this sympathy meetings are being held to collect funds to aid the sufferers.

I am respectfully, your most obedient servant,

WM. LESLIE, *Lord Provost.*

ROCHESTER, N. Y., *October* 16, 1871.

HON. R. B. MASON, *Mayor of Chicago:* —

Dear Sir, — At a special meeting of the "Independent Literary Union" (a body of Jewish young men) it was unanimously resolved to appropriate the sum of one hundred dollars ($100) for the benefit of the sufferers of your devastated city. Therefore I inclose draft for the amount, which please distribute to best advantage for the alleviation of the sufferers.

We hope that God will render his aid to the afflicted in the time of need, and in speedily restoring the city of Chicago.

Be kind enough to acknowledge the receipt of inclosed draft, in order to place the same before our Society.

Yours very respectfully,

SIMON M. ROSENBLATT,
Financial Secretary Independent Literary Union.

RURAL GROVE, N. Y., *October* 16, 1871.

HON. R. B. MASON: —

Dear Sir, — Inclosed you will find draft for the small sum of thirty-four dollars and fifty cents (34\frac{50}{100}$), raised yesterday in an impromptu collection in a small congregation in the M. E. Church, Rural Grove, for the needy sufferers by the late terrible conflagration. We send this as a slight token of our Christian sympathies, humbly commending all the afflicted ones to the kind care of our Heavenly Father.

Yours for God and Humanity,

E. MARSH,

Pastor of the M. E. Church, Rural Grove, N. Y.

PAWLING, N. Y., *October* 16, 1871.

TO THE MAYOR OF CHICAGO: —

Please accept this trifle, two dollars ($2.00) from an anxious heart, and may God bless the poor homeless ones and protect them. How willingly would I give more, but although rich in God's blessing I am poor in this world's goods. Yours truly, M. J. M.

SYRACUSE, N. Y., *October* 16, 1871.

TO THE COMMITTEE FOR DISBURSING THE FUNDS FOR THE RELIEF OF THE CHICAGO SUFFERERS: —

Gentlemen, — I tender you the gross receipts of a Matinee given at my Opera House, Saturday, October 14th, and if agreeable to you should like to have it disposed of among the theatrical profession, who are among the sufferers in your city. By so doing you will greatly oblige the donor. Yours respectfully,

FRANK WILD.

NEW YORK, *October* 16, 1871.

DAVID A. GAGE, ESQ., *City Treasurer, Chicago, Ill.*: —

Sir, — Inclosed you will please find draft of Chemical Bank of this city to your order for ten thousand five hundred and twenty-three dollars and sixty-six cents ($10,523$\frac{66}{100}$). This being the total contributions to Saturday, October 14th, from citizens of New York through New York Herald, nine thousand six hundred and twenty-three dollars and sixty-six cents ($9,623$\frac{66}{100}$), and New York Herald and employés nine hundred dollars ($900).

I will continue to forward you as long as contributions come in. Please acknowledge the inclosed and oblige,

Very respectfully yours,

W. H. HENRY,

Treasurer for New York Herald.

NEW YORK, *October* 16, 1871.

HON. R. B. MASON, *Mayor of Chicago:* —

Sir, — The officials, employés, and laborers, on the new United States Post Office and Court House in this city, through me, desire to present the Chicago sufferers the proceeds of one day's labor and compensation as a small testimony of their sympathy with the sufferers in this great calamity. I inclose my check for three hundred dollars ($300) for that purpose, and beg to remain, Very respectfully yours,

C. T. HULBURD, *Superintendent.*

NEW YORK, *October* 16, 1871.

HON. R. B. MASON, *Mayor, Chicago:* —

Dear Sir, — Please draw on me at sight for three hundred and fifty-four dollars ($354), which sum has been contributed by the employés of this house towards the relief of your suffering ones.

I am yours respectfully,

E. R. SMITH, *with Lord and Taylor.*

249 WEST 43d ST., NEW YORK, N. Y., *October* 16, 1871.

HON. R. B. MASON: —

Inclosed find certificate of deposit for one hundred and seventy-five dollars ($175), being the plate collection of last evening for the relief of those who are in need from the fire in Chicago.

Many of our principal men had given through the various business associations with which they are connected. Please sign and return to me the inclosed receipt. Yours truly,

L. H. KING.

MINERSVILLE, SCHUYLKILL CO., PA., *October* 16, 1871.

TO R. B. MASON, *Mayor of Chicago, Ill.:* —

Dear Sir, — I herewith forward you a draft for twenty-seven dollars ($27) for your suffering fellow citizens, the proceeds of a collection in the English Lutheran Church of this place. Praying that God may provide for the destitute and "temper the wind to the shorn lamb,"

I remain yours, etc.,

R. WEISER,

Pastor of English Lutheran Church, Minersville, Pa.

LEHIGHTON, PA., *October* 16, 1871.

CHICAGO RELIEF AND AID SOCIETY: —

The sum inclosed is the gift of the congregation worshipping in the M. E. Church of Lehighton, Carbon Co., Pa., being a faint expression of our sympathy for the afflicted people of Chicago. Sum inclosed thirteen dollars and seventy-five cents ($$13\frac{75}{100}$).

J. T. Swindells, *Pastor.*

Mayor's Office, Town of Collingwood,
Ontario, Canada, *October* 16, 1871.

To the Mayor of Chicago: —

The townspeople of Collingwood deeply sympathize with the citizens of Chicago in their dire calamity which bears so heavily on them, and extend to them the right hand of friendship in their hour of trouble. Accompanying this you will find five hundred dollars ($500) to assist in meeting their present necessities. Please acknowledge receipt of same.

G. Watson, *Mayor.*

New York, *October* 17, 1871,

To the Hon. Mayor of Chicago: —

Sir, — I took a collection for the sufferers of your ruined city in my congregation in Williamsburg and New York and not knowing what else to do with it I send it to you to be handed to the Treasurer of the Relief Fund.

Will you see that he gets this one hundred and forty-one dollars and fifty-five cents ($$141\frac{55}{100}$) and return me a receipt. Address 125 East 17th Street, New York.

Credit this money to the Progressive Spiritualist societies of New York and Williamsburg. Moses Hull.

Boston, Mass., *October* 17, 1871.

Hon. R. B. Mason, *Mayor of Chicago:* —

Dear Sir, — Herewith please find the sum of four hundred and thirty-eight dollars and fifty-five cents ($$438\frac{55}{100}$) it being the total amount of receipts for the benefit of the sufferers of your city, given at the St. James Theatre on Friday night last, October 13th.

Hoping that, though it is not a great sum, it will do much good, believe us Yours sincerely,

Joseph T. Trowbridge & Co.

Port Jervis, N. Y., *October* 17, 1871.

Mr. R. B. Mason: —

Inclosed you will find six dollars and fifty cents ($$6\frac{50}{100}$) for the relief of the Chicago sufferers from scholars of Room No. 3.

Church Street School.

CHESTER, DELAWARE CO., PA., *October* 17, 1871.

Dear Sir, — I have been requested by a committee of the citizens of this place, of which I am chairman, to say to you or whoever is duly authorized to receive the contributions from our citizens for the relief of the sufferers by the late fire in your city, that we will be able to raise about four thousand dollars ($4,000), and as Chester is a manufacturing city, and the largest contributors are manufacturers, whether the contributions from them would not be more beneficial to send a part, if not all, in such goods as satinets, cloths, jeans, bed-ticking, muslins, shawls, etc., as they could be sent in cases at cash prices and sent free of expense, or whether it would be more acceptable in cash subject to draft. Your early reply is respectfully requested.

Truly yours, JOHN LARKIN, JR.,
Mayor of City of Chester.

TO HON. R. B. MASON.

BOSTON HIGHLANDS, MASS., *October* 17, 1871.

TO HIS HONOR R. B. MASON, *Mayor of Chicago*: —

Dear Sir, — Please accept this small amount, ten dollars ($10), and give it to the little suffering boys and girls. If I was a man, I would give you more, but this is all I could raise from my schoolmates at this time. God bless you, Mr. Mayor, for your kindness to those poor children.

I want Chicago to rise once more, and when I am a man I will come out and help you.

Please inform me if you receive this and oblige,

Yours very respectfully,
ARTHUR HARDY.

NEW YORK CITY, *October* 18, 1871.

BRO. MASON, *Mayor of Chicago*: —

Dear Sir and Bro., — New York Lodge No. 330 F. and A. M., have collected by a deposit in the hat one thousand and thirty dollars and fifty cents ($1,030$\frac{50}{100}$) for the sufferers of your city, and to go to the general relief fund.

Shall we hold it subject to your order or send a certificate of deposit to you, or shall we send it on in small bills? In all probability it will be increased before we hear from you.

The treasurer of this fund may be addressed James R. Elsey, No. 189 Washington Street, New York city.

I feel proud of the Lodge and the modest manner of the donation.

God keep your people from want. Fraternally,

JOHN GRIFFIN, *Master.*

BARMEN, *October* 18, 1871.

HON. R. B. MASON, *Mayor of the City of Chicago*:—

Dear Sir, — With feelings of the deepest sorrow and heartiest sympathy I have read the accounts of the great sufferings of my fellow-citizens at Chicago. Let them know if you please that my heart is with them in this great affliction, and that I will do all in my power to contribute to the appeasing of their grief.

I have the honor to transmit herewith a draft for two thousand dollars ($2,000) gold, which sum I collected at Barmen and Eberfeld.

In the hope to be able to send an equal sum in a few days, I have the honor to be, sir, very respectfully your obedient servant,

EMIL HOECHSTER, *U. S. Consul.*

NEW YORK, *October* 18, 1871.

HON. R. B. MASON:—

Dear Sir, — Last Sunday the "Church of the Strangers" contributed two hundred and ninety-eight dollars and ninety cents (298\frac{90}{100}$) for the relief of the sufferers in Chicago. You can draw upon me at sight for three hundred dollars ($300), or I will forward this amount as you may direct, or have anything purchased in this market which may be most needed. A package or two of clothing will be forwarded at the close of the week. Very respectfully yours,

CHAS. F. DEEMS,
Pastor "Church of the Strangers."

NEW YORK, *October* 18, 1871.

R. B. MASON, ESQ., *Mayor of Chicago*:—

Please find inclosed five hundred and thirteen dollars ($513), a contribution from the employés of the Eighth Avenue Horse Railroad Company of the city of New York.

It is their wish that this money should be distributed to the employés of the horse railroads who have suffered by the fire.

Please acknowledge the receipt of the same.

Yours respectfully,
H. B. WILSON,
Superintendent of the Eighth Avenue Railroad Company.

NEW YORK, *October* 18, 1871.

TO HIS HONOR THE MAYOR OF CHICAGO:—

Dear Sir, — The teachers and pupils of this Institution, represented by an organization known as the Fanwood Literary Association, request your acceptance for the relief of the sufferers by the late disastrous fire in Chicago of two hundred dollars ($200), which they send by express.

Of this, one hundred and seventy-one dollars and forty-nine cents ($\$171\frac{49}{100}$) are the net proceeds of a pantomime entertainment given by the Association at the Institution, on Monday evening the 16th inst., and twenty-nine dollars and fifty-one cents ($\$29\frac{51}{100}$) is composed of contributions from different individuals connected with the Institution.

Probably in no quarter have the recent misfortunes of Chicago excited a livelier sympathy than among the children of silence who compose this household. Their voiceless prayers have ascended to Heaven in behalf of those so suddenly made homeless amd destitute, and their most earnest efforts have been put forth to obtain the means to share with others the happiness of alleviating suffering they so deeply deplore.

Very truly and respectfully your obedient servant,

ISAAC LEWIS PEET,

Principal of the Institution, and Counsellor of the Association.

SENECA FALLS, N. Y., *October* 18, 1871.

HIS HONOR R. B. MASON, *Mayor, and Chairman of the Chicago Relief Committee, Chicago, Ill.:* —

Dear Sir, — About one week since, we forwarded, by the hands of Hon. Geo. B. Daniels, for disbursement amongst the needy sufferers by your late conflagration, the sum of three thousand two hundred and thirty-four dollars and seventy-five cents ($\$3,234\frac{75}{100}$) in cash, being the net result of a one day's collection from our citizens in behalf of your people. We this day forward by railroad freight twenty-three packages marked Chicago Relief Committee, Chicago, Ill., from Seneca Falls Relief Committee.

The collections are from all classes, creeds, and conditions, and all realize how it may be "more blessed to give than to receive." With warm sympathies for your distressed people, and the hope that our offering may prove a present relief to some,

I have the honor to be yours, etc., GEO. W. MEAD,

Treasurer Seneca Falls Relief Committee.

KINDERHOOK, N. Y., *October* 19, 1871.

HON. R. B. MASON, *Mayor of Chicago:* —

Dear Sir, — It affords me much pleasure to inform you that the citizens of Kinderhook Village have subscribed a sum amounting to five hundred and fifty dollars ($550) for the benefit of the needy sufferers by the late fire in your city.

This amount I hold subject to your draft or that of any authorized party connected with the relief movement.

Please advise receipt of this letter and inform me who will be authorized to draw for this amount, Respectfully yours,

WILLIAM R. MESSICK,

President of the Village of Kinderhook, N. Y.

GOLD HILL, NEVADA, *October* 19, 1871.

TO THE HON. R. B. MASON, *Mayor of Chicago*:—

Dear Sir,— Inclosed please find first of exchange on Messrs. Lees & Wallen of New York, for seven hundred and sixty-four dollars and fifty cents ($764 $\frac{50}{100}$) gold coin, it being a donation by the employés of the Crown Point Gold and Silver Mining Company of Gold Hill, Nevada, towards the relief of the sufferers by the late fire which devastated your city. This donation is the free will offering of the employés of this mine, uninfluenced by, and unknown to, any of the officers of the company here, until presented at our office to be forwarded to you, and therefore to be the more appreciated, as coming from the hard working citizens of this State, who, although strangers and separated by thousands of miles, sympathize with you in your suffering, and freely contribute their mite towards your relief.

Please acknowledge the receipt of the same and oblige,

Very respectfully yours,

LEWIS GOODWIN,

Local Secretary, Crown Point Mining Co.

NEW YORK, *October* 19, 1871.

HON. R. B. MASON, *Mayor of Chicago*:—

It affords me great pleasure to announce to you that my benefit for the Chicago sufferers has realized the sum of twenty-three hundred and seventy-nine dollars ($2,379), which amount is in hands of treasurer, Mr. D. S. Greenebaum, of this city. Please confer with Henry Greenebaum, of your city regarding disbursement.

DANIEL E. BANDMAN,

262 *West* 14*th St.*

LANSINGBURG, N. Y., *October* 20, 1871.

HON. R. B. MASON, *Mayor of Chicago*:—

Dear Sir,— I inclose check of the Bank of Lansingburg on National Park Bank of New York for twelve hundred and sixty-two dollars and thirty-four cents ($1,262 $\frac{34}{100}$). This amount is contributed by the citizens of Lansingburg, New York, towards the relief of their fellow-citizens of Chicago, and intrusted to you for that purpose. Please acknowledge its reception.

I sent you thirty (30) barrels of crackers (bill of lading by S. P. Welch, President), did you receive them?

Very respectfully,

F. B. LEONARD,

Treasurer Relief Association.

MILLERSVILLE, PA., *October* 20, 1871.

MR. DAVID A. GAGE: —

Dear Sir, — Inclosed you will find a draft for one hundred and seventy dollars ($170), the contribution of the State Normal School of Pennsylvania, for the relief of the unfortunate people of Chicago.

Please acknowledge the receipt of the same, that we may be sure it has reached you. Yours truly,

EDWARD BROOKS,
Principal State Normal School.

EASTHAMPTON, MASS., *October* 20, 1871.

HON. R. B. MASON, *Mayor of Chicago, Ill.*: —

I inclose draft of our First National Bank on Ninth National Bank of New York for three hundred and twenty dollars ($320), to be used for the relief of those who are suffering from the recent dreadful calamity that has overtaken your city.

This sum is the contribution of the operatives of the Nashawannuck Manufacturing Co. They heartily and voluntarily, upon the news of the fire reaching them, devoted one days earnings as a testimony of their sympathy for those who have so greatly suffered.

Please acknowledge the receipt of the inclosed, and oblige,

E. H. SAWYER,
For employés of the Nashawannuck Mf'g. Co.

WATERFORD, IRELAND, *October* 21, 1871.

HIS HONOR R. B. MASON, *Mayor of Chicago*: —

Dear Sir, — I have had already the gratification to acquaint you that the people of Waterford, in response to a call which I took the liberty of making to them, assembled in public meeting and resolved to aid, by all the means in their power, in mitigating the sufferings which have been cast upon the people of your city by an unparalleled calamity. In the "Waterford News," which I send you by this post, you will see a full report of our proceedings, together with the subscription list, which I am happy to say now amounts to about four hundred pounds (£400), and I am confident of at least another hundred pounds (£100). Compared with the magnitude of your disaster the sum is small, but I trust it will not be taken as a full index of the feelings of our people in your dire distress, for the sympathy pervades all classes, and were our means equal to the disposition of our hearts the amount would be tenfold.

I am authorized by the committee to ask, if your desire is that the sum which may be subscribed here should be forwarded to you in cash, or do you know of any other means by which it could be made more advantageous for the relief of the suffering in your city?

With assurances of the most heartfelt sympathy in your affliction, from myself and my fellow-citizens, I have the honor to remain, with profound esteem, Your faithful servant

HENRY F. SLATTERY,
Mayor of Waterford.

12, ST. VINCENT PLACE, GLASGOW, *October* 21, 1871.

TO THE MAYOR OF CHICAGO:—

Dear Mayor,—Referring to my telegram of the 19th instant, intimating that Messrs. Henderson Brothers would pay you the sum of five thousand pounds sterling (£5,000), to account of the fund at present in course of being subscribed in this city, for the relief of the destitute sufferers from the terrible fire in Chicago, allow me again to express to you and through you to all your suffering people, the warmest sympathy of the citizens of Glasgow. I trust that the loss of life and property may not be so great as we have too much reason to anticipate.

I have little doubt, however, but that your citizens will continue to exhibit the characteristics of a great thriving commercial community, and that the rise of your city from its present calamity will be even more wonderful than its progress in the past.

I have only further to say in behalf of the Glasgow Committee, that the fund is being subscribed here for those who have been left destitute by the conflagration, not for those who may have other means of extricating themselves from their present sufferings.

May I request to hear from you at your convenience.

I am, dear Mayor, yours very truly,
JNO. WATSON, *Acting Chief Magistrate.*

CHARLESTOWN, MASS., *October* 21, 1871.

TO THE MAYOR OF CHICAGO:—

My dear Sir,—The city of Charlestown, in common with all other communities, deeply sympathize with our sister city of Chicago in its sudden and severe calamity.

I am glad to inform you that our people at once devised plans for putting their sympathy into a tangible form of relief. The result of their efforts is the sum of eight thousand dollars ($8,000), which I am authorized to say to you is held subject to your draft, or to such disposition of it as you may direct. Besides this sum I have and am forwarding liberal supplies of clothing to individuals in your city for distribution.

It must be remembered for our credit that a large portion of our resident citizens are merchants in Boston, only separated from us by a narrow river, and they have through very natural business or other associations contributed there, and thus reduced the amount from this city.

The operatives in the navy yard here contributed some three thousand six hundred dollars ($3,600) which went to you by itself. Nearly half of these men are resident here, and of course so much of this money as they represent must be considered fairly as from our city. Other organizations here have also sent their funds separately.

I think I may safely say, therefore, that there has gone from this little city for your aid at least thirteen thousand dollars ($13,000) in all, in addition to the clothing.

We propose to do something also for other western communities who are suffering from like cause with Chicago.

Tendering you the active sympathy and good will of both our government and the people,

I have the honor to remain, your obedient servant,

WM. H. KENT, *Mayor*.

STATE PRISON, CHARLESTOWN, MASS., *October* 12, 1871.

HON. R. B. MASON, *Mayor of Chicago:* —

Dear Sir, — Inclosed please find check on the Bunker Hill National Bank of this city for six hundred and seventeen dollars and thirty-two cents (617\frac{32}{100}$), contributed by the attachés and convicts of this prison for the relief of the sufferers at Chicago.

Very respectfully, GIDEON HAYNES, *Warden*.

SAG HARBOR, LONG ISLAND, N. Y., *October* 21, 1871.

TO THE MAYOR OF CHICAGO, ILL.: —

Dear Sir, — Inclosed please find my draft for the sufferers of the recent fire, from the First Presbyterian Church of this village. Accept it as our offering with our sympathy and prayers. Please let me know if you receive it. Yours for the afflicted,

CHAS. N. BROWNE.

LIVERPOOL, *October* 23, 1871.

TO THE MAYOR OF CHICAGO, U. S. A.: —

Sir, — The members of the Scotch Drapery trade in Liverpool have heard with feelings of sorrow of the terrible fires that have been devastating your city, and they wished, as a body, to evince their sympathies with those who must have suffered so terribly.

They accordingly send to you, per the Mayor of New York, five packages of woolen and cotton goods, which they hope may be found of some little assistance during the rigors of the coming winter.

With profound sympathy for your citizens in their distress, I am sir,

Yours most obediently,

JAS. LAIDLAW.

CONSULATE GENERAL OF THE UNITED STATES OF AMERICA,
FRANKFORT ON THE MAIN, *October* 23, 1871.

HON. R. B. MASON, *Mayor of Chicago:* —

Sir, — I have the pleasure to inform you, that on behalf of the citizens and residents of the city of Frankfort on the Main, I have placed at your disposal the amount of twelve thousand five hundred dollars ($12,500) U. S. Bonds, of the issue of 1862 first series, with the coupons of November attached, being a portion of the amount contributed for the relief of the suffering citizens of your city, which will realize fifteen thousand dollars ($15,000) in U. S. currency.

The German citizens of Frankfort, as well as the Americans resident here, although distant from you in space, are with you in heart, thought, and sympathy, in this hour of your distress and want, and, while the whole world are laboring to relieve your sufferings, they also desire to do all in their power to mitigate the calamity now almost prostrating you. I have the honor to be your obedient servant,

W. PRENTISS WEBSTER, *U. S. Consul-general.*

HALIFAX, N. S., *October* 24, 1871.

TO THE MAYOR OF CHICAGO: —

Dear Sir, — I requested our Mayor on Saturday last to telegraph to you that six thousand dollars ($6,000) collected by the citizens of Halifax was at your disposal, to be added to the sum contributed from all quarters towards the relief of those who have been made homeless by the fire which has destroyed so much of your great and beautiful city.

Allow me to add that this sum but feebly represents the universal feelings of sympathy among us all, for the thousands of the suffering people of Chicago.

The amount would have been much larger, but on the very evening for which the relief meeting was called, a storm of unprecedented violence burst upon our shores, which destroyed so much property of the rich, and swept away the all of so many of the poor, that our hands were stayed from doing as much as we anticipated.

I trust that our small contribution, which goes from willing, sympathizing donors, may be instrumental in relieving some of the more dominant causes of distress, and also in forming a link of kindly feeling between Chicago and Halifax.

Believe me with much esteem and sympathy, yours,

JOHN DOULL,
Treasurer Citizens' Committee for the relief of Chicago.

WEST TROY, N. Y., *October* 24, 1871.

WIRT DEXTER, ESQ., CHICAGO RELIEF AND AID SOCIETY: —

Dear Sir, — I have the honor to inclose two (2) cases of shawls shipped to you, a contribution from the employés of these mills, who also send their heartfelt sympathies for your poor people at this calamitous time.

Yours very sincerely,

ARCH. M. MCLEAN,

In behalf of Messrs. James Roy and Company's employés.

UNITED STATES CONSULATE,
DRESDEN, *October* 24, 1871.

HON. R. B. MASON, *Mayor of Chicago*: —

My dear Sir, — As a small token of the deep sympathy of the residents of Dresden with the people of Chicago in their great calamity, and to aid in the relief of the suffering and destitute, I have received from them the sum of sixteen hundred thalers, which reduced to U. S. currency is thirteen hundred and fifteen dollars ($1,315), which I remit through Messrs. Robert Thode & Co., American bankers, who together with Mr. Jos. Meyer and other friends, will continue to receive subscriptions to be remitted through the Consulate.

With heartfelt sympathy for the distressed, and a just pride as a fellow-countryman in the characteristic energy and public spirit which you all display in such a wonderful manner in repairing the work of the disaster, I am most sincerely,

Your obedient servant,

O. H. IRISH, *U. S. Consul.*

NEW YORK, *October* 24, 1871.

TO HIS HONOR R. B. MASON, *Mayor of Chicago*: —

Dear Sir, — Inclosed please find a draft for one thousand dollars ($1,000) donated by the members of the Musical Mutual Protective Union of New York, in aid of the sufferers of your city.

As I am acting in the name of the above named association as their secretary, you would greatly oblige me by sending an acknowledgment of the receipt of the draft.

I have the honor to be, yours respectfully,

D. SCHAAD, *Secretary.*

LYKENS, PA., *October* 24, 1871.

MR. R. B. MASON: —

Dear Sir, — In behalf of the employés of the Summit Branch Railroad, allow me to tender you and the sufferers of your city our heartfelt sympathy. I have collected from the employés the sum of two hundred and two dollars ($202), which I have deposited in the Miners' Deposit Bank of Lykens, subject to your order, which please accept and distribute as you think best. Yours respectfully,

W. E. RAY, *Superintendent.*

SHAMBURG, PA., *October* 24, 1871.

HON. R. B. MASON, *Chicago, Ill.*: —

In behalf of the citizens of this place we have the pleasure of inclosing herewith New York draft, for three hundred and forty-three dollars ($343), in aid of the destitute sufferers from the late disastrous fire in your city. Accept assurances of our profoundest sympathy, and be assured that our greatest regret is that our number and means prevent our making this contribution larger. We also this day send you box of clothing for same purpose.

Most respectfully yours,

JNO. R. DRUM,
C. S. POOR,
F. W. PERKINS. } *Committee.*

WAPPINGERS FALLS, N. Y., *October* 24, 1871.

R. B. MASON, ESQ., *Mayor of Chicago, Ill.*: —

Dear Sir, — The people of the village of Wappingers Falls, Dutchess Co., N. Y., opened a subscription for the relief of the sufferers by the Chicago fire, and have raised eight hundred and eleven dollars and forty-six cents (811\frac{46}{100}$); two hundred of which has been sent through another channel. I have on deposit the balance, six hundred and eleven dollars and forty-six cents (611\frac{46}{100}$), subject to your draft on me.

Yours truly,

JOSEPH FAULKNER, *President.*

WEST TROY, N. Y., *October* 25, 1871.

HON. R. B. MASON, *Mayor of Chicago, Ill.*: —

Dear Sir, — Our citizens have contributed one thousand dollars ($1,000) for the benefit of your afflicted people, which is in my hands subject to your draft. While we deeply sympathize with the many sufferers in your city, we are not unmindful of the arduous duties imposed upon yourself in consequence of this terrible and widespread calamity.

Very respectfully yours,

J. F. PHELPS, *Treasurer.*

JOHNSTOWN, PA., *October* 25, 1871.

TO HIS HONOR, THE MAYOR OF CHICAGO: —

Inclosed please find forty-six dollars ($46) from Forepaughs' Menagerie, to help the fund for Chicago fire sufferers.

Yours respectfully, BEN. LUSBIE, *Treasurer.*

NYACK, N. Y., *October* 25, 1871.

R. B. MASON, *Mayor of Chicago*: —

Dear Sir, — The Hudson River Sabbath School Teachers' Association convened at Nyack, N. Y., in the Reformed Church, on the 10th inst., and took up an impromptu collection for the Chicago sufferers, the amount of which I here inclose to you.

Will you see that it reaches its destination and acknowledgment made of its receipt.

Address, "Henry V. Voorhees, Nyack, Rockland Co., N. Y."

Yours respectfully,

HENRY V. VOORHEES.

BERLIN, *October* 26, 1871.

HIS HONOR, THE MAYOR OF CHICAGO: —

Sir, — The appalling calamity which has befallen our beloved Chicago, involving such a destruction of use and beauty, of commerce, civilization, and progress, as has never been recorded in human annals, has awakened earnest and genuine sympathy throughout all Germany.

The burning of our great and beautiful city, the grandest and most conspicuous monument of the genius and enterprise of the American people, under free and liberal institutions and government, is justly considered a national, not a mere local calamity. It is felt that a long and cruel train of horrors and suffering must follow the awful destruction that has swept over the ill fated city, and everywhere funds have been and are being raised for the relief of the vast multitudes of your destitute and stricken people. Being one of your citizens, allied to Chicago by many associations of public service and friendship, and glorying in its marvelous growth, prosperity and splendor, the horror of the announcement of its sudden destruction by fire unspeakably shocked and overwhelmed me, but feeling that I must do what little there might be in my power towards aiding and assisting my fellow-citizens in their distress, I promptly took steps to organize a relief committee here, and thanks to the ready responses to my appeals, we have thus far given orders to Messrs. Hardt & Co., of New York, to pay to your order the sum of twenty-five thousand dollars ($25,000), which the committee trusts you have promptly received.

Among the contributors to the fund are found the Emperor and Empress, the Queen Dowager, and the Crown Prince and Crown Princess.

The Empress (to quote the language of the letters transmitting me the donations), "given in grateful remembrance of the sympathy displayed by America during the late war;" and the Crown Prince and Crown Princess, "in grateful acknowledgment of the friendly feelings which America most efficiently manifested for the German warriors during the conflict with France, and in heartfelt sympathy for the inhabitants of Chicago smitten by terrible misfortune."

Our collections are still going on and promise additional results. To enable the committee to properly account to the contributors for the sums received, I am directed to respectfully ask your honor to make suitable acknowledgment of the receipt of the amounts transmitted to you from Berlin. In the meantime we all here feel that the people of Chicago, though grievously tried and well nigh overcome, have not and will not lose hope and heart, and with the help of God, and by their undaunted courage, enterprise, skill, and energy, will rebuild and restore their city to even greater wealth, usefulness, and splendor, — a consummetion most fervently to be desired and hoped for.

I have the honor to be your obedient servant,

H. Kriesmann, *U. S. Consul.*

Town Hall, Leeds, *October* 26, 1871.

To the Right Worshipful, the Mayor of Chicago: —

Dear Mr. Mayor, — I herewith beg to hand you invoices for twenty-one, and bill of lading for nineteen bales of blankets, as the first contribution from the borough of Leeds, in token of our deep sympathy with you in the great calamity which has befallen your city.

The bill of lading for the other two bales shall be forwarded to you on receipt of it from Liverpool.

We had purposed remitting cash, but a communication came from New York stating that all goods for the relief of the sufferers would be admitted, duty free, in Chicago, and that blankets were much needed.

In making the selections we have considered the peculiar circumstances of the case, and have sent blankets of a description which we think best adapted for the immediate wants of your citizens.

With assurances of my deep sympathy with you, believe me, dear Mr. Mayor, Yours, faithfully,

John Barran, *Mayor of Leeds.*

Chicago, Illinois, *October* 27, 1871.

Geo. M. Pullman, Esq., Treasurer Relief and Aid Society, Chicago: —

Sir, — I have the honor to inclose herewith check No. 121,366 on the Assistant Treasurer of the United States, New York, N. Y., for two hundred and three dollars and fifty cents ($\$203\frac{50}{100}$), being subscriptions from the professors, officers, cadets, and residents at the Military Academy of West Point, for the relief of the sufferers by the late fire in Chicago, and to request a receipt for the same.

I am, sir, very respectfully, your obedient servant,

P. H. Sheridan, *Lieutenant-general U. S. Army.*

HEIDELBERG, *October* 29, 1871.

HIS HONOR, THE MAYOR OF CHICAGO:—

Sir,—I inclose herewith a draft for one hundred and sixty dollars ($160), gold (= 400 guilders South German currency), a contribution of the citizens of Baden-Baden towards the relief of your afflicted and suffering fellow-citizens. If there is any arrangement for the acknowledgment of such contributions I shall be most happy to convey to the givers any expression your Honor may be pleased to communicate.

Very complete arrangements have been effected within this consular jurisdiction for collecting relief funds. The amount already subscribed exceeds five thousand dollars ($5,000).

I have the honor to be, sir, most respectfully,

Your obedient servant,

W. H. YOUNG, *U. S. Consul.*

RHENISH PRUSSIA, CREFELD, *October* 30, 1871.

Dear Sir,—Inclosed herewith I have the honor and great satisfaction to remit to your hands two thousand and forty-five dollars ($2,045), gold, as a first part of contributions the citizens of Crefeld placed at your disposal for the benefit and relief of the sufferers by the appalling calamity which has visited the late so prosperous city of Chicago, and as a token of heartfelt sympathy with your afflicted fellow men. The list of subscriptions circulated by me and urged by my best endeavors, showing already an additional amount of donations, and preliminary steps having been taken to have the same opened also in the other places of my district, I may soon expect to be able to forward to you another and similar sum of money.

With great respect, yours most truly,

J. MAGNNE, *U. S. Consular Agent.*

BALTIMORE, MD., *October* 30, 1871.

GEO. M. PULLMAN, ESQ., CHICAGO:—

Dear Sir,—I am instructed to forward to you seven hundred and fifty dollars ($750), the net proceeds of a concert given by the "Baltimore German Liederkranz" for the benefit of the Chicago sufferers. Please distribute the amount among the needy, and give a proportion to the poor Germans that apply to you for aid. Please acknowledge receipt, and be assured of our deep sympathy.

Yours, very respectfully,

F. RAINE.

SUSQUEHANNA DEPOT, PA., *October* 31, 1871.

HON. R. B. MASON, *Mayor, Chicago*: —

Dear Sir, — In common with the spontaneous outburst of praiseworthy and generous liberality of the people of the whole country, I am pleased to inclose you, and through you, my dear sir, to the Aid and Relief Society of your fire-destroyed city, a contribution of the employés of Susquehanna shop, Erie Railway, amounting to six hundred and twenty dollars and twenty cents ($\$620\frac{20}{100}$), to be applied as your society in their judgment may deem best, to the relief of the sufferers by the recent great fire of Chicago, which has left thousands of your citizens houseless, homeless, and penniless. Trusting that it may reach you in safety, and, like the widow's mite, be blessed of God in the little good it may accomplish in the relief of suffering humanity,

I am, with considerations of respect and sympathy,

Very truly,

JAMES B. GREGG, *Master Mechanic.*

NEW YORK, *November* 1, 1871.

HON. R. B. MASON, *Mayor of Chicago*: —

Sir, — When the sad tidings of the destruction of your fair city were spread abroad, the merchants of Washington and West Washington Market, in common with the civilized world, were moved with feelings of deepest sympathy for your people in their day of distress, and at a meeting resolved to raise money for their relief. As the result of our collections I have in hand forty-one hundred and forty-two dollars and fifty cents ($\$4,142\frac{50}{100}$).

Since the destruction of your city, dire calamity by fire has come upon the people of Wisconsin and Michigan, and at a meeting of our merchants it was resolved that the amount collected shall be equally divided among Chicago and the two States mentioned, and in pursuance of directions I have the pleasure now to place at your disposal for distribution, the sum of thirteen hundred and eighty dollars and eighty-four cents ($\$1,380\frac{84}{100}$), being one third the amount collected, and await your suggestions as to how it shall be sent to you. Respectfully,

E. C. SCHANCK,
Secretary and Treasurer.

BASLE, SWITZERLAND, *November* 1, 1871.

HON. R. B. MASON, *Mayor of Chicago*: —

Dear Sir, — I am happy indeed to inform you, that up to date, I have collected from sympathizing citizens of Basle, over sixteen thousand (16,000) francs gold, for the unfortunate inhabitants of Chicago. May this little sum contribute, with the blessing of God, its mite to alleviate suffering, and bring good cheer to some almost desponding souls of your once so happy and prosperous city, truly the Queen of the West.

Please draw upon A. Goettel & Co., New York, for sixteen thousand (16,000) francs. These gentlemen were to-day instructed by Iselin & Strahelin, bankers at Basle, to have this sum at your disposal; the balance, after deducting some expenses, will be forwarded to you at some future day. It may not be uninteresting to you, if I here add, that Basle lies on the very boundary of Switzerland, counts some 40,000 inhabitants, and is proverbial for its liberality. During the late war it contributed largely to the sick and wounded of both armies.

In 1556, Basle itself was almost entirely burnt and destroyed through an earthquake.

Please answer this letter when convenient.

I have the honor to be your obedient servant,

T. C. Erni, *U. S. Consul.*

Commandant's Office, Navy Yard,
Norfolk, Va., *November* 1, 1871.

David Gage, Esq., *Treasurer Chicago Relief Fund, Chicago, Ill.*:—

Dear Sir, — I have the pleasure to send you the inclosed draft for two hundred and thirty-four dollars ($234), a humble contribution from this Yard to the relief of our fellow-citizens, who were sufferers in the late calamity; and I beg you to accept, at the same time, the assurances of our most sincere and affectionate sympathy.

With the highest respect, your obedient servant,

C. H. Davis, *Rear Admiral.*

New Hamburg, N. Y., *November* 1, 1871.

To the Mayor of Chicago:—

Please find inclosed ten dollars ($10), which you will use for the benefit of those in need of help.

The amount has been raised by the scholars of my school without any suggestion upon my part. They have done it entirely among themselves.

Very respectfully,

W. J. Ballard,
Principal Union School.

Church of the Immaculate Conception,
Amenia, Dutchess Co., N. Y., *November* 2, 1871.

Hon. R. B. Mason:—

Dear Sir,— Inclosed please find a draft for one hundred dollars ($100) payable to your order at the Importers' and Traders' National Bank, New York.

Accept it as the generous though small offering of my poor parishioners, collected last Sunday in my little church, for the destitute people suffering by the late fire in your city.

Dispose of it how and where your Honor may judge best, to aid in alleviating the wants of the distressed.

Please acknowledge receipt, and believe me respectfully your obedient servant,

PATRICK W. SANDY, *Pastor.*

CONSULATE OF THE U. S. OF AMERICA,
ASPINWALL, U. S. OF COLUMBIA, *November* 2, 1871.

THE HON. MR. MASON, *Mayor of Chicago:* —

Dear Sir, — It was with profound sorrow that I read the accounts of the terrible calamity which visited Chicago on the 8th and 9th, and following days of October last past. I was more affected from the fact of having visited the "Garden City" but a short time previous to my departure for this country, and having seen the magnificence of the Western Metropolis, which is now laid in ruins.

God will provide for the thousands of homeless, houseless people, for I see that the hearts of millions are affected, and contributions are pouring in from every quarter. I immediately opened a subscription book at this Consulate, but regret exceedingly to say that no one has come forward to enroll his name. However, the American Lodge of Free Masons voted an amount; and the Masons having subscribed independently to the relief of Chicago, it could not be expected that many would subscribe outside, as nearly all our countrymen here belong to the Masonic fraternity. In addition to my Masonic mite, you will please draw on Wm. H. Knoepfel, No. 16 Cedar Street, New York, for twenty-five dollars ($25), and I only regret that I am unable to give as many *thousands*, but the position of Consul, is one which calls daily for the relief of some destitute countrymen, hence my inability to do more.

With feelings of heartfelt sympathy for the distressed people of Chicago, I subscribe myself,

Dear sir, very respectfully,
Your obedient servant,
CHAS. ERASMUS PERRY, *U. S. Consul.*

S. JARLATH'S, TUAM, IRELAND,
November 3, 1871.

TO THE MAYOR OF CHICAGO: —

Dear Sir, — I beg to inclose a draft of fifty pounds (£50) sterling, toward mitigating in some degree the terrible calamity which has so recently and so heavily fallen on the city and people of Chicago. A disaster so appalling in its suddenness, its extent, in the number of its victims and the intensity of their sufferings, must no doubt meet corresponding sympathy in the generous promptness with which relief will continually flow to your city from the charitable and humane of every nation of the earth to which the melancholy story of its awful conflagration, not of its ruin I hope, has been wafted.

At all events we of Ireland who have been tried and trained in the school of misfortune should not be insensible to the distress of others, nor should we forget that when a quarter of a century ago a direful famine swept our land and destroyed our people, it was from all parts of the great American nation our devoted country received its most abundant relief. Accept this humble offering as a pledge of our sincere sympathy with the deep sufferings of your people, and believe me, dear sir,

Your faithful servant,

JOHN, *Archbishop of Tuam.*

SUSQUEHANNA DEPOT, PA.,
November 4, 1871.

MAYOR MASON, *Chicago, Ill.:*—

Dear Sir, — Will you instruct the proper parties connected with the Chicago Aid and Relief Association to draw on me through Curtis & Miller's Banking House of this place for six hundred and eleven dollars and seventy cents ($\$611\frac{70}{100}$), contributed by the citizens of this place in aid of the sufferers of Chicago by the great fire.

We trouble you with this matter because we have not at hand the address of the Treasurer of the Relief Society. Please ask the Treasurer to acknowledge the receipt of the money when received, that we may publish the same for the satisfaction of all parties concerned. Hoping that the needy will be well cared for during the winter,

I remain, yours truly,

M. L. HAWLEY.

U. S. CONSULATE, ZURICH, SWITZERLAND,
November 4, 1871.

HON. R. B. MASON, *Mayor of Chicago:*—

Sir, — It gives me great pleasure to state that the contributions set on foot in this consular district for the relief of Chicago, will amount to nearly forty thousand francs, gold. Thirty thousand (30,000) francs of this sum will be forwarded herewith by the Committee's Cashier, "The Swiss Credit Austalt," in bills on New York. The feeling of sympathy here for the unfortunate city is very general, the contributions being from all classes, rich and poor, in amounts from one to one thousand francs; and I feel that the sum raised would have been much larger were it not for the fact that the people of the district have been compelled to aid very largely their countrymen of the district who suffered by the disastrous overflow of the River Rhine, which occurred in the early summer near here, and laid waste many millions worth of property belonging chiefly to the poor and agricultural classes.

The remainder of the amount subscribed will be forwarded in a few days. I am sir, very respectfully,

Your obedient servant,

S. H. M. BYERS, *U. S. Consul.*

LANCASTER, PENN., *November* 6, 1871.

R. B. MASON, Esq., *Mayor of Chicago:* —

Dear Sir, — Inclosed please find draft for the sum of forty dollars ($40), contributed by the teachers and boys of Lancaster Male Grammar School towards the relief of the suffering school-boys of Chicago.

Respectfully,

R. S. YATES, *Principal.*

NEW YORK, *November* 6, 1871.

HENRY W. KING, Esq., *President Chicago Relief and Aid Society, Chicago, Ill.:* —

Dear Sir, — At the request of our friends Messrs. Garnet, Brown, & Co., of Genoa, Italy, we beg to inclose our check for two hundred and seventy-one dollars and thirty-eight cents ($$271\frac{38}{100}$), being the proceeds of fifty pounds (£50) sterling at the exchange of $122\frac{1}{8}$.

Messrs. Garnet, Brown, & Co. desire this amount appropriated for the benefit of the sufferers by your late fire, and we beg you will make such disposition of it, acknowledging its receipt to our friends above named.

We are your obedient servants,

DUNCAN, SHERMAN, & CO.

NEW YORK, *November* 7, 1871.

GEO. M. PULLMAN, Esq., *Treasurer Chicago Relief and Aid Society:* —

Dear Sir, — I inclose three thousand five hundred and forty-nine dollars and twenty-six cents ($$3,549\frac{26}{100}$), remitted through Messrs. Harris Bros. & Co., by the Corn Trade of the city of London, England, to the President of this Institution, for distribution to the sufferers by the recent disastrous fire in your city. Will you be so kind as to acknowledge the same, through this source, to the contributors and oblige,

Yours very truly,

ISAAC H. REED, *Pres. Pro. Exchange.*

CAMBRIDGE, MASS., *November* 8, 1871.

GEO. M. PULLMAN, Esq., *Treasurer Chicago Relief and Aid Society:* —

Dear Sir, — Inclosed please find a check for eight thousand dollars

($8,000), the same being a contribution by the citizens of Cambridge in aid of the sufferers by the great fire in your city.

Please acknowledge the receipt of the above at your earliest convenience.

Yours truly,

H. R. HARDING,
Mayor of Cambridge, Mass.

LEGATION OF THE UNITED STATES
BERNE, *November* 8, 1871.

THE HON. R. B. MASON, *Mayor of Chicago:* —

Dear Sir, — I inclose herewith a draft from Marcuard & Co., of this city, upon Messrs. H. Arney & Co., of New York, for the sum of fourteen hundred ninety-six dollars and twenty-three cents ($1,496 $\frac{23}{100}$) in gold. This sum is the amount of divers contributions made in Switzerland for the benefit of the sufferers by the great fire in Chicago, and forwarded for transmission to this Legation. The greatest part of it, 6,709 francs, was forwarded to me by Mr. Chas. H. Upton, the United States Consul at Geneva, as the result of contributions made in that city, at Chaux-de-fonds, and at St. Croix. Mr. Upton desired me to suggest, in remitting it to you, that if there were persons of Swiss origin rendered destitute by the fire, it might appropriately be applied to their relief.

Of the other contributors, Messrs. Marcuard & Co., bankers of this city, gave five hundred francs ; three hundred and thirty-four francs were forwarded to me in the name of Swiss citizens who have formerly resided in the United States ; two hundred and three francs were sent by Mr. Th. Renhewitz of Montreux, as the product of a Matinee Musicale and Dramatique, given by the professors and pupils of his school ; and nineteen francs were sent as a collection made at a meeting of laborers at Montreux.

I have the honor to be,

Very truly yours,

HORACE RUBLEE.

OFFICE OF THE "BEAUFORT REPUBLICAN,"
BEAUFORT, S. C., *November* 9, 1871.

GEO. M. PULLMAN, Esq., *Treasurer Relief Society:* —

Dear Sir, — Inclosed please find draft on New York for sixty dollars ($60.00). I regret the amount is so small, but with us it is the "widow's mite." Our community is small, and our people very poor, yet we are all rich in sympathy. I hope it will be acceptable, and that some one will be benefited thereby.

With sorrow for your affliction, I remain

Yours,

G. W. JOHNSON,
Ed. Beaufort Republican.

U. S. S. "GUERRIERE," First Rate. VILLE FRANCHE, FRANCE, *November* 10, 1871.

HON. R. B. MASON, MAYOR OF CHICAGO:—

Sir, — Inclosed herewith please find check on Paris for the sum of eight hundred and ninety-one francs (891 francs), being the contribution of the officers and crew of this ship, for the benefit of the sufferers by the late fire in your city.

Permit me to tender to you on my own behalf, and that of my officers and crew, our heartfelt sympathy for your people in their great calamity.

Respectfully your obedient servant,

J. BLAKELY CREIGHTON, *Captain Commanding.*

ELLANGOWAN, CASTLEHEAD, PAISLEY, *November* 11, 1871.

TO THE HON. THE MAYOR OF CHICAGO:—

Dear Sir, — I had the pleasure of communicating with you on the 8th current, requesting you to draw upon me for six hundred pounds (£600) sterling as an installment of the money raised in this town by a local committee in aid of the sufferers by the late disastrous fire in your city.

Assuring you of the deep sympathy that is felt by all classes in this community for the sufferers by the sad calamity that has befallen the city of Chicago, I am, dear sir,

Yours very truly,

DAVID MURRAY, *Provost.*

MAYOR'S OFFICE, MAYENCE, *November* 15, 1871.

HON. MR. MASON, *Mayor of Chicago*:—

Sir, — We have the honor to forward you, through Mr. Aaron Seeley, the United States consul at this city, a draft for the sum of three thousand one hundred and thirteen dollars and sixty-three cents ($3,113$\frac{63}{100}$) currency, to be placed towards the relief of the unfortunate sufferers caused by the late disastrous fire in your city. This amount was subscribed by the citizens of this city for the above purpose.

We have the honor to remain, very respectfully,

CARL RACHE, *Mayor.*

LEGATION OF THE UNITED STATES, MEXICO, *November* 18, 1871.

HON. HAMILTON FISH, *Secretary of State, Washington*:—

Sir, — I have the honor to inclose the first of a set of exchange, of this date, drawn by the Bank of London, Mexico and South America, payable to your order, for the sum of two thousand four hundred and seventy-two dollars and thirty-eight cents ($2,472$\frac{38}{100}$) in American gold, which was purchased by the amount subscribed in this city and vicinity, in response to my call for aid to the sufferers by the great fires in Chicago and in the State of Wisconsin. This contribution, though not large, will, it is hoped, serve to relieve some who have been brought to want by these great calamities.

You will please appropriate the proceeds to one or both of the objects indicated, in such manner as you may deem most advisable. I inclose a list of the subscribers and the amount paid by each, also a copy of the account of the said bank, showing the amount of premium paid on exchange.

Other remittances will be made from time to time, for the same purpose.

Your obedient servant,

THOMAS H. NELSON.

YORK, PA., *November* 20, 1871.

R. B. MASON:—

Dear Sir,—Inclosed please find check for eighteen dollars ($18) contributed by the pupils of my room towards relieving a mite of the suffering imposed upon your citizens.

Quite a number of my pupils are educating themselves, and their sympathy must be more heartfelt than purse-expressed. With the prayer that He who tempers the wind to the shorn lamb, may be as provident to the homeless thousands of Chicago, permit me to subscribe myself

Yours respectfully,

S. B. HEIGHES, *of York Co. Academy.*

VICTORIA, BRITISH COLUMBIA, *November* 20, 1871.

HON. R. B. MASON, *Mayor of Chicago, Ill.*:—

Sir,—I deeply regret the existence of the occasion which gives me the honor to inclose herewith a draft for five hundred and thirty-five dollars and seventy cents (535\frac{70}{100}$), amount subscribed by residents of Victoria, British Columbia, as a token of their sympathy for the people of your city in these days of her sad trials; and particularly for those in your community who are in distress or suffering. Let me request you to hand the draft to the Chicago Relief and Aid Society and have its reception acknowledged. I am, sir, with high esteem,

Your obedient serva

DAVID ECKSTEIN, *Consul.*

HONOLULU, *November* 20, 1871.

W. C. RALSTON, ESQ., *San Francisco*:—

Dear Sir,—At the first meeting of the Chamber of Commerce of this city after the receipt of the intelligence of the dreadful fires that have devastated Illinois and the neighboring States, a committee was appointed to canvas our community for subscriptions in aid of the sufferers.

An appeal has been made personally by the committee to the residents of Honolulu, and through the papers, to those on the other islands, and as a tangible result of the appeal, I have the pleasure to inclose herewith, as an installment, collected only in Honolulu, first of Bishop & Co.'s exchange on Bank of California for fifteen hundred dollars ($1,500), for distribution where it is most required. I beg also to hand you number of the Hawaiian "Gazette" of the 15th instant, containing the appeal referred to.

Respectfully yours,

ALEX. J. CARTWRIGHT,
Chairman of Committee.

ROBESONIA FURNACES P. O., BERKS CO., PENN.
ROBESONIA, *November* 22, 1871.

TO THE MAYOR OF CHICAGO:—

Hon. Sir,—The ladies of Robesonia, per Mrs. Sarah D. Robeson, shipped by express on the evening of 21st instant, one box containing clothing, bedding, etc. (an invoice of same inclosed), directed to your care, to be distributed to the sufferers by the fire in your city, in such a manner as you think proper. Mrs. Robeson desires me to ask you what articles are still most needed, hoping to be able to furnish you with more goods. Please acknowledge receipt of box, if received, and oblige. Our place is a very small one, but we feel deeply for the calamity that has visited your city. May God's blessing rest upon you, and your efforts to rebuild, and make you a great city again, is our prayer.

Yours truly,

SAMUEL SHEARER.

SECRETARY'S OFFICE, ST. JOHNS, NEWFOUNDLAND,
November 23, 1871.

TO E. M. ARCHIBALD, *Consul-general for the United States:*—

Sir,—I have the honor to transmit to you, by direction of the Government of Newfoundland, a bill of exchange on the National Bank of Commerce, New York, for one thousand dollars ($1,000) gold, and to request you will transmit the amount to the proper authorities for the relief of the fire sufferers at Chicago, and at the same time that you will express to them the deep sympathy that is felt by this government for the citizens of Chicago in their heavy calamity and visitation by fire.

I have honor to be, sir,

Your most obedient servant,

JAMES LYONS NORMAN, *Secretary.*

U. S. Flagship "Lancaster,"
Harbor of Rio de Janeiro, Brazil,
November 24, 1871.

Hon. George M. Robeson, *Secretary of the Navy:* —

Sir, — I have the pleasure to inclose herewith draft for sixty pounds sterling (£60), a contribution from the commander-in-chief, officers, and crew, of the U. S. flagship *Lancaster*, towards the relief of the sufferers by the late fire in Chicago.

Very respectfully, your obedient servant,
J. W. A. Nicholson, *Captain*,
Commanding U. S. Flagship "Lancaster."

The Bank of California, San Francisco,
December 4, 1871.

Hon. R. B. Mason, *Mayor of Chicago:* —

Dear Sir, — I am this morning in receipt of a letter from Alexander J. Cartwright, Esq., of Honolulu, H. I., announcing the result of efforts made in those distant islands for the relief of sufferers by the late fearful conflagrations in your city and neighboring States. A copy of that letter you will find inclosed herewith, and I have also the pleasure of handing you at same time, bank check on New York, No. 38,344, for fifteen hundred dollars ($1,500) gold coin, the amount remitted by Mr. Cartwright, for distribution where most required.

I am, dear sir, yours very truly,
W. C. Ralston, *Cashier.*

Mexico, *December* 7, 1871.

To the Hon. Thomas H. Nelson, *United States Envoy to Mexico:* —

Sir, — The undersigned, in the name of the "German Club in Mexico" have the honor to hand to your Excellency five hundred and fifty-seven dollars ($557), which sum has been collected among the German residents of this capital in aid of the unfortunate sufferers by the fire in Chicago. We beg the favor of your kind offices to remit the amount for the benefit of those for whom it has been subscribed, and remain, sir,

Your obedient servants,
Dr. Semeleder, *President*,
A. Wiesand, *Secretary*, } *of the German Club.*

United States Consulate, Panama,
December 13, 1871.

Wirt Dexter, Esq., *Chairman Relief Committee, Chicago, Ill.*

Sir, — Herewith inclosed you will please find currency draft for the sum of three hundred and fifty dollars ($350) payable to your order.

This money has been collected by myself for your suffering fellow-citizens, and our prayers go with it, hoping that, though it is small in amount, it may be productive of much good. This subscription is independent of the money raised by us in our two Masonic Lodges in this place. You will please acknowledge receipt of this and much oblige,

Truly yours,

OWEN M. LONG, *U. S. Consul.*

DEPARTMENT OF STATE, WASHINGTON,
December 14, 1871.

TO HIS HONOR R. B. MASON, *Mayor of the City of Chicago:—*

Sir,—I transmit herewith a draft on London for sixty pounds (£60) sterling, drawn by Messrs. Warburg & Dotti, of Lisbon, in my favor, and indorsed to George M. Pullman, Treasurer of the Chicago Relief and Aid Society.

This draft accompanied a letter of the 15th ultimo from the United States Minister to Portugal, a copy of which is inclosed, by which it will be seen that the sum abovementioned has been donated by the Countess of Edla, a native of the United States, for the relief of her countrymen who are sufferers by the recent fire in your city.

I will thank you to inform the Department of the receipt of the draft.

I have the honor to be, sir,

Your obedient servant,

HAMILTON FISH.

NEW YORK, *December* 14, 1871.

THE HON. JOSEPH MEDILL, *Mayor of the City of Chicago:—*

Sir,—We are instructed by our old correspondents, Messrs. Auguste Seydoens Sieber & Co. of Paris, to forward to you for the benefit of the sufferers by the fire which recently devastated your city, the sum of one thousand dollars ($1,000) in gold, and for which please find our cheque herein to your order.

Please to acknowledge receipt and oblige

Yours respectfully,

BENKARD & HUTTON.

BUENOS AYRES, *December* 15, 1871.

HON. LYMAN TRUMBULL, *United States Senate Chamber, Washington, D. C.:—*

Dear Sir,—Having been named treasurer of the Committee of the "Chicago Relief Fund" in this city, I have now the pleasure, in accordance with the desire of said committee, to forward you inclosed list of subscribers to said fund, amounting to say seven hundred and eleven dollars and twelve cents (711\frac{12}{100}$), gold, for which amount I beg to hand herein a sight draft of Zimmermand, Fair, & Co., on Mr. Charles F. Zimmermand of New York, made out to your order, with the request that you will kindly collect the same, and have the amount distributed among the sufferers of the late fire in Chicago, as you may think best.

I avail myself of the present opportunity to express in the name of the Committee our sympathy, in this sad visitation which has so devastated one of the fairest cities of the Union, and trust that though small our offering it may nevertheless help to relieve some suffering fellow-being.

Begging you to kindly acknowledge the receipt of the above remittance, I remain,

Yours very respectfully,

JOHN C. ZIMMERMAND, *Treasurer.*

BIRMINGHAM, *December* 16, 1871.

TO THE PRESIDENT OF THE CHICAGO RELIEF AND AID SOCIETY: —

Sir, — Having had the duty, as Mayor of Birmingham, to preside over a public meeting of the principal inhabitants, convened to consider what relief could be sent to your people under their sufferings caused by the late fire, I have now the satisfaction to inform you that the amount raised has been, after the payment of the expenses of collection, nearly four thousand one hundred pounds (£4,100).

Of this sum two thousand pounds (£2,000) was sent through Messrs. J. S. Morgan & Co. of London, and Drexel, Morgan, & Co. of New York, on 16th of October, a further sum of fifteen hundred pounds (£1,500) was forwarded through the same channel on 3d November, and I am directed to inform you that we now hold at your disposal the balance, being nearly six hundred pounds (£600), which we shall be glad to forward in any mode which you may prefer.

I ask you to accept the assurance of my own hearty sympathy, as well as that of this large community, under your great calamity, and

I am, sir, yours most respectfully,

GEORGE B. LLOYD.

UNITED STATES CONSULATE, SANTOS, BRAZIL,
December 20, 1871.

TO HIS HONOR THE MAYOR OF CHICAGO: —

Sir, — I to-day remit to Messrs. Wright & Co. of Rio de Janeiro, the sum of two thousand six hundred and seventy-five milreis (Rs. 2,675), to be by them remitted to you, either direct or through the Chicago Aid Committee there. This is the amount of the subscriptions obtained by me here for the benefit of the unfortunate sufferers by the late terrible conflagration in your city, and I request you to apply it accordingly. The sum is small, but it will go to show you that, although you are seven thousand miles distant, your distress has met with sympathy here and your cry for aid for your sufferers was brought to us over that wire which binds kind hearts together. The people here are very charitable, and would have subscribed far more generously to this fund, but for the fact that they have during this year given very largely for a number of other similar purposes.

I have the honor to be, most respectfully,
Your obedient servant,
WILLIAM T. WRIGHT, *U. S. Consul.*

DEPARTMENT OF STATE, WASHINGTON,
December 21, 1871.

TO HIS HONOR JOSEPH MEDILL, *Mayor of the City of Chicago:* —

Sir, — I transmit herewith a bill of exchange on New York for ten thousand dollars ($10,000), drawn by Bryce, Grace, & Co., of Callao, in my favor, and indorsed to George M. Pullman, Treasurer of the Chicago Relief and Aid Society. The bill of exchange accompanied a dispatch (No. 72), from the United States consul at Callao, from which it will be seen that the sum above mentioned has been contributed by Americans, as well as citizens of Peru, for the relief of those who are sufferers by the recent fire in your city.

I will thank you to acknowledge the receipt of the bill of exchange.

I have the honor to be, sir,
Your obedient servant,
W. HUNTER,
Second Assistant Secretary.

UNITED STATES CONSULATE,
BOMBAY, *December* 22, 1871.

TO THE MAYOR OF CHICAGO, *Chicago, Ill.:* —

Dear Sir, — I have the pleasure to remit you sight bill 39,666, dated December 22, 1871, on the Bank of England, being equivalent of the sum of fifty rupees (Rs. 50), I have received from the Worthy Masters and officers of Lodge Friendship and Harmony, of Egutpoora (a small station in British India), for the use of the sufferers through the late great fire in Chicago, which kindly acknowledge, and use in any way that may seem most fitting to yourself. I have the honor to be, dear sir,

Your most obedient servant,
B. F. FARNHAM, *Consul U. S. A.*

LEGATION OF THE UNITED STATES,
CARACAS, *January* 4, 1872.

TO HON. JOSEPH MEDILL, *Mayor of the City of Chicago*: —

Dear Sir, — I inclose you first of exchange of H. L. Boulton & Co., on John Dallett & Co., of Philadelphia, for two hundred and sixty-nine dollars and forty-eight cents ($\$269\frac{48}{100}$) American gold.

This is the amount of contributions made by myself and a few friends for the benefit of the sufferers by the late fire in your unfortunate city. Please apply the proceeds to the object indicated, and accept the heartfelt condolence and sympathy of the donors for the unfortunate people rendered homeless by the great calamity, and their earnest hope for the rapid rebuilding of your city, and its future prosperity and greatness.

I have the honor to be, sir,

Very respectfully, your obedient servant,

WM. A. PILE.

TOWN HALL, MANCHESTER, ENGLAND, *January* 10, 1872.

TO THE MAYOR OF CHICAGO: —

May I request you to kindly convey to our unfortunate Chicago brethren the assurance that to our contributions for the alleviation, if only in a slight degree, of their sufferings, we desire earnestly to add the expression of our deep sympathy with them in the heavy affliction with which it has pleased Almighty God to visit your great city, and it may be interesting and gratifying to the inhabitants of Chicago to know that the goods we are privileged to send you are purchased with the contributions of every one in our community, inclusive even of the pence of our Ragged School children; and all news received either through the press or by private sources of the gallant struggle in which your brave citizens are engaged for the reëstablishment of your beautiful city, as the great western emporium of commerce, and as one of the centres of civilization in the new world, is read here with the greatest satisfaction.

Very truly,

JOHN GRAVE, *Mayor*.

CORK, IRELAND, *January* 20, 1872.

TO THE MAYOR OF CHICAGO: —

In remitting to you balance of four hundred and sixty-nine pounds (£469) sterling, on the part of the citizens of Cork, I tender to you our deep sympathy, for the misfortune with which God has been pleased to afflict you, and our admiration for the energy and activity (so characteristic of your great nation) which have already done so much to alleviate it.

I am, dear brother Mayor, yours very truly,

JOHN DALY, *Mayor of Cork*.

LEGATION OF THE UNITED STATES,
LONDON, *January* 20, 1872.

THE HON. JOSEPH MEDILL, *Mayor of Chicago* : —

Dear Sir, — You have, through various channels, had information heretofore of the measures taken by Americans in this city to contribute to the relief of the sufferers from the dreadful and calamitous fire which visited your beautiful city.

I have now the pleasure of forwarding to you a copy of the formal report to me of collections and remittances, made by the committee which was appointed at the meeting held here on the 12th of October last. The citizens of Chicago will find in it, I trust, some satisfactory proof of the deep and active sympathy for them which stirred the hearts of their countrymen abroad; and they will not fail to observe also how nobly, generously, and promptly, without even an appeal to them for help, the people of Great Britain claimed to share with American friends the privilege of adding to the fund we sought to raise.

I have the honor to be, very respectfully,

Your obedient servant,

ROBT. C. SCHENCK.

UNITED STATES CONSULATE,
BOMBAY, *January* 22, 1872.

TO THE MAYOR OF CHICAGO, *Chicago, Ill.* : —

Dear Sir, — I have the honor to apprise you that I have this day remitted a sight bill to Messrs. Im Hof & Ertz of your city, for £4 18*s*. 5*d*., equivalent of the sum of fifty rupees (Rs. 50), which I have received from Worthy Master of the Lodge "Cyrus" of this presidency, being contributed for the sufferers through the late fire of your place, which kindly acknowledge and use in the best manner you deem proper.

I have the honor to be, dear sir,

Your obedient servant,

B. F. FARNHAM, *Consul U. S. A.*

CANTON, CHINA, 9*th February*, 1872.

HON. R. B. MASON, *Mayor of Chicago, Ill., U. S. A.* : —

Dear Sir, — Having been appointed by the foreign community of this port, a committee for the purpose of soliciting aid for the sufferers by the fire, which destroyed so large a portion of your city in October of last year, we have now the pleasure to hand you the result of our efforts in the form of the second of exchange, No. $\frac{22}{54}$, of the Oriental Bank Corporation, Hong Kong, on their London office at one month sight, in your favor for two hundred and sixty-three pounds sixteen shillings

(£263 16*s.*) sterling; the first having been forwarded direct to London for acceptance. This is the equivalent, at exchange four shillings forty-three pence and four farthings per dollar (less stamps), of twelve hundred and one dollars and seventy-four cents ($1,201$\frac{74}{100}$), of which six hundred and fifty-five ($655) were subscribed by the foreign, and five hundred and forty-six dollars and seventy-four cents (546\frac{74}{100}$) by the Chinese community.

We regret the insignificance of the amount as compared with the magnitude of the object, and trust it will be accepted more as a token of the sympathy universally felt here by all nationalities for suffering so unparalleled. Our community is very small, most of the merchantile houses being only branches, having heads in Hong Kong and at home, where they subscribed before details of the disaster reached China.

Trusting you will find this small contribution acceptable,

We remain, dear sir, your obedient servants,

R. G. W. JEWELL, *U. S. Consul.*
JOHN CHALMERS,
J. B. CUNNINGHAM.

HONG KONG CHORAL SOCIETY,
HONG KONG, *March* 16, 1872.

TO THE WORSHIPFUL THE MAYOR OF CHICAGO: —

Sir, — I have the honor to inclose first of draft for three hundred and forty-four dollars and nine cents (344\frac{9}{100}$) United States gold coin, on Edward Cunningham, Esq., Boston, being the result of a concert given at this place on behalf of the funds for the relief of the sufferers by the late deplorable catastrophe at your city.

I shall feel obliged if you will dispose of the draft and hand the funds to the treasurer of the said fund, acknowledging the same to,

Sir, yours faithfully,

JAS. B. COUGHTRIE, *Hon. Sec. H. K. C. S.*

PARIS, *March* 27, 1872.

DEAR MR. MAYOR: —

I beg leave to inclose you herewith the draft first of exchange, of Seligiman & Co., of this city, on I. & W. Seligiman & Co., N. Y., for four hundred and forty-six dollars and fifteen cents (446\frac{15}{100}$) in gold. The same is the subscription of the Chamber of Commerce at Havre, for the relief of the sufferers by the Chicago fire, and remitted to me by General Glasgow, our consul at that place. I have requested the General to thank the Chamber for this generous subscription.

Please acknowledge the receipt of same, and

Believe me, very truly yours,

E. B. WASHBURNE.

HENRY W. KING, ESQ.: —

Sir, — The sum inclosed, forty-four pounds, five shillings sixpence (£44 5*s*. 6*d*.) sterling, is a contribution from the Protestant inhabitants of the Italian Vaudois valleys to the Chicago Relief Fund, and is presented by the Rev. Mr. Meille, pastor of the Protestant Vaudois congregation in Turin, through the Hon. George P. Marsh, United States Minister in Italy. Mr. Marsh regrets that a very severe illness, and circumstances consequent upon it, have prevented the remittance of this contribution at an earlier day.

U. S. LEGATION, ROME, *August* 2, 1872.

PROCLAMATIONS, RESOLUTIONS, AND OTHER OFFICIAL DOCUMENTS.

PROCLAMATIONS.

BY THE GOVERNOR OF ILLINOIS.

State of Illinois, Executive Department.

John M. Palmer, *Governor of Illinois, to the People of the State of Illinois:—*

A fire of unexampled magnitude has devastated the city of Chicago, depriving thousands of our citizens of shelter and food and clothing.

Under these painful circumstances I call upon you to open your hearts for the relief of the suffering. Contribute of your abundance everything that you can — food, clothing, money; organize committees and systematize your efforts.

Remember those, our fellow-citizens who have always responded so nobly to every call.

[seal.] In testimony whereof, I have hereunto set my hand and caused the great seal of State to be affixed. Done at the city of Springfield, this 10th day of October, A. D. 1871.

John M. Palmer.

By the Governor,
Edward Rummell, *Secretary of State.*

BY THE GOVERNOR OF ILLINOIS.

State of Illinois, Executive Department.

John M. Palmer, *Governor of Illinois, To all whom these presents shall come, greeting:—*

Whereas, in my judgment, the great calamity that has overtaken Chicago, the largest city of the State; that has deprived many thousands of our citizens of homes and rendered them destitute; that has destroyed many millions in value of property, and thereby disturbing the business of the people and deranging the finances of the State, and interrupting the execution of the laws, is and constitutes "an extraordinary occasion" within the true intent and meaning of the eighth section of the fifth article of the Constitution.

Now, therefore, I, John M. Palmer, Governor of the State of Illinois, do by this, my proclamation, convene and invite the two Houses of the General Assembly in session in the city of Springfield, on Friday, the 13th day of the month of October, in the year of our Lord 1871, at 12 o'clock noon of said day, to take into consideration the following subjects:—

1. To appropriate such sum or sums of money, or adopt such other legislative measures as may be thought judicious, necessary, or proper, for the relief of the people of the city of Chicago.

2. To make provision, by amending the revenue laws or otherwise, for the proper and just assessment and collection of taxes within the city of Chicago.

3. To enact such other laws and to adopt such other measures as may be necessary for the relief of the city of Chicago and the people of said city, and for the execution and enforcement of the laws of the State.

4. To make appropriations for the expenses of the General Assembly, and such other appropriations as may be necessary to carry on the State Government.

[SEAL.] In testimony whereof I have hereunto set my hand and caused the great seal of the State to be affixed. Done at the city of Springfield, this 10th day of October, A. D. 1871.

JOHN M. PALMER.

By the Governor,
EDWARD RUMMELL, *Secretary of State.*

BY THE GOVERNOR OF WISCONSIN.

TO THE PEOPLE OF WISCONSIN:—

Throughout the northern part of this State fires have been raging in the woods for many days, spreading desolation on every side. It is reported that hundreds of families have been rendered homeless by this devouring element, and reduced to utter destitution, their entire crops having been consumed. Their stock has been destroyed, and their farms are but a blackened desert. Unless they receive instant aid from portions not visited by this dreadful calamity, they must perish.

The telegraph also brings the terrible news that a large portion of the city of Chicago is destroyed by a conflagration, which is still raging. Many thousands of people are thus reduced to penury, stripped of their all, and are now destitute of shelter and food. Their sufferings will be

intense, and many may perish unless provisions are at once sent to them from the surrounding country. They must be assisted now.

In the awful presence of such calamities the people of Wisconsin will not be backward in giving assistance to their afflicted fellow-men.

I, therefore, recommend that immediate organized effort be made in every locality to forward provisions and money to the sufferers by this visitation, and suggest to mayors of cities, presidents of villages, town supervisors, pastors of churches, and to the various benevolent societies, that they devote themselves immediately to the work of organizing effort, collecting contributions, and sending forward supplies for distribution.

And I entreat all to give of their abundance to help those in such sore distress.

Given under my hand, at the Capitol, at Madison, this 9th day of October, A. D. 1871.

LUCIUS FAIRCHILD, *Governor of Wisconsin.*

BY THE GOVERNOR OF MICHIGAN.

STATE OF MICHIGAN, EXECUTIVE OFFICE,
LANSING, *October* 9, 1871.

The city of Chicago, in the neighboring State of Illinois, has been visited, in the providence of Almighty God, with a calamity almost unequalled in the annals of history. A large portion of that beautiful and most prosperous city has been reduced to ashes and is now in ruins. Many millions of dollars in property, the accumulation of years of industry and toil, have been swept away in a moment. The rich have been reduced to penury, the poor have lost the little they possessed, and many thousands of people rendered homeless and houseless, and are now without the absolute necessaries of life. I, therefore, earnestly call upon the citizens of every portion of Michigan to take immediate measures for alleviating the pressing wants of that fearfully afflicted city by collecting and forwarding to the Mayor, or proper authorities of Chicago, supplies of food as well as liberal collections of money. Let this sore calamity of our neighbors remind us of the uncertainty of earthly possessions, and that when one member suffers all the members should suffer with it. I cannot doubt that the whole people of the State will most gladly, and most promptly, and most liberally respond to this urgent demand upon their sympathy; but no words of mine can plead so strongly as the calamity itself.

HENRY P. BALDWIN, *Governor of Michigan.*

BY THE GOVERNOR OF IOWA.

To the People of Iowa: —

An appalling calamity has befallen our sister State. Her metropolis — the great city of Chicago — is in ruins. Over one hundred thousand people are without shelter or food, except as supplied by others. A helping hand let us now promptly give. Let the liberality of our people, so lavishly displayed during the long period of national peril, come again to the front, to lend succor in this hour of distress. I would urge the appointment at once of relief committees in every city, town, and township, and I respectfully ask the local authorities to call meetings of the citizens to devise ways and means to render efficient aid. I would also ask the pastors of the various churches throughout the State to take up collections on Sunday morning next, or at such other time as they may deem proper, for the relief of the sufferers. Let us not be satisfied with any spasmodic effort. There will be need of relief of a substantial character to aid the many thousands to prepare for the rigors of the coming winter. The magnificent public charities of that city, now paralyzed, can do little to this end. Those who live in homes of comfort and plenty must furnish this help, or misery and suffering will be the fate of many thousands of our neighbors.

Samuel Merrill, *Governor*.

Des Moines, *October* 10, 1871.

BY THE GOVERNOR OF MISSOURI.

Jefferson City, *October* 9, 1871.

To the People of Missouri: —

A calamity unparalleled in the history of our country has befallen the great city of our sister State. Half of the houses of the people of Chicago are in ashes, and all of its business portion is destroyed. Every bank, railroad depot, insurance office, newspaper establishment, every wholesale house, all its accumulated products and food supply, and nearly every trade appliance and the elevators are reported as utterly consumed. Such disaster will move the hearts of our citizens with the profoundest sympathy. Let us unite likewise in the most generous emulation, and extend the largest possible aid to them in this the hour of misfortune. I, therefore, recommend to all counties, cities, towns, and other corporations, to all business and charitable associations, and to the community at large, to take immediate steps to organize relief committees to express the deep sorrow which Missouri feels at this overwhelming affliction. It was only yesterday that they were united with you in congratulating you on your own soil and in your own chief city whilst their own homes were being destroyed. Let us respond by throwing open wide our own doors to those who are without shelter, by sending bread and raiment at once, and by such contributions ward off further distress, as the generous heart of our own great State will be proud to trânsmit, in recognition, too, of the warm and intimate feeling that has heretofore so closely bound our citizens together. I cannot forbear to extend to all who have been thus stricken down in the midst of an unbounded prosperity the sincerest sympathy of Missouri's sons and daughters in their distress.

Done at the City of Jefferson, this 9th day of October, A. D. 1871.

B. GRATZ BROWN, *Governor of Missouri.*

BY THE GOVERNOR OF OHIO.

CHICAGO, *October* 12, 1871.

TO THE PEOPLE OF OHIO: —

It is believed by the best informed citizens here that many thousands of the sufferers must be provided with the necessaries of life during the cold winter. Let the efforts to raise contributions be energetically pushed. Money, fuel, flour, pork, clothing, and other articles not perishable, should be collected as rapidly as possible — especially money, fuel, and flour. Mr. Joseph Medill, of "The Tribune," estimates the number of those who will need assistance at about seventy thousand.

R. B. HAYES, *Governor of Ohio.*

BY THE MAYOR OF NEW YORK.

MAYOR'S OFFICE, NEW YORK,
Afternoon of October 9, 1871.

A disaster has fallen on the great city of Chicago, which not only has destroyed the best part of its dwellings, and paralyzed its industry and its business, but threatens the gravest consequences to the commerce and prosperity of our country. It has also reduced thousands of people to houselessness and privation. A dispatch from the Mayor of Chicago comes in these words: "Can you send us some aid for a hundred thousand houseless people. Army bread and cheese desirable." I have responded that New York will do everything to alleviate this disaster; and I now call upon the people to make such organization as may be speediest and most effective for the purpose of sending money and clothing and food. I would recommend the immediate formation of general relief committees, who would take charge of all contributions, in order that no time may be lost in carrying relief to those of our fellow citizens who have fallen under this dispensation of Providence. I suggest that the Chamber of Commerce, the Produce Exchange, the Board of Brokers, and the united presidents of the banks, and all religious and charitable associations immediately call a meeting of their respective members, and from them select independent relief committees, who shall solicit subscriptions of money, food, and clothing within their appropriate spheres of action. In the meantime, I am authorized to state that contributions of food and clothing sent to the depots of the Erie and Hudson and Central Railroads (under early and spontaneous offers of Jay Gould and William H. Vanderbilt), in even small quantities, from individuals or business sources, will be at once forwarded through to Chicago free of expense. I cannot too strongly urge upon our citizens immediate attention to this subject.

A. Oakey Hall, *Mayor.*

BILLS AND RESOLVES.

In response to the call of the Governor of Illinois, the Legislature assembled and received from the Executive, October 16, 1871, a further message, covering the subjects to consider which the Legislature had been convened.

Both Houses of the Legislature adjourned to visit Chicago, and after returning, passed the following Act, which having received the Governor's approval became a law.

"*A Bill for an 'Act to relieve the lien of the City of Chicago upon the Illinois and Michigan Canal and revenues, by refunding to said city the amount expended by it in making the improvement contemplated by an Act to provide for the completion of the Illinois and Michigan Canal, upon the plan adopted by the State in* 1836, *approved February* 16, 1865, *together with the interest thereon, as authorized by section five of said Act, and to provide for issuing bonds therefor.*'

" *Whereas* the city of Chicago has expended a large amount of money, to wit: the sum of two and a half millions of dollars, to secure the completion of the Summit division of the Illinois and Michigan Canal, under and pursuant to the provisions of said Act, so approved February

16, A. D. 1865, and Act supplementary thereto; and whereas the said city has a vested lien upon the said canal, with its revenues, subject to any canal debt existing at the time of the passage of said Acts; and whereas said then existing debt due by the State has been fully paid and cancelled; and whereas the canal trustees have delivered to the State of Illinois possession and control of said canal; and whereas it is provided by section five of said Act, as follows: 'The State of Illinois may at any time relieve this lien upon the canal and revenues, by refunding to the City of Chicago the amount expended in making the contemplated improvement and the interest thereon.' Now therefore,

"SEC. 1. *Be it enacted by the People of the State of Illinois, represented in the General Assembly,* That the sum of two million nine hundred and fifty-five thousand three hundred and forty dollars ($2,955,340) with interest thereon, until paid, be and the same is hereby appropriated, for the purpose of relieving the lien as aforesaid, being the principal expended and the interest thereon; which said sum is hereby refunded to said city, and when paid, said city shall execute and deliver to the State of Illinois a proper release of said lien to the satisfaction of the Governor; and the Auditor of State, under the direction of the Governor, is hereby directed to draw his warrants for said sum of money and interest, payable only out of any moneys in the Treasury belonging to the fund hereafter provided, to be known as the 'Canal Redemption Fund.'

"That for the purpose of providing said fund, any funds that are now or may be hereafter in the State Treasury, paid in on the settlement of the Canal Commissioners with the trustees of the Illinois and Michigan Canal, as well as from the revenue of the Canal, also all funds that are now or may hereafter be paid into the State Treasury, known as the "Illinois Central Railroad Fund," shall be transferred by the State Treasurer, upon the Auditor's warrant drawn for that purpose, to said Redemption Fund; that a tax of one and a half mills on each dollar of the assessed value of all the taxable property of the State be levied as a special tax for the years 1871 and 1872, and to meet any deficit in said revenues to meet said appropriation, the Governor, Auditor, and Treasurer are hereby authorized to issue bonds of the State of Illinois, to the amount of two hundred and fifty thousand dollars ($250,000); said bonds to bear interest at the rate of six per cent., per annum, payable semi-annually, in the City of New York, and shall be paid at the pleasure of the State, at any time after three years after the date thereof, and shall be of such denominations as the Governor may deem advisable, and be known as the 'Revenue Deficit Bonds,' and shall be delivered to the city authorities of the City of Chicago, at par, as a part payment on above appropriation. *Provided, however*, that not less than one fifth, nor to exceed one third of said sum, so appropriated, shall be received by said city and be applied in reconstructing the bridges and the public buildings and structures destroyed by fire upon the original sites thereof, as already provided by the Common Council, and the remainder thereof to be applied to the payment of the interest on the bonded debt of such city, and the maintenance of the Fire and Police Department thereof."

"*Whereas*, by reason of a great conflagration in the City of Chicago, the public buildings, bridges, and other public improvements have been totally destroyed, and the business of the courts is suspended, whereby an emergency exists as a reason why this Act shall take effect before the first day of July next, therefore,

"*Be it further enacted*, That this Act shall take effect and be in force from and after its passage."

ACTION OF THE CITY OF SPRINGFIELD, ILLINOIS.

Be it ordained by the City Council of the City of Springfield.

Sec. 1. That the sum of ten thousand dollars ($10,000), or as much thereof as may be necessary, be and the same is hereby appropriated out of any money in the Treasury not otherwise appropriated, for the purpose of relieving the distress occasioned by the terrible calamity which has this day occurred in our neighboring City of Chicago — The same to be expended under the direction of the committee on finance,

Sec. 2. This ordinance shall take effect and be in force from and after its passage.

Passed *October* 9, 1871. Frank Fleury,
City Clerk.

ACTION OF THE CITIZENS OF BOSTON.

Faneuil Hall Meeting, Boston, *October* 10, 1871.

To His Honor R. B. Mason, *Mayor of Chicago:* —

Sir, — Immediately on the receipt of the intelligence of the destructive fire in your city, a meeting of the citizens of Boston was called, and on the 10th instant was held in Faneuil Hall.

The speakers who took part in the meeting were as follows, and in the order given, the Mayor, the Hon. Alexander H. Rice, the Hon. Charles Sumner, the Hon. Wm. Gray, the Rev. Edward E. Hale, the Rev. R. C. Waterston, the Rev. Phillips Brooks, the Hon. Henry Wilson, and the Rev. W. B. Wright.

The following resolutions were adopted with many manifestations of sympathy for your suffering city, and with entire unanimity: —

"The citizens of Boston having received intelligence of the devastation of the city of Chicago, by one of the most terrible conflagrations upon record, have assembled in Fanueil Hall, in response to the invitation of his Honor the Mayor, for the purpose of giving suitable expression to their feelings, and of taking such other action as is demanded by the circumstances of the case: Be it therefore —

"*Resolved*, That the citizens of Boston have heard with unaffected sorrow of the appalling calamity which in the providence of God has just visited the city of Chicago, involving the loss of many lives and the destruction of property to an incalculable amount, leaving hundreds of families houseless and penniless, arresting for a time not only the commercial growth and development of that hitherto prosperous city, but the entire course of its business; and they hereby tender to their brethren and friends thus suddenly and sorely tried, the cordial and heartfelt assurance of their sympathy.

"That they fervently commend their afflicted fellow citizens of Chicago to the paternal care of Him, who alone can adequately minister consolation and relief to them in the time of their overwhelming suffering and sorrow.

"That bearing in mind the marvelous history of Chicago in the past, they would respectfully remind all classes of that community, of the unprecedented success which has attended their tireless energy and unceasing enterprise, and they would urge them to draw strength and encouragement therefrom, in the arduous but not impossible work of restoration and reconstruction which lies before them.

"That the people of Boston and Massachusetts are earnestly invited to unite in an immediate and vigorous effort to relieve the pressing necessities of those families and persons in Chicago who are now suffering in consequence of the destruction of their property and their homes.

"That a committee of citizens be appointed by his Honor the Mayor to make necessary arrangements for the collection of money, and to disburse the same for the relief of the people of Chicago, in such manner as they shall think proper."

A large committee to collect funds was appointed in accordance with the last resolution, and of their doings you will receive reports in due course. With great respect, we are, sir,

Your obedient servants,

WM. GASTON, *Mayor and Chairman.*

HAMILTON A. HILL, *Secretary.*

ACTION OF THE GENERAL ASSEMBLY OF TENNESSEE.

Whereas, Intelligence of the unexampled conflagration in the city of Chicago has been conveyed to this General Assembly, therefore Resolved by the General Assembly of the State of Tennessee, that it is with profound sorrow and painful regret that we receive the melancholy intelligence of the terrible disaster that has befallen the great city of Chicago, whereby thousands of her citizens are thrown out upon the world without food or shelter, and millions of her capital are engulfed in the general ruin.

Resolved, That we tender our sympathies to the citizens of our sister State, the State of Illinois, in this the hour of her fearful calamity and deep distress, and that our strongest compassion is excited in behalf of the suffering victims of this unparalleled misfortune.

Resolved, That we call upon all churches and charitable institutions, corporations and organized associations of every character and description, and all ranks and conditions of people in the State of Tennessee, to contribute to the sufferers of that unfortunate city.

Resolved, That copies of these Resolutions be forwarded to the Governor of Illinois, and the Mayor of the city of Chicago.

Adopted, *October* 11, 1871.

JAMES D. RICHARDSON, *Speaker of the Senate.*
JOHN C. VAUGH, *Speaker of the House.*

MINT OF THE UNITED STATES.

PHILADELPHIA, *October* 11, 1871.

AT a meeting of the officers and employés of the United States Mint, held in the Mint on Wednesday, October 11, 1871, Hon. James Pollock was called upon to preside, and O. C. Bosbyshell made secretary.

The chairman explained the object of the meeting to be, to show some substantial sympathy to the citizens of Chicago left destitute by reason of the late terrible conflagration.

On motion, a committee of three was appointed to draft a series of resolutions expressive of the sense of the meeting. Messrs. Wm. M. Runkel, Wm. S. Steel, and O. C. Bosbyshell were appointed such committee.

During the absence of the committee the chairman took occasion to remark upon the uncertainty of life and property. He described a recent visit to Chicago and dwelt upon its magnificent proportions, and the substantial character of its buildings. To-day it is a smouldering ruin!

The committee on resolutions made the following report, to wit: —

"*Whereas*, The terrible conflagration in the city of Chicago has deprived thousands of our countrymen and fellow-beings of shelter and the common necessities of life; and —

"*Whereas*, We look upon the loss of life and destruction of property as a national calamity, therefore —

"*Resolved*, That in this terrible hour of their affliction the people of Chicago have our deepest sympathy, and with a view that our sympathy may assume a tangible shape, it is —

"*Resolved*, That a committee of seven, representing different departments of the Mint, be appointed to collect funds for the alleviation of the suffering people.

"*Resolved*, That this committee report to the director of the Mint, at 12 o'clock to-morrow, and, as this is an institution of the United States Government, that the funds collected be immediately transmitted to Lieutenant-general P. H. Sheridan, to be expended by him for the benefit of the distressed citizens.

"The undersigned committee appointed by the director of the Mint, to draft a series of resolutions expressive of the sense of the officers and employés of the Mint, beg leave to report the above resolutions, and respectfully recommend the following persons as the committee of seven, namely, Wm. S. Steel, Thos. Mirkil, Miss Caroline Thorn, M. V. B. Davis, James Cowden, John Money, and Chas. Cake.

"Wm. M. Runkel,
"O. C. Bosbyshell,
"Wm. S. Steel. } *Committee.*"

On motion the Resolutions were unanimously adopted, and the persons recommended by the committee were appointed a committee of seven to receive donations.

On motion, adjourned.

James Pollock, *Chairman.*
O. C. Bosbyshell, *Secretary.*

ACTION OF THE CITY OF RICHMOND, VIRGINIA.

In Council of the City of Richmond, October 13, 1871, the following Report was adopted: —

Whereas, The citizens of Richmond, at a meeting held in City Hall, on the 12th instant, adopted the following preamble and resolution, which were presented to the Council by the committee appointed for the purpose, to wit: —

"An appalling and unexampled disaster has befallen the prosperous city of Chicago: that great commercial mart, the pride and ornament of the Northwest, lies in ruins. More than half of her citizens, left houseless and helpless by a terrible and resistless conflagration, wander, in want, in sorrow and despair, around the smouldering embers of their former comfortable and happy homes. Men, women, and children, the aged, the infirm, the sick, stand exposed to the rigors of an approaching winter. This spectacle, while it awakens our liveliest sensibilities, calls for substantial aid. We who know from sad experience how to feel for such distress, will freely contribute, according to our means, to alleviate the privations of that stricken and desolated city. Therefore —

"*Resolved*, That the Council of the City of Richmond be requested to appropriate the sum of ten thousand dollars ($10,000) to the relief of the people of Chicago, and that the chairman appoint a committee of five to present this resolution to the Council."

Be it therefore —

Resolved, That in conformity to the request contained in the resolution of said meeting, this Council hereby appropriates the sum of ten thousand dollars ($10,000), to the relief of the Chicago sufferers.

Resolved, That the president of this Council forward to the proper authorities of Chicago, the sum mentioned above, with a copy of this report; and reiterate on the part of this Council the sentiments of sympathy so fully expressed in the said preamble and resolution.

I certify the foregoing to be a true transcript from the journal of the Council. E. C. HOWARD, *City Clerk*.

ACTION OF THE CITIZENS OF NEWCASTLE-UPON-TYNE.

GUILDHALL, NEWCASTLE-UPON-TYNE,
October 14, 1871.

The following action was taken by the citizens of this town at 12 o'clock, M.: —

Resolved, That the meeting, having heard with the profoundest regret, of the calamity which has overtaken the city of Chicago by the destruction of the greater portion of it by fire, desires to express its deep sympathy with the inhabitants of that city.

Resolved, That with a view of seconding the efforts now being made in this country to aid the sufferers by this calamity, a subscription list be forthwith opened by this town and neighborhood, and that Messrs. Lambton & Co. be requested to act as treasurers.

ACTION OF THE CITY OF MONTREAL.

Extract from the Minutes of a Meeting of the Council of the City of Montreal, held on the 17th of October, 1871.

On motion of Alderman Rodden, seconded by Alderman Davis, it was unanimously —

Resolved, That the terrible calamity with which the city of Chicago has been so suddenly afflicted, carrying with it so unsparingly, death, destruction, and desolation to a city and population so intimately connected with Montreal and its inhabitants by commercial as well as by social ties, is such as to call forth the deepest feelings of sympathy and solicitude from this Council.

That in view of the well understood wishes of the citizens of Montreal, unanimously expressed at the large public meeting which recently took place in this city, that this Council should make a liberal appropriation towards relieving the distress of the sufferers by the fire of Chicago, this Council deem it their duty to contribute the sum of fifty thousand dollars ($50,000) to the Chicago Relief Fund.

ACTION OF THE CHAMBER OF COMMERCE, CARDIFF, WALES.

CHAMBER OF COMMERCE, CARDIFF, WALES,
October 18, 1871.

MAYOR OF CHICAGO: —

The following Resolution was passed to-day at a meeting of this Chamber: —

" That this Chamber desires to express its sympathy with the inhabitants of Chicago now suffering in consequence of the late lamentable fire, as well as with the American nation in the temporary loss of so magnificent a city."

ACTION OF THE CITIZENS OF NOTTINGHAM.

At a public meeting duly convened by the Mayor and held at the Exchange Hall in the town of Nottingham, on Saturday, the 21st day of October, 1871, to express sympathy with the sufferers by the recent disastrous fire at Chicago, John Manning, Esq., Mayor, in the chair: —

It was moved by the Rev. F. Morse, Vicar of St. Marys, seconded by A. J. Mundella, Esq., M. P. and carried unanimously —

"That this meeting has heard with profound regret of the disastrous fire in Chicago, whereby so many American citizens have lost their lives, and thousands of them have been rendered homeless, and property of immense value has been destroyed, and a serious check imposed upon the prosperity of that important city; and this meeting desires to express its sympathy with the sufferers in the terrible losses they have sustained."

JOHN MANNING, *Mayor.*
ALBERT HEYMANN,
Secretary to Chicago Fund.

Countersigned, SAMUEL G. W. MILLER, *Town Clerk.*

ACTION OF THE CITIZENS OF BRISTOL, ENGLAND.

At a public meeting held on Thursday, the 26th of October, 1871, at the Guildhall, Bristol, England, the Right Worshipful the Mayor, T. Canning, Esq., in the chair, the following resolutions were passed unanimously: —

Moved by Lewis Fry, Esq., and seconded by James Ford, Esq., —

"That this meeting desires emphatically to express its deep sympathy with the sufferers by the late calamitous fire in the city of Chicago."

Moved by H. Thomas, Esq., and seconded by W. Terrell, Esq., —

"That whilst gratified at the generous response already made to the appeal for aid by our Chief Magistrate, this meeting, in view of the overwhelming nature of the calamity, urges the unabated and immediate efforts of the citizens to greatly enlarge the subscription list."

Moved by E. Stanton, Esq. (American Consul at Bristol), and seconded by the Rev. W. James, —

"That a vote of thanks be given to the Mayor for presiding, and for the efficient services he has already rendered in receiving contributions, and that he be requested to continue his good offices."

ACTION OF THE CHAMBER OF COMMERCE, NEWPORT, WALES.

NEWPORT CHAMBER OF COMMERCE, TOWN HALL,
NEWPORT, WALES, *October* 26, 1871.

RESOLUTION adopted by the Council of the Newport Chamber of Commerce, at their monthly meeting held this day —

"That the members of this Chamber, many of whom have enjoyed the privilege of an active business intercourse for many years past with American Ship-owners and Merchants, beg to express their deep sympathy with the sufferers by the recent conflagration at Chicago, and have to express an earnest hope that the vast resources and indomitable energies of the American people, coupled with the pecuniary aid which is being actively answered by our countrymen (this town being an item in that respect), will mitigate the personal losses which otherwise might have accrued without the advantages enumerated."

MEETING OF CITIZENS OF THE UNITED STATES AT RIO DE JANEIRO, BRAZIL.

RIO DE JANEIRO, BRAZIL, *November* 20, 1871.

In pursuance of an invitation by the United States Minister, a meeting of United States citizens was held at the Consulate, in this city, on the 20th inst., to secure some measures of relief and subscriptions, in aid of the sufferers by the great fire at Chicago.

Hon. James R. Partridge, United States Envoy, was called to the Chair, and Mr. R. C. Shannon, the Secretary of Legation, acted as Secretary.

Mr. Robert Clinton Wright proposed the following resolutions: —

Resolved, That we have heard with sincere sorrow the painful news of the destruction of a large part of the flourishing city of Chicago on the 8th of October last, by which many lives, and immense amounts of property were lost; one of our most flourishing cities nearly destroyed; and great distress and suffering caused to its inhabitants.

Resolved, That a subscription list be at once opened at the United States Consulate; and that others be placed in the hands of a committee of nine (9) gentlemen, named by the Chairman, who shall personally solicit from their fellow countrymen here their contributions, and who shall receive such as may be offered by others for the relief of the sufferers.

Resolved, — That this Committee make collections of such contributions at once; that the same be reported and paid over to the Hon. James R. Partridge on Friday next, 24th inst., to be by him transmitted by the steamer sailing on the 25th to the order of R. B. Mason, Esq., Mayor of Chicago, with an account of the proceedings of this meeting, and an expression of our sympathy for the sufferers, signed by the Chairman and Secretary.

The resolutions were unanimously adopted.

It was also *Resolved,* that a list should be opened at the Consulate (No. 28 Rua da Alfandega), where the contributions of all others of any nationality would be gladly received, and that notice of the same should be published in the morning journals. The meeting then adjourned.

JAMES R. PARTRIDGE, *Chairman.*
RICHARD C. SHANNON, *Secretary.*

ACTION OF THE HOUSE OF BISHOPS.

The following resolutions were adopted by the House of Bishops of the Protestant Episcopal Church, October 11, 1871: —

Resolved, — That with deep sympathy for our brother in the sore calamity which has befallen the people of his charge, this House unanimously consents to the temporary leave of absence asked by the Bishop of Illinois.

Resolved, — That our brother is requested to convey to the authorities of the city of Chicago the expression of the deep interest taken by this House in the calamitous suffering that has befallen that great city, and its earnest hope that, in response to the appeal already made by this House, a like interest will be felt and manifested by the members of all our churches.

Committees from Boston, New York, St. Louis, Philadelphia, and other cities, were upon the ground during the days immediately succeeding the fire, and rendered timely and efficient assistance to the local Relief Committee. These committees took action to inform their respective cities of the great distress and particular needs of the people, and also to assure them of the trustworthiness of the organization to which they were encouraged to forward their contributions.

As indicating the general character of the action taken by these committees that of the committee from Detroit is subjoined.

ACTION OF THE DETROIT COMMITTEE.

CHICAGO, *October* 11, 1871.

Resolved, — As the sense of the committee appointed by the city of Detroit to distribute material aid to the needy of Chicago, we recommend, after careful investigation, the Chicago Relief and Aid Society as the most wise, well organized, and judicious avenue through which the benefactions of our citizens may be distributed, and we further recommend that in view of the fact that an abundance of provisions for present use are already provided, all further subscriptions be collected in money and deposited in bank to the credit of our Finance Committee for the use of this society as their pressing wants develop and take form.

E. B. WARD, *Chairman of Committee.*

CHAPTER V.

TEMPORARY MEASURES OF RELIEF.

THE authorities of the city came to the performance of an arduous, as well as novel task. Supplies of clothing, of cooked and uncooked provision, were started on their way to supply the wants of the people, whilst yet the flames were laying waste their homes and possessions.

To receive, assort, and distribute these supplies, was a work implying authority, original or delegated, and demanding experience and fidelity on the part of those called to so sacred an administration.

The outside world were as quick to forecast our needs and apprehend the danger of wide-spread suffering, and were as prompt in their action, as were the people of our own city, whose thoughts were not without some selfish occupation, in surveying the extent of their individual losses, and meditating methods for the immediate resumption of business. Sentiments of sympathy had been borne over the wires, letters of condolence had been written, food and raiment shipped, societies, corporations, municipalities, states, and the rulers of nations, had heard the story of our calamity, and had made contributions to supply our needs, while yet all methods to receive and efficiently operate the same, were only tentative.

In the nature of the case, organization and system in the immediate present were out of the question, and the methods employed were characterized by hesitancy in the absence of authority, and of uncertainty by reason of the absence of all precedent in the performance of such a work.

No community has ever had a more surprising illustration of the fact, that in the presence of great emergencies, adequate human resources are never wanting. The proportions of the work enlarged from hour to hour, and the entire compass of human emotions demanded instant comprehension.

Bread was to be furnished to the hungry, and raiment to the insufficiently clad; hope needed a resurrection in the hearts of the despondent, the bereaved needed the ministries of consolation, the sick required the nurse and the physician, the homeless were to be sheltered, the dying were to be proffered the offices of religion, and the dead granted the last ceremonial and service that man renders to his fellow.

Authority was present in the city government. By its hands, organization and system were to be brought as the primary conditions of efficient administration. Social order was the first end to be sought.

In the presence of a lavish abundance, it was a sacred trust to see that no human being was left in want, where human resource or human skill could supply it.

Love was the active sentiment in the community. Human selfishness was for the most part as prostrate as the great structures of wealth and prosperity. It is selfishness that blinds the moral perceptions; it is love that quickens them. Never was spiritual intuition more active, than in this the day of our calamity. Each man knew the need of his fellow, and said, "Thy necessity is like unto mine."

The history of sentiment, of unostentatious mercy illustrated in the throwing open of the homes of the rich and refined, to the thousands whose abode had heretofore been in hovels, but who were now deprived of these, in the sharing of food, raiment, and bedding, in the dividing of what remained of means by those who deemed themselves utterly impoverished, with those whose immediate wants were known to be greater, in the touching words and acts of sympathy and condolence, all this must remain an unwritten record, whilst its memory will be enshrined in our hearts, and hang about us as a glory.

It is not presumed that the account which we here attempt to give of the methods of relief, can possibly portray the conscientious anxiety, the unlooked for efficiency, and the splendid loyalty, which characterized these days and these duties. We can only now for ourselves survey the outlines of these stupendous events, and for others furnish a chart as a guide, should they ever be overtaken by a similar calamity.

The following official communications and documents cover the municipal action and the temporary measures of the citizens, having respect to the work of relief, as furnished by Orrin E. Moore, Chairman, and C. T. Hotchkiss, Secretary of the Citizens Relief Committee:—

RECORD OF PROCEEDINGS OF THE GENERAL RELIEF COMMITTEE, ORGANIZED OCTOBER 6, 1871.

Monday afternoon, October 9, 1871, a number of city officers and prominent citizens met in the Congregational Church, corner of Washington and Ann streets, for consultation regarding the public welfare in the emergency caused by the great conflagration, which, commencing in the West Division the night before, had up to that time twice crossed the river, destroyed the business portion of the South Division, including the City Hall, and was then rapidly approaching the northern limits of the North Division of the city. A call was issued for a meeting that evening at the same place, of the members of the Common Council, the executive officers of the city government, and citizens generally.

At eight o'clock there were present His Honor R. B. Mason, Mayor; T. B. Brown, Mark Sheridan, Commissioners of the Board of Police and Fire Departments; C. N. Holden, Esq., Tax Commissioner; Gen. I. N. Stiles, City Attorney; Gen. C. T. Hotchkiss, City Clerk, and the following named Aldermen, Thomas Wilce, W. B. Bateham, Samuel McCotter, Peter Daggy, H. M. Thompson, M. B. Bailey, S. S. Gardner, I. L. Campbell, Theodore Schintz, Henry Whitbeck, B. G. Gill, James Walsh, and H. O. Glade, and a large number of prominent citizens.

The assemblage was called to order by Mayor Mason, who stated the object of the meeting to be to inaugurate some plan for concert of action between the authorities and citizens, to furnish immediate succor to the large number of our people, who had been rendered homeless and destitute by the terrible conflagration then sweeping over the city, and who, to save their lives, had been driven far out into the open country, north and west of the city limits, where they would be compelled to remain without shelter, food, and in many cases without clothing, until assistance was taken to them. Also, to take charge of and distribute the relief which he was advised was being collected in other cities, and forwarded for the use of the destitute. He also asked coöperation with the city authorities, by organizations amongst the citizens, in maintaining public order, and in preventing as far as possible further devastation by the fire, which, on account of the destruction of the pumping works, would require the greatest vigilance of all persons in every part of the city whose premises had been spared by the flames.

On motion of the Hon. Willard Woodward, His Honor the Mayor was made chairman, and General Hotchkiss secretary of the meeting.

Alderman H. M. Thompson moved that a committee, to consist of six persons, two from each division of the city, to be named by the Mayor, be appointed to act as a General Relief Committee, which motion prevailed. The Mayor nominated Alderman J. H. McAvoy and N. K. Fairbank, Esq., for the South Division, Alderman W. B. Bateham, and Orrin E. Moore, Esq., for the West Division, and Alderman M. A. Devine, and John Herting, Esq., for the North Division, which nominations were unanimously confirmed. On motion of Alderman Bateham, His Honor the Mayor was added to the committee. After general discussion, but no further action, the meeting adjourned.

Tuesday, October 10, 1871. — The General Relief Committee appointed at the meeting of city officers and citizens the night previous, met at the same place on Tuesday morning, and organized by electing Orrin E. Moore, Chairman, C. T. Hotchkiss, Secretary, and C. C. P. Holden, Treasurer, and appointed the following sub-committees: —

J. W. Preston, Esq., President of Board of Trade, in charge of receiving supplies at the railroad stations, and sending the same to depots for storage and distribution.

Hon. R. P. Derrickson, in charge of transportation and distribution of supplies from depots to church and school building committees.

O. C. Gibbs, Esq., of Chicago Aid and Relief Society, in charge of distribution of relief.

G. W. Stamford and Clark Leib, in charge of supplying water to church and school building committees.

A. G. Lane and G. De Clercq in charge of railroad passes to destitute persons wishing to leave the city.

Doctors C. H. Eddy and I. E. Gilman, in charge of hospitals and medical supplies.

Alderman Thomas Wilce in charge of providing barracks for shelter.

The following orders were passed: —

"1. The general headquarters of the General Relief Committee, and all sub-committees, are established at the Congregational Church, corner of Washington and Ann streets, the same having been tendered for that purpose.

"2. The General Committee will remain in constant session at headquarters.

"3. All orders issued by authority of the committee for supplies and other matters, must be signed by the Chairman and Secretary, and entered upon a record to be kept for that purpose by the Secretary."

The following notices were ordered to be printed for distribution: —

"TO THE HOMELESS.

"The headquarters of the General Relief Committee are at the Congregational Church, corner of Washington and Ann streets. All of the public school buildings, as well as churches, are open for the shelter of persons who do not find other accommodations. When food is not found at such buildings, it will be provided by the committee on application at headquarters.

"R. B. MASON, *Mayor*.
J. H. MCAVOY,
N. K. FAIRBANK,
ORRIN E. MOORE,
W. B. BATEHAM,
M. A. DEVINE,
JOHN HERTING,
} *General Relief Committee.*
C. T. HOTCHKISS, *Secretary*."

"NOTICE.

"HEADQUARTERS, GENERAL RELIEF COMMITTEE,
CHICAGO, *October* 10, 1871.

"J. W. Preston, Esq., President of the Board of Trade, is hereby authorized to receive on account of this Committee, all supplies for the relief of the destitute, and distribute the same to depots of supplies established in the city, under the control and upon the order of this Committee.

"He is also authorized to hire or press into service, if necessary, a sufficient number of teams to handle such supplies.

"ORRIN E. MOORE, *Chairman*,
C. T. HOTCHKISS, *Secretary*."

Wednesday, October 11, 1871. — Alderman C. C. P. Holden moved that David A. Gage, City Treasurer, be appointed Treasurer of the Relief Committee, in place of himself, and it was ordered.

His Honor the Mayor submitted the following proclamation, which was approved and ordered placed upon the records: —

"1. All supplies of provisions and clothing will be received and distributed by the General Relief Committee, of which O. E. Moore is Chairman, and C. T. Hotchkiss Secretary. Headquarters of the Committee, corner of Ann and West Washington streets.

"2. All contributions of money will be delivered to the City Treasurer, David A. Gage, who will receipt and keep the same as a Special Relief Fund.

"3. All moneys deposited at other places for the relief of this city, will be drawn for only by the Mayor of this city.

"4. No moneys will be paid out of the Special Relief Fund, except upon the order of the Auditing Committee. George Taylor, City Comptroller, Mancel Talcott, Esq., of the West Division, and Brock McVickar, of the South Division, are hereby appointed such Auditing Committee.

"5. Railroad passes from the city will be issued under the direction of the General Relief Committee, corner of Ann and Washington streets."

Thursday, October 12, 1871. — From reports from all parts of the city, it is believed that every person rendered homeless by the fire was placed under shelter and supplied with food last night.

Also, that supplies in abundance for immediate necessities were being received from every quarter. It is estimated that about seventy thousand (70,000) persons have been relieved by the aid of this Committee.

Wirt Dexter, N. K. Fairbank, and O. C. Gibbs, representing the Chicago Relief and Aid Society, submitted a verbal proposition that the said Society take full charge of the receipt and distribution of all supplies being received for the persons rendered destitute by the fire, throughout the entire city. After full discussion, a resolution, offered by Mr. Fairbank, carrying the same into effect, was adopted. The following is the resolution: —

"*Resolved*, as the sense of this meeting, that the organization of the Chicago Relief and Aid Society be adopted as the means of distributing the food and supplies received for the suffering, and that the present Relief Committee appointed Monday night last, together with the Mayor, Comptroller, City Treasurer, and two other Aldermen from each division of the city, to be selected by the Mayor and President of the Chicago Relief and Aid Society, be added to the direction of said society."

The following circular was submitted by the Secretary, approved, and a copy of the same ordered to be sent to each Committee in charge of distributing relief.

"Committees at school buildings and churches, in charge of distributing food, clothing, and bedding to persons rendered homeless and destitute by the great fire, are directed to limit the issue of supplies to the absolute daily necessities (not always the wants) of persons applying for, and entitled to aid, pending the completion of a larger organization and a more thorough system for the distribution of relief. The Committee respectfully urge upon such Committees the great importance of strictly observing this rule, so that the generous contributions we are now receiving may not be diverted from the purpose for which they are needed, and which was intended by the donors."

Friday, October 13, 1871. — No official action, other than giving special directions for the distribution of relief, as cases presented themselves, was had by the Committee. On account of the great pressure upon the time of every person connected with the operations of the Committee, in the receipt and distribution of relief, it has been impossible to collect sufficient reports to determine the amount and kind of supplies received, and the number of persons receiving aid up to the present time.

ORRIN E. MOORE, *Chairman.*
C. T. HOTCHKISS, *Secretary.*

CHICAGO, *October* 17, 1871.

WIRT DEXTER, ESQ., *Chairman Executive Committee, Chicago Aid and Relief Committee:* —

Sir, — The General Relief Committee of which we were Chairman and Secretary, respectively, with headquarters at the corner of Washington and Ann streets, discontinued all official action as a committee on Saturday evening last, and have since referred all official matters coming to us to your Committee.

We supposed that this fact was generally known, and we now make this formal statement that you may be assured that there has not been, nor can be any conflict on our part to possibly embarrass your Committee in the full control and direction of all matters pertaining to the relief of the destitute in our midst. Respectfully,

ORRIN E. MOORE, *Chairman.*
C. T. HOTCHKISS, *Secretary.*

On Friday, October the 13th, the Mayor issued the proclamation by which the Chicago Relief and Aid Society was constituted the almoner of the world's charity, and to its trust was committed a work of vast importance, various detail, and sacred ministering.

PROCLAMATION.

I have deemed it best for the interest of the city to turn over to the CHICAGO RELIEF AND AID SOCIETY all contributions for the suffering people of this city. This Society is an incorporated and old established organization, having possessed for many years the entire confidence of our community, and is familiar with the work to be done. The regular force of this Society is inadequate to this immense work, but they will rapidly enlarge and extend the same by adding prominent citizens to the respective committees, and I call upon all citizens to aid this organization in every possible way.

I also confer upon them a continuance of the same power heretofore exercised by the Citizens' Committee, namely, the power to impress teams and labor, and procure quarters, so far as may be necessary, for the transportation and distribution of contributions, and care of the sick and disabled. General Sheridan desires this arrangement, and has promised to coöperate with the Association. It will be seen from the plan of the work that is detailed below, that every precaution has been taken in regard to the disposition of contributions.

R. B. MASON, *Mayor.*

CHAPTER VI.

THE RELIEF AND AID SOCIETY.

IN every great city, there is a class of worthy and industrious poor who in their prosperity have a hard struggle to obtain what are deemed the necessaries of life.

In the event of these being overtaken by sickness, accident, the loss of employment, or the destruction of property, they fall behind. And in such domestic emergency, charity, judiciously and opportunely administered, will in many instances rescue them from permanent pauperism, and save the family from being broken up. Added to this class are widows with dependent children; aged and not seldom infirm people, still dependent upon their own toil for subsistence, who during the months of summer are able to earn a comfortable living, but when the winter comes with its increased demand for fuel, clothing, and food, the falling off or entire loss of employment, makes them the most worthy subjects of sympathy and charity.

There are many others who under ordinary circumstances can with rigid economy meet their absolute necessities, but when work stops and winter approaches, or any sudden misfortune befalls them, they are likewise helpless. There are single women, both old and young, who are capable only of doing certain kinds of light work, and who must take such remuneration as they can command, and in whose cases a week's illness brings destitution and want. There are many strangers, frequently whole families, from foreign lands, as well as from remote parts of our own, with but little money and no friends, who arrive in this city, and through failure to find work immediately, are thrown upon this or similar charities for support, or otherwise become public mendicants. As many as possible ought to be kept together in families and in homes, and should be assisted only and to such extent as may be temporarily necessary, and never by such methods as to beget the spirit of dependence, and the loss of self-respect.

These classes of the community should have other and more suitable provision than is usually made by the county or city authorities. They should be subjected to no humiliation, but inspired with the hope of self support, and encouraged in every endeavor to this end. Every failure should be supplemented by the sympathy and material aid of the more fortunate, and the benevolent.

If possible this aid should be tendered through some organized agency, the methods of which should be no obstruction to, but the channel of a kindly and merciful charity, and through which these people could make their wants known, and be supplied to such extent as the case might suggest. It was the intention of its projectors, that the organization known as the Chicago Relief and Aid Society should supply this want of the community, and be the medium of the voluntary benevolence of the people. For many years, through the instrumentalities of this Society, there have been comparatively few street beggars in the city, and by its frequent and public suggestion and request, through the press and otherwise, our citizens have come to understand that it is the part of social economy, as well as civil decency and propriety, to commit to the investigation and treatment of this their own organization, all such cases, in the full assurance that according to its ability their wants will be supplied. The exact domain, functions, and methods, of such an organization as was originally contemplated, can be most readily indicated by embodying the text of its Charter, and the general rules of its administration.

CHARTER.

AN ACT TO INCORPORATE THE CHICAGO RELIEF AND AID SOCIETY.

SECTION 1. *Be it enacted by the People of the State of Illinois, represented in the General Assembly,* That Edwin C. Larned, Mark Skinner, Edward I. Tinkham, Joseph D. Webster, Joseph T. Ryerson, Isaac N. Arnold, Norman B. Judd, John H. Dunham, A. H. Mueller, Samuel S. Greeley, B. F. Cook, N. S. Davis, George W. Dole, George W. Higginson, John H. Kinzie, John Woodbridge, Jr., Erastus S. Williams, Philo Carpenter, George W. Gage, S. S. Hayes, Henry Farnham, William H. Brown, Philip J. Wardner, and their associates and successors, be and they are hereby created a body politic and corporate, under the name of the "*Chicago Relief and Aid Society,*" and by that name to remain in perpetual succession, with power to contract and be contracted with, to sue and be sued, to acquire, hold, and convey property, real, personal, or mixed, to have and use a common seal, and to alter the same at pleasure. to make and alter by-laws for the government of the corporation, its officers, agents, and servants.

SECT. 2. The objects of this corporation shall be strictly of an eleemosynary nature : they shall be to provide a permanent, efficient, and practical mode of administering and distributing the private charities of the city of Chicago ; to examine and establish the necessary means for obtaining full and reliable information of the condition and wants of the poor of said city, and putting into practical and efficient operation the best system of relieving and preventing want and pauperism therein.

SECT. 3. The said corporation shall be located in the city of Chicago, and the persons named in the first section, and their associates, or any ten of them, shall have power to hold a meeting thereof, and organize said institution by the appointment of a Board of Directors, and the establishment of such constitution and by-laws as they shall deem expedient.

SECT. 4. The said corporation shall have power to locate and erect or to lease the necessary building or buildings, and lot or lots, and employ the necessary agents and officers that may be requisite to carry into full effect the purposes of this act ; also to receive, by gift, grant, devise, or bequest, property, real, personal, or mixed, and to hold and use the same for the purposes of the institution.

SECT. 5. All money and property received by said association shall be faithfully applied to the purposes in this act specified; and it shall be lawful for the said corporation to secure the faithful collection, custody, and distribution of its funds and other property by such bonds and other securities as the Board of Directors shall require; and any officer, agent, or member of said corporation who shall fraudulently embezzle or appropriate to his own use any of the funds or property of the said corporation shall be deemed guilty of larceny, and liable to be indicted and punished accordingly.

SECT. 6. The business of said company shall be managed by a Board of Directors, to consist of not less than five members, and by such other officers and agents as said Board shall appoint. The first Board of Directors shall be elected by the persons named in the first section, or such of them, not less than ten, who shall attend a meeting to be held in Chicago, at a time and place of which notice shall be given by any three of said persons, and the persons elected Directors at such time shall hold their offices for one year, and until others are appointed in their places, and shall elect their own officers, and have power to appoint and remove all the other agents, officers, and servants employed by the said corporation.

SECT. 7. This act shall be in force from and after its passage.

SECT. 8. That all property of whatsoever kind and description, belonging to said corporation, shall be and remain free and exempt from all taxes and assessments for state, county, or city purposes.

SECT. 9. It shall be the duty of the said Board of Directors to make a report, at least once a year, to the City Council of Chicago, giving a full account of all their doings, a statement of their receipts and expenditures, verified under oath; also of the property owned by the said corporation, and the uses to which the same is appropriated; also, a list of all the members of said company, and of all persons who have contributed to the objects of the same, with the amount of their respective contributions; together with such information as they may have acquired concerning the condition and wants of the poor of said city, and the plans and intentions of the said corporation; which report shall be published in the official paper of the city, and such other manner, for general circulation, as the City Council shall direct.

SECT. 10. It shall be lawful for the City Council of Chicago to appropriate, from time to time, such sums of money as they shall deem expedient, to aid in carrying out the charitable purposes of said corporation; also to allow said corporation to occupy, without rent, any lot belonging to the city, for the storage of wood, coal, or other supplies intended for charitable distribution, or for any other purpose necessary or desirable to carry out the objects herein specified.

SECT. 11. It shall be the duty of the said corporation to establish, as soon as may be, one or more offices, depots, or stations, in a suitable and convenient place or places, in said city, — of the location of which public notice shall be given, and continued for such time as may be needful, to cause the same to be generally known in the city, — at which places officers or agents of the corporation shall be in attendance for the purpose of carrying out the purposes of this act, in such manner and under such regulations as the Board of Directors may direct.

SECT. 12. The Mayor of the City of Chicago shall, *ex officio*, be a member of the Board of Directors of said corporation.

SECT. 13. It shall be lawful for the Board of Directors to fix the amount (if any) which shall be paid to entitle any person to become a member of said corporation; also, to tax each member of said corporation, annually, a sum not exceeding ten dollars, to aid in defraying the permanent expenses of said corporation; also, to make such persons, whether residing in said city or elsewhere, who shall by their philanthropy and benevolence be adjudged by the Board to be deserving of such distinction, honorary members of said association, and to establish life memberships therein by the payment of such amount as the Board shall determine, which life memberships shall be free from any annual assessments.

SECT. 14. The Board of Directors shall have power to establish such by-laws for the proper management of the business of said Board and such corporation as they may deem expedient, and to alter, add to, and amend the same.

SAMUEL HOLMES,
Speaker of the House of Representatives.

JOHN WOOD,
Speaker of the Senate.

APPROVED, *February* 16, 1857.

WM. H. BISSELL.

CONSTITUTION.

I. In carrying out the objects of this Society as indicated in the act of incorporation, it shall be the end aimed at, not only to afford temporary relief to the destitute, but also by rendering timely counsel and assistance to deserving but indigent persons, to place them above the necessity of aid; and without positively limiting itself to any one class in the distribution of its charities, the Society shall discriminate in favor of those in whom habits of temperance, industry, and thrift, give promise of permanent benefit from the aid furnished, and shall not embrace in the sphere of its operations such as are the proper subjects for the Poorhouse, or for the action of the county officers.

II. Any person may become a member of this Society, by the payment of five dollars ($5.00), into its treasury.

GENERAL RULES.

RULE 1. The object of this Society is to aid such of the poor as through sickness or other misfortune require temporary assistance. The permanently dependent are not regarded as proper subjects, because if they should be relieved, the entire funds of the association would soon be exhausted in the support of a permanent list.

RULE 2. Each applicant for relief is regarded as entitled to charity until a careful examination proves the contrary.

RULE 3. Relief is only to be given after a personal investigation of each case by visitation and inquiry by the Superintendent or authorized visitor.

RULE 4. Necessary articles in small quantities to be given, and only in proportion to immediate need.

RULE 5. Relief to be discontinued to those who manifest a purpose to depend on alms rather than their own exertions for support.

RULE 6. Destitute persons sent from other cities should be referred to the County Agent, to be sent to their former residence. Should we undertake the support of such persons it would be offering a premium to other cities to send their poor to us to be supported.

RULE 7. Able-bodied men are not regarded as proper subjects for relief, but will be furnished employment directly by the Superintendent, or sent to reliable employment agents, with whom the Society coöperates.

RULE 8. Applicants having claims on other charities are to be furnished with a card directing them to the same.

RULE 9. It is an absolute condition of relief by this Society that all persons receiving aid are not to ask alms or assistance of the public, either on the street, at residences, or places of business.

RULE 10. No loans shall be made from the funds of the Society.

RULE 11. As a rule, relief to be administered in supplies rather than money.

RULE 12. Subscribers to the funds of the Society are entitled to send persons applying to them for relief to the rooms of the Society, and will be furnished with cards for that purpose.

RULE 13. In all cases where families or persons have been aided by this Society through a winter, on account of want of employment, and are by us offered situations either in the city or country, adapted to their condition in life, with aid to reach such situations, which they refuse to accept, no further relief shall be extended to them.

BY-LAWS.

1. Any person may become a member of this Association by signing the By-Laws and paying an initiation fee of five dollars.

2. The annual meeting of this society shall be held in the city of Chicago, on the second Monday of November of each and every year, at such place as shall be specified by notice from the Secretary of this Society, to be published in at least one of the American Chicago daily papers three days before the time of such meeting.

3. The members of this Society present at such annual meeting shall select from among their number a Board of Directors, to hold office until the next annual election, or until their successors are chosen.

4. The Board of Directors shall have power to fill vacancies in the Board.

5. The Board of Directors shall hold meetings whenever notified by the President or Secretary; and any three of said Board, together with the President thereof, shall constitute a quorum.

6. The Board of Directors, on being chosen at said annual meeting, shall select one of their number as President of said Board, who shall be the presiding officer of the Board and the chief executive officer of the Society, and shall have the general charge of the business of the Society; also authority and control over the subordinate officers. He shall also have authority to countersign drafts drawn by the Secretary for the general purposes of the Society, subject to the approval of the Board.

7. The Board of Directors shall select a Secretary, whose duty it shall be to keep a full record of all proceedings of the Board and the Society.

8. All money collected or belonging to the Society shall be placed with some depository selected by the Board of Directors, and drawn only in the following manner: By drafts drawn by the Secretary, countersigned by the President, and, in the absence of the President, countersigned by the chairman of the Executive Committee.

9. The failure of any person chosen as a Director to attend three consecutive meetings, without satisfactory excuse to the Board, shall be

deemed sufficient cause for the vacation of his office by a vote of the Board.

10. The Board shall have power to select any three of their number, who shall constitute an Executive Committee, the chairman of which shall have power, in the absence or sickness of the President, or when delegated by him, to draw checks upon the funds of the Society.

In the autumn of 1857, under the above charter, an organization was effected, a Board of Management was elected, and the Constitution, General Rules, and By-laws as embodied above, were adopted.

Committees of citizens were appointed to raise funds, for carrying out the purposes of the Society, and a sufficient amount of money was subscribed and collected, to relieve the wants of all worthy applicants.

In order that the work of this organization may be more fully indicated and comprehended, it may be stated, in brief, that it had its own offices, with a superintendent, one visitor and one messenger, and in addition to these, it employed persons to superintend its Wood-yard and Lodging-house.

At first, voluntary visitors were engaged to examine into the wants and worthiness of applicants, but this was soon found to be an inefficient and unreliable method, and paid visitors were employed by the Society. These constituted the entire working force of the office, and the only salaried employés of the Society.

From year to year, the city was divided into districts, and persons of well known character and influence were designated and requested to canvass for money subscriptions, and other donations.

In illustration of the methods and agencies of the Society, a brief summation of its work for the year 1869, which may be considered as representative, is herein presented.

DISTRICT AND SOLICITING COMMITTEES.

District Number 1.

River Street, and South Water Street from the Lake to the centre of State Street, with the cross streets north to the River. — *Committee:* Simon Reed, William Aldrich, E. S. Wells, and James McKindley.

District Number 2.

Both sides of South Water Street from the centre of State to the centre of La Salle Street. — *Committee:* S. P. Farrington, G. S. Whitaker, E. Frankenthal, F. D. Gray, and W. T. Lewis.

District Number 3.

Both sides of South Water Street from the centre of La Salle to Lake Street Bridge. — *Committee:* Gilbert Hubbard, Geo. E. Purington, and William H. Brooks.

District Number 4.

Both sides of Lake Street from the Central Depot to the centre of State Street, and the cross streets north to South Water Street. — *Committee:* H. A. Hurlbut, Philip Wadsworth, D. B. Fisk, and T. B. Carter.

District Number 5.

Both sides of Lake Street from the centre of State to the centre of La Salle Street and the cross streets north to South Water Street. — *Committee:* John B. Drake, E. P. Dwyer, H. Z. Culver, and J. P. Sharp.

District Number 6.

Both sides of Lake Street from the centre of La Salle to Lake Street Bridge, and the cross streets north to South Water Street. — *Committee:* C. R. Larrabee, H. M. Wilmarth, William H. Whitehead, and Thomas Wallin.

District Number 7.

Both sides of Randolph Street from the Lake to the centre of Dearborn Street, with the cross streets north to Lake Street. — *Committee:* S. D. Kimbark, George M. Pullman, P. Van Schaack, and N. G. Hibbard.

District Number 8.

Both sides of Washington Street from the Lake to the centre of Dearborn Street, with the cross streets north to Randolph Street. — *Committee:* Marshall Field and C. M. Cady.

DISTRICT NUMBER 9.

Both sides of Washington and Randolph streets from the centre of Dearborn to the centre of La Salle, with the cross streets north to Lake Street. — *Committee :* Wirt Dexter, S. B. Gookins, N. K. Fairbanks, and Lewis H. Davis.

DISTRICT NUMBER 10.

Both sides of Randolph and Washington streets from the centre of La Salle to the River and the cross streets north to Lake Street. — *Committee :* Murray Nelson, W. M. Eagan, C. J. Gilbert, W. F. Milligan, John B. Lyon, and P. L. Underwood.

DISTRICT NUMBER 11.

Both sides of Madison and Monroe streets from the Lake to the centre of Clark Street, with the cross streets north to Washington Street. — *Committee :* A. Cowles, John R. Walsh, E. F. Hollister, and D. B. Cook.

DISTRICT NUMBER 12.

Both sides of Madison and Monroe streets from the centre of Clark Street to the River, and the cross streets north to Washington Street. — *Committee :* H. A. Towner, C. B. Goodyear, and M. A. Seymour.

DISTRICT NUMBER 13.

North Water, Kinzie, and Michigan streets from the Lake to the centre of Clark Street, with the cross streets south to the River. — *Committee :* W. N. Mills and A. J. Wright.

DISTRICT NUMBER 14.

North Water, Kinzie, and Michigan streets from the centre of Clark Street west to the North Branch, with the cross streets south to the River. — *Committee :* W. P. Dickinson, A. M. Wright, and N. J. Howe.

DISTRICT NUMBER 15.

RAILROADS. — *Committee :* H. E. Sargent and H. R. Pearson.

DISTRICT NUMBER 16.

PACKERS. — *Committee :* C. H. S. Mixer, S. B. Kent, and B. P. Hutchinson.

DISTRICT NUMBER 17.

BANKS AND BANKERS. — *Committee :* E. I. Tinkham, Ira Holmes, W. F. Coolbaugh, L. J. Gage, and J. Irving Pierce.

DISTRICT NUMBER 18.

ELEVATORS. — *Committee :* George Armour and Charles W. Wheeler.

District Number 19.

Lumbermen. — *Committee:* T. M. Avery, A. C. Calkins, T. W. Harvey, and Jesse Spalding.

District Number 20.

Flouring Mills and Mill Furnishing. — *Committee:* Jirah D. Cole and N. Hawkins.

District Number 21.

Foundries, Manufactories, Iron and Coal Dealers. — *Committee:* J. T. Ryerson, N. S. Bouton, and A. B. Meeker.

District Number 22.

Distillers, Rectifyers, and Brewers. — *Committee:* B. M Ford, E. F. Lawrence, and John Scanlon.

District Number 23.

Insurance, Fire, Marine, and Life. — *Committee:* S. M. Moore, W. E. Rollo, and T. L. Miller.

TABULAR STATEMENT OF WORK.

Total numbers of families aided		1,559
Averaging four and one half persons to each family, or total number of persons		7,015
Total number of Relief Orders issued		5,022
Average number of times each family was aided		3
Number of families aided but once	530	
Number of families aided twice	250	
Number of families aided three times	212	
Number of families aided four times	159	
Number of families aided five times	127	
Number of families aided six times	99	
Number of families aided seven times	64	
Number of families aided eight times	42	
Number of families aided nine times	33	
Number of families aided ten or more times	43	
	——	1,559

Nationalities Represented.

Irish	606
American	317
German	178

English	119	
Scotch	25	
Canadian	11	
French	25	
Welsh	5	
Colored (American)	45	
Hungarian	1	
Greek	1	
Russian	2	
Italian	3	
Scandinavian	190	
Hollander	20	
Belgian	4	
Polander	7	
		1,559

Causes of Destitution.

Widows with dependent children	371	
Sickness and disability	367	
Out of employment	528	
Desertion, or drunkenness of husband	137	
Old age	66	
Other causes	90	
		1,559

RECEIPTS AND DISBURSEMENTS.

Cash.

Received on subscriptions	$33,258.32	
Interest on money in Bank	448.14	
Payment on Lots sold	864.00	
Balance from last year	4,015.10	
Total Cash		$38,585.56

Supplies Received.

From Railroads, 800 tons Coal, @ $4.50	$3,600.00	
From Railroads, 250 cords Wood, @ $7.00	1,750.00	
Wood and Coal from Dealers	263.75	
Coke from Chicago Gas and Coke Co.	75.00	
Provisions, Medicines, Shoes, etc.	383.62	
Second-hand Clothing, valued at	250.00	
		6,322.37
Total Cash and Supplies		$44,907.93

DISBURSEMENTS AND EXPENDITURES.

Cash.

Paid for Fuel, including hauling to yard and delivery to families	$6,446.21	
Clothing and Bedding	331.67	
Provisions and Groceries	9,387.08	
Medicines	277.07	
Shoes	1,470.55	
Meals and Lodgings	934.59	
Printing and Stationery	385.87	
Rent and Office Expenses	662.98	
Rent for Families, Transportations, Delicacies and Nursing for the Sick, Funeral Expenses, Stoves and Furniture	2,140.04	
Salaries to Employés	3,657.65	
Total cash expended		$25,694.61

Supplies donated disbursed.

Wood, Coal, and Coke	$5,688.75	
Provisions, Medicines, and Shoes	383.62	
Second-hand Clothing	250.00	
Supplies donated disbursed		6,322.37
Cash on hand		12,890.95
		$44.907.93

CHAPTER VII.

PLAN OF THE WORK.

IN accordance with the proclamation of the Mayor, this society accepted the enlarged trust created by the emergency, and on the 15th of October, 1871, assumed the care of the sufferers by the Great Fire, and made known the fact of this authority and responsibility in the following dispatch to the Associated Press: —

ASSOCIATED PRESS DISPATCH.

An organization has been perfected for the purpose of receiving and disbursing contributions for our suffering people, consisting of our old established society, the Chicago Relief and Aid Society, aided by prominent citizens.

All bills are to be audited by the Executive Committee of that society, consisting of seven of our best citizens and the Comptroller, and R. B. Mason, present Mayor of Chicago. All checks for funds to be signed both by the Relief and Aid Society and R. B. Mason. In the great destruction that has overwhelmed us we needed a little time to perfect an organization. This we can now say with great confidence has been accomplished.

We most earnestly entreat the friends of suffering humanity not to intermit their efforts, as our want is not for a day but a whole winter.

So far as practicable we suggest that money be raised, so that we can buy the articles which from time to time we most need. All funds should be held subject to the order of the Chicago Relief and Aid Society, to be drawn only upon orders or drafts countersigned by R. B. Mason.

All materials should be consigned to the Chicago Relief and Aid Society at Chicago, great care being taken to mark contents on the packages and send invoice by mail. No more cooked or perishable food is needed at present.

R. B. MASON, *Mayor.*
HENRY W. KING, *President.*
WIRT DEXTER,
Chairman Executive Committee. } *Chicago Relief and Aid Society.*

On the morning of the 19th October, the following communication appeared in the public press of the city: —

CHICAGO, *October* 18, 1871.

In order that the public may understand the condition of the organization for the distribution of contributions for the sufferers by the Chicago fire, it should be known that the Mayor of the City of Chicago, as well as the citizen's committee, have turned over all contributions to the Chicago Relief and Aid Society, and that aside from that Society there is no other authorized to receive contributions for general distribution.

There are many special societies as well as individuals to whom special donations have been directed. These are doing an excellent work and cannot be dispensed with.

Our object is, to direct attention to the fact that there is no conflict in the work, and that contributions for the General Fund should come to this Association.

R. B. MASON, *Mayor.*

On the same date the Relief and Aid Society addressed the subjoined communication to all newspapers: —

CHICAGO, *October* 18, 1871.

TO OUR FRIENDS THROUGHOUT THE CIVILIZED WORLD.

The response to the sufferings of our stricken citizens was so spontaneous and universal, that money, clothing, and provisions were sent not only to the authorities of our city, but to many individuals, some of which, owing to the derangement of all business, may have miscarried.

To the end that these unparalleled contributions may be preserved, judiciously applied, and sacredly accounted for, we ask all persons and committees everywhere to send to this society duplicate statements, so far as possible, of all articles and especially of sums of money sent for our aid, together with the name of the person or society to whom sent.

A complete record of the sources of these contributions, together with the history of their expenditure, will be preserved for future publication.

All newspapers, at home and abroad, are requested to publish this circular. Address

WIRT DEXTER,
Chairman Executive Committee Relief and Aid Society.

The Society established its headquarters at once at Standard Hall, a commodious building in the South Division of the city. A General Plan of work was prepared and presented by Wirt Dexter, Chairman of the Executive Committee, which was adopted by the Society.

GENERAL PLAN OF WORK

OF THE CHICAGO RELIEF AND AID SOCIETY.

COMMITTEE No. 1. On receiving, storing and sorting supplies, and dealing out upon requisitions from other Committees. Murry Nelson, Chairman, aided by Gen. Hardee.

No. 2. Committee on Shelter, to provide tents and barracks. T. M. Avery, Chairman.

No. 3. Committee on Employment, to provide labor for able-bodied applicants. Chairman, N. K. Fairbanks.

No. 4. Committee on Transportation, to provide passes for persons, and freight accommodations for supplies. Chairman, Chas. G. Hammond.

No. 5. Committee on Reception and Correspondence, to receive visitors and answer all dispatches and letters. Chairman, Wirt Dexter.

No. 6. Committee on Distribution of Food, Clothing, and Fuel. O. C. Gibbs, Superintendent of Relief and Aid Society, Chairman.

No. 7. Committee on Sick, Sanitary and Hospital Measures. Dr. H. A. Johnson, Chairman.

No. 8. Executive Committee, consisting of R. B. Mason, the Mayor, and the City Comptroller, the President and Chairman of the Executive Committee of the Chicago Relief and Aid Society, together with the chairman of each of the foregoing committees, shall constitute an Auditing Committee, and have control of all contributions. No bills to be paid unless upon checks or drafts signed by the President or Chairman of the Executive Committee of the Relief and Aid Society, countersigned by R. B. Mason, Mayor.

The chairman of each committee will fill up from citizens who shall tender their services, his own committee, making it as large as the magnitude of the work may require, and be responsible for its doings.

The clergymen of the city are requested to organize an Associate Board of Directors to that of the Relief and Aid Society, and through an executive committee of their own appointment, communicate with our committees.

We recommend the formation of local societies by citizens, and request them through their officers to communicate with the chairmen of the foregoing committees on all matters falling under the respective work of said committees.

The work of distribution as now proceeding will go on until our committees are supplied with force to relieve the present workers; but we request all persons engaged in the work to stop hasty distributions, and give applications as much examination as possible, to the end that we may not waste the generous aid pouring in, as the work of relief is not for a week, or a month, but for the whole of the coming winter, and to a great extent for even a longer period.

The business offices of all the committees except the Executive Committee and Committees of Reception and Correspondence and Transportation, will be at 409 West Washington street, just west of Elizabeth. No relief will be administered at these offices, they being solely for the transaction of Committee business.

Applications for passes on Railroads will be acted upon at one or more places to be designated by the Chairman of that Committee.

The office of the Executive Committee and Committee on Reception and Correspondence, and the general business of the Committee on Transportation will be at Standard Hall, corner Thirteenth Street and Michigan Avenue. Home contributions of money will be receipted for at Standard Hall.

HENRY W. KING, *President.*

WIRT DEXTER,

Chairman Executive Committee Chicago Relief and Aid Society.

This plan was changed only in this respect, that at the following annual meeting of the Society, an Executive Committee was chosen by the Board of Directors from their own number, and invested with power to transact all business subject to the supervision of the Board. This Committee was composed of the heads of the Committees and Departments. No member of the Executive Committee or the Board of Directors has ever received any compensation for his services. The Executive Committee, with one or two exceptions, gave their entire time to the work during most of the winter of 1871–72.

During the early weeks of the winter the Committee gave the entire day to the work of their various departments and held meetings every night at which reports from all the departments were received, plans for the following day were considered, necessary changes in the methods were made, and thus a picture of the situation was constantly in the minds of its members.

Prominent and interested citizens were usually present upon the invitation of the Board, and committees from other cities and towns were frequently present, and were thus enabled to understand the practical operation of the Society and to communicate their impressions to the several constituencies which they represented.

As the work gradually fell into system, the necessity for these meetings became less urgent. To expedite the business of the Executive Committee, and indeed the business generally of the Society, telegraphic communication was established between headquarters and all the warehouses and stations. The convenience was very great, as the distances between the points of communication were long, and the travel through the burnt portions of the city was much impeded, while the expense was small, as the operators were also employed as clerks. For this facility the Society was indebted to the Western Union Telegraph Company, which also forwarded and franked our messages, as did the Atlantic Cable Company in the case of messages of acknowledgement, and orders for supplies.

When it became evident that the amount of the donations received, and of others of which the Society had been notified would enable it to carry forward the work of relief, the Board of Directors authorized the following:

DISPATCH TO THE ASSOCIATED PRESS.

The continued donations since our last report, together with the twenty days of mild weather in January, enable us to say that the resources of the Chicago Relief and Aid Society will meet the wants of the present winter. By resources we mean not only what we have actually received, but various sums of which we have been advised, such as the New York Chamber of Commerce Fund, and the subscriptions of several cities delayed by negotiation of bonds and other causes, which sums, we presume, will be subject to our order when needed. We regard it as a duty to make this announcement the earliest day that it could be made with reasonable assurance of its correctness. We can also say that there will be enough to make temporary provision for our charitable institutions whose resources were cut off by the fire. A careful examination of their affairs is now being made by a committee appointed for that purpose. In our next report, to be published in February, mention will be made of all contributions, both of money and articles, so far as information can be had of the same. Everything received by this Society will be acknowledged, and we ask all other societies of Chicago to send us an account of their receipts. But, as much was given out by various agencies in the first days after the fire without record, we also request all societies and committees elsewhere to send us an account of their donations not mentioned in our next report, to the end that in a still further and final report proper acknowledgment may be made of the entire contributions to our people.

HENRY W. KING, *President.*
WIRT DEXTER, *Chairman Ex. Com.*

CHICAGO, *February* 1, 1872.

CHAPTER VIII.

DEPARTMENT OF GENERAL RELIEF.

SUPPLY AND DISTRIBUTION.

IN the confusion and disorder of the first few days of the fire, the only one practicable rule, and that one of imperative necessity, was that the hungry should be fed. The bountiful supplies which began to pour in from all parts of the country, while the fire was still burning, fortunately made it possible to give food to all who asked it. Churches and school buildings were used as depots and distributing offices, and all who asked received with such order and economy as it was possible to establish in so sudden an emergency. Discrimination, however, was impossible, and bounty fell upon the deserving and the undeserving, as certainly as that the rain falls upon the just and the unjust, for in a calamity that was so universal, and where tens of thousands were faint for want of bread, there was neither the leisure nor the disposition for careful scrutiny. Some waste was inevitable, but it was of more consequence that none should suffer from want than that a few who were not in need should not become successful impostors. But to reduce the work of relief to a system for the sake of economy in the ways and means; to secure to the real sufferers the needed aid; to detect and defeat imposition; to aid in establishing order by withholding encouragement to idleness, was, after giving food to all who said they were hungry, the first object of the Committee. The task was immense, for an army of a hundred thousand, not of men only with some power of endurance, but of men, women, and children, with their aged, their sick, their helpless and their infirm, was suddenly thrown upon the hands of the Society, and there was neither commissariat, nor organization, nor cohesion, nor even distinct and separate locality to fall back upon. The first step was to district the city, and it was accordingly divided into five large districts, made as nearly equal as possible with regard to population.

The public were notified of the location of these depots of distribution, by large posters in all parts of the city, and through the daily press. These were subdivided at first, into thirteen smaller districts, but were rearranged from time to time, as the necessities of the work suggested.

The whole were under the General Superintendent, but to each District was given a Superintendent, with supervision over his whole district, and to each sub-district, a sub-superintendent, with supervision over his immediate depot of supplies.

Sufficient assistance was given to each Superintendent, averaging, at first, about ninety men and women to each district, the duties of a part of whom were to administer to the wants of applicants for food and clothing, courteously and kindly, but with a firm adherence to rules established to guard against extravagant or injudicious distribution, the duplication of relief or pretended want. Another part of this force was made up of a corp of visitors, who were constantly busy in visiting all whose names were registered in the books at the offices of the relief-stations, and in searching for sufferers who needed aid but did not know where to find it. Registration was resorted to at the outset, both as an act of mercy and as a measure of precaution, and a rule was established at the earliest practicable moment, by which none were allowed to take supplies from the depots without full entry of name, residence, condition, and other circumstances which would identify the applicant.

It was the business of the visitor to keep himself constantly informed as to all the persons who were thus entered in his district, and to make periodical returns at the office. He was to learn by observation and inquiry, the exact condition of the registered; whether they were well or ill; whether they were idle or industrious; whether they were voluntarily idle, in which case they were peremptorily cut off from aid; whether they were entitled to entire or only partial support; whether they had other means of support than public bounty; and in short any circumstances in relation to their condition, or habits, or character which would be a guide as to the care which should be given them at the stations. There a ledger account was opened with each of them, in which appeared the returns of the visitors, the supplies given, with their dates, and when they were cut off, if discontinued, and the reasons why.

The Superintendents were required to keep a strict account of all their requisitions of supplies, as well as of their distribution; and as they were accountable for a judicious and energetic discharge of their duties to the General Superintendent, so they held their own subordinates strictly accountable for all their actions. Full and careful reports were made daily from each district, and the Superintendents met with the Executive Committee to make or hear suggestions, to answer criticism or complaints, to report progress and suggest improvement, if possible, in the working machinery. The districts were frequently visited by a general inspector, to examine into their condition and management; and a Committee on Complaints was always ready at headquarters to listen to any complaints of neglect or improper treatment, and to provide for their immediate correction if found, on inquiry, to have been well founded. It took a good deal of time to bring into systematic condition a complicated business of this sort, which was, in fact, getting into running order, under every possible disadvantage of want of preparation, as many large commercial establishments as there are warehouses, bureaus, and relief stations at the various points; but on the whole, the Committee believe that no better plan than that which they adopted could have been devised to carry on the work in their hands, wisely, economically, effectively, and humanely; that the relief given injudiciously or unnecessarily was reduced to the smallest possible percentage, while none were deprived of it who were justly entitled to it. In addition to the several districts of the city proper, there was a sixth district, which included all that portion of Cook county outside the city limits, which was under precisely the same rules and regulations with the rest, and had a similar supervision for such of the sufferers by the fire as found refuge in the other towns in the county.

The subjoined Table is a summary of the statements of the six districts, for the weeks ending November 18th and 25th, and will indicate about the average number of families upon the books at any one date, during the months of the largest distribution of food, fuel, and clothing. It will also indicate the fluctuations which took place in the course of two weeks.

STATEMENT OF FAMILIES AIDED.

For the Week ending November 18, 1871.

DISTRICTS.	Number of Families reported Nov. 11th.	Number added from Nov. 11th to Nov. 18.	TOTAL.	Number discontinued since Nov. 11th.	Number of Families receiving aid Nov. 18.
No. 1	3,305	576	3,881	187	3,602
No. 2	1,876	604	2,480	30	2,450
No. 3	3,543	204	3,747	179	3,568
No. 4	1,995	173	2,168	120	2,048
No. 5	1,740	548	2,288	215	2,073
No. 6	306	none	306	none	306
	12,765	2,105	14,870	733	14,137

For the Week ending November 25, 1871.

DISTRICTS.	Number of Families receiving aid at date of last report, Nov. 18.	Number of Families added during week ending Nov. 25.	TOTAL.	Number of Families to whom aid was discontinued during week ending Nov. 25.	Number of families receiving aid Nov. 25.
No. 1	3,692	384	4,076	720	3,356
No. 2	2,450	541	2,991	165	2,826
No. 3	3,568	166	3,734	240	3,494
No. 4	2,048	150	2,198	112	2,086
No. 5	2,093	440	2,513	249	2,264
No. 6	306	–	306	–	306
Washington Barracks	–	140	140	–	140
Madison St. Barracks	–	137	137	–	136
Harrison St. Barracks	–	316	316	–	316
Clybourne Av. Bar.	–	197	197	–	197
Total	14,137	2,471	16,608	1,486	15,122

The number of different families aided from the time the records were complete to November the 25th, was 23,054. Of these, 3,320 asked only for stove, bedding, and clothing; 19,734 applied for food as well as other necessaries.

The total number of different families aided from October 1871, to May 1873	39,242
Average number in family	4
Total number of persons aided	156,968

In explanation of the above statement of the large number of individuals who received aid at one time or another, to a greater or less extent, it must be remembered that almost the entire business portion of Chicago was destroyed by the fire and thus thousands of families were rendered destitute whose homes were not consumed, but who drew their support from occupation in shops and manufactories of various sorts. Taking the census of 1871 as the basis, the number of those rendered homeless is a matter of easy calculation.

The destruction by the fire was nearly complete in the wards in which it occurred. The fire originated in the Ninth Ward, burning out the northeast corner of that ward. Four blocks of the Tenth Ward had been destroyed the night before. It then crossed the river in the Second Ward, leaving but a dozen buildings in that ward, and destroying twenty-five or more in the Third Ward; it swept every house in the First, Twentieth, Nineteenth, Eighteenth, and Seventeenth Wards, and about four fifths of the Sixteenth Ward. We follow the course of the fire.

Wards.	Inhabitants.
9	2,000
10	250
3	250
2	13,449
1	8,103
20	14,522
19	9,237
18	18,805
17	18,814
16	13,650
Rendered homeless	98,860

CONSOLIDATED TABLE SHOWING TOTAL NUMBER OF FAMILIES ON BOOKS AT DIFFERENT TIMES FROM NOVEMBER 11, 1871, TO MAY 1, 1873.

1871.

Number of families receiving aid November 11		12,765
November 11th to November 18th.		
Added	2,105	
Discontinued	733	
Increase	1,372	
Number of families receiving aid November 18th		14,137
November 18th to November 25th.		
Added	2,471	
Discontinued	1,486	
Increase	985	
Number of families receiving aid November 25th		15,122
November 25th to December 1st.		
Added	1,826	
Discontinued	876	
Increase	950	
Number of families receiving aid December 1st		16,072

December 1st, 1871, to January 1st, 1872.

Added	4,127	
Discontinued	1,976	
Increase	2,151	
Number of families receiving aid January 1st, 1872 . .		18,223

1872.

January 1st to February 1st.

Added	6,329	
Discontinued	4,263	
Increase	2,066	
Number of families receiving aid February 1st . . .		20,289

February 1st to March 1st.

Added	7,263	
Discontinued	5,327	
Increase	1,936	
Number of families receiving aid March 1st		22,225

March 1st to April 1st.

Discontinued	7,562	
Added	3,497	
Decrease	4,065	
Number of families receiving aid April 1st		18,160

April 1st to May 1st.

Discontinued	14,123	
Added	1,412	
Decrease	12,711	
Number of families receiving aid May 1st		5,449

May 1st to September 1st, 1872

Average number of families aided per month	1,587

September 1st, 1872, to May 1st, 1873.

Average number of families aided per month . .	2,116

CONSOLIDATED TABLE SHOWING TOTAL NUMBER OF FAMILIES AIDED FROM OCTOBER, 1871, TO MAY, 1873.

	1871.		
November 11.	Total number of different families aided to date	18,478	
November 18.	New accounts added for week . .	2,105	
November 25.	New accounts added for week . .	2,471	
November 30.	New accounts added for week . .	1,826	
December.	New accounts added for month . .	4,127	
		——	29,007
	1872.		
January.	New accounts added for month . .	3,685	
February.	New accounts added for month . .	2,417	
March.	New accounts added for month . .	1,522	
April.	New accounts added for month . .	345	
May.	New accounts added for month . .	292	
June.	New accounts added for month . .	128	
July.	New accounts added for month . .	117	
August.	New accounts added for month . .	112	
September.	New accounts added for month . .	92	
October.	New accounts added for month . .	221	
November.	New accounts added for month . .	251	
December.	New accounts added for month . .	310	
		——	9,492
	1873.		
January.	New accounts added for month . .	283	
February.	New accounts added for month . .	276	
March.	New accounts added for month . .	125	
April.	New accounts added for month . .	59	
		——	743
Total number of families			39,242
Average number of persons in each family			4
Total number of persons			156,968

ABSTRACT OF NATIONALITIES OF FAMILIES, FROM OCTOBER, 1871, TO MAY, 1873.

Nationality	Families	Nationality	Families
Irish	11,623	Italian	207
German	14,816	Welch	35
American	4,823	Pole	143
English	1,406	Swiss	55
Scandinavian	3,624	Holland	60
French	382	Bohemia	565
Canadian	323	Negro	600
Scotch	526	Belgian	54
		Total	39,242

RATIONS.

Food was given at first indiscriminately, and in uncertain quantities, for want of conveniences in measuring and weighing. As soon as possible, however, it was reduced to fixed rations, and as the system of distribution was perfected, these were given out at intervals of two or three days, and finally of a week. At first, as the people had few conveniences for cooking, bread was given instead of flour, at an increased cost of forty-two cents to the ration. This was afterward almost wholly saved, as most of the applicants were supplied with stoves, and baked their own bread. Crackers, for the first few days, were substituted for bread, when the supply of bread was insufficient. All the crackers used, however, were contributions from abroad. Coffee or tea was given, as the applicant preferred; but tea, which was the cheaper, was the more usually chosen. The following ration for a family of five persons was found to be sufficient for one week: —

EXHIBIT OF THE AMOUNT AND COST OF ONE WEEK'S RATIONS FOR TWO ADULTS AND THREE CHILDREN.

3 pounds Pork, at 5½ cents	.16½
6 pounds Beef, at 5 cents	.30
14 pounds Flour, at 3 cents	.42
1¼ peck Potatoes, at 20 cents	.25
¼ pound Tea, at 80 cents	.20
1½ pounds Sugar, at 11 cents	.16½
1¼ pounds Rice, at 8 cents; or 3½ pounds Beans, at 3¾ cents	.12
1¼ pounds Soap, at 7 cents	.09
1½ pounds Dried Apples, at 8 cents	.12
3 pounds Fresh Beef, at 5 cents	.15
Total	$1.98
If Bread, at 4 cents per pound, was used instead of Flour, the cost was increased	.42
If Crackers, at 7 cents per pound	1.05
If 1½ pounds of Coffee instead of Tea	.17

COAL.

To the cost of the weekly ration of food for a family of five should be added the allowance of one ton of coal a month, or a quarter of a ton a week. Fortunately, for such an exigency as this, the supply of bituminous coal for Chicago was ample, through the Wilmington Coal Company, which owns and works extensive coal mines in Will and Lasalle Counties, Illinois, with sufficient means of transportation at their command over the Alton and St. Louis, and Chicago, Burlington, and Quincy Roads. With Mr. J. M. Walker, president of the latter company, the Committee made a contract for the delivery of coal by the ton or half ton, at the door, for $4.50 per ton. This brought the weekly cost of coal for the family at $1.12½, which added to the cost of the weekly ration, brought the cost of food and fuel at $3.10½. As the demand for fuel was as constant and next in importance to that for food, a large depot of coal from other sources was kept in reserve for emergencies, as in case of interruption to railroad transportation by snow storms, or other causes, during the winter.

CLOTHING.

The demand for clothing was incessant and immense. The larger proportion of those who were sufferers by the fire lost all their personal apparel and their household goods. Immediate and urgent need was only very partially met by the bountiful supplies which were sent forward from all quarters. Much of this supply was of second-hand summer clothing, which was all that people could lay their hands on in the first emergency. It answered a good though only a temporary purpose, and the necessity of substituting for it better and warmer garments was constant and imperative. The markets of this country could not supply the demand for blankets alone. Where the supply of ready-made clothing was insufficient, piece goods were given out in measured quantities to applicants to make up for themselves. In this work great assistance was rendered by associations of ladies, as the Ladies' Relief and Aid Society; the Ladies' Industrial Aid Society of St. John's Church; the Ladies' Christian Union; the Ladies' Society of Park Avenue Church; and the Ladies' Society of The Home of The Friendless; all of these societies employed a large number of sewing women, thrown out of employment by the fire, in making up garments, bed comforters, bed-ticks, and other articles, from piece goods supplied by the Relief Committee, to be returned, thus manufactured, to the several depots for distribution.

PURCHASING COMMITTEE.

The necessity of purchasing food and clothing was imperative even at the outset, notwithstanding the large contributions of both that were made from abroad.

Large as these were, they were not sufficient even when most bountiful, to supply the demands made upon the Committee, and only enabled them to bridge over the interval until supply and demand could be made to balance each other by an organized system. A Purchasing Committee, J. McGregor Adams, Chairman, was therefore appointed, with experienced and responsible merchants to aid him, who, anticipating the wants at the several distributing points, held themselves in readiness at all times, as far as possible, to meet the requisitions of the General Superintendent. Their operations extended to all parts of this country and of England; to replace even partially so much household stuff, the accumulation of years, and to feed so large a multitude, suddenly deprived of their ordinary means of livelihood, was an immense and most difficult work. The supply of manufactured articles in the markets immediately accessible to the committee, was found to be wholly inadequate. Chicago wanted more stoves of a certain pattern, more blankets, more mattresses, more boots and shoes, and more furniture of various kinds than were within its reach to meet the emergency.

The problem was to find and to purchase all these as speedily as possible, and to get them into the hands of those in want. This duty devolved upon the Purchasing Committee, and it required their utmost activity, assisted by a large clerical force, and a most thorough organization, to keep pace with the constant and pressing demands of an impoverished people.

DONATIONS OF CLOTHING.

Of the actual quantity received by gift from abroad and distributed, it is impossible to make a detailed statement, as much was given out in the first calamitous days of destitution to all comers and without count. The

United States Government, through the active efforts of General Sheridan, furnished seven thousand blankets, and five thousand each of undershirts, drawers, and socks. This branch of the work, however, was reduced to a system, like the rest.

The following table is condensed from the reports of the several districts for the week ending November 25th, giving the number distributed of several articles of prime necessity. To it is added the number previously reported: —

DISTRIBUTION OF ARTICLES FOR THE WEEK ENDING NOVEMBER 25, 1871.

District.	Mattresses.	Blankets.	Tons Coal.	Stoves.	Shoes.	Men's Wear.	Women's Wear.	Childrens' Wear.
No. 1	709	667	414	190	5,882	1,266	1,434	3,758
No. 2	628	894	251	165	3,596	1,977	2,423	649
No. 3	270	1,242	433	42	7,046	3,399	2,430	1,246
No. 4	93	605	152	51	1,700	293	760	1,504
No. 5	394	1,172	244	199	4,257	1,454	1,767	1,726
No. 6	37	35	28	17	60	457	81	73
	2,131	4,615	1,522	664	22,531	8,846	8,895	8,984
Previously reported	8,606	20,724	2,131	3,795	–	45,883	57,091	35,953
Total .	10,737	25,339	4,653	4,459	22,581	54,729	65,986	44,937

The above table does not include the stoves and mattresses given out by the Shelter Committee, who furnished both articles to a large proportion of their houses and the barracks. Nor the goods given out by the Special Relief Committee. Neither does it include the furniture and crockery, both large items of expenditure.

PAY-ROLLS.

The cost of handling this large business necessarily varied from week to week, as the number of families asking for aid increased or diminished. The pay-rolls for the week ending November 18th may be taken as a fair average of expenditure for the first months. That for the sixth district, which was that portion of Cook County, outside the city limits, is not included in this table. That, however, was comparatively insignificant, as the number of persons who needed aid there was small. Neither are the expenditures of the Shelter Committee included, as that is properly charged to a separate account, which was closed in a few weeks, and should not be included in the current expenses of the Society. The clerical force employed by that Committee was large, but temporary only.

PAY-ROLLS FOR THE WEEK ENDING NOVEMBER 18, 1871.

Districts.	Persons Employed.	Amount.
No. 1	142	$1,549.00
No. 2	116	1,190.17
No. 3	106	1,347.75
No. 4	50	531.82
No. 5	75	855.66
Special Bureau	9	118.50
Superintendents' Salaries	–	225.00
Warehousemen, Receiving, Storing, and Delivering Supplies	111	1,259.87
Transportation	–	2,148.87
Total for Distribution		$9,226.64
Employment Bureau	2	36.00
Clerks in offices of Treasurer, Auditor, Transportation Committee, Purchasing Committee, and Executive Committee	32	496.34
Total General Business		$9,758.98

The following table shows the total distribution by the Department of General Relief, by months, from October, 1871, to April 20, 1873.

DISTRIBUTION OF

Abstract of Issues from October, 1871,

DESCRIPTION.	Distributed Oct. 1871.	Distributed November.	Distributed December.	Distributed Jan'y 1872.	Distributed February.	Distributed March.	Distributed April.	Distributed May.	Distributed June.	Distributed July.
Rent paid	—	$405.20	$913.50	$2,330.90	$7,605.73	$9,948.52	$2,695.60	$2,212.50	$1,144.00	$1,108.00
Tons Coal	1,500	5,228	6,667	8,418	10,943	6,357½	973	649	249	146
Cords Wood	—	—	—	10¼	28¼	30	—	52¼	7½	8½
Pounds Flour	93,250	262,319	307,128	382,450	14,005	293,819	87,127	59,321	25,893	17,898
Pounds Meal	3,675	10,986	10,735	13,219	14,441	10,390	139	20	35	65
Pounds Pork	19,700	72,271	64,902	65,422	115,680	65,593	1,272	—	—	—
Pounds Beef	63,470	130,455	105,733	109,744	129,748	90,560	—	—	—	—
Pounds Bread	74,700	169,812	191,076	111,237	108,892	39,805	7,919	3,738	3,499	1,667
Pounds Crackers	27,600	70,644	52,152	18,209	4,189	4,423	747	724	258	386
Pounds Fish	3,470	12,853	3,541	1,290	1,933	1,273	391	—	—	—
Pounds Soap	12,480	31,509	35,825	45,359	56,081	27,757	9,209	6,288	2,709	1,900
Pounds Candles	3,725	9,652	12,375	14,599	21,570	9,515	4,293	14,284	6,624	4,323
Pounds Cheese	650	1,122	1,850	460	100	5	2	—	—	—
Pounds Tea	1,875	4,465	5,933	7,321	9,696	5,710	1,813	1,335	493¾	3865
Pounds Coffee	8,525	20,601	14,684	8,483	7,841	9,784	518	154	374½	82½
Pounds Sugar	14,780	34,792	54,605	49,336½	66,429	46,738	9,488	6,818	2,754	1,952
Pounds Bacon	7,440	16,182	18,598	25,389	5,894	—	—	—	—	—
Pounds Hams	550	28	6,410	—	—	—	—	—	—	—
Pounds Butter	280	196	44	73	59	—	—	75	42	39
Pounds Fruit, Dried	2,875	14,946	26,682	38,890	60,227	31,854	2,795	431	48	20¾
Pounds Salt	175	2,123	1,858	262	560	840	1,500	—	—	—
Pounds Rice	8,565	25,922	6,923	5,043	3,940	6,702	2,315	944	390	348¼
Pounds Fresh Beef	—	18,021	146,797	199,152	277,096	116,899	61,190	77,301	28,555	20,300
Pounds Lard	—	13	885	—	—	745	—	—	—	—
Pounds Mutton	—	—	5,921	4,195	—	—	—	—	—	—
Cans Canned Fruit	—	—	—	—	—	—	—	103	43	26
Cans Canned Vegetables	—	—	—	—	—	—	—	28	12	3
Cans Oysters	—	—	—	—	—	—	17	6	1	7
Bushels Potatoes	4,250	9,552	9,551	10,503	13,649	6,950	1,873	1,322½	589½	395½
Bushels Beans	125	733	1,461	2,429	2,183	866	8	1½	—	—
Bushels Onions	250	717	987	2,643	2,799	1,217	2	—	—	—
Pecks Turnips	—	32	—	—	—	—	—	—	—	—
Gallons Vinegar	—	229	53	282	—	81	180	—	—	—
Gallons Syrup	—	872	439	80	—	—	—	—	—	—
Packages Corn Starch	—	—	—	—	—	—	27	13	11	
Packages Farina	—	—	—	—	—	—	—	8	12	9
Packages Ex. Beef	—	—	—	—	—	—	—	21	12	5
Mattresses	3,575	12,224	3,634	2,961	2,581	3,148	101	281	96	23
Pillows	200	935	143	58	128	—	—	—	—	—
White & Gray Blankets	8,775	29,967	13,145	8,479	9,662	3,220	179	547	169	32
Bed and Pillow Ticks	175	84	207	566	774	281	146	—	—	—
Comforts	1,675	3,276	3,548	1,161	725	13	—	—	—	—
Sheets	—	—	1,649	649	665	157	—	—	—	—
Stoves	2,380	4,838	1,646	1,301	1,044	3,362	84	132	43	11
Pieces of Pipe	4,350	7,206	2,458	4,551	4,430	28,338	297	591	177	36
Tables	190	517	2,246	2,006	1.251	2,805	48	141	50	13
Bedsteads	525	1,414	3,025	2,687	1,846	6,718	84	232	72	25
Chairs	775	2,077	4,525	6,607	5,470	11,004	194	555	117	43
Pieces Crockery	5,000	15,668	12,932	3.960	2,451	27,949	111	26	—	—
Wash Tubs	75	230	871	1,919	1,881	4,530	32	88	45	13
Pails	—	—	87	643	759	2,431	22	72	31	12
Wash Boards	—	—	210	1,258	1,469	3,284	21	72	29	6
Tin Ware	—	74	—	—	—	—	—	20	—	—
Dozen Eggs	—	—	—	—	—	—	—	14	5	—
Dozen Lemons	—	—	—	—	—	—	—	36	30	30
Packages Jelly	—	—	—	—	—	—	—	70	34	32
Bottles Wine	—	—	—	—	—	—	—	4	2	12
Pairs Shoes	7,875	28,011	13,138	7,200	8,489	4,342	1,342	300	49	33
Pairs Men's Hose	1,980	4,691	4,279	2,394	2,556	2,235	7	18	—	—
Pairs Women's Hose	3,600	7,334	14,179	4,794	6,292	2,682	256	3	—	—
Knives and Forks	—	—	—	—	—	—	—	—	—	—
Clothes Wringer	—	—	—	—	—	—	—	—	—	—
Men's Clothing	27,600	61,871	18,644	8,513	7,791	2,936	34	36	—	—
Women's Clothing	32,000	73,932	17,833	9,098	9,746	2,754	1,456	13	—	—
Children's Clothing	19,750	49,034	15,789	4,289	8,773	2,263	755	159	—	—
Yards Wool Flannel	3,775	13,376	35,436	18,978	29.218	9,700	244	—	—	—
Yards Canton Flannel	10,450	30,380	28,596	7,171	6,060	2,429	68	—	—	—
Yards Prints	14,600	35,963	75,163	23,452	34,133	18,376	268	—	—	—
Yards Sheeting	13,300	32,144	42,120	23,609	38,266	23,434	—	—	—	—
Yards Jeans	2,300	7,368	24,342	22,086	21,076	9,630	149	—	—	—
Yards Ticking	—	251	134	45	—	—	—	—	—	—
Yards Toweling	—	425	1,109	428	990	1,102	—	—	—	—
Yards Water Proof	—	—	—	—	1,232	1,952	—	—	—	—
Yards Crash	—	—	—	—	286	—	—	—	—	—
Rubber Blankets	—	—	—	—	—	—	—	—	—	—
Heads Cabbage	—	—	—	22	—	—	—	—	—	—
Brooms	—	—	—	6	—	—	—	—	—	—
Pounds Fresh Pork	—	—	—	442	—	—	—	—	—	—

GENERAL RELIEF.

to April 20, 1873, *inclusive.*

Distributed August.	Distributed September.	Distributed October.	Distributed November.	Distributed December.	Distributed Jan'y 1873.	Distributed February.	Distributed March.	Distributed April.	GRAND TOTAL.	DESCRIPTION.
$1,206.00	$1,032.25	$1,247.00	$2,369.00	$3,727.81	$5,448.05	$5,356.15	$5,930.90	$3,504.90	$58,095.41	Rents & Sundry Cash.
162	144½	212½	562¾	1,098½	1,863½	1,566½	765½	240	47,746	Tons Coal.
9¾	4½	¾	8	4½	2	8½	6	44	145	Cords Wood.
19,098	11,992	11,094	19,729	28,258	55,856	53,618	37,447	14,500	2,294,802	Pounds Flour.
96	6½	7	42	194	310	192	71	90	64,613½	Pounds Meal.
—	—	—	—	—	—	—	—	—	404,840	Pounds Salt Pork.
—	—	—	—	—	—	—	—	—	629,710	Pounds Salt Beef.
2,185	903	742	860	869	1,076	1,595	1,934	731	723,240	Pounds Bread.
553	459	447	685	927	1,285	920	704	329	185,641	Pounds Crackers.
—	—	—	—	—	—	—	—	—	24,751	Pounds Salt Fish.
2,078	1,353	1,192	1,926	2,841	5,670	5,846	3,229	1,479	254,731	Pounds Soap.
2,925	1,656	1,386	2,250	3,141	6,300	6,354	4,041	1,499	130,512	Pounds Candles.
38	—	—	—	—	—	—	—	—	4,227	Pounds Cheese.
381¼	264⅞	229⅞	386	570	1,147¾	1,101⅜	673½	259	44,040⅝	Pounds Tea.
139½	100½	79	103	82	161	153	106	66	72,037	Pounds Coffee.
2,026½	1,369	1,176	1,950	2,713	5,723½	5,510	3,370	1,481	313,011½	Pounds Sugar.
—	—	—	—	—	—	—	—	—	73,503	Pounds Bacon.
—	—	—	—	—	—	—	—	—	6,988	Hams.
50	22	19	28	36½	34	39	34	17	1,087½	Pounds Butter.
23	8	2	16	36	24	6½	8½	4	178,896¾	Pounds Dried Fruit.
—	—	—	—	—	—	—	—	—	7,318	Pounds Salt.
501¾	365	318½	451½	686¾	948⅓	696¾	488¾	223	65,772¼	Pounds Rice.
23,344	13,286	13,001	15,995	20,351	44,198	47,456	41,963	19,169	1,184,074	Pounds Fresh Beef.
—	—	—	—	—	—	—	—	—	1,643	Pounds Lard.
—	— A	—	—	—	—	—	—	—	10,116	Pounds Mutton.
29	9	6	6	7	12	3	9	4	257	Cans Canned Fruit.
6	—	—	—	—	4	—	—	—	53	Canned Vegetables.
10	6	1	1	5	5	—	—	—	59	Cans Oysters.
429¾	282⅛	249⅜	409⅝	607¼	1,218⅝	1,162½	718⅛	317¾	64,030⅜	Bushels Potatoes.
—	—	—	—	16 qts	22 qts	—	—	—	7,806½	Bushels Beans.
—	—	—	—	—	—	—	—	—	8,615	Bushels Onions.
—	—	—	—	—	—	—	—	—	32	Pecks Turnips.
—	—	—	—	—	—	—	—	—	825	Gallons Vinegar.
—	—	—	—	—	—	—	—	—	1,391	Gallons Syrup.
3	6	2	3	6	9	11	8	—	99	Packages Corn Starch.
22	8	4	4	10	25	17	6	—	125	Packages Farina.
13	3	1	1	11	34	15	10	—	126	Packages Ex. Beef.
26	—	8	37	53	82	71	—	—	28,901	Mattresses.
—	—	10	—	14	16	8	—	—	1,512	Pillows.
50	—	59	237	510	870	650	168	39	76,758	White & Gray Blank'ts
—	—	4	—	—	—	—	—	4	2,241	Bed and Pillow Ticks.
—	—	—	—	—	—	—	—	—	10,398	Comforts.
—	—	—	—	—	—	—	—	—	3,120	Sheets.
—	—	14	43	37	41	37	5	4	15,022	Stoves.
—	—	—	—	—	—	—	—	—	52,434	Pieces of Pipe.
11	—	2	11	16	13	12	—	—	9,332	Tables.
5	—	4	22	38	43	36	—	—	16,776	Bedsteads.
45	—	10	30	31	62	41	—	—	31,586	Chairs.
2	—	—	—	—	—	—	—	—	68,149	Pieces Crockery.
2	—	8	15	11	10	3	—	—	9,733	Wash Tubs.
4	—	1	5	1	3	—	—	—	4,071	Pails.
5	—	4	9	8	8	3	—	—	6,386	Wash Boards.
—	—	—	—	—	—	—	—	—	94	Tin Ware.
3	3	5	2	2	—	—	—	—	34	Dozen Eggs.
—	6	1	1	—	—	—	—	—	104	Dozen Lemons.
45	21	6	2	6	24	18	10	6	274	Packages Jelly.
10	1	—	—	—	—	—	—	—	29	Bottles Wine.
51	69	250	758	929	1,804	1,868	598	138	77,244	Pairs Shoes.
—	—	—	—	—	—	—	—	—	18,160	Pairs Men's Hose.
—	—	—	—	—	2	—	—	—	39,142	Pairs Women's Hose.
—	—	6	—	9	12	—	—	—	27	Knives and Forks.
—	—	—	—	—	—	1	—	—	1	Clothes Wringer.
—	—	80	435	817	1,465	750	295	65	131,332	Men's Clothing.
—	—	196	1,306	2,645	2,448	480	253	31	154,191	Women's Clothing.
—	—	167	566	532	2,744	1,624	801	98	107,344	Children's Clothing.
—	—	266¼	1,337	984¼	1,145½	54	7	—	114,551	Yards Wool Flannel.
—	—	—	—	—	1,230	4,439	5	—	90,828	Yards Canton Flannel.
—	—	10	10	—	832½	5,188	46½	—	208,042	Yards Prints.
—	—	—	—	—	1,061½	5,202	15	—	179,151½	Yards Sheeting.
—	—	—	—	—	—	—	—	—	86,951	Yards Jeans.
—	—	—	—	—	—	—	—	—	430	Yards Ticking.
—	—	—	—	—	—	—	—	—	4,054	Yards Toweling.
—	—	—	—	—	—	—	—	—	3,184	Yards Water Proof.
—	—	—	—	—	—	—	—	—	286	Yards Crash.
—	—	—	—	—	—	2	—	—	2	Rubber Blankets.
—	—	—	—	—	—	—	—	—	22	Heads Cabbage.
—	—	—	—	—	—	—	—	—	6	Brooms.
—	—	—	—	—	—	—	—	—	442	lbs. Fresh Pork.

CIRCULARS AND ORDERS
ISSUED BY THE DEPARTMENT OF GENERAL RELIEF.

CHICAGO RELIEF AND AID SOCIETY.
HEADQUARTERS DISTRIBUTION OF SUPPLIES.

No. 409 *West Washington Street.*
CHICAGO, *October* 24, 1871.

To all Superintendents, Assistants, and Visitors in the service of the Chicago Relief and Aid Society: —

To us is intrusted the responsibility of the distribution of supplies of food, fuel, and clothing to the needy of our city. With generous donations pouring in on every hand, and with multitudes of sufferers of all classes presenting their claims, in the first hurry and excitement, every tendency will be towards a generous and liberal distribution of supplies; but remember that there are from six to eight months before us in which we will have to fight hunger, cold, and nakedness from the dwellings of our poor.

I am fully justified in saying, that taking into account the amount of relief funds and stores received or reported to date, and those likely to be received hereafter, without the most rigid economy in their disbursement, mid-winter is likely to find us with our treasury bare, with out-door labor, to a large extent, necessarily suspended, and with a city full of poor, looking to us for food and fuel.

You will, therefore, see the pressing necessity that not a single dollar be expended for persons able to provide for themselves, no matter how strongly their claims may be urged by themselves or others. Every carpenter or mason can now earn from three to four dollars per day, every laborer two dollars, every half-grown boy one dollar, every woman capable of doing household work from two to three dollars per week and her board, either in the city or country. Clerks, and persons unaccustomed to out-door labor, if they cannot find such employment as they have been accustomed to, must take such as is offered or leave the city. Any man, single woman, or boy, able to work, and unemployed at this time, is so from choice and not from necessity. You will, therefore, at once commence the work of reëxamination of the cases of all persons who have been visited and recorded upon your books, and will give no aid to any families who are capable of earning their own support, if fully employed (except it be to supply some needed articles of clothing, bedding, or furniture which their earnings will not enable them to procure, and at the same time meet their ordinary expenses of food and fuel).

No aid should be rendered to persons possessed of property, either personal or real, from which they might, by reasonable exertions, procure the means to supply their wants, nor to those who have friends able to relieve them.

Our aid must be held sacred for the aged, infirm, widows and orphans, and to supply to families those actual necessaries of life, which, with the best exertions on their part, they are unable to procure by their labor. You will intrust this work of reëxamination to your most judicious and intelligent visitors, who will act conscientiously and fearlessly in the discharge of their duties.

This circular is issued with the full approval of the Executive Committee, and any failure on the part of any employé of the Society to conform to the instructions above given will be regarded as sufficient cause for his instant dismissal.

O. C. GIBBS,
Gen'l Sup't of Distribution of Supplies.

Approved by the Executive Committee.

WIRT DEXTER, *Chairman.*

CHICAGO RELIEF AND AID SOCIETY.

HEADQUARTERS DISTRIBUTION OF SUPPLIES.

No. 400 *West Washington Street.*
CHICAGO, *October* 24, 1871.

To all Superintendents, Assistants, and Visitors in the Service of the Chicago Relief and Aid Society:—

In the distribution of supplies, give uncooked instead of cooked food, to all families provided with stoves — flour instead of bread, etc.

The Shelter Committee furnish all families for whom they provide houses and barracks, with stove, bedstead, and mattress, and no issue of those articles to such families will be necessary on your part.

Superintendents of Districts and Sub-districts will so keep an account of their disbursements as to give a correct report to me at the end of each week, the number of families aided during the week, and the amount, in gross, of supplies distributed.

Superintendents will also ascertain and report, as early as possible, the amount of furniture, number of stoves, amount of common crockery, etc., which will be needed in their respective districts.

Superintendents will also organize their working-force as early as possible, retaining upon their force those who have proved themselves the most efficient and capable in the discharge of their duties, reducing the number of paid employés to the smallest number consistent with the efficient performance of the work of their districts.

No person in the employ of the Society will be allowed to receive for his own use any supplies of any kind whatever, except it be through the ordinary channels of relief, and recorded on the books of the office in which he is employed.

In all cases of applicants moving into your district from another, you will before giving any relief, ascertain, by inquiry at the office of the district from which they came, if they had been aided in that district, and to what extent.

In the issue of supplies you will discriminate according to the health and condition of the family, furnishing to the aged, infirm, and delicate supplies not ordinarily furnished to those in robust health.

The following has been adopted by the Society as the standard daily ration for a family of five persons; you will vary from the amount according to the income of the family from labor or other sources: —

Bacon or Pork	2 pounds.
or Beef	3 pounds.
Beans	1 pint.
Potatoes	2 quarts.
Bread	3 pounds.
or Flour	2 pounds.
Tea	1 ounce.
or Coffee	2½ ounces.
Sugar	4 ounces.
Rice	4 ounces.
Soap	4 ounces.
Soft Coal	¾ ton per month.

The Department of Sick and Hospitals have adopted the system of Districts and Sub-districts, established by this department, and appointed a medical officer for each district. Visitors will report all cases coming to their knowledge, requiring medical attendance, and the person in charge of each office will have such reports at all times in readiness for the medical officer of the district when he calls. All possible aid must be given the medical officer of the district, and he is to be allowed free access to the office and books of the Society at all times.

The bread now being furnished is contracted for by the pound. You will be furnished with platform scales, and required to weigh and receipt for all bread delivered to you.

Superintendents and Visitors in those districts in which the Shelter Committee have furnished houses to men who were burned out, will inquire carefully into the condition and circumstances of all persons who have been furnished houses by the Shelter Committee, and report to Mr. Avery, Chairman, all cases in which parties have obtained lumber or building material by fraudulent representations.

O. C. Gibbs,
General Superintendent.

CHICAGO RELIEF AND AID SOCIETY.

April 1, 1872.

NOTICE.

On Monday, April 1st, the entire work of the Chicago Relief and Aid Society will be consolidated in one Central Office, at Nos. 215 and 217 East Randolph Street, and will be conducted on the same general plan as previous to the fire.

Only the sick, aged, and infirm, and poor widows with dependent children, will be regarded as subjects for relief. There will be no further issue of stoves, furniture, bedding, nor clothing.

No further appropriations will be made for buildings or anything pertaining to improvement of property or payment of ground rent.

Disapprovals cannot be reconsidered.

By order of the Executive Committee.

Charles L. Allen, *Secretary.*

CHICAGO RELIEF AND AID SOCIETY.

NOTICE TO APPLICANTS.

From present indications the winter is nearly gone, and spring is at hand. Already there is a growing demand for mechanics and laborers of every grade. We intend to close our winter work in these offices as soon as possible, and all who can work must find something to do. This issue of ——————————————————————
closes your account for the present season. The work of this Society will be conducted hereafter on the same general principles and only to the same extent as before the fire. None but the sick, aged, and infirm need apply. No relief will be given in any case where there is an able-bodied man, woman, or children old enough to work.

C. G. Trusdell,
Gen'l Sup't Chicago Relief and Aid Society.

BLANKS

USED BY THE DEPARTMENT OF GENERAL RELIEF.

GENERAL SUPERINTENDENT'S OFFICE,
CHICAGO RELIEF AND AID SOCIETY,
Nos. 215 *and* 217 *Randolph Street.*

Name of Applicant	
Residence	
If burned out, — where and what,	
Amount of Loss	
Amount of Insurance	
Nationality	
Occupation	
Income per week	
Married, Widow, or Single . .	
No. Children, — their ages . .	
Aid Received from Dist. Office .	
From Shelter Committee . . .	
From A. T. Stewart Fund . .	
From Special Relief Committee, Sewing Machine, Money,	
Has Application to any of the above been disapproved?	
Other Sources	
Recommended by	

WANTS,

[*Blank Form of Application.*]

TO THE CHICAGO RELIEF AND AID SOCIETY,

C. G. TRUSDELL, GENERAL SUPERINTENDENT.

215 *and* 217 *E. Randolph Street.*

CHICAGO, 187

I hereby certify that I am personally acquainted with the character and circumstances of

Name,

Residence,

And that in my judgment they are proper subjects of Relief.

[Persons signing this can add any facts of importance.]

MUST BE SIGNED BY TWO RESPONSIBLE CITIZENS.

N. B. Persons signing the above will please understand, that they personally vouch for the merits and necessities of this case.

CHICAGO RELIEF AND AID SOCIETY.

DEPARTMENT OF SPECIAL RELIEF.

CHICAGO, 187

Your case is now under consideration, but before deciding upon it, a personal interview is desired.

Please call, and present this notice between the hours of 10 A. M. and 2 P. M.

Respectfully,

C. G. TRUSDELL, *Superintendent.*

CHICAGO RELIEF AND AID SOCIETY,

C. G. TRUSDELL, GENERAL SUPERINTENDENT.

215 *and* 217 *East Randolph Street.*

FURNISHING DEPARTMENT.

CHICAGO, 187

Your application has been APPROVED for

Call in person and present this notice at our office between 9 A. M. and 3 P. M.

H. F. HAWKES,
Superintendent Furnishing Department.

No.

CHICAGO RELIEF AND AID SOCIETY,

O. C. GIBBS, GENERAL SUPERINTENDENT.

215 *and* 217 *Randolph Street,*

DEPARTMENT OF SPECIAL RELIEF.

CHICAGO, 187

Your application has been APPROVED for

Call in person and present this notice at our office between 10 A. M and 2 P. M.

C. G. TRUSDELL, *Superintendent.*

No.

CHICAGO RELIEF AND AID SOCIETY,

C. G. TRUSDELL, GENERAL SUPERINTENDENT.

215 *and* 217 *East Randolph Street,*

DEPARTMENT OF SPECIAL RELIEF.

CHICAGO, 187

Your application is returned DISAPPROVED, for the following reason:— The restricted Relief afforded by this Society, consequent upon its diminished funds, does not permit of an appropriation in this case.

Disapprovals cannot be reconsidered.

C. H. TRUSDELL,
General Superintendent.

CHICAGO RELIEF AND AID SOCIETY,

215 *and* 217 *Randolph Street,*

CHICAGO, 187

Your case is now under consideration, but before deciding upon it, would like a personal interview.

Please call, and present this notice between the hours of 10 and 12.

Respectfully,

General Superintendent.

CHICAGO RELIEF AND AID SOCIETY,

215 *and* 217 *Randolph Street,*

CHICAGO, 187

Your application is returned DISAPPROVED, for the following reason:—

General Superintendent.

VISITOR'S BLANK.

Name,
Present residence,
Former residence,
Nationality,
Present occupation,
Former occupation,
Rate of wages now received,
Married or single,
Number of children,
Their ages,
How many attend school?
How many children are employed?
What is their occupation?
Total income of family per week,
Were they burned out?
Had they any property, personal or real?
Have they any property now?
Were they insured? For what amount? $
In what company?
Are they receiving aid from any source?
Do they want work?
What kind?
Have they any relatives here or elsewhere?
Are their relatives in condition and disposed to aid them?
Is it a suitable family to be sent out of the city?
Are they willing to go?

☞ Visitors will write in full upon back of this sheet any additional information that may be obtained.

VISITOR'S BLANK.

Name,
Residence,
Where burnt out,
Nationality,
Married or single, Number able to work,
Number of Children, { Boys' Ages, / Girls' Ages,
Occupation,
Total income per week, $
Relatives or friends,

Losses.	Received.	Property Saved.	Wants.
Total $	$		

REMARKS.

Visitor.

FORM OF APPLICATION FOR GENERAL RELIEF.

Name of Man,	Age,
Name of Woman,	Age,
Residence,	Nationality,
Married or Single,	Occupation,
No. Children, Boys, — Ages,	No. at work, and wages,
No. Children, Girls, — Ages,	No. at work, and wages,
Where burnt out,	Am't Ins. What Co.,
Income per week,	Rent paid per Month,
Aided before fire by,	Ground Rent per Year,
How long will aid be required?	Relatives or Friends,

Losses.	Received.	Property Saved and now Owned.	Needs.

REMARKS.

Indorsement on back of above:—

Nos.
Name,
Residence,
Book, Page,

CHICAGO RELIEF AND AID SOCIETY,

FURNISHING DEPARTMENT.

CHICAGO, 187

Deliver to No.

Blankets, White		Nightgowns girls'	
Gray		men's	
Flannel, White		Corsets	
Blue		Hoods, ladies'	
Red		girls'	
Canton		Worsted knit capes, ladies'	
Sheeting		girls'	
Calico		Mitts, ladies'	
Dresses, ladies'		girls'	
girls'		Mittens ladies'	
Skirts, gray flannel, ladies		girls'	
girls'		men's	
red flannel, ladies'		boys'	
girls'		Stockings, ladies'	
Winsey, ladies'		girls'	
girls'		Socks, men's	
Chemises, ladies'		boys'	
girls'		Leggins	
Drawers, colored flannel, ladies'		Handkerchiefs	
girls'		Overcoats, men's	
cotton, ladies'		boys'	
girls'		Coats, men's	
flannel, ladies'		boys'	
girls'		Pants, men's	
Waists, ladies'		boys'	
girls'		Vests, men's	
Sacks, ladies'		boys'	
girls'		Shoes, ladies'	
Cloaks, ladies'		girls'	
girls'		men's	
Aprons, ladies'		boys'	
girls'		Shirts, wool, men's	
Shawls, ladies'		boys'	
girls'		white, men's	
Nightgowns, ladies'		boys'	

CHICAGO RELIEF AND AID SOCIETY,

DEPARTMENT DISTRIBUTION OF SUPPLIES.

CHICAGO, 187

Sir: Below please find statement of Supplies Received this day for distribution in District No. , comprising Sub-districts Nos.

Pounds Flour		Number of Mattresses	
Meal		Pillows	
Pork		Gray Blankets	
Beef		White Blankets	
Bread		Comforts	
Crackers		Sheets	
Fish		Stoves	
Soap		Pieces Pipe	
Candles		Tables	
Cheese		Bedsteads	
Tea		Chairs	
Coffee		Pieces Crockery	
Sugar		Wash Tubs	
Bacon		Pieces Tin Ware	
Hams			
Butter		Pairs Boots	
Fruit		Men's Shoes	
Salt		Boys' Shoes	
Rice		Women's Shoes	
		Children's Shoes	
Bushels Potatoes		Men's Hose	
Beans		Women's Hose	
Onions			
Heads Cabbage		Articles Men's Clothing	
Gallons Vinegar		Women's Clothing	
Molasses		Children's Clothing	
		Yards Cotton Flannel	
		Wool Flannel	
		Prints	
		Sheeting	

Yours respectfully,

SUP'T.

District No.

CHICAGO RELIEF AND AID SOCIETY.

SUPPLY DEPOT AT__________________

CHICAGO, 187

DELIVERED to Wagon No. Teamster

the following Supplies, to be delivered to Superintendent of District No.

	GROCERIES AND PROVISIONS.
....	Barrels Flour.
....	Sacks Flour.
....	Sacks Meal.
....	Barrels Bread.
....	Boxes Bread.
....	Barrels Crackers.
....	Boxes Crackers.
....	Barrels of Irish Potatoes.
....	Barrels Sweet Potatoes.
....	Sacks Potatoes.
....	Barrels Apples.
....	Barrels Onions.
....	Barrels Beans.
....	Barrels Rice.
....	Barrels Sugar.
....	Barrels Ground Coffee.
....	Smoked Hams.
....	Smoked Shoulders.
....	Smoked Sides Bacon.
....	Cabbage.
....	Codfish.
....	Firkins Butter.
....	Chests Tea.
....	Boxes Cheese.
....	Boxes Soap.
....	Salt.
....	Boxes Candles.
....	Boxes Herring.
....	Dried Fruit.
....	Cans Fish and Fruit.
....	
....	
....	
....	
....	
....	
....	

	BEDDING AND FURNITURE.
....	Mattresses.
....	Pillows.
....	Gray Blankets.
....	White Blankets.
....	Comforts.
....	Sheets.
....	Stoves.
....	Pieces Pipe
....	Tables.
....	Bedsteads
....	Chairs.

	SHOES, CLOTHING, AND DRY GOODS.
....	Cases Men's Shoes.
....	Cases Boy's Shoes.
....	Cases Women's Shoes.
....	Cases Misses' Shoes.
....	Cases Children's Shoes.
....	Pairs Men's Hose (assorted).
....	Pairs Women's Hose (assorted).
....	Pairs Children's Hose (assorted).
....	Overcoats.
....	Undercoats.
....	Pants.
....	Vests.
....	Women's Cloaks.
....	Women's and Children's Dresses.
....	Men's Shirts.
....	Men's Drawers.
....	Pieces Sheeting.
....	Pieces Prints.
....	Pieces Flannel.
....	Hats.
....	Caps.
....	Hoods.
....	Shawls.

Received in full the above described Supplies.

Date,

____

Superintendent District No.

CHICAGO RELIEF AND AID SOCIETY.

DEPARTMENT DISTRIBUTION OF SUPPLIES.

Chicago, 187

SIR: Below I hand you Statement showing work performed in District No. comprising Sub-districts Nos. from to

Superintendent.

		Previously Reported.	Total to Date.
Number Cases Visited			
Registered as Worthy of Aid			
Rejected as not Needy or Unworthy			
SUPPLIES DISTRIBUTED.			
Number Tons Coal			
Cords Wood			
Lbs. Flour			
Lbs. Meat			
Loaves Bread			
Lbs. Meal			
Lbs. Crackers			
Lbs. Fish			
Pecks Potatoes			
Qts. Vinegar			
Qts Beans			
Lbs. Rice			
Lbs. Cheese			
Lbs. Sugar			
Lbs. Tea			
Lbs. Coffee			
Lbs. Soap			
Lbs. Candles			
Number Stoves			
Bedsteads			
Chairs			
Tables			
Blankets			
Mattresses			
Comforts			
Pillows			
Number Yds. Fannel			
Yds. Sheeting			
Yds. Prints			
Number Articles Men's Clothing			
Women's Clothing			
Childrens' Clothing			
Pairs Shoes			

Specify in blank spaces any articles or supplies which are not enumerated above.

CHICAGO RELIEF AND AID SOCIETY,

DEPARTMENT DISTRIBUTION OF SUPPLIES.

Chicago, 187

SIR: Below please find statement of Work Performed this day in District No. , comprising Sub-districts Nos.

SUP'T.

New Cases Visited this day, ...
New Cases Registered this day, ...
New Cases Rejected this day, ...
Number of Cases to whom Aid is this day Discontinued,

DISTRIBUTION OF SUPPLIES.

Rent Paid	
Tons Coal	
Cords Wood	
Pounds Flour	
Pounds Meal	
Pounds Pork	
Pounds Beef	
Pounds Bread	
Pounds Crackers	
Pounds Fish	
Pounds Soap	
Pounds Candles	
Pounds Cheese	
Pounds Tea	
Pounds Coffee	
Pounds Sugar	
Pounds Bacon	
Pounds Hams	
Pounds Butter	
Pounds Fruit	
Pounds Salt	
Pounds Rice	
Bushels Potatoes	
Bushels Beans	
Bushels Onions	
Heads Cabbage	
Gallons Vinegar	
Gallons Molasses	

Number of Mattresses	
Pillows	
Gray Blankets	
White Blankets	
Comforts	
Sheets	
Stoves	
Pieces Pipe	
Tables	
Bedsteads	
Chairs	
Pieces Crockery	
Wash Tubs	
Pieces Tin-wrae	
Pairs Boots	
Pairs Men's Shoes	
Pairs Boys' Shoes	
Pairs Women's Shoes	
Pairs Children's Shoes	
Pairs Men's Hose	
Pairs Women's Hose	
Articles Men's Clothing	
Articles Women's Clothing	
Articles Children's Clothing	
Yards Cotton Flannel	
Yards Wool Flannel	
Yards Prints	
Yards Sheeting	

STATEMENT OF WORK IN DISTRICT NO. FOR WEEK ENDING 1872.

Nationalities.	Rations.						Coal.						Clothing.						Furniture.					
	Monday.	Tuesday.	Wednesday	Thursday.	Friday.	Saturday.	Monday.	Tuesday.	Wednesday.	Thursday.	Friday.	Saturday.	Monday.	Tuesday.	Wednesday.	Thursday.	Friday.	Saturday.	Monday.	Tuesday.	Wednesday.	Thursday.	Friday.	Saturday.
Irish,																								
Scandinavian,																								
German,																								
American,																								
English,																								
French,																								
Canadian,																								
Italian,																								
Scotch,																								
Swiss,																								
Holland,																								
Bohemian,																								
Negro,																								
Belgian,																								
Pole,																								
Hungarian,																								
Welsh,																								

Nationalities.	Rations Only.						Coal Only.						Clothing Only.						Furniture Only.					
	Monday.	Tuesday.	Wednesday.	Thursday.	Friday.	Saturday.	Monday.	Tuesday.	Wednesday.	Thursday.	Friday.	Saturday.	Monday.	Tuesday.	Wednesday.	Thursday.	Friday.	Saturday.	Monday.	Tuesday.	Wednesday.	Thursday.	Friday.	Saturday.
Irish,																								
Scandinavian,																								
German,																								
American,																								
English,																								
French,																								
Canadian,																								
Italian,																								
Scotch,																								
Swiss,																								
Holland,																								
Bohemian,																								
Negro,																								
Belgian,																								
Pole,																								
Hungarian,																								
Welsh,																								

CHAPTER IX.

RECEIVING, SORTING, AND STORING SUPPLIES.

IN the matter of receiving and storing, confusion and disorder at the outset were inevitable and unavoidable. The principal railroad depots were destroyed by the fire, and the three hundred and thirty car loads of goods of all kinds which from the 11th to the 16th of October were so lavishly poured in from all parts of the country and which, coming free of freight charges, were without way-bills or invoices, had necessarily to be unloaded from side tracks at remote points of the town, the packages instantly opened and their contents disposed of, or sent without record or count wherever they were most needed. It was a question then, only of feeding the starving and clothing the naked, and not of regularity of business; the law of humanity was paramount to the rules of commerce. General Sheridan had early taken possession of two large warehouses, and these, with full complement of workmen and guards, he presently turned over to a committee, Murray Nelson, chairman, to be assisted by General Hardie. This was the first step out of confusion in this department. About the same time the Skating Rink on the West Side, two large stores, a smaller one, and the Church of the Messiah were taken and occupied, partly as storehouses and partly as points of distribution. They were no more than were needed then, for disorder demands space. But order was gradually evolved out of this chaos, as the heterogeneous mass of contributions gave way to regular, though larger, commercial orders, the railroad arrangements were brought back to something of their former facilities, regular and numerous points of distribution were established, and system generally introduced and maintained. In accordance with the principle of concentration adopted in all the departments of the work, as early as it was at all practicable the general warehouses were reduced to two only, the Rink in the West Division of the city and the Church of the Messiah on the South Side.

The latter was continued especially in view of its being the headquarters at the time of the Special Bureau. When this was abandoned the Rink became the sole depot for all the articles, except vegetables, distributed in the various districts, and which were drawn from it by special requisition of the Superintendents as they were needed.

A large frost-proof building was built for the storage of vegetables, and two large cellars were used for the same purpose.

These several warehouses may be said to have constituted the wholesale department of the Relief work, as the distributing districts were the retail establishments. The aim was to manage all with commercial exactness and economy, and notwithstanding the immense difficulties in the way, a reasonable degree of system and success was early achieved. This is deemed a proper place to make acknowledgment of the contributions of the General Government, the amount of which appears in the subjoined statement.

Consolidated Abstract of Quartermaster, Subsistence Stores, and Money.

Donated and Disbursed by the United States Government, through Captain James Gilliss, A. Q. M., U. S. A., and Colonel Robert McFeely, C. S., U. S. A., at Chicago, for the Relief of Sufferers by the Fire.

Hard Bread.		Flour.		Soft Bread.		Rice.		Hominy.		Coffee.		Tea.		Sugar.		Vinegar.		Candles.		Soap.	
Lbs.	*Oz.*	*Lbs.*	*Oz.*	*Lbs.*	*Oz.*	*Lbs.*	*Oz.*	*Lbs.*	*Oz.*	*Lbs.*	*Oz.*	*Lbs.*	*Oz.*	*Lbs.*	*Oz.*	*Gal.*	*Qt.*	*Lbs.*	*Oz.*	*Lbs.*	*Oz.*
22,365	-	1,045	6	1,000	-	2,264	-	660	-	622	3	7	8	808	8	6	3	8	10	927	6

Salt.		Pepper.		Bacon.		Beans.		Potatoes.		Hospital Tents.	Blankets.	Flannel Shirts.	Drawers.	Socks.	Shoes.	Water Barrels.	Cash Value, Stores.	Pay Roll, Employés.
Lbs.	*Oz.*	*Lbs.*	*Oz.*	*Lbs.*	*Oz.*	*Lbs.*	*Oz.*	*Lbs.*	*Oz.*	*No.*	*No.*	*No.*	*Pairs.*	*Pairs.*	*Pairs.*	*No.*		
25	14	1	11	1,087	8	37	8	1,082	-	195	10,000	4,000	4,000	4,000	1,500	39	$93,162.67½	$3,575.73

All but ten (10) of the hospital tents were returned in a damaged condition.

The subsistence stores were distributed to meet the pressing wants of the sufferers for the two or three days after the fire, before donations of food were received sufficient to meet the demand. The amount disbursed on account of pay-roll of employés was for men hired by General Hardie to unload cars containing donations prior to the time the Relief and Aid Society took charge of the receipt and distribution of stores and money.

The water barrels were bought to bring water from the lake to distributing depots while the supply of water for the city was cut off.

CHAPTER X.

TRANSPORTATION.

THE business of transportation was under the direction of a special committee of which C. G. Hammond was appointed chairman. During the early weeks of its labors the work of this committee was necessarily enormous, and the expenditures for transportation heavy.

At the same time these labors were much increased by the perplexing duty of providing passes for the large number of persons who wished to leave Chicago and were without the means of doing so. It was absolutely necessary, though by no means easy, to discriminate among the multitude who asked for passes, as there was danger of giving to undeserving persons and imposing upon the generosity and good nature of the Railroad Companies who had thrown open their roads as a part of the general relief.

At first passes were issued by this Committee which were honored by the different roads; after the immediate pressure of the first few weeks had passed, the Committee only gave recommendations for passes, which were usually accepted by the roads. At a still later period in the work of the Committee an arrangement was made with the superintendents of the different roads by which half fare passes were issued upon the recommendation of the chairman of this Committee, which arrangement still holds good with most of the roads, the recommendation for half fare being signed by the General Superintendent of the Society. It is only now in exceptional cases, however, that applications for passes receive favorable attention except upon the recommendation of the Superintendent of the Employment Bureau, in the case of persons being sent to the country to labor.

A careful record of names of persons and destinations has from the first been kept, and is an interesting voucher of one of the incidents of the Great Fire.

NUMBER OF PASSES ISSUED AND PERSONS TRANSPORTED,

FROM OCTOBER 13 TO OCTOBER 31, 1871, INCLUSIVE.

Date.	Number Passes.	Number Persons.
1871.		
October 13 and 14 . .	35	76
16 . .	390	885
17 . .	452	1,000
18 . .	452	666
19 . .	310	1,083
20 . .	218	484
21 . .	133	276
23 . .	160	315
24 . .	165	348
25 . .	130	259
26 . .	104	206
27 . .	68	115
28 . .	78	155
30 . .	65	140
31 . .	6	9
Total	2,766	6,017

NUMBER OF PASSES ISSUED AND PERSONS TRANSPORTED, BY MONTHS,

FROM OCTOBER 13, 1871, TO MAY 1, 1873.

Date.	Number Passes.	Number Persons.
1871.		
October	2,766	6,017
November	134	221
December	127	207
1872.		
January	126	198
February	81	117
May	27	35
June	17½	22
July	15½	20
August	36	42
September	29½	38
October	31	41
November	35	44
December	45½	55
1873.		
January	55	69
February	55	66
March	45	56
April	33	41
Total	3,659	7,289

Total amount paid by the Society for Passenger Fares, from October 13, 1871, to May 1, 1873 . . . . } $14,118.79

CHAPTER XI.

SHELTER.

THE first immediate necessity to be relieved, of course, was food, and in some measure, clothing. But close following upon it was need of shelter, for it was plain that the thousands who lay upon the ground, on the prairie whither they had fled, in the door-yards and empty lots of the city, must have immediate protection.

The homes left by the fire, were already full of either friends or strangers.

The suburbs of Chicago are comparatively few, and for the most part distant, and only few of the families found immediate shelter in these. Had a like fire occurred in London or Boston, it would have been possible to have sheltered the hundred thousand homeless people in the immediate suburbs, in either of these cities, until definite and adequate temporary arrangements could have been made for them.

The Churches and School-houses which were at first thrown open to those who had no better place of refuge, could of course, be only unsuitable, and at best, temporary resting places.

The exigency was imperative. We were on the verge of the most inclement season of the year, and those familiar with the great severity of our winters, and our exposed situation between the open prairie on the one side and the lake on the other, can understand how the question of shelter pressed upon us. Some rude barracks were, at the outset, put up by the Citizens' Committee, which could only answer for immediate protection from the weather, but such structures, even if well built, were open to grave objections as the homes of forty or fifty thousand people in the winter. So large a number brought into promiscuous and involuntary association, would almost certainly engender disease and promote idleness, disorder, and vice, and be dangerous to themselves and to the neighborhood in which they might be placed. Such buildings could only be put up by sufferance upon land to which the occupants could obtain no title, could have no interest in improving, and from which they would undoubtedly be removed in the spring, if not sooner, by the actual owners. To construct barracks for the houseless, therefore, was only to postpone the solution of the problem for a few months, to find us then with a large class of permanent poor still without homes, and demoralized by a winter of dependence and evil communications. A small number, under stringent police and sanitary rule, might be kept in health and comfort and order in barracks, but the system would be manifestly a bad one for so large a number of people, and particularly for the class who made much the larger proportion of those who were sufferers by the fire. These were mechanics and the better class of laboring people, thrifty, domestic, and respectable, whose skill and labor were indispensable in rebuilding the city, and most of whom had accumulated enough to become the owners of their own homesteads either as proprietors or lessees of the lots. To restore them to these homes would be to raise them at once from depression and anxiety, if not despair, to hope, renewed energy, and comparative prosperity. With all the incentives to industry left them, and with the conscious pride and independence of still living under their own roof-tree, they would thus settle for themselves, and in the best way, the question of title to land, and restore value to their real estate by proving it to be as desirable for occupation as before the fire.

It was decided, therefore, to put in barracks the minimum number who could not otherwise be provided for, and to provide small but comfortable houses for the rest; much the larger proportion who had families, and who had owned or had leases of the lots where they had previously resided. Messrs. T. M. Avery and T. W. Harvey, members of the Executive Committee of this Society, were at once put at the head of a Shelter Committee, and the result of their labors was even more successful and encouraging than the most sanguine had anticipated.

ISOLATED HOUSES.

The Bureau of the Shelter Committee was very thoroughly organized with an efficient corps of clerks and examiners, to whom the claim of the applicant was made for a careful and thorough examination, with all possible checks to detect imposition, while all were listened to with the utmost sympathy and patience. The houses given were of two sizes; one of 20 × 16 feet for families of more than three persons; the other of 12 × 16 feet for families of three only. The floor joists were of 2 × 6 inches timber, covered with a flooring of planed and matched boards; the studding was of 2 × 4 inches, covered with inch boards and battened on the outside or with planed and matched flooring; the inside walls were lined with thick felt paper; and each house had a double iron chimney, two four-panelled doors, three windows, and a partition to be put up where the occupant pleased.

HOUSE WITH TWO ROOMS.

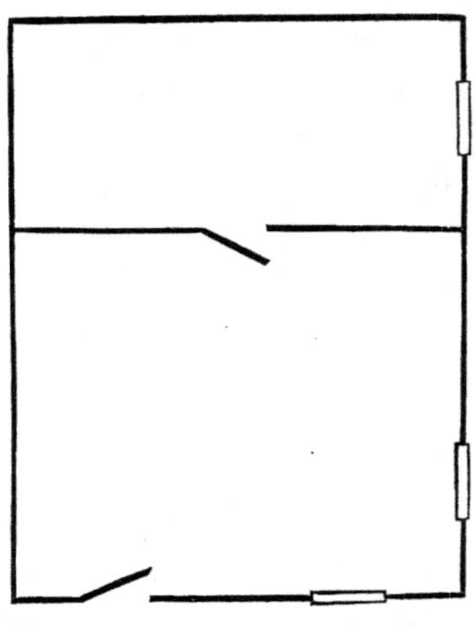

Dimensions.

Size . . . . 16 × 20
Height of Sides . . . . 8 feet
Studs . . 16 inches from centres

Material.

Studs . .	86 pieces	2 × 4	8
Joists for 2 Floors	22 pieces	2 × 6	16
Rafters .	12 pieces	2 × 4	10
Plates and Ridge	3 pieces	2 × 4	20
Sills . . .	2 pieces	2 × 6	20
Girders . .	6 pieces	2 × 4	16

Sides . . . 650 feet 8 ft. boards
Floor . 400 feet matched boards
Floor Attic { 350 feet rough boards
Roof . . { 800 feet common boards 10 ft. long.
Partition . { 200 feet dressed and matched boards, 8 ft. long.
Battens . . 85 pieces 8 feet long.
Two Doors and Frames.
Door Trimmings.
Three Windows and Frames, glazed, etc.
40 pounds 10 d. Nails. 10 pounds 20 d. Nails. 7 pounds 8 d. Nails.

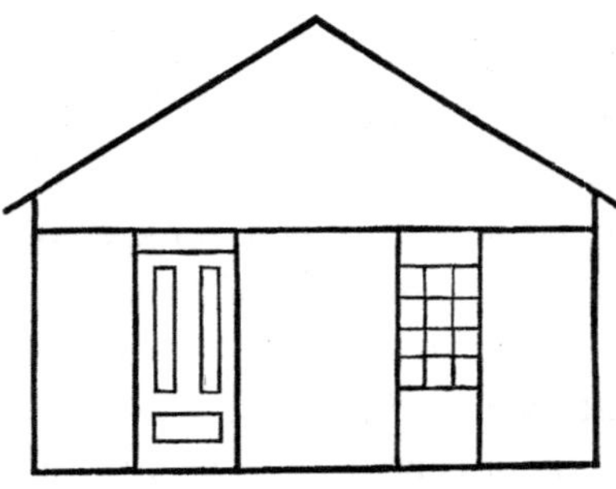

HOUSE WITH ONE ROOM.

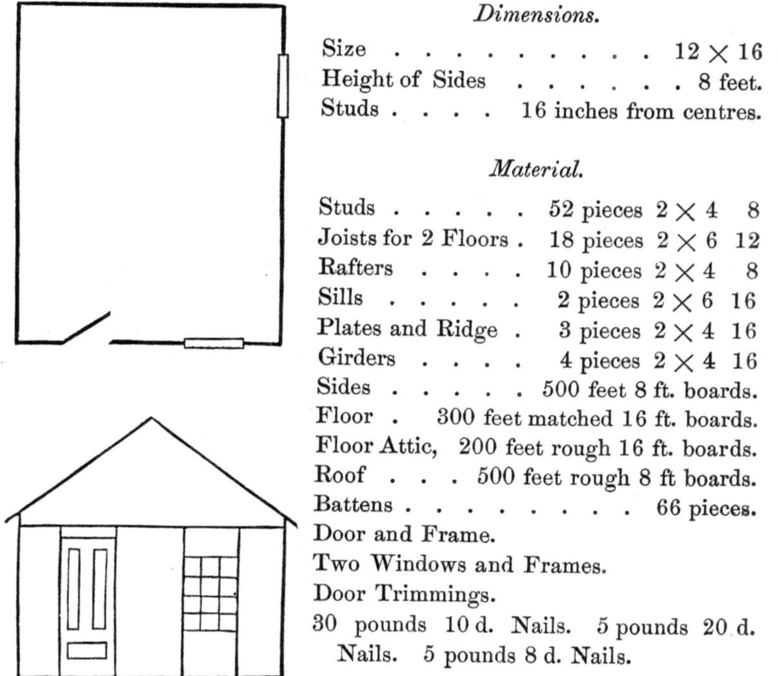

Dimensions.

Size	12 × 16
Height of Sides	8 feet.
Studs	16 inches from centres.

Material.

Studs	52 pieces	2 × 4	8
Joists for 2 Floors	18 pieces	2 × 6	12
Rafters	10 pieces	2 × 4	8
Sills	2 pieces	2 × 6	16
Plates and Ridge	3 pieces	2 × 4	16
Girders	4 pieces	2 × 4	16

Sides . . . . . . 500 feet 8 ft. boards.
Floor . 300 feet matched 16 ft. boards.
Floor Attic, 200 feet rough 16 ft. boards.
Roof . . . 500 feet rough 8 ft boards.
Battens . . . . 66 pieces.
Door and Frame.
Two Windows and Frames.
Door Trimmings.
30 pounds 10 d. Nails. 5 pounds 20 d. Nails. 5 pounds 8 d. Nails.

Afterward many were shingled, plastered, etc.

The establishment was completed in a simple but sufficient way for comfortable living by the addition of a cooking stove and utensils, several chairs, a table, bedstead, bedding, and sufficient crockery for the use of the family; and the total cost of the house when thus furnished was one hundred and twenty-five dollars. The majority of those who received the prepared material for these houses were mechanics enough to put them together for themselves, or had the means to hire builders; but for the large class of widows, infirm, or otherwise helpless persons, the house was built and put in complete readiness for the proposed tenant by the Committee.

The total number of houses built by the Shelter Committee, from October 18, 1871, to May 1, 1873, was 7,983

This provided, at the usual estimate of five to a family, respectable and comfortable homes for from thirty-five to forty thousand persons.

It will be seen by the following table, that of this number, 5,226 houses had been built within a month from the time the Committee began its labors.

ABSTRACT OF HOUSES CONSTRUCTED

FROM OCTOBER 18 TO NOVEMBER 17, 1871, INCLUSIVE.

Date.		Number.	Date.		Number.
October . .	18	116	November .	3	98
	19	127		4	131
	20	272		6	127
	21	317		7	56
	23	355		8	133
	24	371		9	88
	25	413		10	135
	26	429		11	114
	27	367		13	134
	28	284		14	147
	30	273		15	80
	31	149		16	121
November . .	1	154		17	106
	2	129			
			Total . . .		5,226

The actual rental of these houses may be estimated as worth ten dollars per month, based upon what the Society was then, and in many instances is still paying for similar accommodations to keep people from being turned out of doors.

The cost of these "Shelter Houses," exclusive of furniture, was about one hundred dollars.

The rental therefor for ten months would cover the entire original cost. It must not be understood, however, that this was a rental actually charged and received, for in no case was rent taken from the occupants of these houses.

The stock of lumber destroyed in Chicago by the fire was not less than sixty-five millions of feet, and the supply destroyed in the lumber regions, ready for shipment to this market, was also immense. The price of lumber consequently rapidly enhanced, and by the 26th of October was twenty dollars per thousand. By the wise forethought and activity of the Shelter Committee, this rise in value was anticipated, and all their purchases were made at an average price of sixteen dollars and fifty cents per thousand. They used quite thirty-five millions of feet with this large saving in cost.

THE BARRACKS.

Besides the isolated houses, there were, in different sections of the city, four barracks, in which were lodged one thousand families. They were mainly of the class who had not hitherto lived in houses of their own, but in rooms in tenement houses. Each family in these barracks had two separate rooms to itself, and they were furnished in precisely the same way with the isolated houses. Their occupants were undoubtedly very nearly, if not quite, as comfortable as they were before the fire, and as only one thousand two hundred and fifty people were gathered together in one community, and those were under the constant and careful supervision of medical and police superintendents, their moral and sanitary condition was unquestionably better than that which had heretofore obtained in that class.

This statement is confirmed by the fact that but one death occurred in the barracks during the first month.

These houses were not only built and given outright to the applicants found to be worthy, but were likewise supplied with all necessary furniture.

The table, which is here subjoined, illustrates the kind and extent of this furnishing.

ABSTRACT OF ISSUES OF STOVES AND FURNITURE,
FROM DECEMBER 1 TO DECEMBER 30, 1871, INCLUSIVE.

1871. December.	Stoves.	Stove Furniture.	Mattresses.	Bedsteads.	Chairs.	Tables.	Tubs.	Wash Boards.	Pails.	Pipe.	Elbows.	Tin Ware.	Crockery.
1	96	258	185	180	394	67	16	15	9	335	71	13	495
2	103	289	141	126	264	62	35	34	13	216	52	9	340
4	105	315	142	140	266	69	18	15	15	332	87	13	285
5	87	261	151	118	285	67	26	18	13	224	58	15	201
6	100	300	163	184	327	78	45	37	24	263	81	9	303
7	04	282	120	139	278	88	57	57	24	311	79	24	349
8	90	270	121	147	320	81	56	51	26	306	82	11	336
9	107	321	141	165	379	107	62	58	31	332	84	18	379
11	96	288	132	163	437	109	55	52	24	357	94	9	290
12	83	249	140	140	371	97	61	60	28	293	82	9	144
13	91	273	119	152	345	108	72	66	33	319	73	18	-
14	81	243	140	155	364	109	67	56	34	259	72	5	-
15	54	162	96	118	260	82	53	51	24	182	48	6	16
16	65	195	104	103	371	88	47	44	21	222	58	4	-
18	53	159	81	108	261	77	54	50	22	173	47	2	-
19	39	117	57	62	171	48	30	28	15	125	43	2	-
20	40	120	56	54	150	40	36	29	25	137	43	18	4
21	47	141	64	72	174	60	38	28	9	155	46	17	-
22	49	147	47	63	145	50	20	21	6	176	50	7	-
23	36	108	53	51	135	52	41	35	18	124	32	14	-
25	6	18	14	8	10	5	7	6	-	14	4	2	-
26	39	117	58	56	150	39	38	36	7	131	41	18	-
27	57	171	91	85	202	63	48	37	3	149	42	22	-
28	38	114	44	43	90	30	30	22	10	128	32	13	-
29	25	75	58	40	83	39	16	7	7	116	15	20	-
30	40	120	53	55	151	50	27	19	8	144	40	24	-
Total	1,721	5,113	2,571	2,727	6,283	1,765	1,055	932	449	5,523	1,456	322	3,143

The working method of this Committee will be explained somewhat more fully by the Blanks and Forms used, and which are here inserted.

The number of applicants for shelter was so great that we divided the burnt district into sixteen divisions, and established a depot in each division to receive the applications. The following blank was filled by the clerk in charge of the district office, and when found correct, was sent to the central office, 409 West Washington Street, for approval by the Shelter Committee.

Office No.

HEADQUARTERS SHELTER COMMITTEE.

409 *West Washington Street.*

1. Name,
2. Former residence,
3. Where located now,
4. Number of family,
5. If burned out,
6. Do you own lot or lease?
   Is it encumbered? Amount,
7. Location of lot where you will build,
8. What occupation,
9. Refer to whom,
10. Are you insured — what company?
    Amount of insurance,
11. Had you any money in bank?
    What bank? Amount in bank,
12. Any other property,

I certify that the above is well known to me, that he has been burned out, owns no house *now*, and that he is worthy and deserving of assistance.

Name,
Place of business,
Or residence,

No.

OFFICE SHELTER COMMITTEE.

409 *West Washington Street.*

Deliver to

2 doors 2 ft. 6 in. × 6 ft. 6 in., 1¼ in., second quality.
1 outside frame, 5½ in. jambs.
1 inside frame, 3 in. jambs.
3 windows, 12 lights, 8 × 10, glazed, plain.
3 window frames, 5½ in. jambs.

This voucher will be required in settlement.

No.

OFFICE OF SHELTER COMMITTEE, OF THE CHICAGO RELIEF AND AID SOCIETY,

Corner Sedgwick and Division Streets.

Send bill to Standard Hall with this order.

CHICAGO, 187 .

MESSRS.

Please deliver to

Street.

26 pieces	2 × 4	16 ft.
18 pieces	2 × 6	12 ft.
2 pieces	2 × 6	16 ft.
2 pieces	6 × 8	16 ft.
2 pieces	6 × 8	12 ft.

300 feet common boards, 16 ft.
900 feet dressed and matched fencing, 16 ft.
260 feet cull boards or fencing.
2 pieces 16 ft. D. stock boards, dressed.
2 pieces 12 ft. D. stock boards, dressed.
3¼ thousand extra No. 1 shingles.

HOUSE 12 × 16. DELIVER.

No.

OFFICE OF SHELTER COMMITTEE OF THE CHICAGO RELIEF AND AID SOCIETY,

Corner Sedgwick and Division Streets.

Send bill to Standard Hall with this order.

CHICAGO, 187 .

MESSRS.

Please deliver to

Street.

30 pieces	2 × 4	16 ft.
22 pieces	2 × 6	16 ft.
11 pieces	3 × 4	20 ft.
2 pieces	6 × 8	20 ft.
3 pieces	6 × 8	16 ft.

2 pieces 16 ft. D. stock boards, dressed.
3 pieces 14 ft. D. stock boards, dressed.
320 feet common boards, 14 or 16 ft.
1,500 feet dressed and matched fencing, 16 ft.
400 feet cull boards or fencing.
4 thousand extra No. 1 shingles.

HOUSE 16 × 20. DELIVER.

No.

OFFICE OF SHELTER COMMITTEE OF THE CHICAGO RELIEF AND AID SOCIETY,

Corner Sedgwick and Division Streets,

Send bill to Standard Hall with this order.

CHICAGO, 187 .

MESSRS.

Please deliver to

Street.

36 pieces	2 × 4	16 ft.
27 pieces	2 × 6	18 ft.
14 pieces	2 × 4	22 ft.
2 pieces	2 × 6	22 ft.
2 pieces	6 × 8	24 ft.
2 pieces	6 × 8	18 ft.
1 piece	6 × 8	16 ft.

430 feet common boards.
530 feet cull fencing.
1,750 feet dressed and matched fencing.
7 pieces 12 ft. D. stocks, dressed 1 S.
$5\frac{1}{4}$ thousand extra No. 1 shingles.

HOUSE 18 × 24. DELIVER.

SHELTER COMMITTEE.

409 *Washington Street.*

T. M. AVERY.
T. W. HARVEY.

Built.	Size.	Stories.	Brick, Frame, Stone, } Battened, Sided.	No. Family.
	×			

How occupied.	Nationality.	Able to pay.	When.	Note.	Rec.

Built on

REMARKS.

No.

FORM OF RECEIPT GIVEN BY APPLICANT.

CHICAGO, 187 .

THIS IS TO CERTIFY, that I have this day received from the CHICAGO RELIEF AND AID SOCIETY material for one house to be erected at

ISSUES OF FURNITURE,

For the Week ending 187 .

BY WHOM ISSUED.	Stoves.	Stove Furniture.	Mattresses.	Bedsteads.	Chairs.	Tables.	Tubs.	Wash Boards.	Pails.	Pipe.	Elbows.	Crockery.	Cutlery.	Chimney Tops.
Shelter Committee														
District No. 1 .														
District No. 2 .														
District No. 5 .														

CHAPTER XII.

SPECIAL RELIEF.

THE Special Committee was formed to provide a suitable agency for supplying the necessities of those sufferers by the fire whose needs could not be adequately and properly met by the District Distributing Relief Depots. The great throng of persons who crowded those depots in the earlier periods of the relief work made them unsuitable places for the sick, aged, and infirm, or for those whose previous condition in life unfitted them to endure the exposure and suffering incident to such modes of receiving relief. There were also many cases whose necessities could be adequately provided for only by the payment of money, which was not then intrusted to the District Superintendents.

To meet these necessities the Special Committee was organized. It was appointed by a meeting of the pastors of the various Churches, and the representative officers of the various Benevolent Associations of the city, convened for that purpose, upon the invitation of the Executive Committee of the Relief and Aid Society. Although the selection of the Committee was delegated to the persons above named, in the hope of thereby inducing a closer union and more active participation with the work on the part of the appointing body, the Special Committee so appointed was, from the first, strictly a department of the Executive Board, represented in such Board by its Chairman, and subject to its instructions and control.

The Special Committee, as originally appointed, was composed of the following persons: E. C. Larned, Rev. Laird Collier, Rev. E. P. Goodwin, B. G. Caulfield, Louis Wahl, Geo. R. Chittenden, Mrs. Joseph Medill, Mrs. David A. Gage, Mrs. J. Mason Loomis, and Mrs. J. E. Tyler; of whom E. C. Larned was appointed Chairman, and Rev. Laird Collier, Secretary. Some of the above members resigned, others withdrew from any active participation in the work, and several additions were subsequently made.

On the 13th February, 1872, E. C. Larned resigned and Rev. Laird Collier was appointed Chairman and E. K. Hubbard was chosen Secretary of the Committee; W. E. Doggett, A. Keith, and N. S. Bouton became members of the Committee. The members who continued actively connected with the Committee until the close of its work were Rev. Laird Collier, E. K. Hubbard, A. Keith, W. E. Doggett, Orrington Lunt, and N. S. Bouton.

From the formation of the Committee until the 6th day of December, 1871, its work of Relief included the supplying of clothing, fuel, food, and furniture, as well as money.

In the earlier portion of its work the Committee relied entirely upon the certificates of the pastors of churches, and authorized officers of organized Benevolent Associations, for the evidence that the applicant's condition and needs had been duly investigated, and for a correct statement of the kind and amount of relief required. To facilitate such investigations, suitable blanks were prepared, containing appropriate inquiries respecting the applicant's property, circumstances, losses, and present condition. Experience soon demonstrated that we could not rely with sufficient confidence upon this method of investigation, as affording reliable evidence of the nature and amount of the applicant's needs; and, subsequently, the course was adopted, of sending all applications which were suitably recommended, to the District in which the applicant resided, for the case to be personally investigated and reported upon in writing by one of the official visitors in the employ of the Society.

As soon as the proper arrangements were made authorizing applications for supplies to be made by letter to the District Superintendents, without requiring the personal attendance of the applicant, the necessity for any further action upon this class of applications was obviated, and the Special Committee, in pursuance of instructions to that effect from the Executive Board, ceased to entertain any new applications of this nature after the 10th day of December, 1871.

The whole number of families which were furnished with supplies by this Committee, up to that date, was 1,474, amounting, at the usual average, to about 7,000 persons.

The amounts of supplies issued will be found specified in detail in the tabular statement annexed.

The estimated cost of such supplies amounted to about the sum of $90,000.

The action of the Special Bureau, in the matter of furnishing supplies, met a great and pressing need.

There was a class of sufferers by the fire, consisting of persons before that event in comfortable circumstances, who were suddenly reduced to conditions of the greatest privation and distress. This class of our population were the keenest sufferers of all. They were not accustomed to exposures and hardships which were easily borne by the laboring people, and at the same time the change in their condition and circumstances was greater and more disastrous. They were borne in a single night from homes of comfort and plenty into absolute destitution. Nothing could exceed the misery which they were compelled to undergo; many of these families received aid from the Special Relief Department which was of the greatest benefit to them, and was afforded with a warmth of good-will, and an earnest sympathy and kindness, which served in some degree to relieve the painful experiences necessarily incident to applications for assistance by persons who had previously been independent in their circumstances.

The nature and extent of the work of this Committee in furnishing aid by the payment of money was modified from time to time, as the experience of the special needs of the sufferers by the fire became more enlarged, and the demands upon the funds for affording necessary shelter and supplies of food, fuel, clothing, and furniture were lessened.

At the commencement of its work, under instructions issued to this Committee by the Executive Board, the payment of money was for some time strictly limited to affording aid in paying rent, and in the purchase of sewing machines, and in the relief of pressing necessities occasioned by sickness or some other cause.

On the 29th of December, 1871, the work of this Committee in this field was enlarged by the Executive Board, by virtue of the following resolution:—

"That the amount of money which the Special Committee be authorized to grant in special cases, without the previous action of the Executive Committee, be two hundred dollars.

"That the Special Committee are instructed that while the general rule heretofore adopted, forbidding grants of money to be made for the purpose of aiding parties to reëstablish themselves in business, be enforced, so far as relates to affording aid in purchasing stocks of goods or articles for sale, it may be so far modified as to authorize the Special Committee, in their discretion, to aid persons in the purchase of tools, machinery, furniture, fixtures, or professional books, which are necessary for engaging in any business which has a sufficiently assured prospect of providing a support for the applicant and his family."

A large proportion of the special work of relief consisted in affording aid to destitute sewing women, who lost their machines by the fire, in obtaining sewing machines. By arrangements made with most of the sewing machine companies, persons who were deemed entitled to such aid were allowed a discount of forty per cent, from the regular retail prices of the respective machines.

This Committee advanced to the Sewing Machine Company (in the greater proportion of such cases) the sum of twenty dollars towards such purchase, leaving the applicant to pay the remainder of the price, which, on a seventy (70) dollar machine, amounted to twenty-two dollars, for the payment of which a liberal credit was granted by the companies.

In cases of special destitution, or where the peculiar circumstances of the applicant or her family were such as to render it expedient, the whole price of the machine, less the agreed discount, was paid.

By a subsequent arrangement with the *Singer*, *Wheeler & Wilson*, and *Howe* companies, a discount of fifty per cent. was allowed on their machines in all cases where the Committee should advance, in cash, one half of the retail price of the machine.

The applicant in every case designated in the application the kind of machine desired.

This form of relief was, in the opinion of the Committee, productive of great good. It rendered a large number of worthy and industrious sewing women, whose means of subsistence had been wholly destroyed by the fire, at once self-supporting.

In addition to giving aid in the purchase of sewing machines, money was granted in various amounts, to meet the respective needs of applicants, in aid of their reëstablishment in some kind of business or mechanical employment which afforded a fair promise of yielding a support to the applicant and his family. The aid thus given was strictly limited to the purposes specified in the foregoing resolution of the Executive Committee.

The relief effected in this department of its work was

very varied. Carpenters, masons, tinners, bookbinders, locksmiths, tailors, shoemakers, and workers in almost every branch of mechanical industry, were supplied with tools; machinery of various kinds was furnished; surgeons, dentists, and engineers were supplied with the instruments of their respective callings. Many persons were aided with furniture and means to open boarding-houses.

The aim of the Committee in this class of cases was, by aiding the applicant with the needful tools and appliances for prosecuting some kind of business or industrial pursuit to enable him, at the earliest practicable period, to obtain a support, and relieve him from the necessity of any further application for assistance.

The relief thus afforded extended to a class in our community who, while they were the severest sufferers by the fire, had hitherto received less than any other from the relief funds.

Money which simply placed in the applicant's possession the means of earning his own support, could be received without humiliation and without injury; and the machinery and appliances which were thus purchased were not lost, but constituted lasting additions to the productive industry of the community.

ABSTRACT OF DISBURSEMENTS ON ACCOUNT OF SPECIAL RELIEF.

FROM NOVEMBER 6, 1871, TO MAY 1, 1873.

Special Relief	$281,489.03
Sewing Machines	138,855.26
Rent	6,371.80
Tools	10,742.00
Total	$437,458.09

Number of Machines Full paid	2,353
Number of Machines on which $20 was paid	2,065
Number of Machines on which Balances paid	791
Total Machine Orders	5,299

Number of Approved Applications	9,962
Number of Disapproved Applications	6,337
Total Number of Cases examined	16,299

ABSTRACT OF NATIONALITIES

WHO RECEIVED AID FROM SPECIAL RELIEF FROM NOVEMBER 6, 1871, TO MAY 1, 1873.

German	5,013
Irish	4,230
American	2,933
English	1,385
Scandinavian	1,189
Scotch	570
French	365
Canadian	244
Italian	111
Negro	81
Bohemian	67
Welsh	62
Swiss	27
Pole	22
Total	16,299

STATEMENT OF GOODS

ISSUED BY THE SPECIAL RELIEF COMMITTEE, FROM NOVEMBER 6 TO DECEMBER 12, 1871.

573 Dresses (Ladies).
398 Hats and Hoods (Ladies).
724 Shawls (Ladies).
1,276 pairs Shoes (Ladies).

7,134 pieces Underwear (Ladies).
1,706 Skirts (Ladies).
343 Cloaks (Ladies).

786 pairs Boots and Shoes (Mens.)
498 Overcoats (Mens).
858 Pants (Mens).
4204 pieces Underwear (Mens).
741 Coats (Mens).
693 Vests (Mens).

Groceries.

1566 pounds Sugar.
162 barrels Flour.
264½ pounds Tea.
836 pounds Coffee.
286 pounds Rice.
310 pounds Meal.
115 Hams.
227 bushels Potatoes.
781 pounds Sundries.

Furniture.

449 Bedsteads.
333 Tables.
1,393 Chairs.

Crockery.

5,113 pieces Crockery and China.
2,300 pieces Knives, Forks, and Spoons.

Coal.

235 tons Hard Coal.
157½ tons Soft Coal.

Stoves.

429 Heating and Cooking.

Bedding, etc.

1,645 Blankets.
610 Pillow Slips.
363 Pillows.

855 Comforts.
961 Mattresses.
1,178 Sheets.
307 Towels.

PIECE GOODS.

1,023 yards Waterproof.
1,400 yards Delaine.
1,890 yards Linsey.
2,649 yards Alpaca.
7,820½ yards Muslin.
8,251½ yards Flannel.
2,934 yards Canton Flannel.
4,122 yards Sheeting.
2,707 yards Calico.

SUNDRY DRY GOODS.

433 Articles.

CIRCULARS AND BLANKS.

CHICAGO RELIEF AND AID SOCIETY.

COMMITTEE OF SPECIAL RELIEF.

Church of the Messiah.

NOTICE TO APPLICANTS FOR RELIEF.

All applications to this Committee for special relief must be certified by the pastor of a church, or proper officer of some organized benevolent society, or by a member of the Executive Committee of the Relief and Aid Society, or of this Committee, who shall state in such certificate that the condition and needs of the applicant have been duly investigated, to the satisfaction of the person so certifying, and stating what amount and kind of relief should be afforded to such applicant.

In every application the name, residence, and relief district in which such applicant lives, should be plainly written.

Such application should state whether the applicant is married or single, the number of persons in the applicant's family, the age and sex of each member, and should set forth in detail the articles which are wanted, and the number, amount, or quantity of such articles. In applications for clothing, the kind of clothing, and number of pieces needed of each kind, should be distinctly stated, the proper sizes where necessary (as of boots, shoes, and other articles) given.

Applications for groceries should state specifically the articles wanted, and amounts of each article ; and where crockery, or furniture, or bedding is needed, the specific articles wanted, and the number of such articles, should be stated.

The Committee desire to call the attention of the applicant specially to the following points, in regard to which information will be desired, and which should be stated: —

The present and former occupation of the applicant, whether burned out and what loss they suffered, amount of insurance and in what company, what property applicant has, and what aid they have received from any source, or expect to receive.

Careful attention to these requirements will save the applicant delay and trouble, and insure prompt action in the case.

E. C. Larned, *Chairman.*
Laird Collier, *Secretary.*

NOTICE TO APPLICANTS FOR MONEY.

1. Every application for relief by payment of money must in addition to answering the questions upon the printed blanks, give a brief statement in writing, showing the special grounds which make such money relief necessary, and must be certified by a clergyman or the proper officer of an organized benevolent society.

2. No application for money will be entertained from any person who has received relief from the District Depots, unless such applicant shall bring a letter signed by the Superintendent of his District, and approved by the General Superintendent, recommending such application.

3. Except in cases of emergency requiring immediate action, no application for the payment of money will be acted upon until the condition and needs of the applicant have been investigated by a visitor.

Applications for sewing machines (unless certified by a member of this Committee or by the Executive Committee) will not be acted upon until they have been referred to the District Superintendent for investigation and report.

4. Every applicant will be notified by mail whether his application has been approved or rejected, and until he receives such notice it will not be necessary for him to make any further call upon the Committee.

COMMITTEE OF SPECIAL RELIEF.

CHURCH OF THE MESSIAH, *Corner Wabash Avenue and Hubbard Court.*

TO PASTORS AND REPRESENTATIVES OF BENEVOLENT ASSOCIATIONS: —

To correct any misapprehensions that may exist respecting the Department of Special Relief, the Committee having such relief in charge desire to call attention to the following facts: —

1. It is not designed that this department shall supersede, supplement, or in anywise interfere with the relief work of the general Society. It is meant exclusively to provide for those peculiar and delicate cases which it is not possible to meet satisfactorily in the ordinary way.

2. All pastors of churches, of whatever name, and all accredited representatives of relief organizations of every form, are persons duly authorized to indorse applications, and their indorsement will in all cases be satisfactory guaranty of the worthiness of the applicant. But the Committee particularly request, as a means of greatly facilitating their arduous work, that all applications, so far as possible, be made through these channels. And they further urge that pastors of churches appoint visitors, whose duty it shall be to investigate the cases of those who apply, and to search out such needy and deserving persons as from motives of delicacy will not be likely to make their wants known.

3. All applications should be made in writing, and should state specifically the place of residence before and since the fire, the nature and extent of the losses suffered, and the particular articles or form of aid desired. Ministers and others can have blanks to keep on hand for this purpose by applying to the Committee.

4. The headquarters of the Committee, and their Depot of Supplies, are at the Church of the Messiah, corner Wabash Avenue and Hubbard Court, where all applications, when duly indorsed, should be presented. So far as may be possible, these will be responded to at once, so that parties may take their supplies with them. In all other cases the articles will be delivered at the place named by the applicant.

To avoid misapprehension as to the powers of the Committee, it is desirable to state that no application for money to build up any form of business destroyed by the fire can be entertained, and that, as a general rule, relief by payment of money is only extended in a few exceptional cases.

E. C. LARNED, *Chairman.*
LAIRD COLLIER, *Secretary.*

CHICAGO RELIEF AND AID SOCIETY.

COMMITTEE OF SPECIAL RELIEF.

STANDARD HALL, *Corner Michigan Avenue and Thirteenth Street.*

LAIRD COLLIER, *Chairman.*
E. K. HUBBARD, *Secretary.*

CHICAGO, 1872.

The persons making the application must answer fully the following questions: —

1. What is your occupation?
2. Where did you live before the fire?
3. Where do you live now?
4. Are you married or single?
5. Number of children and ages?
6. What is the total income of family per week?
7. What property have you?
8. What relief have you received, and from what sources?
9. State fully what you now desire, and the precise reasons why you ask relief in this form.

STATEMENT:

Name of Applicant,
Residence,

☞ The above must be indorsed by two well-known citizens:
(*Signed.*)

The indorsement on the back of the above was as follows: —

No.
Application for $
Of
Residence,
Order issued, 1872.
$ paid.
Approved.

Chairman.
Secretary.

CHICAGO RELIEF AND AID SOCIETY.

COMMITTEE OF SPECIAL RELIEF,

STANDARD HALL, *Corner Michigan Avenue and Thirteenth Street.*

E. C. LARNED, *Chairman.*
LAIRD COLLIER, *Secretary.*

CHICAGO, 187 .

Application is made by now residing at who states that she owned a Sewing Machine, which was destroyed by the fire at that she understands the use of such machine, and would be able to contribute largely to her own support if she could obtain a sewing machine, but that she is destitute of means to purchase one, and desires a Sewing Machine.

☞ The individual applying for Sewing Machine will fill in the blanks in this application, and sign it here. *Applicant's name,*

REMARKS: —

☞ Have your Pastor, Priest, or some other prominent person sign the following recommendation: —

CHICAGO, 187 .

The undersigned is acquainted with the above named and believes to be a deserving person, and that the facts above stated are correct.

[SIGNED]

Present this application at this Office between the hours of 9 A. M. and 1 P. M. (Sundays excepted).

The indorsement on back of above was: —

No.
Application for
Sewing Machine.
Of
Order issued 187
$ paid.

CHICAGO RELIEF AND AID SOCIETY.

COMMITTEE OF SPECIAL RELIEF.

STANDARD HALL, *Corner Michigan Avenue and Thirteenth Street.*

E. C. LARNED, *Chairman.*
LAIRD COLLIER, *Secretary.*

CHICAGO, 1872.

Application is made by who resides at for assistance in the payment of rent. Applicant states that was burned out in the late fire, and suffered a loss of all had, and is now without property or income of any description.

That is paying the sum of $ per month. That after diligent inquiry is unable to obtain any suitable quarters for a less sum, and desires month rent. $

That if the Committee shall aid applicant to pay the above month rent, believes that will be able to furnish own support, in whole or in part.

☞ The individual applying for rent, will fill in the blanks in this application, and sign it here. *Applicant's name,*

REMARKS: —

☞ Have this recommendation signed by two prominent citizens.

We hereby certify that we are acquainted with the above named ; that is renting as above stated, and we believe to be an honest and worthy person, whose statements are entitled to credit.

Send application through the mail to Special Relief Committee, Standard Hall, corner Michigan Avenue and Thirteenth Street.

The indorsement on back of above was: —

No.
Application for Rent of
Approved for $
Money paid
Order drawn on Geo. M. Pullman.

☞ The applicant must make out for himself a list or a bill of the tools, or instruments he wants; name the price of each tool, and pin the list to this application, or he will receive no attention.

CHICAGO RELIEF AND AID SOCIETY.

COMMITTEE OF SPECIAL RELIEF.

STANDARD HALL, *Corner Michigan Avenue and Thirteenth Street.*

E. C. LARNED, *Chairman.*
LAIRD COLLIER, *Secretary.*

CHICAGO, 1872.

Application is made by a now residing at who states that he owned which destroyed by the fire at that he understands the use of such and would be able to contribute largely to his own support if he could obtain them, and he is destitute of means to purchase them, and desires

☞ The individual applying for Tools or Instruments will fill in the blanks in this application, and sign it here. *Applicant's name,*

☞ Have this recommendation signed by two prominent citizens.

CHICAGO, 1872.

The undersigned are acquainted with the above named and believe him to be a deserving person, and that the facts above stated are correct. [SIGNED]

Send application through the mail to Special Relief Committee, Standard Hall, corner Michigan Avenue and Thirteenth Street.

The indorsement on back of above was: —

No.
Application for
Of
Order issued 1872.
$ paid.

CHAPTER XIII.

SICK, SANITARY, AND HOSPITAL MEASURES.

IMMEDIATELY after the fire, the Board of Health began to gather the sick and injured who could not find refuge in private families, into churches and school-houses where they were tenderly cared for by physicians and citizens, who very generally tendered their services. In order that there might be as little delay as possible, the sanitary policemen were authorized by the Mayor to impress teams for the transportation of the sick from the prairies and vacant lots whither they had been driven by the flames. At the headquarters of the Citizen's Committee, corner of West Washington and Ann streets, Drs. Rauch and Johnson, of the Board of Health, and Dr. J. E. Gilman of the Citizen's Committee were constantly engaged in assigning physicians and providing medicines and stores for the churches and other buildings used as temporary hospitals.

When the Relief and Aid Society took charge of the General Relief work in accordance with the proclamation of the Mayor, it assigned to Dr. H. A. Johnson the special duty of organizing and directing this department, with authority to associate with himself such members of the medical profession as he should think best. The following gentlemen comprised the Committee as finally constituted: Dr. H. A. Johnson, chairman, and Drs. B. McVickar, R. Ludlam, M. J. Asche, J. H. Rauch, M. Manheimer, Ernst Schmidt, B. C. Miller, and Rev. H. N. Powers. Dr. J. E. Gilman was appointed secretary.

For several weeks the committee held daily meetings, and weekly meetings were held during the entire winter.

VISITATION.

The city was divided into districts and sub-districts, with the same boundaries and the same offices as those of the Superintendents of Distribution.

To each of these divisions a Medical Superintendent and a sufficient number of visiting physicians were appointed. Their duties were defined in the following circular: —

TO MEDICAL OFFICERS.

First. Each visiting physician will establish an office in connection with the depot of distribution in his district.

Second. He will, at a specified hour, morning and evening, visit the office and answer such calls as may be left by the Superintendent of Distribution, the visitors, and the Medical Superintendent of the district.

Third. He will supply himself with a case and medicines for the use of those only who are the proper subjects of relief by this Society.

Fourth. He will affix to each prescription that he may send to the dispensing chemist, his signature, with a statement that this prescription is on account of the Chicago Relief and Aid Society.

Fifth. He will especially examine into the sanitary condition of his district, the quantity and quality of food, clothing, dwellings, etc., and all matters having a bearing upon public or private health.

Sixth. He will report daily to the Medical Superintendent of his district, the name, age, sex, and nativity of each patient, with the name of the disease, result of treatment, number of visits to each patient, and such other information as the Medical Superintendent may, from time to time, require.

Seventh. Each Medical Superintendent will have the immediate direction of the medical service and sanitary interest of his district, and will be held responsible for the faithful performance of this work. He will assign visiting physicians to sub-districts, and require of them daily reports of their work. These reports he will condense and present weekly to the Committee. He will admit patients to hospital, and in cases of emergency, visit patients at their homes.

The General Superintendent directed visitors to report all cases coming to their knowledge requiring medical attendance, and the person in charge of each office had such reports at all times in readiness for the medical officer of the district, when he called. All possible aid was given the medical officer of the district, and he was allowed free access to the office and books of the Society at all times.

MEDICAL DISPENSARIES.

In addition to this provision for the visitation of the sick at their homes, dispensaries were established at convenient points, where such patients as were able to apply in person for advice were treated, and where medicines were dispensed upon the prescriptions of any physician certifying that his services in the case were gratuitous. In the North Division of the city there was only one of these institutions; in the West Division there were three, and in the South Division two. Medicines were also dispensed, and out-patients treated at all of the hospitals.

The physicians to these dispensaries were men of approved character and professional standing.

HOSPITALS.

For the relief of such patients as could not safely be treated in their homes or quarters, and who could not apply at a dispensary, hospital accommodations were provided. Fortunately the principal hospitals of the city were in the unburned district. Arrangements were made with all these institutions by which patients were received on account of this Society, without charge for medical and surgical attendance, nursing and general care; the Society furnishing only medicines, rations, and furniture for such relief patients as were received on its account. These hospitals were as follows: —

The Providence Hospital, located just beyond the northern limits of the city. The Women's and Children's Hospital, formerly located on North State Street, but after the fire at No. 598 West Adams Street. This was mainly a lying-in-hospital. The Chicago Eye and Ear Infirmary, under the care of Dr. E. L. Holmes, before the fire on Pierson Street in the North Division, now at 579 West Adams Street. St. Luke's Hospital, on Indiana Avenue between Fourteenth and Sixteenth streets. The Hahnemann Hospital, on Cottage Grove Avenue near Twenty-ninth Street. Mercy Hospital, corner of Calumet Avenue and Twenty-sixth Street, and the County Hospital, on Arnold Street, near Eighteenth Street.

In addition to these accommodations, hospitals were constructed in connection with the barracks in the West and North Divisions of the city. Patients were admitted to hospitals upon the order of the medical officers of the Chicago Relief and Aid Society, the Sanitary Superintendent of the Board of Health, and the County Physician.

Supplies to hospitals and dispensaries were issued upon requisitions indorsed by the chief medical officer of the institution, and approved by the Chairman of the Committee on Sick, Sanitary, and Hospital Measures.

The dispensaries and hospitals reported daily to the chairman of this committee the number of patients treated, number of deaths, number of recoveries, and as often as required, the names of relief patients under treatment. With the daily reports from the visiting physicians and these reports from hospitals and dispensaries, the Committee was able to give at any time the name and address, age, sex, nationality, disease, and the result of treatment of every patient under its care.

BURIALS.

Arrangements were made with the county authorities by which, at a small cost to the Relief Society, all who died while under the care of this department were furnished a coffin and hearse to any of the cemeteries in the vicinity of the city.

HOW MEDICAL RELIEF WAS OBTAINED.

To obtain medical relief, it was only necessary to make application to some one of the Superintendents of Distribution, to a Visitor of that bureau, or to a Medical Superintendent.

SANITARY REGULATIONS AND CONDITION.

The sanitary questions connected with houses and barracks were carefully considered, and the suggestions of this Committee were adopted by the Committee on Shelter. The barracks were subject to a careful daily inspection by sanitary officers, and regulations best calculated to maintain health were rigidly enforced. The statistics indicate that these quarters were probably more healthy than those occupied by the same class of tenants before the fire. Up to November 30, only one death had occurred among a population of five thousand in barracks.

SMALL-POX.

For four years our city had experienced a singular immunity from small-pox. We could hope to maintain this only by the same measures hitherto used, namely, vaccination and revaccination. In order to accomplish this it was found necessary to make satisfactory vaccination a condition upon which supplies were issued. The blanks published with this report explain sufficiently the mode of doing the work. About sixty-four thousand persons were vaccinated by the officers of the Society.

During the winter of 1871–72 small-pox was epidemic throughout the country. Many of the smaller as well as larger cities suffered severely from it. The mortality in Chicago from this cause during the whole winter was low. Of the comparatively few cases that did occur many were brought in from the country, while many more were emigrants. Thirty of these were from the ill-fated steamer Allemania, arriving at New York with the disease on board. It seems hardly possible to exaggerate the disaster that in all human probability was averted by this systematic and thoroughly executed plan of the Committee. The results of about thirty thousand vaccinations and revaccinations will be found in the tables published herewith.

TYPHOID FEVER.

Soon after the fire in the more densely crowded portions of the city, where, in many instances, several families were compelled to occupy one small badly ventilated house, typhoid fever made its appearance. These districts were carefully inspected, and the Shelter Committee provided other quarters whenever deemed necessary by the medical officers. The disease did not spread. It disappeared, as usual, with the advance of winter.

CHANGE IN PLAN OF WORK.

The Relief and Aid Society had appropriated nearly $200,000 for the various hospitals of the city on condition that these hospitals should, upon the order of the Society, receive, care for, and provide for all the medical and surgical wants of one patient for each $1,000 appropriated. In other words the appropriation constituted an endowment of about two hundred beds, subject to the control of the Relief Society. About the 1st of February,

1872, the issue of rations to hospitals was therefore discontinued and, to such sick as needed hospital care, permits, or orders were given upon which they were admitted into these institutions. The plan of visitation was materially modified. The district medical officers were discontinued and the work was done by the dispensaries, the Society furnishing medicines and meeting such incidental expenses as were necessary for their support. In addition to the aid given to the dispensaries proper, a small monthly salary was paid to those physicians who were employed by the dispensaries in visiting patients at their homes. The prescribing physicians at the dispensaries received no compensation whatever. On the 15th of March, 1872, Dr. John Reid, who had served as medical superintendent of the First District, was appointed General Medical Superintendent, and continued to perform the duties of that office till May 1st, 1873. The reports from the dispensaries and hospitals were made regularly, and the general record of this department of the Society's work maintained with uniformity till May 1st, 1873.

AUXILIARY AID.

On the 25th of November, 1871, the following circular was prepared and issued, earnestly inviting the coöperation of the citizens in providing for the sick proper nourishment, delicacies, and such care as could not be given by the physician.

MEDICAL RELIEF.

The Sick, Sanitary, and Hospital Committee of the Chicago Relief and Aid Society desire to secure the personal coöperation of benevolent citizens in the important and responsible work that comes under their supervision. The visiting and dispensing Physicians are unable, from the nature of their engagements, to provide in all cases such treatment and attentions as would best conduce to the welfare of their patients. Not seldom the sick are in need of some article of diet or simple luxury, which if opportunity furnished, would not only be grateful to the sufferer, but instrumental in his recovery. It is believed that there are among us many persons of benevolent character and valuable sanitary experience who would be willing to give some personal attention to these cases, if the way could be pointed out to them, and if they could be assured that their services would be welcomed by the physicians in charge.

The Committee wish to inform all such persons that their ministrations to the sick depending upon the Relief and Aid Society, in their respective neighborhoods, is sincerely desired and would be gratefully accepted. Pastors, Churches, and Charitable Societies are requested to organize visitors in localities in which they are situated for efficient aid in this particular. Sometimes such immediate provision for the sick is needed as cannot be procured in time through the ordinary channels of relief, which might be speedily furnished in the way that is proposed. Where the expense attending such ministrations is of a kind to be at all burdensome to visitors it will be paid out of the funds of the Society. What is aimed at is such an alert, kind, and intelligent care of the sick as shall be most promotive of their speedy convalescence. Such as desire are respectfully requested to put themselves in communication with the Medical Superintendents and Medical Officers of this Committee, who may be found at the Depot of Distribution.

HORATIO N. POWERS, } *Special Committee.*
R. LUDLAM. }

In response to this circular the "Ladies Aid Society" and many individuals not connected with any organization, rendered, under the direction of the medical officers, timely and valuable services. In every case a record was made and a report rendered of the kind and amount of aid supplied. The tables herewith published, with few exceptions, perhaps sufficiently explain themselves. The nomenclature of disease adopted by the physicians was not found to be in all respects the same, but it is believed that the results are not materially affected by that fact. Wherever a doubt existed as to the meaning of the reporter, a personal inquiry was addressed to him upon the subject and the assignment of the case determined by his reply. It will be seen that some terms are used in a general sense. Diphtheria, for instance, embraces not only diphtheritic inflammation of the fauces, but also the same form of disease of the larynx. Without discussing the propriety of the grouping of these two forms of the disease under the same name, it has seemed almost a necessity, as croup, diphtheritic croup, membranous croup, and dipththeria, have been used by different reporters apparently for the designation of the same disease. On the contrary, spasmodic croup or false croup has been placed under the general term of laryngitis.

The physicians reporting these cases were without exception men of thorough medical education, many of them of large experience in hospital and private practice and there is every reason to rely upon the accuracy of their diagnosis. The statistics of mortality are absolutely accurate, as a single death could not have escaped the knowledge of the Department, even though the patient had been transferred before the termination of the case to the care of a physician not connected with the Society. No burial could take place without a registry or permit from the Board of Health, and the mortuary record of the Society was constantly compared with the official registration.

It is believed that these tables contain information not readily accessible in any other form. They present a picture of the sanitary condition and vital force of about one hundred thousand of our citizens during the year 1872,—not only the deaths but the diseases and the mortality from each disease at different ages and in the two sexes.

This represents much more nearly the work of physicians in private practice than either the statistics of hospitals or dispensaries, or of army practice, and so far as is known to the chairman of the Committee furnishes the largest collected and tabulated record of the kind in existence. The meteorological record is taken from the official register of the Board of Health of the city of Chicago. The direction and force of the wind is an approximation arrived at by taking the daily record for the first half of the month and giving only the average for the period, and repeating the same process for the last half.

The daily reports contain, besides the information here given, the nationality and as far as possible the occupation of each patient. These reports are also complete for the whole period from October 16th, 1871, to May 1st, 1873, covering 89,724 cases.

The blanks used by the Committee need no explanation.

RECORD OF PATIENTS RECEIVED

In the Hospitals, on Orders of the Chicago Relief and Aid Society, from October 16, 1871, to May 1, 1873.

Hospital.	Patients received in Hospitals from October 9, 1871, to October 16, 1871.	Patients admitted since October 16, 1871.	Patients died.	Total Patients treated.	Patients remaining in the Hospitals, May 1, 1873.
Mercy	124	245	23	369	31
St. Luke	29	162	20	191	8
St. Joseph	25	194	29	219	10
Women and Children's	27	198	8	225	15
Hahnemann . . .	12	86	2	98	1
Eye and Ear . . .	5	39	–	44	–
Total	222	924	82	1,146	65

RECORD OF PATIENTS TREATED,

PRESCRIPTIONS FILLED, AND VACCINATIONS PERFORMED AT THE DISPENSARIES UNDER CHARGE OF THE CHICAGO RELIEF AND AID SOCIETY, FROM OCTOBER 16, 1871, TO MAY 1, 1873.

DISPENSARY.	Patients Treated.	Prescriptions Filled.	Vaccinations Performed.	Medical Director.
Central	14,448	20,168	4,527	P. Adolphus.
North Star . . .	14,335	23,174	2,354	John Reid.
Davis Free . . .	11,809	18,133	916	D. T. Nelson.
Herrick	9,171	12,270	1,438	J. W. Hutchins.
Hahnemann . .	1,288	1,860	235	T. S. Hoyne.
Women and Children's . . .	103	194	45	M. A. Thompson.
Eye and Ear . .	744	860	–	E. L. Holmes.
Total	51,898	76,659	9,515	

RECORD OF PATIENTS TREATED

AND VISITS MADE BY THE VISITING PHYSICIANS OF THE CHICAGO RELIEF AND AID SOCIETY, FROM OCTOBER 16, 1871, TO MAY 1, 1873.

DISTRICTS.	Medical Superintendents.	Patients treated at Residence.	Visits made at Residence.	Vaccinations performed at Residence.	Vaccinations performed at District Supply Headquarters.
1	John Reid . . .	13,313	17,470	334	12,074
2	William Wagner	6,611	10,598	1,016	21,386
3	R. G. Bogue . .	4,661	7,230	561	4,191
4	Edwin Powell . .	6,494	7,550	313	3,924
5	J. W. Freer . .	5,601	8,530	1,070	9,549
	Total	36,680	51,378	3,294	51,124

Grand Total of Patients treated	89,724
Grand Total of Prescriptions filled	76,660
Grand Total of Vaccinations performed	63,933
Grand Total of Visits made	51,378
Grand Total of Deaths	519
Per cent. of Deaths to Patients	0.58

TABLE OF THE DISEASES AND MORTALITY

Of Male and Female Patients under Five (5) Years of Age, for the Year 1872.

1872.	January.					February.					March.				
	Sexes.			Deaths.		Sexes.			Deaths.		Sexes.			Deaths.	
List of Diseases.	Male.	Female.	Total.	Male.	Female.	Male.	Female.	Total.	Male.	Female.	Male.	Female.	Total.	Male.	Female.
Epilepsy	–	3	3	–	–	1	1	2	–	–	1	–	1	–	–
Convulsions . . .	5	7	12	1	1	15	6	21	2	1	7	8	15	4	1
Chorea	–	–	–	–	–	–	–	–	–	–	2	7	9	–	–
Meningitis . . .	2	2	4	1	1	3	–	3	–	–	1	–	1	–	–
Paralysis, Partial .	–	2	2	–	–	1	2	3	–	–	1	–	1	–	–
Spinal Curvature .	1	1	2	–	–	–	1	1	–	–	1	–	1	–	–
Neuralgia . . .	2	4	6	–	–	1	2	3	–	–	–	2	2	–	–
Conjunctivitis . .	17	8	25	–	–	11	6	17	–	–	2	2	4	–	–
Granular Lids . .	4	–	4	–	–	2	1	3	–	–	–	2	2	–	–
Keratitis	–	1	1	–	–	1	1	2	–	–	3	4	7	–	–
Coryza	2	4	6	–	–	5	3	8	–	–	1	2	3	–	–
Catarrh	28	10	38	–	–	18	10	28	–	–	7	3	10	–	–
Tonsillitis . . .	12	12	24	–	–	10	11	21	–	–	2	4	6	–	–
Pharyngitis . . .	2	7	9	1	1	4	2	6	–	–	5	8	13	–	–
Diphtheria . . .	–	5	5	–	–	–	10	10	–	–	3	3	6	–	1
Laryngitis . . .	13	24	37	–	–	6	8	14	–	1	5	9	14	–	–
Bronchitis . . .	98	78	176	2	–	138	107	245	1	1	64	44	108	–	–
Bronchitis Chronic	29	15	44	–	–	51	21	72	–	–	17	7	24	–	–
Bronchitis with Diarrhœa	9	12	21	–	–	27	15	42	–	–	15	6	21	–	–
Pertussis	23	12	35	–	–	29	13	42	–	–	14	7	21	–	–
Pneumonia . . .	29	40	69	1	–	10	20	30	1	4	13	8	21	2	3
Pleuritis	–	1	1	–	–	1	3	4	–	–	–	1	1	–	–
Dyspepsia . . .	–	2	2	–	–	2	6	8	–	–	8	4	12	–	–
Ulcer of Stomach .	–	–	–	–	–	–	–	–	–	–	3	1	4	–	–
Cholera Infantum	–	–	–	–	–	–	–	–	–	–	5	4	9	–	–
Diarrhœa	19	29	48	–	–	37	32	69	–	–	24	14	38	–	–
Diarrhœa, Chronic	13	8	21	–	–	14	11	25	2	–	10	8	18	–	–
Dysentery . . .	5	4	9	–	–	9	3	12	–	–	7	3	10	–	–
Cholera Morbus .	–	–	–	–	–	–	–	–	–	–	–	–	–	–	–
Enteritis	2	4	6	–	–	2	8	10	–	–	4	12	16	1	1
Constipation . .	3	6	9	–	–	4	8	12	–	–	8	10	18	–	–
Helminthiasis . .	21	25	46	–	–	22	10	32	–	–	6	4	10	–	–
Jaundice	9	3	12	–	–	12	5	17	–	–	7	4	11	–	–
Ascites	–	–	–	–	–	–	–	–	–	–	–	–	–	–	–
Anasarca	–	2	2	–	–	1	2	3	–	–	–	2	2	–	–
Cystitis	–	–	–	–	–	–	–	–	–	–	–	–	–	–	–
Incontinence of Urine	2	–	2	–	–	1	–	1	–	–	3	1	4	–	–
Phthisis	3	6	9	–	–	9	3	12	1	1	9	5	14	–	1
Rheumatism . .	12	14	26	–	–	17	8	25	–	–	8	2	10	–	–
Rheumatism Chronic	4	2	6	–	–	12	3	15	–	–	2	1	3	–	–
Erysipelas . . .	5	1	6	–	–	3	–	3	–	–	1	–	1	–	–
Ephemeral Fever .	18	25	43	–	–	10	10	20	–	–	4	6	10	–	–
Intermittent Fever	13	8	21	–	–	13	6	19	–	–	9	12	21	–	–
Intermittent with Diarrhœa . . .	6	3	9	–	–	5	1	6	–	–	3	1	4	–	–
Remittent Fever .	14	10	24	–	–	15	11	26	2	–	26	15	41	–	–
Typhoid Fever . .	9	2	11	–	–	10	3	13	–	1	9	3	12	–	–
Cerebro-spinal Meningitis	–	–	–	–	–	–	–	–	–	–	–	–	–	–	–
Total	434	402	836	6	3	532	373	905	9	9	320	239	559	7	7

January.				February.				March.			
Mean Therm.	Rain Fall.	Direction and Force of Wind.		Mean Therm.	Rain Fall.	Direction and Force of Wind.		Mean Therm.	Rain Fall.	Direction and Force of Wind.	
26°	.670	S. W. h.	N. W. g.	27°	.690	S. W. g.	S. E. g.	29°	3.220	N. E. h.	N. W. g.

TABLE OF THE DISEASES AND MORTALITY

OF MALE AND FEMALE PATIENTS UNDER FIVE (5) YEARS OF AGE, FOR THE YEAR 1872.— *Continued.*

1872.	April.					May.					June.				
	Sexes.			Deaths.		Sexes.			Deaths.		Sexes.			Deaths.	
List of Diseases.	Male.	Female.	Total.	Male.	Female.	Male.	Female.	Total.	Male.	Female.	Male.	Female.	Total.	Male.	Female.
Epilepsy	–	–	–	–	–	–	–	–	–	–	–	–	–	–	–
Convulsions . . .	7	4	11	2	1	5	7	12	1	1	7	7	14	–	–
Chorea	2	4	6	–	–	–	–	–	–	–	2	3	5	–	–
Meningitis . . .	1	–	1	1	–	1	–	1	1	–	1	–	1	–	–
Paralysis, Partial .	1	–	1	–	–	–	1	1	–	–	1	1	2	–	–
Spinal Curvature .	1	–	1	–	–	–	–	–	–	–	–	–	–	–	–
Neuralgia . . .	–	–	–	–	–	–	–	–	–	–	–	–	–	–	–
Conjunctivitis . .	1	–	1	–	–	–	3	3	–	–	6	3	9	–	–
Granular Lids . .	–	–	–	–	–	–	1	1	–	–	2	–	2	–	–
Keratitis	2	4	6	–	–	–	1	1	–	–	–	2	2	–	–
Coryza	–	–	–	–	–	–	–	–	–	–	–	–	–	–	–
Catarrh	3	4	7	–	–	2	4	6	–	–	–	2	2	–	
Tonsillitis . . .	–	–	–	–	–	–	1	1	–	–	–	–	–	–	–
Pharyngitis . . .	7	4	11	3	2	–	1	1	–	–	–	1	1	–	–
Diphtheria . . .	–	2	2	–	2	–	–	–	–	–	–	4	4	–	–
Laryngitis . . .	1	4	5	–	–	2	4	6	–	–	–	2	2	–	–
Bronchitis . . .	19	14	33	–	–	9	5	14	–	–	5	4	9	–	–
Bronchitis, Chronic	7	3	10	–	–	–	–	–	–	–	–	–	–	–	–
Bronchitis with Diarrhœa . . .	4	1	5	–	–	1	–	1	–	–	–	–	–	–	–
Pertussis	2	–	2	2	–	1	3	4	–	–	3	3	6	–	–
Pneumonia . . .	9	4	13	–	2	5	9	14	–	–	7	5	12	–	–
Pleuritis	–	–	–	–	–	–	–	–	–	–	–	–	–	–	–
Dyspepsia . . .	5	2	7	–	–	1	–	1	–	–	–	2	2	–	–
Ulcer of Stomach .	2	–	2	–	–	2	–	2	–	–	–	–	–	–	–
Cholera Infantum	9	5	14	–	–	10	5	15	–	–	7	12	19	1	4
Diarrhœa	17	8	25	2	1	6	2	8	–	–	24	15	39	–	
Diarrhœa Chronic	4	2	6	–	–	2	–	2	–	–	8	3	11	–	–
Dysentery . . .	8	6	14	–	–	5	7	12	–	–	13	10	23	–	–
Cholera Morbus .	–	–	–	–	–	–	1	1	–	–	10	2	12	–	–
Enteritis	10	8	18	–	1	3	8	11	–	–	2	5	7	–	–
Constipation . .	5	9	14	–	–	5	6	11	–	–	1	4	5	–	–
Helminthiasis . .	8	7	15	–	–	7	8	15	–	–	11	4	15	–	–
Jaundice	4	1	5	–	–	6	3	9	–	–	–	–	–	–	–
Ascites	–	–	–	–	–	–	–	–	–	–	–	–	–	–	–
Anasarca	–	1	1	–		1	–	1	–	–	–	–	–	–	–
Cystitis	–	–	–	–	–	–	–	–	–	–	–	–		–	–
Incontinence of Urine	1	–	1	–	–	1	–	1	–	–	–	–	–	–	–
Phthisis	4	8	12	2	–	4	1	5	1	–	7	4	11	–	–
Rheumatism . .	1	–	1	–	–	6	2	8	–	–	1	–	1	–	–
Rheumatism, Chronic	–	–	–	–	–	–	–	–	–	–	1	–	1	–	–
Erysipelas . . .	–	–	–	–	–	–	1	1	–	–	1	–	1	–	–
Ephemeral Fever .	1	–	1	–	–	–	2	2	–	–	–	–	–	–	–
Intermittent Fever	8	2	10	–	–	4	–	4	–	–	5	1	6	–	–
Intermittent with Diarrhœa . . .	5	1	6	–	–	1	–	1	–	–	4	1	5	–	–
Remittent Fever .	9	3	12	–	–	5	2	7	–	–	7	1	8	–	–
Typhoid Fever . .	5	1	6	–	–	–	–	–	–	–	2	–	2	–	
Cerebro-spinal Meningitis	–	–	–	–	–	–	–	–	–	–	2	–	2	1	
Total	173	112	285	12	9	95	88	183	3	1	140	101	241	2	4

April.				May.				June.			
Mean Therm.	Rain Fall.	Direction and Force of Wind.		Mean Therm.	Rain Fall.	Direction and Force of Wind.		Mean Therm.	Rain Fall.	Direction and Force of Wind.	
48°	2.990	S. W. h.	N. E. h.	57½°	3.285	S. W. g.	S. E. h.	70⅛°	3.410	S. W. g.	N. W. g.

TABLE OF THE DISEASES AND MORTALITY

Of Male and Female Patients under Five (5) Years of Age, for the Year 1872.— *Continued.*

1872.	July.					August.					September.				
	Sexes.			Deaths.		Sexes.			Deaths.		Sexes.			Deaths.	
List of Diseases.	Male.	Female.	Total.	Male.	Female.	Male.	Female.	Total.	Male.	Female.	Male.	Female.	Total.	Male.	Female.
Epilepsy	–	–	–	–	–	–	–	–	–	–	1	3	4	–	–
Convulsions	9	4	13	1	–	9	5	14	–	1	4	12	16	–	–
Chorea	–	–	–	–	–	–	–	–	–	–	–	–	–	–	–
Meningitis	1	–	1	–	–	1	3	4	–	–	2	–	2	–	–
Paralysis, Partial	1	–	1	–	–	1	2	3	–	–	–	–	–	–	–
Spinal Curvature	–	–	–	–	–	–	1	1	–	–	1	–	1	–	–
Neuralgia	1	1	2	–	–	–	–	–	–	–	–	1	1	–	–
Conjunctivitis	9	3	12	–	–	–	2	2	–	–	7	1	8	–	–
Granular Lids	–	–	–	–	–	–	1	1	–	–	–	–	–	–	–
Keratitis	1	2	3	–	–	2	1	3	–	–	–	1	1	–	–
Coryza	–	–	–	–	–	–	–	–	–	–	–	–	–	–	–
Catarrh	9	5	14	–	–	5	1	6	–	–	–	2	2	–	–
Tonsillitis	–	–	–	–	–	–	–	–	–	–	3	6	9	–	–
Pharyngitis	–	1	1	–	–	–	1	1	–	–	4	1	5	–	–
Diphtheria	1	2	3	–	–	–	1	1	–	–	1	5	6	–	–
Laryngitis	2	1	3	–	–	–	4	4	–	–	1	6	7	–	–
Bronchitis	3	–	3	–	–	3	1	4	–	–	11	10	21	–	–
Bronchitis, Chronic	–	–	–	–	–	–	–	–	–	–	9	3	12	–	–
Bronchitis with Diarrhœa	2	–	2	–	–	1	–	1	–	–	6	2	8	–	–
Pertussis	5	7	12	–	–	7	1	8	–	1	9	6	15	1	–
Pneumonia	2	9	11	–	–	4	1	5	–	–	9	2	11	–	–
Pleuritis	–	–	–	–	–	–	–	–	–	–	–	1	1	–	–
Dyspepsia	2	1	3	–	–	2	2	4	–	–	–	–	–	–	–
Ulcer of Stomach	1	1	2	–	–	–	1	1	–	–	–	–	–	–	–
Cholera Infantum	18	27	45	2	8	38	30	68	5	7	19	10	29	1	2
Diarrhœa	33	18	51	1	–	33	10	43	1	1	37	22	59	–	–
Diarrhœa, Chronic	9	6	15	1	–	10	6	16	–	–	9	3	12	–	–
Dysentery	11	4	15	1	–	14	6	20	–	–	14	8	22	–	–
Cholera Morbus	8	3	11	–	–	11	2	13	–	–	5	–	5	–	–
Enteritis	–	5	5	–	–	1	4	5	–	–	2	10	12	–	–
Constipation	5	2	7	–	–	–	4	4	–	–	1	4	5	–	–
Helminthiasis	12	6	18	–	–	7	3	10	–	–	12	5	17	–	–
Jaundice	–	–	–	–	–	–	–	–	–	–	–	–	–	–	–
Ascites	–	–	–	–	–	–	–	–	–	–	2	3	5	–	–
Anasarca	–	–	–	–	–	–	–	–	–	–	–	–	–	–	–
Cystitis	–	–	–	–	–	–	–	–	–	–	–	–	–	–	–
Incontinence of Urine	1	–	1	–	–	1	1	2	–	–	–	1	1	–	–
Phthisis	2	–	2	–	–	4	–	4	–	–	3	3	6	–	–
Rheumatism	5	1	6	–	–	2	–	2	–	–	3	–	3	–	–
Rheumatism, Chronic	–	–	–	–	–	2	–	2	–	–	–	1	1	–	–
Erysipelas	–	1	1	–	–	2	–	2	–	–	–	–	–	–	–
Ephemeral Fever	–	2	2	–	–	2	–	2	–	–	1	1	2	–	–
Intermittent Fever	1	1	2	–	–	3	–	3	–	–	3	1	4	–	–
Intermittent with Diarrhœa	1	–	1	–	–	5	2	7	–	–	–	2	2	–	–
Remittent Fever	6	–	6	–	–	6	2	8	–	–	11	5	16	–	–
Typhoid Fever	–	–	–	–	–	8	4	12	–	–	7	6	13	–	–
Cerebro-spinal Meningitis	1	1	2	–	–	3	1	4	–	1	1	1	2	–	–
Total	162	114	276	6	8	187	103	290	6	11	198	148	346	2	2

July.				August.				September.			
Mean Therm.	Rain Fall.	Direction and Force of Wind.		Mean Therm.	Rain Fall.	Direction and Force of Wind.		Mean Therm.	Rain Fall.	Direction and Force of Wind.	
72½°	4.050	S. W. h.	N. W. g.	72°	2.560	N. W. g.	S. W. g.	64°	6.430	S. W. g.	S. E. g

TABLE OF THE DISEASES AND MORTALITY

Of Male and Female Patients under Five (5) Years of Age, for the Year 1872. — *Continued.*

1872. List of Diseases.	October. Sexes. Male.	October. Sexes. Female.	October. Total.	October. Deaths. Male.	October. Deaths. Female.	November. Sexes. Male.	November. Sexes. Female.	November. Total.	November. Deaths. Male.	November. Deaths. Female.	December. Sexes. Male.	December. Sexes. Female.	December. Total.	December. Deaths. Male.	December. Deaths. Female.	Total Patients.	Total Deaths.
Epilepsy	1	2	3	–	–	–	1	1	–	–	–	2	2	–	–	16	–
Convulsions	7	3	10	1	1	7	5	12	1	1	5	6	11	1	–	161	22
Chorea	–	–	–	–	–	–	–	–	–	–	–	–	–	–	–	20	–
Meningitis	3	1	4	–	1	2	–	2	–	–	2	2	4	–	–	28	5
Paralysis, Partial	–	–	–	–	–	2	2	4	–	–	1	–	1	–	–	19	–
Spinal Curvature	–	1	1	–	–	1	1	2	–	–	2	1	3	–	–	13	–
Neuralgia	–	2	2	–	–	2	1	3	–	–	–	2	2	–	–	21	–
Conjunctivitis	5	3	8	–	–	9	4	13	–	–	19	13	32	–	–	134	–
Granular Lids	–	1	1	–	–	4	–	–	–	–	1	–	1	–	–	15	–
Keratitis	–	1	1	–	–	2	–	2	–	–	2	2	4	–	–	33	–
Coryza	–	2	2	–	–	1	3	4	–	–	3	6	9	–	–	32	–
Catarrh	8	6	14	–	–	18	8	26	–	–	41	10	51	–	–	204	–
Tonsillitis	–	–	–	–	–	4	8	12	–	–	4	9	13	–	–	86	–
Pharyngitis	3	1	4	–	–	3	3	6	–	–	5	3	8	–	–	66	7
Diphtheria	1	3	4	1	1	4	12	16	–	–	15	10	25	–	–	82	5
Laryngitis	4	9	13	–	1	5	14	19	–	–	19	25	44	–	–	168	2
Bronchitis	19	9	28	–	–	29	19	48	–	–	64	40	104	–	–	793	4
Bronchitis, Chronic	9	2	11	–	–	10	3	13	–	–	24	12	36	–	–	222	–
Bronchitis with Diarrhœa	6	4	10	–	–	9	3	12	–	–	11	2	13	–	–	136	–
Pertussis	8	8	16	–	–	10	4	14	–	–	29	13	42	–	–	217	4
Pneumonia	7	7	14	–	–	29	18	47	–	–	29	19	48	–	–	295	13
Pleuritis	3	5	8	–	–	2	4	6	–	–	4	3	7	–	–	28	–
Dyspepsia	–	–	–	–	–	1	1	2	–	–	2	–	2	–	–	43	–
Ulcer of Stomach	–	–	–	–	–	–	–	–	–	–	–	–	–	–	–	11	–
Cholera Infantum	9	4	13	–	–	–	–	–	–	–	–	–	–	–	–	212	30
Diarrhœa	17	10	27	–	–	32	11	43	–	–	33	26	59	–	–	509	6
Diarrhœa, Chronic	9	2	11	–	–	9	2	11	–	–	14	7	21	–	–	169	3
Dysentery	11	4	15	–	–	13	8	21	–	–	6	6	12	–	–	185	1
Cholera Morbus	–	–	–	–	–	–	–	–	–	–	–	–	–	–	–	42	–
Enteritis	–	5	5	–	1	4	12	16	–	–	3	11	14	1	–	125	5
Constipation	2	5	7	–	–	3	8	11	–	–	7	6	13	–	–	116	–
Helminthiasis	8	7	15	–	–	8	4	12	–	–	22	10	32	–	–	237	–
Jaundice	8	1	9	–	–	10	2	12	–	–	13	4	17	–	–	92	–
Ascites	–	–	–	–	–	–	–	–	–	–	–	–	–	–	–	5	–
Anasarca	–	–	–	–	–	–	–	–	–	–	–	–	–	–	–	9	–
Cystitis	–	–	–	–	–	–	–	–	–	–	–	3	3	–	–	3	–
Incontinence of Urine	1	–	1	–	–	1	–	1	–	–	1	–	1	–	–	16	–
Phthisis	9	3	12	–	–	5	7	12	–	–	7	7	14	–	–	113	6
Rheumatism	3	1	4	–	–	5	3	8	–	–	6	4	10	–	–	104	–
Rheumatism, Chronic	2	–	2	–	–	2	2	4	–	–	7	2	9	–	–	43	–
Erysipelas	–	–	–	–	–	3	1	4	–	–	5	1	6	–	–	25	–
Ephemeral Fever	7	2	9	–	–	8	8	16	–	–	4	8	12	–	–	119	–
Intermittent Fever	13	6	19	–	–	11	5	16	–	–	12	4	16	–	–	141	–
Intermittent with Diarrhœa	3	–	3	–	–	1	–	1	–	–	2	–	2	–	–	47	–
Remittent Fever	9	3	12	–	–	9	5	14	–	–	9	5	14	–	–	188	2
Typhoid Fever	11	3	14	–	–	12	4	16	–	–	9	10	19	–	–	118	1
Cerebro-spinal Meningitis	–	2	2	–	–	–	–	–	–	–	–	–	–	–	–	12	2
Total	206	128	334	2	5	286	196	482	1	1	442	294	736	2	–	5,473	118

October. Mean Therm.	October. Rain Fall.	October. Direction and Force of Wind.		November. Mean Therm.	November. Rain Fall.	November. Direction and Force of Wind.		December. Mean Therm.	December. Rain Fall.	December. Direction and Force of Wind.	
52°	.650	N. E. g.	S. W. h.	32½°	.800	N. W. h.	N. W. g.	19°	.430	N. W. g.	S. W. g

ADDITIONAL TABLE OF THE SICKNESS AND MORTALITY

Of Patients Unclassified as to Sex, under Five (5) Years of Age, for the Year 1872.

1872.	January.		February.		March.		April.		May.		June.		July.		August.		September.		October.		November.		December.			
List of Diseases.	Patients.	Deaths.	Patients.	Deaths.	Patients.	Deaths.	Patients.	Deaths.	Patients.	Deaths..	Patients.	Deaths.	Patients.	Deaths.	Patients.	Deaths.	Patients.	Deaths.	Patients.	Deaths.	Patients.	Deaths.	Patients.	Deaths.	Total Patients.	Total Deaths.
Abscess	6	-	5	-	7	-	3	-	2	-	1	-	3	-	4	-	1	-	-	-	2	-	1	-	35	-
Furoncle	3	-	1	-	1	-	-	-	1	-	1	-	-	-	-	-	1	-	2	-	1	-	3	-	14	-
Inflammation of Mamma	4	-	3	-	1	-	1	-	-	-	1	-	-	-	-	-	-	-	-	-	2	-	5	-	17	-
Ulcer of Leg	4	-	2	-	1	-	1	-	1	-	1	-	1	-	-	-	1	-	-	-	1	-	-	-	13	-
Frost-bite	10	-	6	-	-	-	-	-	-	-	-	-	-	-	-	-	-	-	-	-	16	-	19	-	51	-
Contusion	4	-	6	-	3	-	1	-	2	-	1	-	2	-	2	-	1	-	2	-	4	-	5	-	33	-
Incised Wound	5	-	6	-	3	-	2	-	1	-	1	-	-	-	1	-	-	-	-	-	3	-	5	-	27	-
Fracture of Ulna	4	-	2	-	3	-	2	-	1	-	1	-	1	-	-	-	2	-	1	-	3	-	5	-	25	-
Periostitis	3	-	3	-	1	-	1	-	1	-	2	-	1	-	-	-	-	-	1	-	2	-	4	-	19	-
Synovitis	3	-	3	-	2	-	1	-	3	-	1	-	1	-	-	-	-	-	-	-	4	-	7	-	25	-
Atrophy	5	-	2	-	2	-	-	-	2	-	1	-	2	-	2	-	1	-	2	-	-	-	-	-	19	-
Anæmia	1	-	3	-	2	-	1	-	1	-	2	-	2	-	-	-	-	-	1	-	3	-	1	-	17	-
Debility	10	-	6	-	4	-	1	-	2	-	4	-	2	-	10	-	15	-	4	-	14	-	11	-	83	-
Inanition	2	-	3	-	5	-	2	-	3	1	2	1	2	1	1	-	5	1	-	-	1	-	2	-	28	4
Malaise	3	-	3	-	1	-	1	-	2	-	-	-	1	-	-	-	-	-	-	-	1	-	3	-	15	-
Hysteria	1	-	2	-	1	-	1	-	1	-	1	-	1	-	-	-	3	-	-	-	1	-	1	-	13	-
Cephalalgia	2	-	4	-	2	-	4	-	3	-	1	-	2	-	-	-	2	-	-	-	3	-	2	-	25	-
Hydrocephalus	3	1	5	-	12	2	7	1	1	-	2	-	13	-	19	-	-	-	3	1	2	-	3	-	70	5
Odontalgia	10	-	12	-	11	-	7	-	3	-	2	-	1	-	4	-	6	-	5	-	14	-	19	-	94	-
Otalgia	5	-	7	-	6	-	1	-	1	-	1	-	-	-	-	-	2	-	-	-	5	-	9	-	37	-
Otitis	17	-	17	-	7	-	1	-	2	-	3	-	4	-	-	-	4	-	-	-	13	-	16	-	84	-
Strabismus	1	-	2	-	1	-	1	-	-	-	2	-	1	-	-	-	1	-	2	-	3	-	5	-	19	-
Stomatitis	14	-	16	-	10	-	12	-	2	-	6	-	3	-	-	-	-	-	2	-	12	-	14	-	91	-
Parotiditis	24	-	38	-	13	-	12	-	6	-	3	-	1	-	1	-	-	-	6	-	15	-	19	-	138	-
Angina	8	-	6	-	1	-	1	-	1	-	-	-	-	-	1	-	1	-	-	-	2	-	6	-	27	-
Gastritis	1	-	3	-	5	-	6	-	3	-	3	1	-	-	3	-	-	-	5	-	3	-	6	-	38	1
Gastralgia	7	-	4	-	1	-	2	-	1	-	1	-	-	-	-	-	-	-	5	-	6	-	9	-	36	-
Colic	16	-	14	-	19	-	8	-	4	-	2	-	5	-	6	-	9	-	11	-	21	-	35	-	150	-
Peritonitis	4	-	5	-	2	-	1	-	-	-	2	-	-	-	-	-	1	-	1	-	3	-	5	-	24	-
Hœmaturia	1	-	3	-	1	-	-	-	-	-	1	-	-	-	-	-	-	-	2	-	3	-	5	-	16	-
Urethritis	2	-	6	-	3	-	1	-	-	-	-	-	-	-	-	-	-	-	3	-	5	-	9	-	29	-
Orchitis	3	-	2	-	1	-	1	-	-	-	-	-	-	-	-	-	2	-	1	-	3	-	4	-	17	-
Total	186	1	200	-	132	2	83	1	50	1	49	2	49	1	54	-	58	1	59	1	171	-	238	-	1,329	10

ADDITIONAL TABLE OF THE SICKNESS AND MORTALITY

OF PATIENTS, UNCLASSIFIED AS TO SEX, UNDER FIVE (5) YEARS OF AGE, FOR THE YEAR 1872. — *Continued.*

1872.	January.		February.		March.		April.		May.		June.		July.		August.		September.		October.		November.		December.			
List of Diseases.	Patients.	Deaths.	Patients.	Deaths.	Patients.	Deaths.	Patients.	Deaths.	Patients.	Deaths.	Patients.	Deaths.	Patients.	Deaths.	Patients.	Deaths.	Patients.	Deaths.	Patients.	Deaths.	Patients.	Deaths.	Patients.	Deaths.	Total Patients.	Total Deaths.
Vaginitis	12	–	8	–	7	–	1	–	2	–	3	–	1	–	1	–	1	–	2	–	9	–	19	–	66	–
Vaginal Hœmorrhage	2	–	6	–	4	–	3	–	4	–	2	–	4	–	6	–	12	–	3	–	1	–	8	–	55	–
Encephaloid Tumor	3	–	2	–	1	–	1	–	–	–	1	–	–	–	2	–	3	–	1	–	4	–	5	–	23	–
Adenitis	15	–	14	–	6	–	1	–	2	–	2	–	2	–	3	–	–	–	–	–	13	–	19	–	77	–
Scrofula	39	–	24	–	18	–	11	–	4	–	6	–	4	–	1	–	6	–	4	–	16	–	17	–	150	–
Potts' Disease	2	–	1	–	1	–	1	–	2	–	–	–	–	–	–	–	1	–	–	–	2	–	3	–	13	–
Morbus Coxarius	6	–	9	–	5	–	3	1	2	1	–	–	–	–	–	–	1	–	1	–	4	–	5	–	36	2
Tabes Mesenterica	1	–	1	–	1	–	–	–	1	–	–	–	1	–	1	–	1	1	–	–	1	–	1	–	9	1
Marasmus	1	–	2	–	1	–	–	–	1	–	–	–	–	–	1	–	–	–	2	–	4	–	3	–	15	–
Sciatica	–	–	–	–	–	–	–	–	1	–	1	–	2	–	1	–	1	–	1	–	–	–	–	–	7	–
Cellulitis	3	–	2	–	1	–	1	–	–	–	1	–	–	–	–	–	–	–	2	–	3	–	4	–	17	–
Rubeola	20	–	12	–	4	–	3	–	3	–	6	–	1	–	2	–	4	–	11	–	14	–	25	–	105	–
Varicella	21	–	19	–	13	–	–	–	–	–	–	–	–	–	–	–	–	–	14	–	16	–	19	–	102	–
Roseola	4	–	3	–	2	–	–	–	–	–	–	–	–	–	–	–	–	–	6	–	2	–	3	–	20	–
Scarlatina	17	1	28	2	8	–	2	–	1	1	2	–	–	–	–	–	–	–	6	–	11	–	23	–	98	4
Syphilis	11	–	7	–	4	–	3	–	2	–	6	–	2	–	2	–	2	–	2	–	2	–	6	–	49	–
Syphilis, Secondary	2	–	3	–	1	–	–	–	1	–	2	–	–	–	–	–	–	–	1	–	1	–	2	–	14	–
Syphilitic Eruption	2	–	1	–	2	–	1	–	–	–	–	–	–	–	–	–	–	–	2	–	3	–	4	–	15	–
Erythema	–	–	–	–	4	–	5	–	3	–	1	–	–	–	–	–	–	–	–	–	–	–	–	–	13	–
Eczema	19	–	28	–	21	–	6	–	6	–	10	–	4	–	4	–	4	–	8	–	12	–	16	–	138	–
Herpes	6	–	6	–	4	–	1	–	–	–	–	–	1	–	–	–	2	–	3	–	5	–	9	–	37	–
Impetigo	–	–	.	–	2	–	3	–	1	–	1	–	1	–	1	–	1	–	–	–	–	–	–	–	10	–
Urticaria	6	–	5	–	1	–	1	–	–	–	1	–	1	–	–	–	1	–	1	–	2	–	3	–	22	–
Prurigo	2	–	2	–	1	–	1	–	–	–	–	–	–	–	–	–	–	–	1	–	2	–	3	–	12	–
Tinea Capitis	6	–	7	–	2	–	1	–	–	–	–	–	–	–	–	–	1	–	2	–	3	–	5	–	27	–
Porrigo	6	–	10	–	3	–	2	–	–	–	1	–	–	–	–	–	–	–	4	–	6	–	9	–	41	–
Psoriasis	6	–	2	–	1	–	1	–	–	–	–	–	1	–	–	–	1	–	3	–	5	–	12	–	32	–
Total	212	1	202	2	118	–	52	1	36	2	46	–	25	–	26	–	42	1	80	–	141	–	223	–	1,203	7
Brought forward from page 225	186	1	200	–	132	2	83	1	50	1	49	2	49	1	54	–	58	1	59	1	171	–	238	–	1,329	10

Male Patients, Classified	3,175	Deaths of Male Patients	58
Female Patients, Classified	2,298	Deaths of Female Patients	60
Patients, Unclassified by Sexes	2,532	Deaths of Unclassified Patients	17
Total Patients	8,005	Total Deaths	135

TABLE OF THE DISEASES AND MORTALITY

Of Male and Female Patients, from the Age of Five to Ten Years, for the Year 1872.

1872.	January.					February.					March.				
	Sexes.			Deaths.		Sexes.			Deaths.		Sexes.			Deaths.	
List of Diseases.	Male.	Female.	Total.	Male.	Female.	Male.	Female.	Total.	Male.	Female.	Male.	Female.	Total.	Male.	Female.
Epilepsy	–	2	2	–	–	1	–	1	–	–	1	1	2	–	–
Convulsion	5	7	12	–	–	3	2	5	–	–	–	2	2	–	–
Chorea	–	–	–	–	–	–	–	–	–	–	–	–	–	–	–
Meningitis	4	2	6	–	–	4	3	7	–	–	3	1	4	1	1
Paralysis	1	–	1	–	–	1	–	1	–	–	–	1	1	–	–
Paralysis, Partial	2	–	2	–	–	–	1	1	–	–	2	1	3	–	–
Hemiplegia	–	1	1	–	–	–	1	1	–	–	–	1	1	–	–
Spinal Disease	1	1	2	–	–	–	1	1	–	–	1	1	2	–	–
Neuralgia	2	2	4	–	–	1	5	6	–	–	–	2	2	–	–
Conjunctivitis	7	8	15	–	–	7	3	10	–	–	5	4	9	–	–
Granular Lids	5	1	6	–	–	4	2	6	–	–	2	1	3	–	–
Keratitis	2	2	4	–	–	1	3	4	–	–	1	3	4	–	–
Catarrh	32	13	45	–	–	24	16	40	–	–	17	8	25	–	–
Epistaxis	–	–	–	–	–	–	–	–	–	–	–	–	–	–	–
Tonsillitis	4	8	12	–	–	4	9	13	–	–	4	5	9	–	–
Pharyngitis	4	2	6	–	–	2	2	4	–	–	7	2	9	–	–
Diphtheria	3	5	8	–	–	3	4	7	–	–	–	1	1	–	–
Laryngitis	5	14	19	–	–	9	4	13	–	–	1	7	8	–	2
Bronchitis	48	29	77	1	–	53	34	87	–	–	19	18	37	–	–
Bronchitis, Chronic	7	2	9	–	–	9	3	12	–	–	4	1	5	–	–
Asthma	2	–	2	–	–	4	1	5	–	–	2	–	2	–	–
Pertussis	13	2	15	–	–	6	6	12	–	–	4	2	6	–	–
Pneumonia	12	4	16	–	1	9	7	16	–	1	14	4	18	–	1
Pleuritis	1	4	5	–	–	5	4	9	–	–	5	2	7	–	–
Heart Disease	2	2	4	–	–	1	2	3	–	–	1	3	4	–	–
Dyspepsia	3	9	12	–	–	6	7	13	–	–	3	1	4	–	–
Diarrhœa	14	7	21	–	–	7	4	11	–	–	9	4	13	–	–
Cholera Morbus	–	–	–	–	–	–	–	–	–	–	–	–	–	–	–
Enteritis	1	5	6	–	–	1	4	5	–	–	1	3	4	–	–
Dysentery	7	12	19	–	–	13	4	17	–	–	7	4	11	–	–
Constipation	7	11	18	–	–	4	7	11	–	–	6	5	11	–	–
Hœmorrhoids	–	1	1	–	–	2	–	2	–	–	1	–	1	–	–
Helminthiasis	17	5	22	–	–	14	11	25	–	–	14	7	21	–	–
Jaundice	6	1	7	–	–	4	1	5	–	–	2	–	2	–	–
Bright's Disease	–	–	–	–	–	–	–	–	–	–	–	–	–	–	–
Ascites	1	–	1	–	–	1	–	1	–	–	2	1	3	–	–
Cystitis	–	2	2	–	–	–	2	2	–	–	–	1	1	–	–
Dysuria	–	1	1	–	–	–	1	1	–	–	–	1	1	–	–
Incontinence of Urine	3	–	3	–	–	3	2	5	–	–	–	1	1	–	–
Phthisis	9	5	14	1	–	10	6	16	–	–	4	8	12	–	–
Rheumatism	13	5	18	–	–	5	9	14	1	–	10	8	18	–	–
Rheumatism, Chronic	1	–	1	–	–	2	–	2	–	–	1	–	1	–	–
Erysipelas	7	–	7	–	–	4	2	6	–	–	1	1	2	–	–
Ephemeral Fever	21	10	31	–	–	19	17	36	–	–	6	14	20	–	–
Intermittent Fever	29	12	41	–	–	14	7	21	–	–	9	7	16	–	–
Remittent Fever	7	2	9	–	–	6	4	10	–	–	7	5	12	–	–
Typhoid Fever	12	4	16	1	–	9	6	15	1	–	7	5	12	1	–
Cerebro-spinal Meningitis	–	–	–	–	–	–	–	–	–	–	–	–	–	–	–
Total	320	208	523	3	1	275	207	482	2	1	183	147	330	2	4

January.				February.				March.			
Mean Therm.	Rain Fall.	Direction and Force of Wind.		Mean Therm.	Rain Fall.	Direction and Force of Wind.		Mean Therm.	Rain Fall.	Direction and Force of Wind.	
26°	.670	S. W. h.	N. W. g.	27°	.690	S. W. g.	S. E. g.	29°	3.220	N. E. h.	N. W. g.

TABLE OF THE DISEASES AND MORTALITY

OF MALE AND FEMALE PATIENTS, FROM THE AGE OF FIVE TO TEN YEARS, FOR THE YEAR 1872. — *Continued.*

1872.	April.					May.					June.				
	Sexes.			Deaths.		Sexes.			Deaths.		Sexes.			Deaths.	
List of Diseases.	Male.	Female.	Total.	Male.	Female.	Male.	Female.	Total.	Male.	Female.	Male.	Female.	Total.	Male.	Female.
Epilepsy . . .	–	–	–	–	–	–	–	–	–	–	–	–	–	–	–
Convulsion . .	1	–	1	–	–	–	–	–	–	–	–	–	–	–	–
Chorea	–	–	–	–	–	–	–	–	–	–	2	–	2	–	–
Meningitis . . .	1	–	1	–	–	–	–	–	–	–	1	–	1	–	–
Paralysis . . .	–	–	–	–	–	–	–	–	–	–	–	–	–	–	–
Paralysis, Partial .	1	–	1	–	–	–	–	–	–	–	1	1	2	–	–
Hemiplegia . . .	–	–	–	–	–	–	–	–	–	–	–	–	–	–	–
Spinal Disease . .	1	–	1	–	–	–	–	–	–	–	–	–	–	–	–
Neuralgia . . .	–	–	–	–	–	–	–	–	–	–	–	–	–	–	–
Conjunctivitis . .	3	1	4	–	–	3	–	3	–	–	2	–	2	–	–
Granular Lids . .	1	1	2	–	–	3	1	4	–	–	1	–	1	–	–
Keratitis . . .	1	–	1	–	–	–	1	1	–	–	1	1	2	–	–
Catarrh	3	3	6	–	–	2	–	2	–	–	–	1	1	–	–
Epistaxis . . .	–	–	–	–	–	–	–	–	–	–	–	–	–	–	–
Tonsillitis . . .	1	–	1	–	–	3	2	5	–	–	–	–	–	–	–
Pharyngitis . .	–	–	–	–	–	–	–	–	–	–	–	–	–	–	–
Diphtheria . .	–	–	–	–	–	–	1	1	–	–	–	–	–	–	–
Laryngitis . . .	1	–	1	–	–	–	2	2	–	–	–	–	–	–	–
Bronchitis . . .	9	4	13	1	–	11	7	18	–	–	4	3	7	–	–
Bronchitis, Chronic	3	–	3	–	–	1	–	1	–	–	–	–	–	–	–
Asthma	–	–	–	–	–	–	–	–	–	–	–	–	–	–	–
Pertussis . . .	–	1	1	–	–	–	–	–	–	–	2	1	3	–	–
Pneumonia . . .	6	7	13	–	–	8	8	16	–	–	7	4	11	–	–
Pleuritis . . .	–	1	1	–	–	–	–	–	–	–	2	1	3	–	–
Heart Disease . .	–	1	1	–	–	–	1	1	–	–	–	–	–	–	–
Dyspepsia . . .	1	3	4	–	–	–	–	–	–	–	–	2	2	–	–
Diarrhœa . . .	6	5	11	–	–	4	8	12	–	–	8	7	15	–	–
Cholera Morbus .	–	–	–	–	–	–	–	–	–	–	–	–	–	–	–
Enteritis . . .	1	1	2	–	–	–	–	–	–	–	–	–	–	–	–
Dysentery . . .	–	1	1	–	–	2	–	2	–	–	–	–	–	–	–
Constipation . .	2	9	11	–	–	9	4	13	–	–	2	–	2	–	–
Hœmorrhoids . .	1	–	1	–	–	–	–	–	–	–	–	–	–	–	–
Helminthiasis . .	3	1	4	–	–	1	–	1	–	–	5	1	6	–	–
Jaundice . . .	1	–	1	–	–	1	1	2	–	–	2	1	3	–	–
Bright's Disease .	–	–	–	–	–	–	–	–	–	–	–	–	–	–	–
Ascites	–	–	–	–	–	1	1	2	–	–	–	–	–	–	–
Cystitis	–	–	–	–	–	–	–	–	–	–	–	–	–	–	–
Dysuria	–	1	1	–	–	–	–	–	–	–	–	1	1	–	–
Incontinence of Urine	1	–	1	–	–	1	–	1	–	–	1	–	1	–	–
Phthisis . . .	8	4	12	1	–	3	2	5	–	–	1	–	1	–	–
Rheumatism . .	2	–	2	–	–	–	–	–	–	–	2	–	2	–	–
Rheumatism, Chronic	–	–	–	–	–	–	–	–	–	–	1	–	1	–	–
Erysipelas . . .	–	–	–	–	–	–	–	–	–	–	1	–	1	–	–
Ephemeral Fever .	6	4	10	–	–	2	–	2	–	–	3	1	4	–	–
Intermittent Fever	3	2	5	–	–	4	1	5	–	–	1	3	4	–	–
Remittent Fever .	1	2	3	–	–	–	–	–	–	–	–	–	–	–	–
Typhoid Fever . .	5	6	11	1	1	–	–	–	–	–	7	5	12	1	–
Cerebro-spinal Meningitis . . .	–	–	–	–	–	–	–	–	–	–	–	1	1	–	–
Total	73	58	131	3	1	59	40	99	–	–	57	34	91	1	–

April.				May.				June.			
Mean Therm.	Rain Fall.	Direction and Force of Wind.		Mean Therm.	Rain Fall.	Direction and Force of Wind.		Mean Therm.	Rain Fall.	Direction and Force of Wind.	
48°	2.990	S. W. h.	N. E. h.	57½°	3.285	S. W. g.	S. E. h.	70⅓°	3.410	S. W. g.	N. W. g.

TABLE OF THE DISEASES AND MORTALITY

Of Male and Female Patients, from the Age of Five to Ten Years, for the Year 1872.— *Continued.*

1872.	July.					August.					September.				
	Sexes.			Deaths.		Sexes.			Deaths.		Sexes.			Deaths.	
List of Diseases.	Male.	Female.	Total.	Male.	Female.	Male.	Female.	Total.	Male.	Female.	Male.	Female.	Total.	Male.	Female.
Epilepsy	–	–	–	–	–	–	–	–	–	–	1	–	1	–	–
Convulsion	–	–	–	–	–	–	–	–	–	–	–	–	–	–	–
Chorea	–	–	–	–	–	–	–	–	–	–	–	–	–	–	–
Meningitis	1	1	2	–	–	–	–	–	–	–	–	–	–	–	–
Paralysis	–	–	–	–	–	–	–	–	–	–	–	–	–	–	–
Paralysis, Partial	–	1	1	–	–	–	1	1	–	–	1	1	2	–	–
Hemiplegia	–	1	1	–	–	–	1	1	–	–	–	–	–	–	–
Spinal Disease	–	–	–	–	–	–	–	–	–	–	–	–	–	–	–
Neuralgia	–	–	–	–	–	–	1	1	–	–	–	–	–	–	–
Conjunctivitis	–	1	1	–	–	1	–	1	–	–	–	–	–	–	–
Granular Lids	1	1	2	–	–	1	1	2	–	–	1	1	2	–	–
Keratitis	–	1	1	–	–	1	1	2	–	–	–	1	1	–	–
Catarrh	1	1	2	–	–	–	–	–	–	–	–	–	–	–	–
Epistaxis	–	2	2	–	–	–	–	–	–	–	–	–	–	–	–
Tonsillitis	–	–	–	–	–	–	1	1	–	–	–	1	1	–	–
Pharyngitis	–	–	–	–	–	–	–	–	–	–	–	–	–	–	–
Diphtheria	–	–	–	–	–	–	1	1	–	–	–	1	1	–	–
Laryngitis	–	–	–	–	–	–	–	–	–	–	–	–	–	–	–
Bronchitis	4	1	5	–	–	3	3	6	–	–	9	4	13	–	–
Bronchitis, Chronic	–	–	–	–	–	–	–	–	–	–	–	–	–	–	–
Asthma	–	–	–	–	–	1	–	1	–	–	–	–	–	–	–
Pertussis	2	–	2	–	–	3	3	6	–	–	3	1	4	–	–
Pneumonia	6	5	11	–	–	6	8	14	–	–	8	7	15	–	–
Pleuritis	1	1	2	–	–	–	–	–	–	–	–	–	–	–	–
Heart Disease	2	1	3	–	–	1	1	2	–	–	1	–	1	–	–
Dyspepsia	–	–	–	–	–	1	1	2	–	–	1	–	1	–	–
Diarrhœa	9	7	16	–	–	6	6	12	–	–	10	8	18	–	–
Cholera Morbus	3	1	4	–	–	2	1	3	–	–	–	–	–	–	–
Enteritis	–	2	2	–	–	–	1	1	–	–	–	–	–	–	–
Dysentery	–	1	1	–	–	–	1	1	–	–	2	–	2	–	–
Constipation	3	6	9	–	–	2	4	6	–	–	1	1	2	–	–
Hœmorrhoids	–	–	–	–	–	–	–	–	–	–	–	–	–	–	–
Helminthiasis	4	2	6	–	–	3	5	8	–	–	1	3	4	–	–
Jaundice	–	–	–	–	–	–	–	–	–	–	4	2	6	–	–
Bright's Disease	2	–	2	–	–	1	–	1	–	–	–	–	–	–	–
Ascites	–	–	–	–	–	1	–	1	–	–	–	1	1	–	–
Cystitis	–	–	–	–	–	–	–	–	–	–	–	–	–	–	–
Dysuria	–	–	–	–	–	–	1	1	–	–	–	–	–	–	–
Incontinence of Urine	–	–	–	–	–	1	–	1	–	–	–	–	–	–	–
Phthisis	–	–	–	–	–	2	–	2	–	–	1	1	2	–	1
Rheumatism	–	–	–	–	–	1	–	1	–	–	1	–	1	–	–
Rheumatism, Chronic	–	–	–	–	–	1	–	1	–	–	–	–	–	–	–
Erysipelas	1	–	1	–	–	–	–	–	–	–	–	–	–	–	–
Ephemeral Fever	–	–	–	–	–	–	–	–	–	–	4	2	6	–	–
Intermittent Fever	–	–	–	–	–	3	–	3	–	–	3	2	5	–	–
Remittent Fever	2	–	2	–	–	–	–	–	–	–	4	2	6	–	–
Typhoid Fever	2	–	2	–	–	11	5	16	–	1	8	3	11	1	–
Cerebro-spinal Meningitis	1	1	2	1	–	1	–	1	–	–	–	1	1	–	1
Total	45	37	82	1	–	53	47	100	–	1	64	43	107	1	2

July.				August.				September.			
Mean Therm.	Rain Fall.	Direction and Force of Wind.		Mean Therm.	Rain Fall.	Direction and Force of Wind.		Mean Therm.	Rain Fall.	Direction and Force of Wind.	
72½°	4.050	S. W. h.	N. W. g.	72°	2.560	N. W. g.	S. W. g.	64°	6.430	S. W. g.	S. E. g.

TABLE OF THE DISEASES AND MORTALITY

Of Male and Female Patients, from the Age of Five to Ten Years, for the Year 1872. — *Continued.*

1872.	October.					November.					December.					Total Patients.	Total Deaths.
	Sexes.			Deaths.		Sexes.			Deaths.		Sexes.			Deaths.			
List of Diseases.	Male.	Female.	Total.	Male.	Female.	Male.	Female.	Total.	Male.	Female.	Male.	Female.	Total.	Male.	Female.		
Epilepsy	–	–	–	–	–	1	–	–	–	–	–	–	–	–	–	6	–
Convulsion	–	2	2	–	–	–	1	2	–	–	–	1	1	–	–	25	–
Chorea	–	–	–	–	–	–	–	–	–	–	–	–	–	–	–	2	–
Meningitis	1	–	1	–	–	–	–	–	–	–	–	–	–	–	–	22	2
Paralysis	–	–	–	–	–	1	–	1	–	–	–	–	–	–	–	4	–
Paralysis, Partial	1	1	2	–	–	–	1	1	–	–	–	–	–	–	–	16	–
Hemiplegia	–	–	–	–	–	–	–	–	–	–	–	–	–	–	–	5	–
Spinal Disease	–	–	–	–	–	–	–	–	–	–	–	1	1	–	–	7	–
Neuralgia	–	–	–	–	–	–	–	–	–	–	–	2	2	–	–	15	–
Conjunctivitis	–	–	–	–	–	–	–	–	–	–	1	1	2	–	–	47	–
Granular Lids	–	1	1	–	–	1	1	2	–	–	1	–	1	–	–	32	–
Keratitis	1	1	2	–	–	1	–	1	–	–	1	1	2	–	–	25	–
Catarrh	1	–	1	–	–	9	2	11	–	–	16	4	20	–	–	153	–
Epistaxis	–	–	–	–	–	–	–	–	–	–	–	–	–	–	–	2	–
Tonsillitis	–	–	–	–	–	2	1	3	–	–	1	1	2	–	–	47	–
Pharyngitis	1	1	2	–	–	–	–	–	–	–	–	2	2	–	–	23	–
Diphtheria	–	–	–	–	–	–	1	1	–	–	–	2	2	–	–	22	–
Laryngitis	2	3	5	–	–	3	7	10	–	–	7	9	16	–	1	74	3
Bronchitis	6	2	8	–	–	24	19	43	–	–	47	27	74	–	–	388	1
Bronchitis, Chronic	1	–	1	–	–	3	–	3	–	–	7	2	9	–	–	43	–
Asthma	2	–	2	–	–	2	1	3	–	–	1	–	1	–	–	16	–
Pertussis	3	–	3	–	–	3	1	4	–	–	7	2	9	–	–	65	–
Pneumonia	9	4	13	–	–	7	5	12	–	–	7	5	12	–	–	167	4
Pleuritis	–	–	–	–	–	–	–	–	–	–	1	–	1	–	–	28	–
Heart Disease	–	–	–	–	–	1	–	1	–	–	–	1	1	–	–	21	–
Dyspepsia	1	1	2	–	–	–	–	–	–	–	–	–	–	–	–	40	–
Diarrhœa	7	6	13	–	–	8	4	12	–	–	6	8	14	–	–	168	–
Cholera Morbus	–	–	–	–	–	–	–	–	–	–	–	–	–	–	–	7	–
Enteritis	–	–	–	–	–	–	–	–	–	–	–	–	–	–	–	20	–
Dysentery	1	1	2	–	–	7	5	12	–	–	8	4	12	–	–	80	–
Constipation	2	3	5	–	–	6	5	11	–	–	6	5	11	–	–	110	–
Hœmorrhoids	–	2	2	–	–	–	2	2	–	–	–	–	–	–	–	9	–
Helminthiasis	1	7	8	–	–	5	4	9	–	–	4	3	7	–	–	121	–
Jaundice	3	2	5	–	–	8	1	9	–	–	5	1	6	–	–	46	–
Bright's Disease	1	–	1	–	–	–	–	–	–	–	–	–	–	–	–	4	–
Ascites	1	1	2	–	–	–	–	–	–	–	2	–	2	–	–	13	–
Cystitis	–	–	–	–	–	–	–	–	–	–	–	1	1	–	–	6	–
Dysuria	–	1	1	–	–	–	–	–	–	–	–	1	1	–	–	8	–
Incontinence of Urine	1	–	1	–	–	1	–	1	–	–	2	–	2	–	–	17	–
Phthisis	–	–	–	–	–	8	6	14	1	–	11	6	17	1	–	95	5
Rheumatism	3	1	4	–	–	9	7	16	–	–	13	6	19	–	–	95	1
Rheumatism, Chronic	1	–	1	–	–	2	–	2	–	–	2	1	3	–	–	12	–
Erysipelas	–	–	–	–	–	2	1	3	–	–	5	–	5	–	–	25	–
Ephemeral Fever	–	–	–	–	–	5	7	12	–	–	9	10	19	–	–	140	–
Intermittent Fever	4	2	6	–	–	11	6	17	–	–	16	10	26	–	–	149	–
Remittent Fever	9	4	13	–	–	9	8	17	–	–	10	6	16	–	–	88	–
Typhoid Fever	7	3	10	–	–	9	3	12	–	–	10	4	14	–	–	131	8
Cerebro-spinal Meningitis	–	–	–	–	–	–	–	–	–	–	–	–	–	–	.	5	2
Total	70	49	119	–	–	148	99	247	1	–	206	127	333	1	1	2,644	26

October.				November.				December.			
Mean Therm.	Rain Fall.	Direction and Force of Wind.		Mean Therm.	Rain Fall.	Direction and Force of Wind.		Mean Therm.	Rain Fall.	Direction and Force of Wind.	
52°	.650	N. E. g.	S. W. h.	32½°	.800	N. W. h.	N. W. g.	19°	.430	N. W. g.	S. W. g.

ADDITIONAL TABLE OF THE SICKNESS AND MORTALITY

OF PATIENTS, UNCLASSIFIED AS TO SEX, FROM THE AGE OF FIVE TO TEN YEARS, FOR THE YEAR 1872.

1872.	JANUARY.	FEBRUARY.	MARCH.	APRIL.	MAY.	JUNE.	JULY.	AUGUST.	SEPTEMBER.	OCTOBER.	NOVEMBER.	DECEMBER.	
LIST OF DISEASES.	Patients.	Patients.	Patients.	Patients.	Patients.	Patients.	Patients.	Patients.	Patients.	Patients.	Patients.	Patients.	Total Patients.
Abscess	3	5	2	1	6	4	5	–	3	–	4	3	36
Furoncle	4	2	1	–	–	–	–	–	–	2	5	6	20
Ulcer	10	6	4	2	1	1	1	2	1	1	2	1	32
Frost-bite	15	10	–	–	–	–	–	–	–	–	4	19	48
Contusion	4	2	1	–	–	1	1	1	–	–	–	2	12
Incised wound	8	12	4	2	1	1	1	2	–	2	3	2	38
Fracture of Clavicle	4	5	2	1	–	–	1	–	–	–	–	–	13
Fracture of Radius	–	–	–	–	–	–	–	–	1	–	–	–	1
Fracture of Tibia	5	2	4	1	–	–	–	–	1	–	–	–	13
Necrosis	1	2	1	–	–	–	–	–	1	–	–	1	6
Synovitis	2	3	2	1	1	2	1	2	1	1	2	3	21
Hernia	–	–	–	–	2	1	2	–	–	–	–	–	5
Hernia Inguinal	5	6	3	1	–	–	–	1	–	1	5	9	31
Atrophy	1	2	1	1	–	–	–	2	–	1	2	–	10
Anæmia	1	2	1	1	3	2	2	–	–	–	3	–	15
Debility	11	14	12	3	2	–	1	–	1	–	12	11	67
Inanition	1	2	1	1	–	2	–	1	2	1	1	1	13
Malaise	2	3	2	–	–	–	–	–	–	1	2	3	13
Cephalalgia	3	6	2	2	–	–	–	–	–	–	3	2	18
Hydrocephalus	–	–	–	–	2	–	–	–	–	–	–	–	2
Odontalgia	17	20	7	2	2	3	1	1	2	12	11	12	90
Otalgia	4	2	1	–	–	–	–	1	–	1	2	4	15
Otitis	2	1	4	5	2	1	1	–	–	1	1	2	20
Stomatitis	2	2	1	–	–	–	–	–	–	1	2	2	10
Parotiditis	6	5	4	2	–	1	–	–	–	6	9	13	46
Gastritis	2	1	1	1	–	1	–	2	1	2	4	2	17
Gastralgia	2	2	2	1	–	–	–	–	3	–	–	2	12
Colic	5	4	2	1	–	–	–	–	–	1	5	6	24
Total	120	121	65	29	22	20	17	15	17	34	82	106	648

ADDITIONAL TABLE OF THE SICKNESS AND MORTALITY

Of Patients, unclassified as to Sex, from the Age of Five to Ten Years, for the Year 1872. — *Continued.*

1872. List of Diseases.	January. Patients.	January. Deaths.	February. Patients.	February. Deaths.	March. Patients.	March. Deaths.	April. Patients.	April. Deaths.	May. Patients.	May. Deaths.	June. Patients.	June. Deaths.	July. Patients.	July. Deaths.	August. Patients.	August. Deaths.	September. Patients.	September. Deaths.	October. Patients.	October. Deaths.	November. Patients.	November. Deaths.	December. Patients.	December. Deaths.	Total Patients.	Total Deaths.
Vaginitis	4	-	6	-	2	-	1	-	-	-	1	-	-	-	1	-	-	-	1	-	3	-	5	-	24	-
Tumor of Neck	-	-	-	-	-	-	-	-	-	-	-	-	-	-	-	-	1	-	-	-	-	-	-	-	1	-
Adenitis	12	-	7	-	8	-	4	-	2	-	5	-	3	-	1	-	1	-	-	-	3	-	5	-	51	-
Scrofula	9	-	13	-	6	-	2	-	4	-	4	-	1	-	-	-	3	-	1	-	2	-	4	-	49	-
Morbus Coxarius	7	-	4	-	5	-	1	-	-	-	2	-	1	-	3	-	1	-	2	-	1	-	3	-	30	-
Lumbago	2	-	3	-	1	-	-	-	-	-	-	-	-	-	2	-	2	-	-	-	3	-	4	-	17	-
Coxalgia	4	-	2	-	1	-	2	-	-	-	-	-	-	-	-	-	-	-	-	-	4	-	6	-	19	-
Tabes Mesenterica	1	-	-	-	2	-	-	-	-	-	-	-	-	-	-	-	-	-	-	-	-	-	-	-	3	-
Rubeola	9	-	4	-	6	-	1	-	1	-	-	-	-	-	-	-	-	-	1	-	4	-	3	-	29	-
Varicella	9	-	8	-	2	-	-	-	-	-	-	-	-	-	-	-	-	-	-	-	4	-	3	-	26	-
Scarlatina	15	-	11	2	4	1	1	-	1	-	1	-	1	-	-	-	2	-	5	1	2	-	6	1	49	5
Syphilis	1	-	2	-	1	-	1	-	1	-	1	-	1	-	1	-	1	-	1	-	1	-	1	-	13	-
Syphilis Secondary	2	-	2	-	1	-	1	-	-	-	1	-	-	-	1	-	-	-	1	-	1	-	-	-	10	-
Syphilis Tertiary	1	-	-	-	2	-	-	-	-	-	-	-	-	-	-	-	1	-	-	-	-	-	-	-	4	-
Erythema	2	-	1	-	2	-	1	-	-	-	-	-	-	-	-	-	2	-	2	-	-	-	1	-	11	-
Eczema	15	-	16	-	9	-	8	-	4	-	1	-	1	-	4	-	3	-	2	-	15	-	17	-	95	-
Crustea Lactea	2	-	1	-	1	-	1	-	-	-	-	-	1	-	1	-	1	-	2	-	1	-	1	-	12	-
Herpes	2	-	3	-	2	-	1	-	2	-	1	-	-	-	3	-	1	-	2	-	1	-	2	-	20	-
Pemphigus	1	-	2	-	1	-	2	-	1	-	2	-	1	-	1	-	1	-	2	-	1	-	1	-	16	-
Impetigo	2	-	3	-	3	-	2	-	1	-	1	-	1	-	-	-	1	-	2	-	1	-	1	-	18	-
Scabies	1	-	1	-	1	-	-	-	-	-	-	-	-	-	-	-	1	-	-	-	1	-	1	-	6	-
Urticaria	2	-	1	-	1	-	-	-	1	-	1	-	-	-	1	-	-	-	-	-	-	-	1	-	8	-
Tinea Capitis	5	-	7	-	7	-	3	-	-	-	-	-	-	-	1	-	-	-	1	-	2	-	5	-	31	-
Pytiriasis	2	-	4	-	3	-	1	-	-	-	-	-	1	-	-	-	-	-	2	-	1	-	-	-	14	-
Psoriasis	1	-	2	-	1	-	1	-	-	-	-	-	-	-	1	-	-	-	1	-	1	-	1	-	9	-
Pediculi Capitis	1	-	2	-	1	-	1	-	-	-	1	-	1	-	-	-	1	-	2	-	1	-	2	-	13	-
Total	112	-	105	2	73	1	35	-	18	-	22		13		21	-	23	-	30	1	53	-	73	1	578	5

Male Patients classified	1,553
Female Patients classified	1,091
Patients unclassified by Sexes	1,226
Total Patients	3,870

Deaths of Male Patients	15
Deaths of Female Patients	11
Deaths of unclassified Patients	5
Total Deaths	31

TABLE OF THE DISEASES AND MORTALITY

Of Male and Female Patients, from the Age of Ten to Twenty Years, for the Year 1872.

1872.	January.					February.					March.				
	Sexes.			Deaths.		Sexes.			Deaths.		Sexes.			Deaths.	
List of Diseases.	Male.	Female.	Total.	Male.	Female.	Male.	Female.	Total.	Male.	Female.	Male.	Female.	Total.	Male.	Female.
Epilepsy	4	3	7	–	–	2	4	6	–	–	3	5	8	–	–
Convulsions	10	11	21	–	–	10	9	19	–	–	10	5	15	–	–
Chorea	3	3	6	–	–	1	4	5	–	–	–	2	2	–	–
Congestion of Brain	2	–	2	–	–	1	2	3	–	–	–	1	1	–	1
Meningitis	7	3	10	–	–	6	4	10	–	1	4	1	5	–	1
Paralysis	2	1	3	–	–	4	–	4	–	–	1	1	2	–	–
Paralysis, Partial	9	7	16	–	–	6	4	10	–	–	2	4	6	–	–
Hemiplegia	1	1	2	–	–	2	1	3	–	–	–	1	1	–	–
Spinal Disease	4	1	5	–	–	2	4	6	–	–	1	1	2	–	–
Neuralgia	7	14	21	–	–	1	9	10	–	–	1	3	4	–	–
Conjunctivitis	16	11	27	–	–	13	8	21	–	–	8	1	9	–	–
Granular Lids	17	12	29	–	–	10	7	17	–	–	8	2	10	–	–
Keratitis	2	3	5	–	–	5	6	11	–	–	1	3	4	–	–
Coryza	–	1	1	–	–	–	1	1	–	–	1	1	2	–	–
Catarrh	48	33	81	–	–	35	32	67	–	–	5	8	13	–	–
Epistaxis	2	2	4	–	–	2	1	3	–	–	–	2	2	–	–
Tonsilitis	21	24	45	–	–	16	25	41	–	–	4	15	19	–	–
Pharyngitis	19	13	32	–	–	13	11	24	–	–	10	4	14	–	–
Diphtheria	–	2	2	–	–	–	3	3	–	–	–	2	2	–	–
Laryngitis	2	7	9	–	–	1	8	9	–	–	2	5	7	–	–
Bronchitis	104	79	183	–	–	80	66	146	–	–	70	52	122	–	–
Bronchitis, Chronic	12	4	16	–	–	7	4	11	–	–	5	4	9	–	–
Bronchitis with Diarrhœa	7	2	9	–	–	4	–	4	–	–	2	–	2	–	–
Asthma	6	1	7	–	–	2	–	2	–	–	1	–	1	–	–
Pertussis	19	6	25	–	–	12	6	18	–	–	5	1	6	–	–
Congestion of Lungs	3	1	4	–	–	3	–	3	–	–	2	–	2	–	–
Pneumonia	24	11	35	1	–	8	11	19	–	–	3	9	12	1	1
Pleuritis	7	9	16	–	–	8	6	14	–	–	2	6	8	–	–
Heart Disease	4	10	14	–	–	4	9	13	–	–	2	4	6	–	–
Dyspepsia	9	23	32	–	–	12	23	35	–	–	5	17	22	–	–
Ulcer of Stomach	1	1	2	–	–	3	1	4	–	–	2	1	3	–	–
Diarrhœa	19	6	25	–	–	13	9	22	–	–	8	4	12	–	–
Cholera Morbus	–	–	–	–	–	–	–	–	–	–	–	–	–	–	–
Enteritis	2	4	6	–	–	3	7	10	–	–	1	3	4	–	–
Dysentery	2	–	2	–	–	1	–	1	–	–	4	2	6	–	–
Constipation	3	9	12	–	–	3	6	9	–	–	2	6	8	–	–
Hœmorrhoids	2	4	6	–	–	4	1	5	–	–	1	1	2	–	–
Helminthiasis	15	6	21	–	–	10	9	19	–	–	4	4	8	–	–
Hepatitis	–	2	2	–	–	–	2	2	–	–	1	1	2	–	–
Congestion of Liver	–	–	–	–	–	–	–	–	–	–	–	–	–	–	–
Jaundice	3	–	3	–	–	4	–	4	–	–	5	–	5	–	–
Nephritis	–	2	2	–	–	–	3	3	–	–	1	1	2	–	–
Bright's Disease	2	–	2	–	–	1	–	1	–	–	2	–	2	–	–
Ascites	–	2	2	–	–	1	–	1	–	–	1	–	1	–	–
Cystitis	2	5	7	–	–	2	4	6	–	–	–	1	1	–	–
Dysuria	–	2	2	–	–	–	1	1	–	–	–	3	3	–	–
Incontinence of Urine	4	2	6	–	–	7	2	9	–	–	2	–	2	1	–
Phthisis	9	12	21	–	–	4	8	12	–	–	5	4	9	–	–
Rheumatism	25	24	49	–	–	22	18	40	–	–	19	11	30	–	–
Rheumatism, Chronic	2	1	3	–	–	3	2	5	–	–	2	–	2	–	–
Erysipelas	7	2	9	–	–	5	1	6	–	–	4	1	5	–	
Ephemeral Fever	19	15	34	–	–	9	8	17	–	–	9	8	17	–	–
Intermittent Fever	30	32	62	–	–	52	30	82	–	–	17	17	34	–	–
Remittent Fever	13	10	23	–	–	11	6	17	–	–	7	4	11	–	–
Typhoid Fever	8	2	10	2	–	13	6	19	–	–	7	3	10	1	1
Cerebro-spinal Meningitis	–	–	–	–	–	–	–	–	–	–	1	–	1	–	–
Total	539	441	980	3	–	441	392	833	–	1	263	235	498	3	4

January.				February.				March.			
Mean Therm.	Rain Fall.	Direction and Force of Wind.		Mean Therm.	Rain Fall.	Direction and Force of Wind.		Mean Therm.	Rain Fall.	Direction and Force of Wind.	
26°	.670	S. W. h.	N. W. g.	27°	.690	S. W. g.	S. E. g.	29°	3.220	N. E. h.	N. W. g.

TABLE OF THE DISEASES AND MORTALITY
Of Male and Female Patients, from the Age of Ten to Twenty Years, for the Year 1872.— *Continued.*

1872.	April.					May.					June.				
	Sexes.		Total.	Deaths.		Sexes.		Total.	Deaths.		Sexes.		Total.	Deaths.	
List of Diseases.	Male.	Female.		Male.	Female.	Male.	Female.		Male.	Female.	Male.	Female.		Male.	Female.
Epilepsy	–	–	–	–	–	–	1	1	–	–	–	–	–	–	–
Convulsions	–	–	–	–	–	3	3	6	–	–	1	1	2	–	–
Chorea	1	–	1	–	–	1	–	1	–	–	–	2	2	–	–
Congestion of Brain	–	2	2	–	–	–	–	–	–	–	–	–	–	–	–
Meningitis	2	2	4	–	–	–	–	–	–	–	1	–	1	1	–
Paralysis	1	–	1	–	–	–	–	–	–	–	–	–	–	–	–
Paralysis, Partial	1	1	2	–	–	–	–	–	–	–	–	1	1	–	–
Hemiplegia	–	1	1	–	–	–	1	1	–	–	1	1	2	–	–
Spinal Disease	–	1	1	–	–	–	–	–	–	–	–	–	–	–	–
Neuralgia	1	6	7	–	–	–	3	3	–	–	–	–	–	–	–
Conjunctivitis	10	4	14	–	–	–	1	1	–	–	5	2	7	–	–
Granular Lids	2	–	2	–	–	–	–	–	–	–	1	1	2	–	–
Keratitis	–	1	1	–	–	–	1	1	–	–	–	1	1	–	–
Coryza	–	1	1	–	–	–	–	–	–	–	–	–	–	–	–
Catarrh	2	4	6	–	–	–	1	1	–	–	–	–	–	–	–
Epistaxis	–	–	–	–	–	–	1	1	–	–	–	–	–	–	–
Tonsillitis	8	1	4	–	–	–	2	2	–	–	1	3	4	–	–
Pharyngitis	8	8	11	–	–	1	1	2	–	–	2	3	5	–	–
Diphtheria	–	1	1	–	–	–	1	1	–	–	–	–	–	–	–
Laryngitis	1	2	3	–	–	1	2	3	–	–	–	–	–	–	–
Bronchitis	32	25	57	–	–	7	2	9	–	–	4	5	9	–	–
Bronchitis, Chronic	2	–	2	–	–	1	–	1	–	–	1	–	1	–	–
Bronchitis with Diarrhœa	–	1	1	–	–	–	–	–	–	–	1	–	1	–	–
Asthma	1	–	1	–	–	1	–	1	–	–	1	–	1	–	–
Pertussis	–	1	1	–	–	1	–	1	–	–	1	1	2	–	–
Congestion of Lungs	–	–	–	–	–	1	–	1	–	–	–	–	–	–	–
Pneumonia	1	5	6	–	–	1	2	3	–	–	1	3	4	–	–
Pleuritis	–	2	2	–	–	1	1	2	–	–	–	2	2	–	–
Heart Disease	2	3	5	–	–	–	–	–	–	–	–	1	1	–	–
Dyspepsia	4	3	7	–	–	–	2	2	–	–	1	2	3	–	–
Ulcer of Stomach	1	–	1	–	–	–	–	–	–	–	–	–	–	–	–
Diarrhœa	3	2	5	–	–	–	1	1	–	–	2	6	8	–	1
Cholera Morbus	–	–	–	–	–	–	–	–	–	–	–	2	2	–	–
Enteritis	–	2	2	–	–	–	1	1	–	–	–	3	3	–	–
Dysentery	1	3	4	–	–	–	–	–	–	–	–	–	–	–	–
Constipation	1	3	4	–	–	–	–	–	–	–	–	2	2	–	–
Hœmorrhoids	–	1	1	–	–	–	–	–	–	–	1	1	2	–	–
Helminthiasis	3	2	5	–	–	–	2	2	–	–	1	–	1	–	–
Hepatitis	–	2	2	–	–	–	–	–	–	–	–	–	–	–	–
Congestion of Liver	–	–	–	–	–	–	–	–	–	–	–	–	–	–	–
Jaundice	–	–	–	–	–	–	–	–	–	–	–	–	–	–	–
Nephritis	–	1	1	–	–	–	1	1	–	–	–	1	1	–	–
Bright's Disease	–	–	–	–	–	–	–	–	–	–	–	–	–	–	–
Ascites	–	1	1	–	–	–	–	–	–	–	–	–	–	–	–
Cystitis	–	–	–	–	–	–	–	–	–	–	–	–	–	–	–
Dysuria	–	–	–	–	–	–	–	–	–	–	–	–	–	–	–
Incontinence of Urine	1	1	2	–	–	2	–	2	–	–	–	1	1	–	–
Phthisis	4	2	6	–	–	1	3	4	2	–	4	4	8	–	–
Rheumatism	5	6	11	–	–	5	3	8	–	–	3	1	4	–	–
Rheumatism, Chronic	2	–	2	–	–	–	–	–	–	–	1	–	1	–	–
Erysipelas	3	1	4	–	–	2	–	2	–	–	2	–	2	–	–
Ephemeral Fever	3	1	4	–	–	2	1	3	–	–	–	–	–	–	–
Intermittent Fever	14	7	21	–	–	5	2	7	–	–	3	–	3	–	–
Remittent Fever	2	–	2	–	–	1	–	1	–	–	1	1	2	–	–
Typhoid Fever	2	–	2	2	–	1	–	1	–	–	–	–	–	–	–
Cerebro-spinal Meningitis	1	–	1	–	–	1	–	1	–	–	2	–	2	–	–
Total	115	110	225	2	–	39	39	78	2	–	42	51	93	1	1

April.				May.				June.			
Mean Therm.	Rain Fall.	Direction and Force of Wind.		Mean Therm.	Rain Fall.	Direction and Force of Wind.		Mean Therm.	Rain Fall.	Direction and Force of Wind.	
48°	2.990	S. W. h	N. E. h.	57½°	3.285	S. W. g	S. E. h.	70⅛°	3.410	S. W. g.	N. W. g.

TABLE OF THE DISEASES AND MORTALITY

Of Male and Female Patients, from the Age of Ten to Twenty Years, for the Year 1872. — *Continued.*

1872.	July.					August.					September.				
	Sexes.			Deaths.		Sexes.			Deaths.		Sexes.			Deaths.	
List of Diseases.	Male.	Female.	Total.	Male.	Female.	Male.	Female.	Total.	Male.	Female.	Male.	Female.	Total.	Male.	Female.
Epilepsy	–	–	–	–	–	–	–	–	–	–	–	–	–	–	–
Convulsions	2	–	2	–	–	–	–	–	–	–	–	1	1	–	–
Chorea	–	2	2	–	–	3	–	3	–	–	–	2	2	–	–
Congestion of Brain	–	1	1	–	–	–	1	1	–	–	–	–	–	–	–
Meningitis	1	1	2	–	–	–	2	2	–	–	1	–	1	–	–
Paralysis	–	–	–	–	–	–	1	1	–	–	–	–	–	–	–
Paralysis, Partial	2	1	3	–	–	–	–	–	–	–	2	–	2	–	–
Hemiplegia	–	1	1	–	–	–	1	1	–	–	–	1	1	–	–
Spinal Disease	–	1	1	–	–	1	–	1	–	–	–	1	1	–	–
Neuralgia	–	–	–	–	–	–	–	–	–	–	–	–	–	–	–
Conjunctivitis	2	2	4	–	–	–	–	–	–	–	–	3	3	–	–
Granular Lids	–	–	–	–	–	4	–	4	–	–	1	1	2	–	–
Keratitis	1	1	2	–	–	–	–	–	–	–	–	–	–	–	–
Coryza	–	–	–	–	–	–	–	–	–	–	–	–	–	–	–
Catarrh	1	1	2	–	–	1	–	1	–	–	–	–	–	–	–
Epistaxis	–	–	–	–	–	1	–	1	–	–	–	–	–	–	–
Tonsillitis	1	–	1	–	–	2	–	2	–	–	2	2	4	–	–
Pharyngitis	1	–	1	–	–	3	2	5	–	–	–	1	1	–	–
Diphtheria	–	–	–	–	–	–	–	–	–	–	–	–	–	–	–
Laryngitis	1	–	1	–	–	–	–	–	–	–	–	1	1	–	–
Bronchitis	4	2	6	–	–	3	–	3	–	–	2	5	7	–	–
Bronchitis, Chronic	–	1	1	–	–	–	–	–	–	–	–	–	–	–	–
Bronchitis with Diarrhœa	–	–	–	–	–	1	1	2	–	–	–	1	1	–	–
Asthma	–	1	1	–	–	–	1	1	–	–	–	–	–	–	–
Pertussis	–	–	–	–	–	–	–	–	–	–	–	2	2	–	–
Congestion of Lungs	–	–	–	–	–	–	–	–	–	–	1	2	3	–	–
Pneumonia	–	2	2	–	1	–	–	–	–	–	–	2	2	–	–
Pleuritis	1	1	2	–	–	–	3	3	–	–	1	2	3	–	–
Heart Disease	–	1	1	–	–	–	–	–	–	–	–	–	–	–	–
Dyspepsia	2	5	7	–	–	2	2	4	–	–	–	4	4	–	–
Ulcer of Stomach	2	–	2	–	–	–	–	–	–	–	1	–	1	–	–
Diarrhœa	7	9	16	–	–	18	6	24	–	–	4	2	6	–	–
Cholera Morbus	3	4	7	–	–	3	5	8	–	–	3	1	4	–	–
Enteritis	–	2	2	–	–	–	2	2	–	–	–	3	3	–	–
Dysentery	1	3	4	–	–	5	1	6	1	–	6	4	10	–	–
Constipation	–	1	1	–	–	1	–	1	–	–	–	–	–	–	–
Hœmorrhoids	–	–	–	–	–	2	–	2	–	–	–	–	–	–	–
Helminthiasis	–	2	2	–	–	5	–	5	–	–	5	1	6	–	–
Hepatitis	–	1	1	–	–	2	1	3	–	–	–	–	–	–	–
Congestion of Liver	–	–	–	–	–	–	–	–	–	–	–	–	–	–	–
Jaundice	–	–	–	–	–	–	–	–	–	–	–	–	–	–	–
Nephritis	–	1	1	–	–	1	–	1	–	–	–	–	–	–	–
Bright's Disease	1	–	1	–	–	–	–	–	–	–	–	–	–	–	–
Ascites	–	–	–	–	–	–	–	–	–	–	–	–	–	–	–
Cystitis	–	–	–	–	–	–	–	–	–	–	–	–	–	–	–
Dysuria	–	–	–	–	–	–	–	–	–	–	–	–	–	–	–
Incontinence of Urine	2	1	3	–	–	1	–	1	–	–	–	–	–	–	–
Phthisis	2	5	7	–	–	2	–	2	–	–	1	1	2	1	–
Rheumatism	6	1	7	–	–	3	–	3	–	–	3	1	4	–	–
Rheumatism, Chronic	–	–	–	–	–	1	–	1	–	–	–	–	–	–	–
Erysipelas	–	–	–	–	–	1	–	1	–	–	–	–	–	–	–
Ephemeral Fever	1	–	1	–	–	–	–	–	–	–	–	1	1	–	–
Intermittent Fever	5	1	6	–	–	9	1	10	–	–	23	25	48	–	–
Remittent Fever	5	–	5	–	–	4	–	4	–	–	8	4	12	–	–
Typhoid Fever	2	–	2	–	–	6	2	8	–	–	8	2	10	–	–
Cerebro-spinal Meningitis	–	–	–	–	–	2	–	2	–	–	–	–	–	–	–
Total	56	55	111	–	1	87	32	119	1	–	72	76	148	1	–

July.				August.				September.			
Mean Therm.	Rain Fall.	Direction and Force of Wind.		Mean Therm.	Rain Fall.	Direction and Force of Wind.		Mean Therm.	Rain Fall.	Direction and Force of Wind.	
72½°	4.050	S. W. h.	N. W. g	72°	2.560	N. W. g.	S. W. g	64°	6.430	S. W. g.	S. E. g.

TABLE OF THE DISEASES AND MORTALITY

Of Male and Female Patients, from the Age of Ten to Twenty Years, for the Year 1872. — *Continued.*

1872.	October.					November.					December.						
	Sexes.			Deaths.		Sexes.			Deaths.		Sexes.			Deaths.			
List of Diseases.	Male.	Female.	Total.	Male.	Female.	Male.	Female.	Total.	Male	Female.	Male.	Female.	Total.	Male.	Female.	Total Patients.	Total Deaths.
Epilepsy	–	–	–	–	–	1	–	1	–	–	–	1	1	–	–	24	–
Convulsions	–	–	–	–	–	4	–	4	–	–	3	2	5	–	–	75	–
Chorea	1	–	1	–	–	–	–	–	–	–	–	1	1	–	–	26	–
Congestion of Brain	2	–	2	–	–	2	1	3	–	–	–	–	–	–	–	15	1
Meningitis	–	–	–	–	–	2	–	2	–	–	–	–	–	–	–	37	3
Paralysis	2	–	2	–	–	–	–	–	–	–	–	1	1	–	–	14	–
Paralysis, Partial	–	–	–	–	–	–	1	1	–	–	–	–	–	–	–	41	–
Hemiplegia	–	2	2	–	–	–	1	1	–	–	–	1	1	–	–	17	–
Spinal Disease	1	–	1	–	–	–	–	–	–	–	–	–	–	–	–	18	–
Neuralgia	–	2	2	–	–	–	2	2	–	–	–	2	2	–	–	51	–
Conjunctivitis	3	2	5	–	–	8	3	11	–	–	5	2	7	–	–	109	–
Granular Lids	1	–	1	–	–	2	–	2	–	–	1	–	1	–	–	70	–
Keratitis	3	1	4	–	–	3	2	5	–	–	2	2	4	–	–	38	–
Coryza	–	2	2	–	–	–	–	–	–	–	–	–	–	–	–	7	–
Catarrh	2	–	2	–	–	2	–	2	–	–	7	6	13	–	–	188	–
Epistaxis	1	–	1	–	–	–	–	–	–	–	–	–	–	–	–	12	–
Tonsillitis	5	7	12	–	–	1	2	3	–	–	3	7	10	–	–	147	–
Pharyngitis	7	5	12	–	–	8	6	14	–	–	13	6	19	–	–	140	–
Diphtheria	1	2	3	–	–	–	2	2	–	–	1	4	5	–	–	19	–
Laryngitis	–	1	1	–	–	3	6	9	–	–	3	6	9	–	–	52	–
Bronchitis	10	2	12	–	–	16	13	29	–	–	43	17	60	–	–	643	–
Bronchitis, Chronic	1	–	1	–	–	1	2	3	–	–	9	5	14	–	–	59	–
Bronchitis with Diarrhœa	–	–	–	–	–	–	2	2	–	–	3	8	11	–	–	33	–
Asthma	1	–	1	–	–	–	1	1	–	–	9	3	12	–	–	29	–
Pertussis	1	–	1	–	–	–	–	–	–	–	9	4	13	–	–	69	–
Congestion of Lungs	1	–	1	–	–	2	3	5	–	–	3	1	4	–	–	23	–
Pneumonia	4	2	6	–	–	1	4	5	–	–	12	8	20	–	–	114	4
Pleuritis	–	4	4	–	–	–	1	1	–	–	10	6	16	–	–	73	–
Heart Disease	–	1	1	–	–	–	1	1	–	–	3	9	12	–	–	54	–
Dyspepsia	–	5	5	–	–	1	2	3	–	–	5	10	15	–	–	139	–
Ulcer of Stomach	–	–	–	–	–	1	–	1	–	–	–	–	–	–	–	14	–
Diarrhœa	4	3	7	–	–	1	–	1	–	–	12	6	18	–	–	145	1
Cholera Morbus	–	–	–	–	–	–	–	–	–	–	–	1	–	–	–	21	–
Enteritis	1	2	3	1	–	1	1	2	–	–	–	3	3	–	–	41	1
Dysentery	2	–	2	–	–	1	1	2	–	–	–	2	2	–	–	39	1
Constipation	1	1	2	–	–	–	1	1	–	–	3	9	12	–	–	52	–
Hœmorrhoids	1	2	3	–	–	1	3	4	–	–	5	–	5	–	–	30	–
Helminthiasis	1	1	2	–	–	5	2	7	–	–	9	6	15	–	–	93	–
Hepatitis	–	1	1	–	–	–	2	2	–	–	–	1	1	–	–	16	–
Congestion of Liver	–	–	–	–	–	1	–	1	–	–	–	–	–	–	–	1	–
Jaundice	1	–	1	–	–	2	–	2	–	–	1	–	1	–	–	16	–
Nephritis	1	–	1	–	–	–	–	–	–	–	–	1	1	–	–	14	–
Bright's Disease	–	–	–	–	–	–	–	–	–	–	–	–	–	–	–	6	1
Ascites	1	–	1	–	–	–	–	–	–	–	–	–	–	–	–	6	–
Cystitis	–	–	–	–	–	–	–	–	–	–	–	1	1	–	–	15	–
Dysuria	–	–	–	–	–	–	–	-	–	–	–	–	–	–	–	6	–
Incontinence of Urine	2	–	2	–	–	–	–	–	–	–	2	2	4	–	–	32	–
Phthisis	4	1	5	–	–	3	–	3	1	–	14	4	18	1	–	97	5
Rheumatism	5	2	7	–	–	2	3	5	–	–	17	13	30	–	–	198	–
Rheumatism Chronic	–	–	–	–	–	–	–	–	–	–	3	3	6	–	–	20	–
Erysipelas	–	–	–	–	–	–	1	1	–	–	3	2	5	–	–	35	–
Ephemeral Fever	2	–	2	–	–	2	–	2	–	–	12	9	21	–	-	102	–
Intermittent Fever	18	7	25	–	–	9	3	12	–	–	26	25	51	–	–	361	–
Remittent Fever	5	–	5	–	–	3	2	5	–	–	10	8	18	–	–	105	–
Typhoid Fever	2	–	2	1	–	2	3	5	1	1	5	4	9	–	1	78	10
Cerebro-spinal Meningitis	–	–	–	–	–	–	–	-	–	–	–	–	–	–	–	7	–
Total	98	58	156	2	–	91	77	168	2	1	266	211	477	1	1	3,886	27

October.				November.				December.			
Mean Therm.	Rain Fall.	Direction and Force of Wind.		Mean Therm.	Rain Fall.	Direction and Force of Wind.		Mean Therm.	Rain Fall.	Direction and Force of Wind.	
52°	.650	N. E. g.	S. W. h.	32½°	.800	N. W. h.	N. W. g.	19°	.430	N. W. g.	S. W. g.

ADDITIONAL TABLE OF THE SICKNESS AND MORTALITY

Of Patients, Unclassified as to Sex, from the Age of Ten to Twenty Years, for the Year 1872.

1872.	Jan.	Feb.	Mar.	April.	May.	June.	July.	Aug.	Sept.	Oct.	Nov.	Dec.	
List of Diseases.	Patients.	Patients.	Patients.	Patients.	Patients.	Patients.	Patients.	Patients.	Patients.	Patients.	Patients.	Patients.	Total Patients.
Abscess	14	6	2	–	4	3	1	3	4	3	5	6	51
Furoncle	4	5	3	–	–	–	2	–	–	–	–	–	14
Ulcer	29	18	6	–	–	5	7	3	2	1	1	13	85
Ulcer of Leg	5	6	4	2	–	1	–	2	–	1	1	4	26
Frost-bite	25	16	1	–	–	–	–	–	–	–	16	18	76
Contusion or Contused wound	15	15	5	–	3	–	2	2	–	1	1	7	51
Incised wound	8	11	8	4	1	4	6	1	2	1	1	3	50
Paronychia	3	2	4	2	1	2	1	2	–	2	–	3	22
Varix	1	2	1	–	1	–	1	–	2	–	1	1	10
Fracture of Clavicle	5	6	1	–	–	–	–	–	–	2	–	–	14
Fracture of Radius	–	–	–	–	–	–	1	1	–	–	–	–	2
Dislocation of Shoulder	2	2	2	1	–	–	–	–	–	1	–	1	9
Periostitis	6	9	4	1	–	–	1	–	1	2	–	1	25
Necrosis	11	13	9	7	1	1	1	2	1	1	2	5	54
Arthritis	1	2	1	1	1	1	1	1	–	2	1	1	13
Synovitis	5	3	2	1	–	1	2	–	1	–	1	–	16
Hernia	1	2	2	1	–	–	3	4	2	2	1	1	19
Hernia Inguinal	9	6	4	3	2	–	2	3	1	–	–	11	41
Atrophy	11	12	3	1	–	2	1	1	1	1	1	11	45
Anæmia	12	10	6	2	–	1	2	4	–	3	1	12	53
Debility	14	9	6	1	–	2	2	4	5	–	1	16	60
Inanition	3	2	1	1	–	–	–	1	–	1	–	1	10
Malaise	7	7	6	5	–	–	2	–	2	–	–	3	32
Hysteria	2	4	8	5	2	–	1	1	2	–	1	1	27
Cephalalgia	12	10	16	12	14	9	5	1	1	1	9	15	105
Vertigo	4	3	2	–	1	–	–	1	–	2	–	1	14
Pareplegia	2	3	2	1	–	–	–	1	–	2	–	1	12
Odontalgia	46	34	44	25	16	11	6	3	2	2	14	39	242
Otalgia	6	5	1	1	1	–	2	1	1	2	3	6	29
Otitis	15	12	10	4	2	4	3	2	2	2	1	3	60
Strabismus	1	2	1	1	–	–	1	1	–	–	1	2	10
Stomatitis	4	2	2	1	–	2	–	1	3	3	1	2	21
Parotiditis	2	1	1	1	–	–	2	–	1	1	1	1	11
Angina	2	1	1	1	–	–	1	–	1	1	1	2	11
Carditis	1	2	1	–	–	–	1	2	–	1	–	1	9
Gastritis	4	5	2	1	–	–	2	–	–	3	–	–	17
Gastralgia	4	6	2	1	–	–	1	1	1	1	–	1	18
Fistula in Ano	1	2	1	1	1	–	–	1	–	2	–	1	10
Colic	8	5	3	1	–	3	–	2	3	1	–	1	27
Tympanitis	1	1	2	1	–	–	1	–	1	–	1	–	8
Nephralgia	1	2	1	1	–	1	1	–	1	–	1	–	9
Gonorrhœa	3	4	1	1	–	1	–	–	–	–	1	–	11
Total	310	268	182	92	51	54	65	52	43	48	69	195	1,429

ADDITIONAL TABLE OF THE SICKNESS AND MORTALITY

F PATIENTS, UNCLASSIFIED AS TO SEX, FROM THE AGE OF TEN TO TWENTY YEARS, FOR THE YEAR 1872. — *Continued.*

1872.	JAN.	FEB.	MARCH.		APRIL.	MAY.		JUNE.	JULY.	AUG.	SEPT.	OCT.	NOV.	DEC.		
ST OF DISEASES.	Patients.	Patients.	Patients.	Death.	Patients.	Patients.	Death.	Patients.	Patients.	Patients.	Patients.	Patients.	Patients.	Patients.	Total Patients.	Total Deaths.
ethritis . .	2	4	5	-	1	-	-	2	-	1	1	2	-	1	19	-
bo . . .	9	6	2	-	1	-	-	2	1	2	1	6	9	12	51	-
etritis . .	-	-	-	-	-	-	-	-	-	1	-	-	1	-	2	-
erine disease	15	17	10	-	5	3	-	2	2	3	1	3	2	13	76	-
ortion . .	21	22	19	-	5	2	-	4	1	2	2	-	-	11	89	-
ucorrhea .	5	7	6	-	1	-	-	1	-	1	-	-	-	-	21	-
lorosis . .	6	8	5	-	2	1	-	3	-	2	1	-	-	-	28	-
nenorrhea .	12	14	19	-	3	6	-	13	8	2	2	3	2	12	96	-
smenorrhea	4	3	7	-	2	1	-	1	2	-	2	1	-	2	25	-
norrhagia .	3	4	2	-	1	-	-	-	1	-	1	-	1	-	13	-
aritis . .	2	1	1	-	1	-	-	-	1	-	1	-	1	-	8	-
mor of Neck	3	4	1	-	-	-	-	-	1	3	-	-	-	-	12	-
mor of Jaw	2	1	1	-	-	-	-	-	-	-	-	-	1	1	6	-
itre . . .	-	-	-	-	-	-	-	-	-	-	1	1	1	3	6	-
lenitis . .	14	9	6	-	3	3	-	3	6	1	3	3	2	12	65	-
rofula . .	12	14	7	-	3	1	-	7	4	2	1	2	3	14	70	-
tt's disease .	1	2	1	-	1	1	-	1	1	-	-	1	-	1	10	-
rbus Coxarius . . .	9	8	4	-	3	1	1	-	2	3	1	4	1	1	37	1
ite Swellings	2	2	1	-	1	-	-	-	1	-	1	-	1	-	9	-
bes Mesenterica . .	1	2	2	-	-	-	-	-	-	-	-	-	2	3	10	-
rticollis . .	2	3	2	-	1	-	-	1	-	1	-	1	-	-	11	-
mbago . .	3	4	3	-	-	-	-	-	-	2	-	1	3	1	17	-
atica . .	1	1	2	-	-	-	-	1	1	2	-	1	-	1	10	-
xalgia . .	4	2	2	-	1	1	-	-	-	1	2	1	1	2	17	-
beola . .	15	19	15	-	9	1	-	1	1	1	2	2	12	14	92	-
ricella . .	15	10	6	-	1	-	-	4	2	5	-	4	6	14	67	-
rlatina . .	14	9	3	1	-	1	-	-	1	2	1	2	2	11	46	1
acco poisoning . .	1	2	2	-	1	-	-	-	-	-	-	-	-	-	6	-
hilis . .	9	6	5	-	4	2	-	2	1	2	4	4	1	2	42	-
hilis Secondary . .	1	2	1	-	1	1	-	1	2	2	1	1	2	3	18	-
hilis Tertiary . . .	1	1	1	-	-	1	-	-	-	1	-	1	1	1	8	-
thema . .	2	4	1	-	1	3	-	-	1	-	1	-	1	1	15	-
ema . .	12	14	19	-	0	1	-	1	1	3	1	1	12	12	87	-
stea Lactea	1	1	1	-	11	-	-	-	-	-	-	-	-	-	4	-
pes . . .	9	9	6	-	2	3	-	2	1	4	6	5	12	12	71	-
phigus .	2	3	2	-	1	-	-	-	-	1	-	1	-	1	11	-
petigo . .	3	5	1	-	1	1	-	-	-	-	2	1	-	1	15	-
bies . .	7	5	3	-	1	1	-	-	-	-	1	3	2	5	28	-
icaria . .	3	4	3	-	2	-	-	-	2	-	-	1	-	1	16	-
ea Capitas	13	13	9	-	6	2	-	2	1	1	3	3	3	9	65	-
iriasis . .	4	6	2	-	2	1	-	1	2	1	1	2	1	2	25	-
riasis . .	1	1	1	-	1	2	-	1	1	1	1	2	1	2	15	-
Total .	246	252	189	1	79	40	1	56	48	53	45	63	87	181	1,339	2

Male Patients classified	2,109	Deaths of Male Patients	18
Female Patients classified	1,777	Deaths of Female Patients	9
Patients unclassified by Sexes	2,768	Deaths of unclassified Patients	2
Total Patients	6,654	Total Deaths	29

TABLE OF THE DISEASES AND MORTALITY

Of Male and Female Patients, from the Age of Twenty to Forty Years, for the Year 1872.

1872.	January.					February.					March.				
List of Diseases.	Sexes.		Total.	Deaths.		Sexes.		Total.	Deaths.		Sexes.		Total.	Deaths.	
	Male.	Female.		Male.	Female.	Male.	Female.		Male.	Female.	Male.	Female.		Male.	Female.
Epilepsy	3	9	12	–	–	7	8	15	–	–	3	6	9	–	–
Convulsions	2	4	6	–	–	3	2	5	–	–	5	7	12	–	–
Chorea	5	–	5	–	–	5	2	7	–	–	4	–	4	–	–
Congestion of Brain	2	–	2	–	–	1	–	1	–	–	1	–	1	–	–
Hydrocepalus	1	–	1	–	–	–	–	–	–	–	2	–	2	–	–
Encephalitis	4	5	9	–	–	4	4	8	–	–	1	3	4	–	–
Meningitis	7	3	10	–	–	8	4	12	–	–	2	4	6	–	–
Locomotor-ataxia	4	1	5	–	–	4	–	4	–	–	2	–	2	–	–
Paralysis	3	2	5	–	–	5	1	6	–	–	2	1	3	–	–
Paralysis, Partial	6	3	9	–	–	8	2	10	–	–	3	3	6	–	–
Hemiplegia	1	3	4	–	–	3	3	6	–	–	2	–	2	–	–
Spinal Disease	5	–	5	–	–	4	2	6	–	–	8	1	9	–	–
Neuralgia	31	52	83	–	–	28	34	62	–	–	8	35	43	–	–
Ophthalmia	4	–	4	–	–	4	1	5	–	–	3	1	4	–	–
Conjunctivitis	20	9	29	–	–	15	6	21	–	–	9	3	12	–	–
Granular Lids	4	1	5	–	–	3	1	4	–	–	1	2	3	–	–
Keratitis	14	8	22	–	–	6	9	15	–	–	4	9	13	–	–
Opacity of Cornea	6	4	10	–	–	6	–	6	–	–	2	–	2	–	–
Iritis	1	5	6	–	–	2	5	7	–	–	1	3	4	–	–
Ozœna	–	–	–	–	–	–	–	–	–	–	–	–	–	–	–
Coryza	1	3	4	–	–	2	1	3	–	–	1	1	2	–	–
Catarrh	72	60	132	–	–	40	59	99	–	–	9	22	31	–	–
Epistaxis	1	3	4	–	–	5	1	6	–	–	2	–	2	–	–
Tonsillitis	5	7	12	–	–	3	12	15	–	–	3	8	11	–	–
Pharyngitis	19	10	29	–	–	13	22	35	–	–	7	8	15	–	–
Diphtheria	1	4	5	–	1	4	8	12	–	–	4	5	9	–	–
Laryngitis	2	7	9	–	–	1	5	6	–	–	1	3	4	–	–
Bronchitis	200	111	311	–	–	147	125	272	–	–	121	81	202	–	–
Bronchitis, Chronic	13	8	21	–	–	14	11	25	–	–	11	8	19	–	–
Bronchitis with Diarrhœa	20	11	31	–	–	14	10	24	–	–	8	7	15	–	–
Asthma	15	14	29	–	–	15	4	19	–	–	6	4	10	–	–
Pertussis	13	6	19	–	–	7	10	17	–	–	5	11	16	–	–
Congestion of Lungs	8	2	10	–	–	7	2	9	–	–	3	1	4	–	–
Pneumonia	30	37	67	1	–	26	21	47	–	1	10	11	21	1	–
Emphysema Pulm.	2	–	2	–	–	1	–	1	–	–	1	–	1	–	–
Pleuritis	22	20	42	–	–	14	14	28	–	–	8	15	23	–	–
Total	547	412	959	1	1	429	389	818	–	1	263	263	526	1	–

TABLE OF THE DISEASES AND MORTALITY

Of Male and Female Patients, from the Age of Twenty to Forty Years, for the Year 1872. — *Continued.*

1872.	April.					May.					June.				
	Sexes.			Deaths.		Sexes.			Deaths.		Sexes.			Deaths.	
List of Diseases.	Male.	Female.	Total.	Male.	Female.	Male.	Female.	Total.	Male.	Female.	Male.	Female.	Total.	Male.	Female.
Epilepsy . . .	–	2	2	–	–	2	1	3	–	–	1	–	1	–	–
Convulsions . .	3	1	4	–	–	1	–	1	–	–	3	–	3	–	–
Chorea	1	–	1	–	–	1	–	1	–	–	1	1	2	–	–
Congestion of Brain	1	–	1	–	–	1	–	1	–	–	1	–	1	–	–
Hydrocephalus .	1	–	1	–	–	1	–	1	–	–	–	–	–	–	–
Encephalitis . .	–	1	1	–	–	–	–	–	–	–	–	–	–	–	–
Meningitis . . .	1	–	1	1	–	–	–	–	2	–	–	–	–	–	–
Locomotor-ataxia .	–	–	–	–	–	2	–	2	–	–	1	–	1	–	–
Paralysis . . .	2	–	2	–	–	1	–	1	–	–	1	–	1	–	–
Paralysis, Partial .	1	–	1	–	–	1	3	4	–	–	2	–	2	–	–
Hemiplegia . .	–	1	1	–	–	–	–	–	–	–	–	–	–	–	–
Spinal Disease . .	3	1	4	–	–	–	–	–	–	–	–	–	–	–	–
Neuralgia . . .	4	11	15	–	–	3	4	7	–	–	1	3	4	–	–
Ophthalmia . .	1	1	2	–	–	1	–	1	–	–	1	1	2	–	–
Conjunctivitis . .	6	3	9	–	–	3	2	5	–	–	5	3	8	–	–
Granular Lids . .	1	1	2	–	–	3	1	4	–	–	1	–	1	–	–
Keratitis . . .	1	3	4	–	–	3	4	7	–	–	2	4	6	–	–
Opacity of Cornea	1	–	1	–	–	–	–	–	–	–	–	–	–	–	–
Iritis	–	1	1	–	–	–	–	–	–	–	–	2	2	–	–
Ozœna	–	–	–	–	–	–	–	–	–	–	–	–	–	–	–
Coryza	1	–	1	–	–	–	–	–	–	–	–	1	1	–	–
Catarrh	4	4	8	–	–	–	3	3	–	–	1	4	5	–	–
Epistaxis . . .	–	–	–	–	–	–	–	–	–	–	–	–	–	–	–
Tonsillitis . . .	2	3	5	–	–	–	2	2	–	–	–	1	1	–	–
Pharyngitis . .	1	3	4	–	–	1	3	4	–	–	2	1	3	–	–
Diphtheria . . .	–	2	2	–	–	–	–	–	–	–	–	–	–	–	–
Laryngitis . . .	–	2	2	–	–	1	1	2	–	–	2	2	4	–	–
Bronchitis . . .	38	26	64	–	–	36	30	66	–	–	15	16	31	–	–
Bronchitis, Chronic	7	4	11	–	–	5	5	10	–	–	2	3	5	–	–
Bronchitis with Diarrhœa . .	5	6	11	–	–	4	1	5	–	–	–	2	2	–	–
Asthma	2	–	2	–	–	6	1	7	–	–	2	–	2	–	–
Pertussis . . .	4	5	9	–	–	–	2	2	–	–	1	–	1	–	–
Congestion of Lungs	1	–	1	–	–	1	–	1	–	–	–	–	–	–	–
Pneumonia . .	4	6	10	–	–	5	8	13	1	–	1	4	5	1	–
Emphysema Pulm.	1	–	1	–	–	–	–	–	–	–	–	–	–	–	–
Pleuritis . . .	2	3	5	–	–	1	3	4	–	–	3	4	7	–	–
Total	99	90	189	1	–	83	74	157	3	–	49	52	101	1	–

TABLE OF THE DISEASES AND MORTALITY

Of Male and Female Patients, from the Age of Twenty to Forty Years, for the Year 1872. — *Continued.*

1872.	July.					August.					September.				
	Sexes.		Total.	Deaths.		Sexes.		Total.	Deaths.		Sexes.		Total.	Deaths.	
List of Diseases.	Male.	Female.		Male.	Female.	Male.	Female.		Male.	Female.	Male.	Female.		Male.	Female.
Epilepsy	–	–	–	–	–	–	–	–	–	–	–	–	–	–	–
Convulsions	1	1	2	–	–	–	–	–	–	–	3	1	4	–	–
Chorea	–	1	1	–	–	3	–	3	–	–	1	–	1	–	–
Congestion of Brain	1	–	1	–	–	1	–	1	–	–	1	–	1	–	–
Hydrocephalus	2	–	2	–	–	–	–	–	–	–	2	–	2	–	–
Encephalitis	–	–	–	–	–	–	–	–	–	–	–	1	1	–	–
Meningitis	1	–	1	–	–	2	–	2	–	–	3	1	4	–	–
Locomotor-ataxia	–	–	–	–	–	–	–	–	–	–	–	–	–	–	–
Paralysis	1	–	1	–	–	–	–	–	–	–	–	1	1	–	–
Paralysis, Partial	2	1	3	–	–	2	–	2	–	–	–	1	1	–	–
Hemiplegia	–	2	2	–	–	–	–	–	–	–	–	–	–	–	–
Spinal Disease	–	–	–	–	–	1	–	1	–	–	2	1	3	–	–
Neuralgia	1	7	8	–	–	1	8	9	–	–	1	7	8	–	–
Ophthalmia	1	–	1	–	–	–	–	–	–	–	–	–	–	–	–
Conjunctivitis	8	1	9	–	–	3	2	5	–	–	4	2	6	–	–
Granular Lids	3	–	3	–	–	–	–	–	–	–	1	1	2	–	–
Keratitis	2	3	5	–	–	2	–	2	–	–	3	5	8	–	–
Opacity of Cornea	1	–	1	–	–	–	–	–	–	–	2	–	2	–	–
Iritis	–	–	–	–	–	–	–	–	–	–	–	1	1	–	–
Ozœna	–	–	–	–	–	–	1	1	–	–	–	–	–	–	–
Coryza	1	1	2	–	–	–	–	–	–	–	1	–	1	–	–
Catarrh	–	–	–	–	–	–	2	2	–	–	2	–	2	–	–
Epistaxis	–	–	–	–	–	–	–	–	–	–	–	–	–	–	–
Tonsillitis	1	1	2	–	–	1	2	3	–	–	2	4	6	–	–
Pharyngitis	5	4	9	–	–	9	4	13	–	–	2	3	5	–	–
Diphtheria	–	1	1	–	–	–	–	–	–	–	–	2	2	–	–
Laryngitis	–	2	2	–	–	2	–	2	–	–	–	–	–	–	–
Bronchitis	14	6	20	–	–	12	4	16	–	–	31	19	50	–	–
Bronchitis, Chronic	4	2	6	–	–	3	–	3	–	–	7	5	12	–	–
Bronchitis with Diarrhœa	2	–	2	–	–	1	3	4	–	–	1	2	3	–	–
Asthma	3	–	3	–	–	–	–	–	–	–	1	–	1	–	–
Pertussis	–	–	–	–	–	2	7	9	–	–	2	4	6	–	–
Congestion of Lungs	–	–	–	–	–	1	–	1	–	–	–	–	–	–	–
Pneumonia	2	3	5	2	–	4	4	8	–	–	3	4	7	–	1
Emphysema Pulm.	–	–	–	–	–	–	–	–	–	–	1	–	1	–	–
Pleuritis	–	2	2	–	–	2	1	3	–	–	2	3	5	–	–
Total	56	38	94	2	–	52	38	90	–	–	78	68	146	–	1

TABLE OF THE DISEASES AND MORTALITY

Of Male and Female Patients, from the Age of Twenty to Forty Years, for the Year 1872. — *Continued.*

1872.	October.					November.					December.					Total Patients.	Total Deaths.
	Sexes.		Total.	Deaths.		Sexes.		Total.	Deaths.		Sexes.		Total.	Deaths.			
List of Diseases.	Male.	Female.		Male.	Female.	Male.	Female.		Male.	Female.	Male.	Female.		Male.	Female.		
Epilepsy . . .	–	1	1	–	–	–	–	–	–	–	6	3	9	–	–	52	–
Convulsions . .	2	–	2	–	–	3	–	3	–	–	1	–	1	–	–	43	–
Chorea	–	1	1	–	–	1	2	3	–	–	1	–	1	–	–	30	–
Congestion of Brain	–	–	–	–	–	1	–	1	–	–	2	–	2	–	–	13	–
Hydrocephalus .	–	–	–	–	–	–	–	–	–	–	–	–	–	–	–	9	–
Encephalitis . .	–	–	–	–	–	–	–	–	–	–	–	–	–	–	–	23	–
Meningitis . . .	1	–	1	–	–	1	–	1	–	–	1	1	2	–	–	40	3
Locomotor-ataxia .	–	–	–	–	–	–	–	–	–	–	–	–	–	–	–	14	–
Paralysis . . .	5	–	5	–	–	2	–	2	–	–	2	–	2	–	–	29	–
Paralysis, Partial .	2	–	2	–	–	–	–	–	–	–	1	1	2	–	–	42	–
Hemiplegia . . .	–	–	–	–	–	–	–	–	–	–	–	2	2	–	–	17	–
Spinal Disease . .	1	–	1	–	–	1	–	1	–	–	6	1	7	–	–	37	–
Neuralgia . . .	–	5	5	–	–	2	17	19	–	–	8	22	30	–	–	293	–
Ophthalmia . .	1	–	1	–	–	–	–	–	–	–	–	–	–	–	–	20	–
Conjunctivitis . .	–	2	2	–	–	4	1	5	–	–	7	2	9	–	–	120	–
Granular Lids . .	–	–	–	–	–	–	–	–	–	–	–	–	–	–	–	24	–
Keratitis . . .	2	4	6	–	–	–	2	2	–	–	2	3	5	–	–	95	–
Opacity of Cornea	1	–	1	–	–	2	–	2	–	–	1	–	1	–	–	26	–
Iritis	–	2	2	–	–	–	–	–	–	–	–	1	1	–	–	24	–
Ozœna	–	–	–	–	–	–	–	–	–	–	–	1	1	–	–	2	–
Coryza	–	1	1	–	–	–	–	–	–	–	1	1	2	–	–	17	–
Catarrh	1	7	8	–	–	4	8	12	–	–	24	24	48	–	–	350	–
Epistaxis . . .	–	–	–	–	–	–	–	–	–	–	–	1	1	–	–	13	–
Tonsillitis . . .	2	2	4	–	–	4	9	13	–	·	4	5	9	–	–	83	–
Pharyngitis . .	–	3	3	–	–	1	2	3	–	–	1	3	4	–	–	127	–
Diphtheria . . .	–	1	1	–	–	–	2	2	–	–	–	1	1	–	–	35	1
Laryngitis . . .	–	1	1	–	–	2	1	3	–	–	–	–	–	–	–	35	–
Bronchitis . . .	34	33	67	–	–	104	82	186	–	–	145	110	255	–	–	1,540	–
Bronchitis, Chronic	5	4	9	–	–	13	14	27	–	–	18	13	31	–	–	179	–
Bronchitis with Diarrhœa . . .	–	2	2	–	–	1	–	1	–	–	2	–	2	–	–	102	–
Asthma	3	1	4	–	–	7	2	9	–	–	12	5	17	–	–	103	–
Pertussis . . .	3	7	10	–	–	3	3	6	–	–	14	5	19	–	–	114	–
Congestion of Lungs	1	–	1	–	–	9	–	9	–	–	5	1	6	–	–	42	–
Pneumonia . . .	2	7	9	–	–	10	9	19	–	–	15	14	29	–	–	240	8
Emphysema Pulm.	–	–	–	–	–	–	–	–	–	–	2	–	2	–	–	8	–
Pleuritis . . .	1	3	4	–	–	2	2	4	–	–	2	7	9	–	–	136	–
Total	67	87	154	–	–	177	156	333	–	–	283	227	510	–	–	4,077	12

TABLE OF THE DISEASES AND MORTALITY

OF MALE AND FEMALE PATIENTS, FROM THE AGE OF TWENTY TO FORTY YEARS, FOR THE YEAR 1872. — *Continued.*

1872.	January.					February.					March.				
	Sexes.		Total.	Deaths.		Sexes.		Total.	Deaths.		Sexes.		Total.	Deaths.	
List of Diseases.	Male.	Female.		Male.	Female.	Male.	Female.		Male.	Female.	Male.	Female.		Male.	Female.
Heart Disease . .	20	7	27	–	2	10	9	19	–	–	8	2	10	–	–
Endocarditis . .	–	–	–	–	–	–	–	–	–	–	–	–	–	–	–
Dyspepsia . . .	23	47	70	–	–	23	22	45	–	–	8	11	19	–	–
Ulcer of Stomach .	3	–	3	–	–	5	–	5	–	–	5	1	6	–	–
Cancer of Stomach	3	–	3	–	–	1	–	1	–	–	1	–	1	–	–
Diarrhœa . . .	21	21	42	–	–	22	14	36	–	–	21	26	47	–	–
Diarrhœa, Chronic	5	4	9	1	–	2	3	5	–	–	2	4	6	–	–
Cholera Morbus .	–	1	1	–	–	–	–	–	–	–	1	–	1	–	–
Enteritis . . .	2	7	9	–	–	2	7	9	–	–	3	9	12	–	–
Dysentery . . .	3	4	7	–	–	3	5	8	–	–	11	10	21	–	–
Constipation . .	10	28	38	–	–	9	20	29	–	–	6	15	21	–	–
Hœmorrhoids . .	15	23	38	–	–	22	9	31	–	–	7	12	19	–	–
Helminthiasis . .	10	2	12	–	–	8	5	13	–	–	4	6	10	–	–
Tænia	1	4	5	–	–	5	1	6	–	–	1	2	3	–	–
Hepatitis . . .	2	4	6	–	–	2	4	6	–	–	–	3	3	–	–
Congestion of Liver	3	1	4	–	–	4	1	5	–	–	–	1	1	–	–
Jaundice . . .	–	–	–	–	–	–	–	–	–	–	–	–	–	–	–
Nephritis . . .	2	5	7	–	–	5	3	8	–	–	1	3	4	–	–
Bright's Disease .	5	1	6	–	–	3	2	5	–	–	2	–	2	–	–
Ascites	3	6	9	–	–	1	5	6	–	2	2	1	3	–	–
Anasarca . . .	1	5	6	–	–	1	3	4	–	–	2	1	3	–	–
Cystitis	–	5	5	–	–	1	5	6	–	–	–	2	2	–	–
Dysuria	2	3	5	–	–	2	4	6	–	–	–	4	4	–	–
Incontinence of Urine	9	3	12	–	–	7	2	9	–	–	2	3	5	–	–
Gravel	2	3	5	–	–	1	4	5	–	–	1	3	4	–	–
Phthisis . . .	47	28	75	2	2	40	21	61	2	1	23	15	38	1	1
Rheumatism . .	114	75	189	–	–	106	80	186	–	–	103	67	170	–	–
Rheumatism, Chronic	11	4	15	–	–	5	4	9	–	–	3	3	6	–	–
Erysipelas . . .	8	4	12	–	–	8	7	15	–	–	5	4	9	–	–
Ephemeral Fever .	13	16	29	–	–	9	12	21	–	–	8	11	19	–	-
Intermittent Fever	69	98	167	–	–	60	72	132	–	–	29	46	75	–	–
Remittent Fever .	59	35	94	–	–	47	33	80	–	–	13	12	25	–	·
Typhoid Fever . .	20	9	29	–	–	12	7	19	–	–	9	3	12	1	–
Cerebro-spinal Meningitis	–	–	–	–	–	–	–	–	–	–	–	–	–	–	–
Total	486	453	939	3	4	426	364	790	2	3	281	280	561	2	1

January.					February.					March.				
Mean Therm.	Rain Fall.	Direction and Force of Wind.			Mean Therm.	Rain Fall.	Direction and Force of Wind.			Mean Therm.	Rain Fall.	Direction and Force of Wind.		
26°	.670	S. W. h.	N. W. g.		27°	.690	S. W. g.	S. E. g.		29°	3.220	N. E. h.	N. W. g.	

TABLE OF THE DISEASES AND MORTALITY

OF MALE AND FEMALE PATIENTS, FROM THE AGE OF TWENTY TO FORTY YEARS, FOR THE YEAR 1872.— *Continued.*

1872.	April.					May.					June.				
	Sexes.		Total.	Deaths.		Sexes.		Total.	Deaths.		Sexes.		Total.	Deaths.	
List of Diseases.	Male.	Female.		Male.	Female.	Male.	Female.		Male.	Female.	Male.	Female.		Male.	Female.
Heart Disease	4	1	5	1	–	–	1	1	1	1	–	1	1	–	–
Endocarditis	–	–	–	–	–	4	2	6	–	–	–	–	–	–	–
Dyspepsia	2	9	11	–	–	3	8	11	–	–	9	13	22	–	–
Ulcer of Stomach	1	–	1	–	–	–	–	–	–	–	1	–	1	–	–
Cancer of Stomach	–	1	1	–	–	1	–	1	–	–	1	–	1	–	–
Diarrhœa	10	7	17	–	–	3	5	8	–	–	5	3	8	–	–
Diarrhœa, Chronic	–	1	1	–	–	1	–	1	–	–	1	–	1	1	–
Cholera Morbus	2	4	6	–	–	4	1	5	–	–	13	6	19	–	–
Enteritis	1	3	4	–	–	–	1	1	–	–	–	–	–	–	–
Dysentery	6	5	11	–	–	–	3	3	–	–	5	5	10	–	–
Constipation	2	8	10	–	–	2	8	10	–	–	1	6	7	–	–
Hœmorrhoids	2	3	5	–	–	1	4	5	–	–	–	2	2	–	–
Helminthiasis	–	3	3	–	–	–	1	1	–	–	3	1	4	–	–
Tænia	1	–	1	–	–	–	2	2	–	–	1	3	4	–	–
Hepatitis	–	2	2	–	–	–	2	2	–	–	–	2	2	–	–
Congestion of Liver	1	–	1	–	–	–	–	–	–	–	1	–	1	–	–
Jaundice	–	–	–	–	–	–	–	–	–	–	–	–	–	–	–
Nephritis	1	2	3	–	–	–	1	1	–	–	–	2	2	–	–
Bright's Disease	1	–	1	–	–	–	–	–	–	–	1	–	1	–	–
Ascites	2	–	2	–	–	3	2	5	–	–	1	–	1	–	–
Anasarca	1	–	1	–	–	–	1	1	–	–	–	–	–	–	–
Cystitis	–	1	1	–	–	–	1	1	–	–	1	1	2	–	–
Dysuria	–	2	1	–	–	–	1	1	–	–	–	1	1	–	–
Incontinence of Urine	2	2	4	–	–	–	–	–	–	–	–	–	–	–	–
Gravel	1	–	1	–	–	1	–	1	–	–	–	1	1	–	–
Phthisis	12	12	24	–	1	11	9	20	2	1	10	15	25	3	2
Rheumatism	50	30	80	–	–	23	17	40	–	–	12	10	22	–	–
Rheumatism, Chronic	2	–	2	–	–	4	4	8	–	–	6	3	9	–	–
Erysipelas	–	–	–	–	–	–	–	–	–	–	5	2	7	–	–
Ephemeral Fever	2	6	8	–	–	–	2	2	–	–	1	2	3	–	–
Intermittent Fever	20	6	26	–	–	35	17	52	–	–	13	22	35	–	–
Remittent Fever	4	2	6	–	–	5	1	6	–	–	2	–	2	–	–
Typhoid Fever	4	2	6	–	–	4	1	5	–	–	2	1	3	–	–
Cerebro-spinal Meningitis	–	–	–	–	–	–	–	–	–	–	–	–	–	–	–
Total	134	112	246	1	1	105	95	200	3	2	95	102	197	4	2

April.				May.				June.			
Mean Therm.	Rain Fall.	Direction and Force of Wind.		Mean Therm.	Rain Fall.	Direction and Force of Wind.		Mean Therm.	Rain Fall.	Direction and Force of Wind.	
48°	2.990	S. W. h.	N. E. h.	57½°	3.285	S. W. g.	S. E. h.	70⅛°	3.410	S. W. g.	N. W. g.

TABLE OF THE DISEASES AND MORTALITY

OF MALE AND FEMALE PATIENTS, FROM THE AGE OF TWENTY TO FORTY YEARS, FOR THE YEAR 1872. — *Continued.*

1872.	July.					August.					September.				
	Sexes.		Total.	Deaths.		Sexes.		Total.	Deaths.		Sexes.		Total.	Deaths.	
LIST OF DISEASES.	Male.	Female.		Male.	Female.	Male.	Female.		Male.	Female.	Male.	Female.		Male.	Female.
Heart Disease	2	3	5	1	–	1	3	4	–	–	2	4	6	–	–
Endocarditis	–	–	–	–	–	–	–	–	–	–	–	–	–	–	–
Dyspepsia	12	9	21	–	–	3	17	20	–	–	2	14	16	–	–
Ulcer of Stomach	–	–	–	–	–	–	–	–	–	–	2	–	2	–	–
Cancer of Stomach	–	–	–	–	–	1	–	1	–	–	–	–	–	–	–
Diarrhœa	29	20	49	–	–	19	37	56	–	–	18	10	28	–	1
Diarrhœa, Chronic	4	2	6	–	–	4	5	9	–	–	5	4	9	–	–
Cholera Morbus	29	16	45	–	–	26	13	39	–	–	4	1	5	–	–
Enteritis	1	2	3	–	–	4	2	6	–	–	2	3	5	–	–
Dysentery	5	4	9	–	–	9	5	14	–	–	9	4	13	1	–
Constipation	1	7	8	–	–	1	9	10	–	–	–	5	5	–	–
Hœmorrhoids	1	2	3	–	–	–	2	2	–	–	2	2	4	–	–
Helminthiasis	–	1	1	–	–	1	4	5	–	–	1	5	6	–	–
Tænia	1	3	4	–	–	2	–	2	–	–	2	1	3	–	–
Hepatitis	–	1	1	–	–	–	–	–	–	–	–	1	1	–	–
Congestion of Liver	1	–	1	–	–	1	–	1	–	–	–	–	–	–	–
Jaundice	–	–	–	–	–	–	–	–	–	–	3	–	3	–	–
Nephritis	–	1	1	–	–	2	–	2	–	–	1	2	3	–	–
Bright's Disease	–	–	–	–	–	1	–	1	–	–	–	–	–	–	–
Ascites	2	1	3	–	1	–	1	1	–	–	1	–	1	–	1
Anasarca	–	–	–	–	–	1	–	1	–	–	–	2	2	–	–
Cystitis	1	1	2	–	–	–	1	1	–	–	–	1	1	–	–
Dysuria	–	2	2	–	–	–	–	–	–	–	–	1	1	–	–
Incontinence of Urine	4	1	5	–	–	2	–	2	–	–	4	1	5	–	–
Gravel	–	–	–	–	–	–	–	–	–	–	–	–	–	–	–
Phthisis	17	9	26	3	2	8	8	16	3	–	24	15	39	1	–
Rheumatism	15	8	23	–	–	11	7	18	–	–	14	10	24	–	–
Rheumatism, Chronic	1	–	1	–	–	7	2	9	–	–	2	2	4	–	–
Erysipelas	4	1	5	–	–	1	–	1	–	–	3	1	4	–	–
Ephemeral Fever	1	1	2	–	–	3	1	4	–	–	–	–	–	–	–
Intermittent Fever	17	21	38	–	–	31	12	43	–	–	64	30	94	–	–
Remittent Fever	3	–	3	–	–	8	3	11	–	–	15	11	26	–	–
Typhoid Fever	2	–	2	–	–	10	5	15	2	1	14	11	25	2	–
Cerebro-spinal Meningitis	2	–	2	–	–	2	1	3	–	–	2	–	2	–	–
Total	155	116	271	4	3	159	138	297	5	1	196	141	337	4	2

July.				August.				September.			
Mean Therm.	Rain Fall.	Direction and Force of Wind.		Mean Therm.	Rain Fall.	Direction and Force of Wind.		Mean Therm.	Rain Fall.	Direction and Force of Wind.	
72½°	4.050	S. W. h.	N. W. g.	72°	2.560	N. W. g.	S. W. g.	64°	6.430	S. W. g.	S. E. g.

TABLE OF THE DISEASES AND MORTALITY

OF MALE AND FEMALE PATIENTS, FROM THE AGE OF TWENTY TO FORTY YEARS, FOR THE YEAR 1872.— *Continued.*

1872.	October.					November.					December.					Total Patients.	Total Deaths.
	Sexes.		Total.	Deaths.		Sexes.		Total.	Deaths.		Sexes.		Total.	Deaths.			
List of Diseases	Male.	Female.		Male.	Female.	Male.	Female.		Male.	Female.	Male.	Female.		Male.	Female.		
Heart Disease	2	4	6	–	–	–	–	–	*1	–	3	1	4	1	–	88	8
Endocarditis	–	–	–	–	–	–	–	–	–	–	1	1	2	–	–	8	–
Dyspepsia	2	13	15	–	–	3	9	12	–	–	4	6	10	–	–	272	–
Ulcer of Stomach	–	–	–	–	–	1	–	1	–	–	1	–	1	–	–	20	–
Cancer of Stomach	1	–	1	–	–	–	–	–	–	–	2	–	2	–	–	12	–
Diarrhœa	4	6	10	–	–	4	3	7	–	–	4	7	11	–	–	319	1
Diarrhœa, Chronic	–	2	3	–	–	1	–	1	–	–	1	1	2	–	–	53	2
Cholera Morbus	1	2	3	–	–	–	–	–	–	–	–	–	–	–	–	124	–
Enteritis	–	2	2	–	–	–	2	2	–	1	1	5	6	–	–	59	1
Dysentery	7	3	10	–	–	4	5	9	1	–	7	4	11	1	–	126	3
Constipation	3	3	6	–	–	1	6	7	–	–	3	12	15	–	–	166	–
Hœmorrhoids	–	3	3	–	–	–	–	–	–	–	–	–	–	–	–	112	–
Helminthiasis	2	4	6	–	–	1	5	6	–	–	3	7	10	–	–	77	–
Tænia	–	3	3	–	–	–	1	1	–	–	1	1	2	–	–	36	–
Hepatitis	–	–	–	–	–	–	–	–	–	–	–	1	1	–	–	24	–
Congestion of Liver	1	–	1	–	–	–	–	–	–	–	2	–	2	–	–	17	–
Jaundice	2	–	2	–	–	1	–	1	–	–	6	–	6	–	–	12	–
Nephritis	1	1	2	–	–	–	1	1	–	–	2	1	3	–	–	37	–
Bright's Disease	1	–	1	–	–	–	–	–	–	–	1	–	1	–	–	18	–
Ascites	2	–	2	–	–	2	1	3	–	–	5	–	5	1	–	41	5
Anasarca	–	1	1	–	–	–	1	1	–	–	2	4	6	–	–	26	–
Cystitis	1	2	3	–	–	–	1	1	–	–	–	2	2	–	–	27	–
Dysuria	1	–	1	–	–	1	2	3	–	–	–	2	2	–	–	28	–
Incontinence of Urine	8	2	10	–	–	–	1	1	–	–	4	–	4	–	–	57	–
Gravel	–	–	–	–	–	–	–	–	–	–	–	–	–	–	–	17	–
Phthisis	15	14	29	1	–	14	5	19	1	–	19	10	29	2	–	401	31
Rheumatism	18	14	32	–	–	14	12	26	–	–	44	33	77	–	–	887	–
Rheumatism, Chronic	3	–	3	–	–	3	1	4	–	–	9	6	15	–	–	85	–
Erysipelas	1	1	2	–	–	4	–	4	–	–	5	1	6	–	–	65	–
Ephemeral Fever	–	–	–	–	–	4	5	9	–	–	10	9	19	–	–	116	
Intermittent Fever	43	25	68	–	–	20	21	41	–	–	49	38	87	–	–	858	
Remittent Fever	12	5	17	–	–	6	2	8	–	–	9	7	16	–	–	294	
Typhoid Fever	13	3	16	4	–	14	4	18	2	1	19	10	29	1	–	179	14
Cerebro-spinal Meningitis	–	–	–	–	–	–	–	–	–	–	–	–	–	–	–	7	–
Total	145	113	258	5	–	98	88	186	5	2	217	169	386	6	–	4,668	65

October.				November.				December.			
Mean Therm.	Rain Fall.	Direction and Force of Wind.		Mean Therm.	Rain Fall.	Direction and Force of Wind.		Mean Therm.	Rain Fall	Direction and Force of Wind.	
52°	.650	N. E. g.	S. W. h.	32½°	.800	N. W. h	N. W. g.	19°	.430	N. W. g.	S. W. g.

Male Patients, Classified	4,680	Deaths of Male Patients	53
Female Patients, Classified	4,065	Deaths of Female Patients	24
Patients, Unclassified by Sexes	5,301	Deaths of Unclassified Patients	2
Total Patients	14,046	Total Deaths	79

* Case from previous month.

ADDITIONAL TABLE OF THE SICKNESS AND MORTALITY

Of Patients, Unclassified as to Sex, from the Age of Twenty to Forty Years, for the Year 1872.

1872.	Jan.	Feb.	Mar.	April.	May.	June.	July.	Aug.	Sept.	Oct.	Nov.	Dec.	
List of Diseases.	Patients.	Patients.	Patients.	Patients.	Patients.	Patients.	Patients.	Patients.	Patients.	Patients.	Patients.	Patients.	Total Patients.
Abscess . .	41	30	12	9	9	8	8	7	8	6	9	29	176
Furoncle . .	4	9	3	1	-	-	-	1	-	2	-	1	21
Ulcers . . .	59	38	21	9	10	14	12	5	9	10	9	20	216
Inflammation of Mamma . .	4	6	3	1	-	-	-	-	-	-	-	1	15
Ulcer of Leg .	15	17	9	5	4	4	3	3	4	6	2	4	76
Frost-bite . .	29	15	-	-	-	-	-	-	-	-	-	21	65
Contusion or Contused wound	33	40	23	6	5	4	8	9	10	4	7	16	165
Incised wound	11	9	5	1	-	5	-	4	1	1	-	6	43
Punctured wound . .	2	1	2	1	-	-	2	1	1	-	-	1	11
Paronychia .	1	2	1	1	-	-	-	4	-	2	-	-	11
Onychia . .	2	3	1	1	-	-	-	-	-	-	1	-	8
Varix . . .	3	4	2	1	-	-	2	-	1	1	-	2	16
Varicose Veins	18	16	11	6	3	1	-	3	1	5	6	5	75
Fracture of Clavicle . . .	9	4	2	1	1	2	3	-	-	-	-	5	27
Fracture of Ulna	4	5	2	-	-	-	3	-	-	2	-	-	16
Fracture of Tibia	19	12	2	1	1	-	-	2	1	1	-	-	39
Dislocation of Shoulder .	6	5	12	4	1	3	2	-	4	2	3	1	43
Periostitis . .	·12	15	6	2	1	2	-	-	-	-	-	-	38
Caries . . .	1	2	1	1	1	-	1	-	-	1	-	1	9
Necrosis . .	13	10	6	2	1	1	1	3	2	-	6	-	45
Arthritis . .	6	4	3	1	1	-	1	1	2	1	1	6	27
Synovitis . .	6	9	5	1	1	-	-	-	2	2	4	5	35
Hernia . . .	9	17	14	7	5	7	1	6	1	4	6	13	90
Hernia Inguinal	9	10	4	2	-	1	-	-	3	-	-	4	33
Hernia Umbilical	19	10	6	1	1	-	-	2	1	2	-	-	42
Atrophy . .	9	2	3	1	-	-	-	1	2	4	2	1	25
Anæmia . .	19	20	10	7	4	2	4	10	3	3	10	16	108
Debility . .	87	60	42	17	19	12	21	20	12	8	11	11	320
Malaise . .	15	10	9	6	-	2	1	3	1	-	1	2	50
Hysteria . .	9	6	4	2	2	4	2	6	5	4	3	4	51
Cephalalgia .	21	19	11	6	7	6	5	9	6	2	4	9	105
Vertigo . .	2	3	2	1	-	1	-	2	-	1	1	-	13
Odontalgia .	53	62	32	20	9	1	2	5	16	20	19	27	266
Otalgia . . .	4	3	2	1	-	-	-	-	1	4	-	-	15
Otitis . . .	15	21	7	3	5	3	2	2	-	-	-	-	58
Stomatitis . .	2	2	3	1	4	-	-	-	2	1	5	2	22
Angina . . .	4	5	3	1	1	-	1	-	1	1	-	2	19
Cardialgia . .	2	1	-	1	-	1	1	2	2	2	1	-	13
Gastritis . .	16	10	9	2	3	3	1	2	-	-	1	1	48
Gastralgia . .	10	8	2	1	2	-	2	3	-	-	-	-	28
Fistula in Ano	9	8	3	1	-	-	2	-	1	2	1	-	27
Colic . . .	11	9	6	2	3	1	5	12	3	2	7	2	63
Total . .	623	542	304	138	104	88	96	128	106	106	120	218	2,573

ADDITIONAL TABLE OF THE SICKNESS AND MORTALITY OF PATIENTS, UNCLASSIFIED AS TO SEX, FROM THE AGE OF TWENTY TO FORTY YEARS, FOR THE YEAR 1872. — *Continued.*

1872.	JAN.	FEB.	MAR.	APRIL.		MAY.	JUNE.	JULY.	AUG.	SEPT.	OCT.	NOV.	DEC.	Total Patients.	Total Deaths.
ST OF DISEASES.	Patients.	Patients.	Patients.	Patients.	Deaths.	Patients.	Patients.	Patients.	Patients.	Patients.	Patients.	Patients.	Patients.		
ephralgia .	12	4	2	1	–	–	–	–	2	–	1	–	1	23	–
onorrhœa .	12	9	6	4	–	1	4	3	1	3	1	3	4	51	–
rethritis . .	6	7	4	1	–	–	1	2	–	2	1	2	1	27	–
ıbo . . .	21	11	6	5	–	2	3	1	3	1	2	5	9	69	–
rchitis . .	4	5	2	–	–	–	2	2	–	1	–	–	1	17	–
etritis . .	130	105	65	88	2	59	52	35	31	26	12	24	14	641	2
terine Disease	45	41	19	10	–	12	28	8	3	9	5	7	15	202	–
bortion . .	95	41	42	25	–	10	5	9	3	6	2	5	10	253	–
eucorrhœa .	41	29	12	4	–	4	3	2	2	1	3	2	2	105	–
aginitis . .	–	–	–	–	–	–	2	–	2	1	2	1	–	8	–
rolapsus Uteri . .	35	33	37	20	–	23	7	11	6	15	12	11	9	219	–
splacement of Uterus . .	5	4	2	1	–	1	–	–	2	–	1	–	1	17	–
ılorosis . .	11	9	5	2	–	1	2	1	2	1	–	1	4	39	–
menorrhœa .	23	19	9	5	–	–	2	5	3	2	6	8	15	97	–
ysmenorrhea	3	5	3	2	–	1	5	2	2	3	1	4	5	36	–
enorrhagia .	10	12	9	2	–	–	4	3	–	2	1	1	4	48	–
varitis . .	6	7	2	1	–	–	–	–	–	–	–	–	–	16	–
ımors . .	15	14	9	4	–	1	2	1	4	3	4	5	6	68	–
ıcephaloid Tumors . .	2	3	2	1	–	–	–	–	–	–	–	–	1	9	–
itre . . .	–	2	2	2	–	1	–	–	–	–	–	–	–	7	–
lenitis . .	24	24	14	6	–	5	1	–	1	3	8	1	8	90	–
rofula . .	7	6	4	1	–	3	1	1	1	4	–	3	2	33	–
orbus Coxarius . . .	4	5	2	1	–	1	3	1	1	–	2	2	3	25	–
ımbago . .	29	18	9	4	–	3	2	6	6	1	1	2	4	85	–
iatica . .	7	5	3	1	–	–	2	4	–	1	1	1	1	26	–
xalgia . .	4	5	2	1	–	2	1	1	2	1	1	3	2	25	–
ıbeola . .	–	–	–	–	–	–	–	–	–	–	–	1	2	3	–
arlatina . .	19	14	2	3	–	–	–	–	–	5	2	3	4	52	–
philis . .	21	14	17	8	–	6	6	5	4	2	6	9	7	105	–
philis, Secondary . .	4	5	6	1	–	2	11	10	6	3	4	4	3	59	–
philis, Tertiary	6	4	3	2	–	1	1	–	–	–	1	2	–	20	–
ancre . .	1	2	1	2	–	2	2	2	1	1	1	3	2	20	–
pia . . .	–	–	–	–	–	3	–	–	1	–	2	–	–	6	–
ythema . .	4	3	4	1	–	–	–	–	4	–	1	–	2	19	–
zema . .	9	7	6	3	–	1	–	2	–	2	2	2	5	39	–
rpes . . .	3	5	2	2	–	2	–	–	–	–	–	1	2	17	–
nphigus .	2	1	2	1	–	–	–	–	1	–	1	–	–	8	–
petigo . .	7	6	4	1	–	–	1	–	2	2	1	1	4	29	–
bies . .	3	4	2	1	–	–	1	–	–	–	2	–	–	13	–
ticaria . .	9	6	5	2	–	1	1	–	2	3	–	–	2	31	–
ea Capitis	2	6	6	1	–	1	1	2	2	2	1	2	4	30	–
riasis . .	12	9	6	1	–	2	–	–	–	2	–	4	5	41	–
'otal . .	653	509	338	221	2	151	156	119	100	108	86	123	164	2,728	2

TABLE OF THE DISEASES AND MORTALITY

OF MALE AND FEMALE PATIENTS, FROM THE AGE OF FORTY TO SIXTY YEARS, FOR THE YEAR 1872.

1872.	January.					February.					March.				
	Sexes.		Total.	Deaths.		Sexes.		Total.	Deaths.		Sexes.		Total.	Deaths.	
List of Diseases.	Male.	Female.		Male.	Female.	Male.	Female		Male.	Female.	Male.	Female.		Male.	Female.
Epilepsy	2	1	3	–	–	2	1	3	–	–	1	2	3	–	–
Convulsions	4	2	6	–	–	5	4	9	–	–	3	1	4	–	–
Congestion of Brain	–	1	1	–	–	2	–	2	–	–	–	–	–	1	–
Paralysis	4	1	5	–	–	–	2	2	–	–	1	2	3	–	–
Paralysis, Partial	1	1	2	–	–	4	2	6	–	–	2	3	5	–	–
Hemiplegia	–	–	–	–	–	–	–	–	–	–	–	–	–	–	–
Spinal Disease	2	–	2	–	–	3	1	4	–	–	2	–	2	–	–
Neuralgia	8	33	41	–	–	2	18	20	–	–	14	35	49	–	–
Conjunctivitis	4	6	10	–	–	3	3	6	–	–	6	3	9	–	–
Granular Lids	1	2	3	–	–	1	–	1	–	–	1	–	1	–	–
Keratitis	1	2	3	–	–	–	3	3	–	–	2	1	3	–	–
Iritis	–	–	–	–	–	–	–	–	–	–	–	–	–	–	–
Ozœna	–	–	–	–	–	–	–	–	–	–	–	–	–	–	–
Catarrh	15	5	20	–	–	15	14	29	–	–	4	8	12	–	–
Epistaxis	–	–	–	–	–	–	2	2	–	–	–	–	–	–	–
Tonsillitis	5	14	19	–	–	4	8	12	–	–	6	3	9	–	–
Pharyngitis	3	6	9	–	–	3	7	10	–	–	1	3	4	–	–
Laryngitis	2	4	6	–	–	–	1	1	–	–	–	2	2	–	–
Bronchitis	76	45	121	–	–	76	65	141	–	–	59	42	101	2	1
Bronchitis, Chronic	12	9	21	–	–	11	8	19	–	–	10	6	16	–	–
Asthma	13	6	19	–	–	11	5	16	–	–	3	–	3	–	–
Pertussis	3	6	9	–	–	7	2	9	–	–	2	–	2	–	–
Congestion of Lungs	1	–	1	–	–	1	–	1	–	–	–	–	–	–	–
Pneumonia	7	8	15	3	–	10	6	16	–	–	3	7	10	1	–
Pleuritis	28	10	38	–	–	19	13	32	–	–	4	14	18	–	–
Heart Disease	6	3	9	–	–	4	3	7	–	–	3	1	4	–	–
Endocarditis	1	–	1	–	–	1	–	1	–	–	1	–	1	–	–
Dyspepsia	9	20	29	–	–	3	15	18	–	–	2	7	9	–	–
Cancer of Stomach	–	–	–	–	–	–	–	–	–	–	–	–	–	–	–
Diarrhœa	10	6	16	–	–	11	5	16	–	–	3	11	14	1	–
Cholera Morbus	–	–	–	–	–	–	–	–	–	–	–	–	–	–	–
Enteritis	–	2	2	–	1	–	1	1	–	–	–	1	1	–	–
Dysentery	5	1	6	–	–	2	–	2	–	–	2	3	5	–	–
Constipation	1	18	19	–	–	9	16	25	–	–	3	13	16	–	–
Hœmorrhoids	3	7	10	–	–	3	10	13	–	–	3	4	7	–	–
Hepatitis	1	4	5	–	–	3	4	7	–	–	3	2	5	–	–
Jaundice	–	–	–	–	–	–	–	–	–	–	–	–	–	–	–
Nephritis	–	2	2	–	–	1	2	3	–	–	1	–	1	–	–
Bright's Disease	2	–	2	–	–	2	–	2	–	–	1	–	1	–	–
Ascites	1	–	1	–	–	1	1	2	–	–	–	1	1	–	–
Cystitis	–	–	–	–	–	–	–	–	–	–	–	–	–	–	–
Incontinence of Urine	3	1	4	–	–	5	1	6	–	–	2	–	2	–	–
Gravel	–	–	–	–	–	–	–	–	–	–	–	–	–	–	–
Phthisis	25	14	39	3	1	19	12	31	–	2	15	4	19	1	1
Rheumatism	105	57	162	–	–	70	52	122	–	–	43	17	60	–	–
Rheumatism, Chronic	15	4	19	–	–	8	3	11	–	–	2	1	3	–	–
Erysipelas	3	3	6	–	–	2	2	4	–	–	1	–	1	–	–
Ephemeral Fever	3	2	5	–	–	5	1	6	–	–	–	1	1	–	–
Intermittent Fever	19	16	35	–	–	17	12	29	–	–	27	17	44	–	–
Remittent Fever	8	11	19	–	–	10	7	17	–	–	9	3	12	–	–
Typhoid Fever	4	1	5	–	–	6	3	9	–	–	4	2	6	2	–
Total	416	334	750	6	2	361	315	676	–	2	249	220	469	8	2

January.				February.				March.			
Mean Therm.	Rain Fall.	Direction and Force of Wind.		Mean Therm.	Rain Fall.	Direction and Force of Wind.		Mean Therm.	Rain Fall.	Direction and Force of Wind.	
26°	.670	S. W. h.	N. W. g.	27°	.690	S. W. g.	S. E. g.	29°	3.220	N. E. h.	N. W. g.

TABLE OF THE DISEASES AND MORTALITY

Of Male and Female Patients, from the Age of Forty to Sixty Years, for the Year 1872. — *Continued.*

1872.	April.					May.					June.				
	Sexes.		Total.	Deaths.		Sexes.		Total.	Deaths.		Sexes.		Total.	Deaths.	
List of Diseases.	Male.	Female.		Male.	Female.	Male.	Female.		Male.	Female.	Male.	Female.		Male.	Female.
Epilepsy	–	1	1	–	–	–	2	2	–	–	1	1	2	–	–
Convulsions	–	–	–	–	–	2	–	2	–	–	1	–	1	–	–
Congestion of Brain	–	–	–	–	–	–	–	–	–	–	–	–	–	–	–
Paralysis	1	–	1	–	–	2	1	3	–	–	–	–	–	–	–
Paralysis, Partial	4	2	6	–	–	–	1	1	–	–	–	–	–	–	–
Hemiplegia	–	–	–	–	–	–	–	–	–	–	–	–	–	–	–
Spinal Disease	1	–	1	–	–	–	–	–	–	–	–	–	–	–	–
Neuralgia	2	3	5	–	–	1	9	10	–	–	–	5	5	–	–
Conjunctivitis	1	2	3	–	–	–	1	1	–	–	1	1	2	–	–
Granular Lids	1	–	1	–	–	2	–	2	–	–	–	–	–	–	–
Keratitis	–	2	2	–	–	–	2	2	–	–	–	1	1	–	–
Iritis	–	–	–	–	–	–	–	–	–	–	–	–	–	–	–
Ozœna	–	–	–	–	–	–	–	–	–	–	–	–	–	–	–
Catarrh	3	1	4	–	–	2	4	6	–	–	–	–	–	–	–
Epistaxis	–	–	–	–	–	–	1	1	–	–	–	–	–	–	–
Tonsillitis	1	–	1	–	–	–	–	–	–	–	–	–	–	–	–
Pharyngitis	–	–	–	–	–	2	–	2	–	–	–	–	–	–	–
Laryngitis	–	1	1	–	–	–	3	3	–	–	–	1	1	–	–
Bronchitis	13	28	41	–	–	16	23	39	–	–	5	2	7	–	–
Bronchitis, Chronic	2	2	4	–	–	1	2	3	–	–	2	–	2	–	–
Asthma	–	–	–	–	–	9	3	12	–	–	4	1	5	–	–
Pertussis	1	–	1	–	–	–	–	–	–	–	–	–	–	–	–
Congestion of Lungs	–	–	–	–	–	–	–	–	–	–	2	–	2	–	–
Pneumonia	4	1	5	–	–	2	1	3	–	–	2	–	2	1	–
Pleuritis	2	6	8	–	–	1	2	3	–	–	–	1	1	–	–
Heart Disease	–	1	1	–	1	2	2	4	–	–	3	4	7	–	–
Endocarditis	–	–	–	–	–	–	–	–	–	–	–	–	–	–	–
Dyspepsia	–	5	5	–	–	4	8	12	–	–	5	12	17	–	–
Cancer of Stomach	–	–	–	–	–	1	–	1	–	–	–	–	–	–	–
Diarrhœa	18	6	24	–	–	2	–	2	–	–	8	2	10	–	–
Cholera Morbus	2	–	2	–	–	–	–	–	–	–	–	–	–	–	–
Enteritis	–	–	–	–	–	–	1	1	–	–	–	1	1	–	–
Dysentery	7	2	9	–	–	–	–	–	–	–	2	–	2	–	–
Constipation	1	4	5	–	–	5	5	10	–	–	2	6	8	–	–
Hœmorrhoids	1	1	2	–	–	1	2	3	–	–	5	3	8	–	–
Hepatitis	2	–	2	–	–	–	–	–	–	–	1	–	1	–	–
Jaundice	–	–	–	–	–	–	–	–	–	–	–	–	–	–	–
Nephritis	–	1	1	–	–	1	–	1	–	–	–	–	–	–	–
Bright's Disease	–	–	–	–	–	–	–	–	–	–	3	–	3	2	–
Ascites	1	–	1	–	–	–	1	1	–	–	2	1	3	1	–
Cystitis	–	–	–	–	–	–	1	1	–	–	–	–	–	–	–
Incontinence of Urine	–	1	1	–	–	–	–	–	–	–	–	–	–	–	–
Gravel	–	–	–	–	–	–	–	–	–	–	–	–	–	–	–
Phthisis	8	4	12	3	–	11	3	14	2	–	10	3	13	2	–
Rheumatism	10	12	22	–	–	25	25	50	–	–	15	16	31	–	–
Rheumatism, Chronic	1	–	1	–	–	4	3	7	–	–	2	3	5	–	–
Erysipelas	–	–	–	–	–	2	1	3	–	–	4	1	5	–	–
Ephemeral Fever	–	1	1	–	–	2	–	2	–	–	1	–	1	–	–
Intermittent Fever	14	12	26	–	–	16	8	24	–	–	14	8	22	–	–
Remittent Fever	5	1	6	–	–	1	2	3	–	–	4	2	6	–	–
Typhoid Fever	1	1	2	–	–	–	–	–	–	–	1	–	1	–	–
Total	107	101	208	3	1	117	117	234	2	–	100	75	175	6	–

April.				May.				June.			
Mean Therm.	Rain Fall.	Direction and Force of Wind.		Mean Therm.	Rain Fall.	Direction and Force of Wind.		Mean Therm.	Rain Fall.	Direction and Force of Wind.	
48°	2.990	S. W. h.	N. E. h.	57½°	3.285	S. W. g.	S. E. h.	70⅛°	3.410	S. W. g.	N. W. g.

TABLE OF THE DISEASES AND MORTALITY

Of Male and Female Patients, from the Age of Forty to Sixty Years, for the Year 1872. — *Continued.*

1872.	July.					August.					September.				
	Sexes.		Total.	Deaths.		Sexes.		Total.	Deaths.		Sexes.		Total.	Deaths.	
List of Diseases.	Male.	Female.		Male.	Female.	Male.	Female.		Male.	Female.	Male.	Female.		Male.	Female.
Epilepsy	1	–	1	–	–	2	–	2	–	–	1	–	1	–	–
Convulsions	2	–	2	–	–	–	1	1	–	–	1	–	1	–	–
Congestion of Brain	–	–	–	–	–	–	–	–	–	–	2	1	3	–	–
Paralysis	–	–	–	–	–	1	–	1	1	–	3	–	3	–	–
Paralysis, Partial	1	–	1	–	–	2	–	2	–	–	2	–	2	–	–
Hemiplegia	1	–	1	–	–	–	–	–	–	–	–	–	–	–	–
Spinal Disease	1	–	1	–	–	–	–	–	–	–	–	–	–	–	–
Neuralgia	5	3	8	–	–	–	1	1	–	–	2	1	3	–	–
Conjunctivitis	2	–	2	–	–	1	1	2	–	–	–	2	2	–	–
Granular Lids	–	1	1	–	–	–	–	–	–	–	–	–	–	–	–
Keratitis	–	2	2	–	–	1	2	3	–	–	3	1	4	–	–
Iritis	2	–	2	–	–	–	–	–	–	–	–	–	–	–	–
Ozœna	–	–	–	–	–	–	–	–	–	–	–	–	–	–	–
Catarrh	1	–	1	–	–	5	3	8	–	–	–	2	2	–	–
Epistaxis	–	–	–	–	–	–	–	–	–	–	–	1	1	–	–
Tonsillitis	–	–	–	–	–	2	–	2	–	–	3	–	3	–	–
Pharyngitis	1	1	2	–	–	2	4	6	–	–	2	–	2	–	–
Laryngitis	–	1	1	–	–	–	–	–	–	–	2	–	2	–	–
Bronchitis	4	4	8	–	–	3	–	3	–	–	3	4	7	–	–
Bronchitis, Chronic	1	2	3	–	–	1	–	1	–	–	2	2	4	–	–
Asthma	3	1	4	–	–	4	3	7	–	–	4	3	7	–	–
Pertussis	–	–	–	–	–	–	–	–	–	–	–	1	1	–	–
Congestion of Lungs	–	–	–	–	–	–	–	–	–	–	–	–	–	–	–
Pneumonia	2	1	3	–	–	–	–	–	–	–	5	7	12	–	–
Pleuritis	–	1	1	–	–	3	2	5	–	–	3	2	5	–	–
Heart Disease	–	1	1	1	–	–	–	–	–	–	–	–	–	–	–
Endocarditis	–	–	–	–	–	–	–	–	–	–	–	1	1	–	–
Dyspepsia	6	5	11	–	–	5	5	10	–	–	2	6	8	–	–
Cancer of Stomach	–	–	–	–	–	1	–	1	–	–	–	–	–	–	–
Diarrhœa	7	7	14	–	–	15	8	23	–	–	4	4	8	–	–
Cholera Morbus	8	2	10	–	–	3	1	4	1	–	1	2	3	–	–
Enteritis	–	1	1	–	–	–	2	2	–	–	2	1	3	–	–
Dysentery	3	4	7	–	–	6	3	9	–	–	5	7	12	–	–
Constipation	.	2	2	–	–	2	6	8	–	–	1	3	4	–	–
Hœmorrhoids	2	1	3	–	–	–	–	–	–	–	–	2	2	–	–
Hepatitis	–	3	3	–	–	2	3	5	–	–	2	–	2	–	–
Jaundice	–	1	1	–	–	–	–	–	–	–	–	1	1	–	–
Nephritis	2	–	2	–	–	–	–	–	–	–	1	–	1	–	–
Bright's Disease	6	–	6	1	–	1	–	1	–	–	–	–	–	–	–
Ascites	2	3	5	–	–	1	1	2	–	–	–	–	–	–	–
Cystitis	1	–	1	–	–	–	–	–	–	–	–	–	–	–	–
Incontinence of Urine	1	–	1	–	–	1	1	2	–	–	1	–	1	–	–
Gravel	–	–	–	–	–	–	1	1	–	–	–	–	–	–	–
Phthisis	9	4	13	2	1	6	1	7	–	–	4	2	6	–	–
Rheumatism	12	7	19	–	–	3	8	11	–	–	10	11	21	–	–
Rheumatism, Chronic	5	2	7	–	–	2	1	3	–	–	–	–	–	–	–
Erysipelas	4	3	7	–	–	–	2	2	–	–	–	–	–	–	–
Ephemeral Fever	2	–	2	–	–	1	–	1	–	–	1	3	4	–	–
Intermittent Fever	11	6	17	–	–	9	6	15	–	–	21	9	30	–	–
Remittent Fever	1	1	2	–	–	3	–	3	–	–	9	3	12	–	–
Typhoid Fever	–	–	–	–	–	3	2	5	–	–	6	4	10	2	–
Total	109	70	179	4	1	91	68	159	2	–	108	86	194	2	–

July.				August.				September.			
Mean Therm.	Rain Fall.	Direction and Force of Wind.		Mean Therm.	Rain Fall.	Direction and Force of Wind.		Mean Therm.	Rain Fall.	Direction and Force of Wind.	
72½°	4.050	S. W. h.	N. W. g.	72°	2.560	N. W. g.	S. W. g.	64°	6.430	S. W. g.	S. E. g.

TABLE OF THE DISEASES AND MORTALITY

OF MALE AND FEMALE PATIENTS, FROM THE AGE OF FORTY TO SIXTY YEARS, FOR THE YEAR 1872. — *Continued.*

1872.	October.					November.					December.					Total Patients.	Total Deaths.
	Sexes.		Total.	Deaths.		Sexes.		Total.	Deaths.		Sexes.		Total.	Deaths.			
List of Diseases.	Male.	Female.		Male.	Female.	Male.	Female.		Male.	Female.	Male.	Female.		Male.	Female.		
Epilepsy . . .	–	–	–	–	–	–	–	–	–	–	2	1	3	–	–	21	–
Convulsions . .	1	–	1	–	–	–	–	–	–	–	4	1	5	–	–	32	–
Congestion of Brain	–	–	–	–	–	–	–	–	–	–	1	–	1	–	–	7	1
Paralysis . . .	4	1	5	–	–	1	1	2	–	–	2	–	2	–	–	27	1
Paralysis, Partial .	1	–	1	–	–	–	1	1	–	–	–	–	–	–	–	27	–
Hemiplegia . . .	–	–	–	–	–	–	–	–	–	–	1	–	1	–	–	2	–
Spinal Disease . .	–	–	–	–	–	–	–	–	–	–	–	–	–	–	–	10	–
Neuralgia . . .	–	2	2	–	–	1	4	5	–	–	7	12	19	–	–	168	–
Conjunctivitis . .	1	1	2	–	–	1	1	2	–	–	–	1	1	–	–	42	–
Granular Lids . .	–	–	–	–	–	–	–	–	–	–	–	–	–	–	–	9	–
Keratitis . . .	1	1	2	–	–	3	–	3	–	–	2	1	3	–	–	31	–
Iritis	–	–	–	–	–	–	–	–	–	–	–	–	–	–	–	2	–
Ozœna	–	–	–	–	–	–	–	–	–	–	–	1	1	–	–	1	–
Catarrh	1	3	4	–	–	7	4	11	–	–	7	9	16	–	–	113	–
Epistaxis . . .	–	–	–	–	–	–	–	–	–	–	–	1	1	–	–	5	–
Tonsillitis . . .	–	1	1	–	–	–	1	1	–	–	3	1	4	–	–	52	–
Pharyngitis . .	–	–	–	–	–	1	1	2	–	–	–	–	–	–	–	37	–
Laryngitis . . .	2	–	2	–	–	–	–	–	–	–	–	–	–	–	–	19	–
Bronchitis . . .	8	6	14	–	–	39	23	62	–	–	53	22	75	–	–	619	3
Bronchitis, Chronic	–	1	1	–	–	5	3	8	–	–	4	2	6	–	–	88	–
Asthma	10	–	10	–	–	5	2	7	–	–	13	2	15	–	–	105	–
Pertussis . . .	–	–	–	–	–	–	–	–	–	–	–	–	–	–	–	22	–
Congestion of Lungs	–	–	–	–	–	5	–	5	–	–	6	1	7	–	–	16	–
Pneumonia . . .	4	2	6	–	–	18	8	26	–	–	22	8	30	–	–	128	5
Pleuritis . . .	3	1	4	–	–	1	–	1	–	–	8	3	11	–	–	127	–
Heart Disease . .	1	–	1	–	–	–	–	–	–	–	–	–	–	–	1	34	3
Endocarditis . .	–	–	–	–	–	–	–	–	–	–	–	–	–	–	–	4	–
Dyspepsia . . .	–	5	5	–	–	4	2	6	–	–	2	5	7	–	–	137	–
Cancer of Stomach	–	–	–	–	–	–	–	–	–	–	1	–	1	–	–	3	–
Diarrhœa . . .	1	3	4	–	–	1	–	1	–	–	2	–	2	–	–	134	1
Cholera Morbus .	–	–	–	–	–	–	–	–	–	–	–	–	–	–	–	19	1
Enteritis . . .	–	–	–	–	–	2	–	2	–	–	–	–	–	–	–	14	1
Dysentery . . .	4	1	5	–	–	–	–	–	–	–	–	1	1	–	–	58	–
Constipation . .	–	2	2	–	–	1	–	1	–	–	1	5	6	–	–	106	–
Hœmorrhoids . .	2	–	2	–	–	–	1	1	–	–	1	–	1	–	–	52	–
Hepatitis . . .	1	2	3	–	–	–	–	–	–	–	–	–	–	–	–	33	–
Jaundice . . .	–	–	–	–	–	–	–	–	–	–	–	–	–	–	–	2	–
Nephritis . . .	1	–	1	–	–	–	–	–	–	–	–	–	–	–	–	12	–
Bright's Disease .	–	–	–	–	–	–	–	–	–	–	–	–	–	–	–	15	3
Ascites	3	–	3	–	–	5	2	7	–	–	3	–	3	2	–	29	3
Cystitis	–	1	1	–	–	3	–	3	–	–	–	–	–	–	–	6	–
Incontinence of Urine	–	–	–	–	–	2	–	2	–	–	1	–	1	–	–	20	–
Gravel	–	–	–	–	–	–	–	–	–	–	–	–	–	–	–	1	–
Phthisis . . .	13	8	21	–	–	8	6	14	2	2	18	9	27	3	–	216	25
Rheumatism . .	12	7	19	–	–	15	11	26	–	–	37	19	56	–	–	599	–
Rheumatism, Chronic	3	–	3	–	–	3	5	8	–	–	3	4	7	–	–	74	–
Erysipelas . . .	2	–	2	–	–	1	1	2	–	–	6	2	8		–	40	–
Ephemeral Fever .	–	–	–	–	–	–	–	–	–	–	2	–	2	–	–	25	–
Intermittent Fever	21	11	32	–	–	7	5	12	–	–	5	3	8	–	–	294	–
Remittent Fever .	2	2	4	–	–	3	–	3	–	–	–	–	–	–	–	87	–
Typhoid Fever . .	–	–	–	–	–	1	–	1	–	–	–	–	–	1	–	39	5
Total	102	61	163	–	–	143	82	225	2	2	217	114	331	6	1	3,763	52

October.				November.				December.			
Mean Therm.	Rain Fall.	Direction and Force of Wind.		Mean Therm.	Rain Fall.	Direction and Force of Wind.		Mean Therm.	Rain Fall.	Direction and Force of Wind.	
52	.650	N. E. g.	S. W. h.	32½°	.800	N. W. h.	N. W. g.	19°	.430	N. W. g.	S. W. g.

ADDITIONAL TABLE OF THE DISEASES AND MORTALITY

Of Patients Unclassified as to Sex, from 40 to 60 Years of Age, for the Year 1872.

1872. List of Diseases.	January. Patients.	January. Deaths.	February. Patients.	February. Deaths.	March. Patients.	March. Deaths.	April. Patients.	April. Deaths.	May. Patients.	May. Deaths.	June. Patients.	June. Deaths.	July. Patients.	July. Deaths.	August. Patients.	August. Deaths.	September. Patients.	September. Deaths.	October. Patients.	October. Deaths.	November. Patients.	November. Deaths.	December. Patients.	December. Deaths	Total Patients.	Total Deaths.
Abscess	6	-	9	-	4	-	5	-	2	-	3	-	1	-	3	-	3	-	-	-	4	-	5	-	45	-
Fourncle	-	-	-	-	-	-	-	-	-	-	-	-	-	-	1	-	-	-	-	-	-	-	-	-	1	-
Ulcer	28	-	33	-	19	-	10	-	6	-	9	-	25	-	6	-	7	-	11	-	13	-	22	-	189	-
Frost-bite	29	-	21	-	-	-	-	-	-	-	-	-	-	-	-	-	-	-	-	-	-	-	25	-	75	-
Contusion	21	-	14	-	6	-	2	-	3	-	3	-	10	-	3	-	7	-	4	-	2	-	4	-	79	-
Contused Wound	4	-	5	-	2	-	1	-	1	-	-	-	-	-	-	-	2	-	-	-	-	-	-	-	15	-
Incised Wound	4	-	5	-	2	-	1	-	1	-	-	-	-	-	1	-	-	-	1	-	-	-	1	-	16	-
Paronychia	-	-	-	-	-	-	-	-	-	-	1	-	-	-	-	-	-	-	-	-	-	-	-	-	1	-
Varix	-	-	-	-	-	-	-	-	-	-	-	-	-	-	-	-	-	-	-	-	-	-	2	-	2	-
Varicose Veins	2	-	5	-	3	-	1	-	1	-	-	-	2	-	1	-	3	-	1	-	2	-	1	-	22	-
Fracture of Clavicle	5	-	4	-	2	-	-	-	-	-	-	-	2	-	-	-	1	-	-	-	-	-	6	-	20	-
Fracture of Radius	5	-	4	-	2	-	-	-	-	-	-	-	-	-	-	-	-	-	-	-	-	-	-	-	11	-
Fracture of Tibia	2	-	1	-	1	-	1	-	1	-	1	-	1	-	-	-	-	-	-	-	-	-	-	-	8	-
Periostitis	-	-	-	-	-	-	-	-	-	-	-	-	-	-	1	-	-	-	-	-	-	-	1	-	2	-
Necrosis	2	-	3	-	2	-	1	-	2	-	1	-	3	-	1	-	-	-	-	-	-	-	3	-	18	-
Synovitis	2	-	1	-	1	-	1	-	1	-	-	-	1	-	-	-	-	-	1	-	2	-	-	-	10	-
Hernia, Inguinal	15	-	24	-	20	-	13	-	8	-	5	-	2	-	5	-	4	-	1	-	7	-	9	-	113	-
Anæmia	2	-	1	-	2	-	1	-	2	-	1	-	-	-	1	-	-	-	2	-	-	-	2	-	14	-
Debility	22	-	19	-	21	-	10	1	19	-	23	-	15	-	7	-	14	-	11	-	11	-	9	1	181	2
Malaise	9	-	8	-	4	-	1	-	-	-	-	-	-	-	-	-	1	-	-	-	-	-	-	-	23	-
Hysteria	5	-	7	-	2	-	1	-	-	-	2	-	1	-	3	-	2	-	-	-	-	-	-	-	23	-
Cephalalgia	5	-	2	-	1	-	1	-	1	-	3	-	-	-	-	-	1	-	1	-	-	-	-	-	15	-
Vertigo	2	-	1	-	2	-	1	-	-	-	1	-	-	-	1	-	-	-	-	-	-	-	-	-	8	-
Hydrocephalus	-	-	-	-	-	-	-	-	-	-	1	-	-	-	-	-	-	-	-	-	-	-	-	-	1	-
Softening of Brain	-	-	2	-	-	-	-	-	-	-	-	-	1	-	-	-	-	-	-	-	-	-	1	-	4	-
Odontalgia	21	-	20	-	11	-	6	-	13	-	5	-	-	-	6	-	2	-	3	-	5	-	2	-	94	-
Otalgia	19	-	15	-	10	-	4	-	-	-	2	-	-	-	2	-	-	-	-	-	-	-	5	-	57	-
Otitis	4	-	5	-	2	-	1	-	1	-	-	-	1	-	-	-	-	-	-	-	-	-	-	-	14	-
Stomatitis	3	-	2	-	1	-	1	-	-	-	-	-	-	-	-	-	-	-	-	-	-	-	-	-	7	-
Angina	-	-	-	-	-	-	-	-	1	-	-	-	-	-	-	-	2	-	-	-	-	-	-	-	3	-
Hœmoptysis	-	-	-	-	-	-	-	-	-	-	-	-	-	-	-	-	-	-	-	-	1	-	-	-	1	-
Pericarditis	-	-	-	-	-	-	-	-	1	-	1	-	-	-	-	-	-	-	-	-	-	-	-	-	2	-
Total	217	-	211	-	120	-	63	1	64	-	62	-	65	-	42	-	49	-	36	-	47	-	98	1	1,074	2

ADDITIONAL TABLE OF DISEASES AND MORTALITY.—*Continued.*

1872.	January.		February.		March.		April.		May.		June.		July.		August.		September.		October.		November.		December.			
List of Diseases.	Patients.	Deaths.	Patients.	Deaths.	Patients.	Deaths.	Patients.	Deaths.	Patients.	Deaths.	Patients.	Deaths.	Patients.	Deaths.	Patients.	Deaths.	Patients.	Deaths.	Patients.	Deaths.	Patients.	Deaths.	Patients.	Deaths.	Total Patients.	Total Deaths.
Cardialgia	-	-	-	-	-	-	-	-	-	-	-	-	-	-	2	-	-	-	-	-	-	-	-	-	2	-
Gastritis	2	-	3	-	1	-	1	-	5	-	1	-	1	-	1	-	-	-	2	-	-	-	-	-	17	-
Gastralgia	1	-	2	-	1	-	1	-	-	-	-	-	3	-	3	-	1	-	1	-	-	-	-	-	13	-
Fistula in Ano	2	-	1	-	1	-	-	-	-	-	-	-	-	-	-	-	1	-	-	-	-	-	-	-	5	-
Colic	4	-	2	-	2	-	1	-	-	-	-	-	-	-	-	-	-	-	-	-	-	-	3	-	12	-
Gonorrhœa	2	-	2	-	1	-	-	-	-	-	-	-	1	-	-	-	1	-	-	-	1	-	-	-	8	-
Orchitis	-	-	-	-	-	-	-	-	-	-	-	-	-	-	-	-	1	-	-	-	-	-	3	-	4	-
Metritis	1	-	1	-	1	-	1	-	4	-	8	-	12	-	11	-	14	-	14	-	7	-	14	-	88	-
Uterine Disease	26	-	41	-	29	-	12	-	9	-	15	-	3	-	2	-	1	-	2	-	4	-	6	-	150	-
Abortion	4	-	6	-	2	-	1	-	-	-	2	-	-	-	1	-	-	-	-	-	-	-	-	-	16	-
Leucorrhœa	4	-	5	-	3	-	1	-	1	-	1	-	2	-	2	-	2	-	2	-	-	-	4	-	27	-
Displacement of Uterus	1	-	2	-	1	-	-	-	4	-	2	-	-	-	-	-	-	-	-	-	3	-	3	-	16	-
Chlorosis	-	-	-	-	-	-	-	-	1	-	1	-	-	-	-	-	-	-	-	-	-	-	-	-	2	-
Amenorrhœa	2	-	1	-	1	-	1	-	-	-	2	-	-	-	-	-	-	-	-	-	-	-	-	-	7	-
Dysmenorrhœa	-	-	-	-	-	-	-	-	-	-	-	-	1	-	2	-	2	-	2	-	-	-	-	-	7	-
Menorraghia	6	-	9	-	5	-	2	-	1	-	4	-	3	-	1	-	-	-	1	-	1	-	1	-	34	-
Adenitis	7	-	7	-	2	-	1	-	3	-	-	-	1	-	1	-	-	-	4	-	3	-	-	-	29	-
Scrofula	4	-	2	-	5	-	1	-	1	-	1	-	2	-	2	-	3	-	-	-	1	-	3	-	25	-
Marasmus	-	-	-	-	-	-	-	-	-	-	-	-	1	-	-	-	1	-	-	-	-	-	-	-	2	-
Lumbago	15	-	13	-	6	-	1	-	-	-	5	-	2	-	4	-	1	-	1	-	1	-	3	-	52	-
Sciatica	6	-	5	-	6	-	2	-	1	-	-	-	1	-	-	-	3	-	1	-	-	-	1	-	26	-
Coxalgia	1	-	2	-	1	-	-	-	-	-	-	-	-	-	-	-	-	-	-	-	-	-	-	-	4	-
Scarlatina	2	-	1	-	5	-	2	-	-	-	1	-	-	-	-	-	-	-	-	-	-	-	-	-	11	-
Syphilis	10	-	7	-	5	-	2	-	3	-	9	-	5	-	4	-	9	-	2	-	2	-	2	-	60	-
Syphilis, Secondary	4	-	3	-	2	-	1	-	1	-	3	-	5	-	1	-	2	-	1	-	2	-	1	-	26	-
Syphilis, Tertiary	1	-	1	-	1	-	-	-	1	-	2	-	1	-	-	-	1	-	-	-	-	-	1	-	[illegible]	-
Erythema	-	-	-	-	-	-	-	-	-	-	-	-	-	-	-	-	-	-	-	-	-	-	2	-	2	-
Eczema	4	-	7	-	2	-	1	-	3	-	1	-	4	-	-	-	1	-	-	-	2	-	3	-	28	-
Urticaria	-	-	-	-	-	-	-	-	-	-	-	-	1	-	1	-	1	-	-	-	-	-	-	-	3	-
Prurigo	-	-	-	-	-	-	-	-	-	-	1	-	-	-	-	-	1	-	1	-	-	-	-	-	3	-
Psoriasis	2	-	3	-	2	-	1	-	1	-	-	-	-	-	-	-	2	-	1	-	-	-	-	-	12	-
Herpes	2	-	3	-	1	-	-	-	-	-	-	-	-	-	-	-	-	-	1	-	-	-	1	-	8	-
Total	113	-	129	-	86	-	33	-	39	-	59	-	49	-	38	-	48	-	36	-	27	-	51	-	708	-

Male Patients, Classified, 2,120; Female Patients, Classified, 1,643; Patients, Unclassified by Sexes, 1,782; Total Patients, 5,545.
Deaths of Male Patients, 41; Deaths of Female Patients, 11; Deaths of Unclassified Patients, 2; Total Deaths, 54.

TABLE OF THE DISEASES AND MORTALITY

OF MALE AND FEMALE PATIENTS, FROM THE AGE OF SIXTY YEARS AND UPWARDS, FOR THE YEAR 1872.

1872.	January.					February.					March.				
	Sexes.		Total.	Deaths.		Sexes.		Total.	Deaths.		Sexes.		Total.	Deaths.	
List of Diseases.	Male.	Female.		Male.	Female.	Male.	Female.		Male.	Female.	Male.	Female.		Male.	Female.
Bronchitis . . .	15	10	25	-	-	17	12	29	-	-	16	5	21	1	-
Bronchitis, Chronic	6	4	10	-	-	7	4	11	-	-	6	6	12	-	-
Asthma	6	4	10	-	-	6	7	13	-	-	10	5	15	-	-
Congestion of Lungs	1	-	1	-	-	1	-	1	-	-	1	-	1	-	-
Pneumonia . . .	2	5	7	-	-	2	3	5	-	-	3	1	4	-	-
Emphysema Pulm.	-	-	-	-	-	-	-	-	-	-	-	1	1	-	-
Pleuritis . . .	1	1	2	-	-	1	1	2	-	-	-	1	1	-	-
Heart Disease . .	3	-	3	-	-	2	-	2	-	-	1	-	1	1	-
Endocarditis . .	-	-	-	-	-	-	-	-	-	-	-	-	-	-	-
Dyspepsia . . .	3	3	6	-	-	3	4	7	-	-	4	2	6	-	-
Cancer of Stomach	-	-	-	-	-	1	-	1	-	-	1	-	1	-	-
Diarrhœa	-	-	-	-	-	1	-	1	-	-	6	3	9	-	-
Diarrhœa, Chronic	-	-	-	-	-	-	-	-	-	-	4	2	6	1	-
Cholera Morbus .	-	-	-	-	-	-	-	-	-	-	-	-	-	-	-
Enteritis	-	-	-	-	-	-	-	-	-	-	-	-	-	-	-
Dysentery . . .	-	-	-	-	-	1	-	1	-	-	-	1	1	-	-
Constipation . .	3	6	9	-	-	2	5	7	-	-	4	2	6	-	-
Hœmorrhoids . .	1	-	1	-	-	-	2	2	-	-	1	-	1	-	-
Peritonitis . . .	-	-	-	-	-	1	-	1	-	-	-	-	-	-	-
Hepatitis	-	1	1	-	-	-	1	1	-	-	-	-	-	-	-
Renal Calculi . .	-	1	1	-	-	-	1	1	-	-	-	-	-	-	-
Nephritis	1	-	1	-	-	1	-	1	-	-	-	-	-	-	-
Bright's Disease .	1	-	1	-	-	1	-	1	-	-	-	-	-	-	-
Ascites	2	1	3	-	-	1	4	5	-	-	3	3	6	1	-
Anasarca	-	-	-	-	-	-	-	-	-	-	-	-	-	-	-
Cystitis	-	1	1	-	-	-	-	-	-	-	1	-	1	-	-
Dysuria	-	-	-	-	-	-	-	-	-	-	1	-	1	-	-
Incontinence of									-	-	2	-	2	-	-
Urine	2	-	2	-	-	2	1	3	-	-	2	-	2	-	-
Gravel	2	-	2	-	-	1	2	3	-	-	2	-	2	-	-
Phthisis	4	5	9	-	1	4	11	15	-	-	5	1	6	1	-
Rheumatism . .	20	11	31	-	-	17	20	37	-	-	15	8	23	-	-
Rheumatism, Chronic	3	2	5	-	-	7	4	11	-	-	4	2	6	-	-
Erysipelas . . .	1	-	1	-	-	4	1	5	-	-	-	2	2	-	-
Intermittent Fever	6	3	9	-	-	1	5	6	-	-	4	3	7	-	-
Remittent Fever .	1	3	4	-	-	3	2	5	-	-	1	5	6	-	-
Typhoid Fever . .	2	-	2	-	-	2	1	3	-	-	2	-	2	-	-
Total	86	61	147	-	1	90	91	181	-	-	97	53	150	5	-

January.				February.				March.			
Mean Therm.	Rain Fall.	Direction and Force of Wind.		Mean Therm.	Rain Fall.	Direction and Force of Wind.		Mean Therm.	Rain Fall.	Direction and Force of Wind.	
26°	.670	S. W. h.	N. W. g.	27°	.690	S. W. g.	S. E. g.	29°	3.220	N. E. h.	N. W. g.

TABLE OF THE DISEASES AND MORTALITY

Of Male and Female Patients, from the Age of Sixty Years and upwards, for the Year 1872. — *Continued.*

1872.	April.					May.					June.				
List of Diseases.	Sexes.		Total.	Deaths.		Sexes.		Total.	Deaths.		Sexes.		Total.	Deaths.	
	Male.	Female.		Male.	Female.	Male.	Female.		Male.	Female.	Male.	Female.		Male.	Female.
Bronchitis . . .	14	5	19	–	–	3	2	5	–	–	4	2	6	–	–
Bronchitis, Chronic	2	1	3	–	–	–	–	–	–	–	1	–	1	–	–
Asthma	2	–	2	–	–	4	1	5	–	–	–	–	–	–	–
Congestion of Lungs	1	–	1	–	–	–	–	–	–	–	–	–	–	–	–
Pneumonia . . .	1	1	2	–	–	1	–	1	–	–	1	–	1	–	–
Emphysema . .	–	–	–	–	–	–	–	–	–	–	–	–	–	–	–
Pleuritis	1	–	1	–	–	1	–	1	–	–	–	1	1	–	–
Heart Disease . .	1	–	1	1	–	–	–	–	–	–	–	–	–	–	–
Endocarditis . .	–	–	–	–	–	–	–	–	–	–	–	–	–	–	–
Dyspepsia . . .	2	1	3	–	–	3	1	4	–	–	1	–	1	–	–
Cancer of Stomach	–	–	–	–	–	–	–	–	–	–	–	–	–	1	–
Diarrhœa . . .	11	5	16	–	–	–	–	–	–	–	–	–	–	–	–
Diarrhœa, Chronic	6	3	9	–	–	1	–	1	–	–	–	–	–	–	–
Cholera Morbus .	–	–	–	–	–	–	–	–	–	–	2	–	2	–	–
Enteritis	–	–	–	–	–	–	–	–	–	–	–	–	–	–	–
Dysentery . . .	1	–	1	–	–	–	–	–	–	–	–	–	–	–	–
Constipation . .	5	2	7	–	–	3	2	5	–	–	4	2	6	–	–
Hœmorrhoids . .	1	–	1	–	–	–	–	–	–	–	–	–	–	–	–
Peritonitis . . .	–	–	–	–	–	–	–	–	–	–	–	–	–	–	–
Hepatitis	–	–	–	–	–	–	–	–	–	–	–	–	–	–	–
Renal Calculi . .	–	–	–	–	–	–	–	–	–	–	–	–	–	–	–
Nephritis	–	–	–	–	–	–	–	–	–	–	–	–	–	–	–
Bright's Disease .	–	–	–	–	–	–	–	–	–	–	–	–	–	–	–
Ascites	2	–	2	–	–	–	–	–	–	–	2	1	3	1	–
Anasarca	–	–	–	–	–	1	–	1	–	–	–	–	–	–	–
Cystitis	–	–	–	–	–	–	–	–	–	–	–	–	–	–	–
Dysuria	–	–	–	–	–	–	–	–	–	–	–	–	–	–	–
Incontinence of Urine	1	–	1	–	–	–	–	–	–	–	–	–	–	–	–
Gravel	–	–	–	–	–	–	–	–	–	–	1	–	1	–	–
Phthisis	2	1	3	–	1	1	–	1	1	–	1	1	2	1	–
Rheumatism . .	11	5	16	–	–	3	2	5	–	–	2	1	3	–	–
Rheumatism, Chronic	2	1	3	–	–	1	–	1	–	–	1	1	2	–	–
Erysipelas . . .	–	–	–	–	–	–	–	–	–	–	1	1	2	–	–
Intermittent Fever	4	2	6	–	–	2	–	2	–	–	1	–	1	–	–
Remittent Fever .	3	1	4	–	–	–	–	–	–	–	–	–	–	–	–
Typhoid Fever . .	1	–	1	–	–	–	–	–	–	–	–	–	–	–	–
Total	74	28	102	1	1	24	8	32	1	–	21	10	31	3	–

April.				May.				June.			
Mean Therm.	Rain Fall.	Direction and Force of Wind.		Mean Therm.	Rain Fall.	Direction and Force of Wind.		Mean Therm.	Rain Fall.	Direction and Force of Wind.	
48°	2.990	S. W. h.	N. E. h.	57½°	3.285	S. W. g.	S. E. h.	70⅜°	3.410	S. W. g.	N. W. g.

TABLE OF THE DISEASES AND MORTALITY

OF MALE AND FEMALE PATIENTS, FROM THE AGE OF SIXTY YEARS AND UPWARDS, FOR THE YEAR 1872. — *Continued.*

1872.	July.					August.					September.				
	Sexes.			Deaths.		Sexes.			Deaths.		Sexes.			Deaths.	
List of Diseases.	Male.	Female.	Total.	Male.	Female.	Male.	Female.	Total.	Male.	Female.	Male.	Female.	Total.	Male.	Female.
Bronchitis	3	3	6	–	–	1	1	2	–	–	1	1	2	–	–
Bronchitis, Chronic	1	–	1	1	–	–	–	–	–	–	1	1	2	–	–
Asthma	1	–	1	–	–	1	–	1	–	–	–	–	–	–	–
Congestion of Lungs	–	–	–	–	–	1	–	1	–	–	–	–	–	–	–
Pneumonia	–	–	–	–	–	–	–	–	–	–	–	–	–	–	–
Emphysema	–	–	–	–	–	–	–	–	–	–	–	–	–	–	–
Pleuritis	–	–	–	–	–	–	–	–	–	–	–	–	–	–	–
Heart Disease	–	2	2	–	–	–	–	–	–	–	1	–	1	–	–
Endocarditis	–	–	–	–	–	–	–	–	–	–	–	–	–	–	–
Dyspepsia	2	1	3	–	–	3	1	4	–	–	–	2	2	–	–
Cancer of Stomach	–	–	–	–	–	1	–	1	–	–	–	–	–	–	–
Diarrhœa	7	4	11	–	–	1	1	2	–	–	3	2	5	–	–
Diarrhœa, Chronic	–	–	–	–	–	–	–	–	–	–	–	–	–	–	–
Cholera Morbus	1	1	2	–	–	2	–	2	–	–	–	1	1	–	–
Enteritis	–	–	–	–	–	–	–	–	–	–	–	–	–	–	–
Dysentery	2	1	3	–	–	–	–	–	–	–	2	–	2	–	–
Constipation	–	–	–	–	–	–	1	1	–	–	–	–	–	–	–
Hœmorrhoids	1	1	2	–	–	–	–	–	–	–	–	–	–	–	–
Peritonitis	–	–	–	–	–	–	–	–	–	–	–	–	–	–	–
Hepatitis	–	–	–	–	–	–	–	–	–	–	–	–	–	–	–
Renal Calculi	–	–	–	–	–	–	–	–	–	–	–	–	–	–	–
Nephritis	–	–	–	–	–	–	–	–	–	–	1	–	1	–	–
Bright's Disease	1	–	1	–	–	–	–	–	–	–	1	–	1	–	–
Ascites	1	–	1	–	–	–	–	–	–	–	1	1	2	1	–
Anasarca	1	–	1	–	–	1	–	1	–	–	–	–	–	–	–
Cystitis	–	–	–	–	–	–	–	–	–	–	–	–	–	–	–
Dysuria	–	–	–	–	–	–	–	–	–	–	–	–	–	–	–
Incontinence of Urine	–	–	–	–	–	–	–	–	–	–	–	–	–	–	–
Gravel	–	–	–	–	–	–	–	–	–	–	–	–	–	–	–
Phthisis	2	1	3	2	1	2	1	3	1	1	1	–	1	–	–
Rheumatism	4	2	6	–	–	1	–	1	–	–	2	–	2	1	–
Rheumatism, Chronic	1	–	1	–	–	–	–	–	–	–	–	–	–	–	–
Erysipelas	2	1	3	–	–	–	–	–	–	–	–	–	–	–	–
Intermittent Fever	–	–	–	–	–	2	1	3	–	–	3	1	4	–	–
Remittent Fever	–	1	1	–	–	–	–	–	–	–	2	–	2	–	–
Typhoid Fever	–	–	–	–	–	–	–	–	–	–	2	–	2	–	–
Total	30	18	48	3	1	16	6	22	1	1	21	9	30	2	–

July.				August.				September.			
Mean Therm.	Rain Fall.	Direction and Force of Wind.		Mean Therm.	Rain Fall.	Direction and Force of Wind.		Mean Therm.	Rain Fall.	Direction and Force of Wind.	
72½°	4.050	S. W. h.	N. W. g.	72°	2.560	N. W. g.	S. W. g.	64°	6.430	S. W. g.	S. E. g.

TABLE OF THE DISEASES AND MORTALITY

Of Male and Female Patients, from the Age of Sixty Years and upwards, for the Year 1872. — *Continued.*

1872.	October.					November.					December.					Total Patients.	Total Deaths.
	Sexes.		Total.	Deaths.		Sexes.		Total.	Deaths.		Sexes.		Total.	Deaths.			
List of Diseases.	Male.	Female.		Male.	Female	Male.	Female.		Male.	Female.	Male.	Female.		Male.	Female.		
Bronchitis . . .	4	2	6	–	–	4	2	6	–	–	5	2	7	–	–	134	1
Bronchitis, Chronic	1	1	2	–	–	3	1	4	–	–	1	1	2	–	–	48	1
Asthma	4	1	4	–	–	4	1	5	–	–	1	1	2	–	–	59	–
Congestion of Lungs	1	–	1	–	–	–	–	–	–	–	–	–	–	–	–	6	–
Pneumonia . . .	–	–	–	–	–	–	1	1	–	–	1	1	2	–	–	23	–
Emphysema . .	–	–	–	–	–	–	–	–	–	–	–	–	–	–	–	1	–
Pleuritis . . .	–	–	–	–	–	–	–	–	–	–	–	–	–	–	–	8	–
Heart Disease . .	–	1	1	1	1	–	–	–	–	–	2	1	3	–	–	14	5
Endocarditis . .	–	–	–	–	–	–	–	–	–	–	1	–	1	–	–	1	–
Dyspepsia . . .	–	1	1	–	–	1	1	2	–	–	–	1	1	–	–	40	–
Cancer of Stomach	1	–	1	–	–	–	–	–	–	–	–	1	1	–	–	5	1
Diarrhœa . . .	3	1	4	–	–	–	–	–	–	–	1	2	3	–	–	51	–
Diarrhœa, Chronic	1	–	1	–	–	–	–	–	–	–	–	–	–	–	–	17	1
Cholera Morbus .	–	–	–	–	–	–	–	–	–	–	–	–	–	–	–	7	–
Enteritis . . .	–	–	–	–	–	–	–	–	–	–	–	1	1	–	–	1	–
Dysentery . . .	–	–	–	–	–	1	–	1	1	–	1	1	2	1	–	11	2
Constipation . .	–	–	–	–	–	1	1	2	–	–	1	3	4	–	–	47	–
Hœmorrhoids . .	–	–	–	–	–	–	–	–	–	–	2	–	2	–	–	9	–
Peritonitis . . .	–	–	–	–	–	–	–	–	–	–	–	–	–	–	–	1	–
Hepatitis . . .	–	–	–	–	–	–	–	–	–	–	–	–	–	–	–	2	–
Renal Calculi . .	–	–	–	–	–	–	–	–	–	–	–	–	–	–	–	2	–
Nephritis . . .	1	1	2	–	–	–	–	–	–	–	–	1	1	–	–	6	–
Bright's Disease .	–	–	–	–	–	1	–	1	1	–	1	–	1	–	–	6	1
Ascites	–	–	–	–	–	–	–	–	–	–	1	–	1	–	–	23	3
Anasarca . . .	–	–	–	–	–	–	–	–	–	–	–	1	1	–	–	4	–
Cystitis	–	–	–	–	–	–	–	–	–	–	–	–	–	–	–	2	–
Dysuria	–	–	–	–	–	–	–	–	–	–	–	–	–	–	–	1	–
Incontinence of Urine	–	–	–	–	–	–	–	–	–	–	–	–	–	–	–	8	–
Gravel	–	–	–	–	–	–	–	–	–	–	–	–	–	–	–	8	–
Phthisis	–	–	–	–	–	–	–	–	–	–	5	2	7	1	–	50	11
Rheumatism . .	3	1	4	1	–	4	2	6	–	–	8	4	12	–	–	146	2
Rheumatism, Chronic	1	1	2	–	–	–	–	–	–	–	1	1	2	–	–	33	–
Erysipelas . . .	–	–	–	–	–	–	–	–	–	–	–	–	–	–	–	13	–
Intermittent Fever	–	–	–	–	–	–	–	–	–	–	1	1	2	–	–	40	–
Remittent Fever .	–	–	–	–	–	–	–	–	–	–	1	–	1	–	–	23	–
Typhoid Fever . .	–	–	–	–	–	–	–	–	–	–	–	–	–	–	–	10	–
Total	20	10	30	2	1	19	9	28	2	–	34	25	59	2	1	860	28

October.				November.				December.			
Mean Therm.	Rain Fall.	Direction and Force of Wind.		Mean Therm.	Rain Fall.	Direction and Force of Wind.		Mean Therm.	Rain Fall.	Direction and Force of Wind.	
52°	.650	N. E. g.	S. W. h.	32½°	.800	N. W. h.	N. W. g.	19°	.430	N. W. g.	S. W. g.

ADDITIONAL TABLE OF THE SICKNESS AND MORTALITY

OF PATIENTS, UNCLASSIFIED AS TO SEX, FROM THE AGE OF SIXTY YEARS AND UPWARDS, FOR THE YEAR 1872.

1872.	JAN.	FEB.		MAR.		APRIL		MAY	JUN.	JUL.	AUG.	SEP.	OCT.	NOV.		DEC.			
LIST OF DISEASES.	Patients.	Patients.	Deaths.	Patients.	Death.	Patients.	Death.	Patients.	Patients.	Patients.	Patients.	Patients.	Patients.	Patients.	Death.	Patients.	Deaths.	Total Patients.	Total Deaths.
Abscess	1	2	–	1	–	1	–	1	–	1	–	1	–	–	–	1	–	9	–
Ulcer	12	16	–	10	–	4	–	3	3	6	1	3	2	2	–	5	–	67	–
Inflammation of Mamma	1	1	–	–	–	–	–	–	–	–	–	–	–	–	–	–	–	2	–
Frost-bite	9	5	–	–	–	–	–	–	–	–	–	–	–	1	–	2	–	17	–
Concussion	–	–	–	–	–	–	–	1	–	–	–	1	–	1	–	–	–	3	–
Contusion	2	2	–	3	–	1	–	1	–	–	1	–	–	2	–	–	–	12	–
Contused wound	1	–	–	1	–	–	–	–	–	1	–	–	2	–	–	–	–	5	–
Incised wound	1	2	–	1	–	–	–	–	–	–	–	–	–	–	–	–	–	4	–
Paronychia	–	–	–	–	–	–	–	–	–	–	–	2	–	–	–	–	–	2	–
Periostitis	–	–	–	–	–	–	–	–	1	–	–	–	–	–	–	–	–	1	–
Exostosis	–	–	–	1	–	–	–	–	–	–	–	–	–	–	–	–	–	1	–
Caries	–	–	–	1	–	–	–	1	–	–	–	1	1	–	–	–	–	4	–
Necrosis	–	1	–	–	–	–	–	–	1	–	–	–	–	–	–	–	–	2	–
Arthritis	1	–	–	1	–	–	–	–	–	–	1	–	1	–	–	1	–	5	–
Synovitis	–	1	–	–	–	1	–	–	–	–	–	–	–	–	–	–	–	2	–
Hernia	5	8	–	3	–	2	–	3	–	1	1	–	1	–	–	1	–	25	–
Anæmia	–	–	–	–	–	1	–	1	2	1	–	–	–	–	–	–	–	5	–
Debility, or Old Age	46	25	2	17	1	10	1	10	10	10	6	4	3	2	1	6	1	149	6
Malaise	1	1	–	1	–	–	–	–	–	–	–	–	–	–	–	–	–	3	–
Hysteria	–	–	–	–	–	–	–	–	1	–	–	–	–	–	–	–	–	1	–
Cephalalgia	2	1	–	1	–	1	–	2	1	–	–	–	–	–	–	–	–	8	–
Softening of Brain	1	–	–	–	–	1	–	–	–	–	–	1	–	–	–	1	1	4	1
Meningitis	–	–	–	–	–	–	–	1	1	–	–	–	–	–	–	–	–	2	–
Paralysis	2	3	–	1	–	–	–	–	1	–	–	–	–	1	–	1	–	9	–
Paralysis, partial	–	1	–	2	–	1	–	–	–	–	–	–	–	–	–	–	–	4	–
Hemiplegia	–	–	–	–	–	–	–	–	–	1	–	–	–	–	–	–	–	1	–
Spinal disease	–	–	–	–	–	–	–	–	–	–	–	–	1	–	–	–	–	1	–
Neuralgia	4	5	–	2	–	1	–	1	–	–	1	–	–	–	–	4	–	18	–
Odontalgia	2	3	–	4	–	1	–	1	1	–	–	–	–	1	–	1	–	14	–
Otalgia	–	–	–	–	–	1	–	1	–	–	–	–	–	–	–	–	–	2	–
Otitis	–	1	–	–	–	–	–	–	–	1	–	–	–	–	–	–	–	2	–
Total	91	78	2	50	1	26	1	27	22	22	11	13	11	10	1	23	2	384	7

Total of Male Patients for the year 1872, classified	14,168
Total of Female Patients for the year 1872, classified	11,203
Total of Patients for the year 1872, unclassified by Sexes	14,181
Grand Total Patients for the year 1872	39,552
Total Deaths of Male Patients, for the year 1872	207
Total Deaths of Female Patients, for the year 1872	121
Total Deaths of unclassified Patients, for the year 1872	35
Grand Total Deaths for the year 1872	363

ADDITIONAL TABLE OF THE SICKNESS AND MORTALITY OF PATIENTS, UNCLASSIFIED AS TO SEX, FROM THE AGE OF SIXTY YEARS AND UPWARDS, FOR THE YEAR 1872. — *Continued.*

1872.	JAN.	FEB.	MAR.	APRIL	MAY	JUNE	JULY	AUG.	SEPT.	OCT.	NOV.	DEC.	
LIST OF DISEASES.	Patients.	Patients.	Patients.	Patients.	Patients.	Patients.	Patients.	Patients.	Patients.	Patients.	Patients.	Patients.	Total Patients.
Conjunctivitis	2	3	1	1	–	–	–	1	–	1	2	–	11
Granular Lids	1	2	1	–	–	–	–	–	–	–	–	–	4
Catarrh . .	12	16	12	8	4	1	–	–	–	–	4	6	63
Stomatitis . .	–	–	–	–	1	–	–	–	–	–	–	–	1
Quinsy . . .	1	1	1	–	–	–	–	–	–	–	–	–	3
Pharyngitis .	–	1	–	–	1	1	–	–	–	–	–	–	3
Diphtheria .	–	1	–	1	–	–	–	–	–	–	–	–	2
Laryngitis . .	–	–	–	–	–	–	–	–	–	–	1	–	1
Trachitis . .	1	1	1	–	–	–	–	–	–	–	–	–	3
Pyrosis . .	–	–	–	–	1	–	–	–	–	–	–	–	1
Gastralgia . .	1	1	1	–	–	1	1	–	–	–	–	–	5
Orchitis .	1	1	–	–	–	–	–	–	–	–	–	–	2
Uterine disease	1	1	–	–	–	–	1	–	–	–	–	–	3
Leucorrhea .	–	1	–	–	1	–	–	–	–	–	–	–	2
Tumors . .	2	1	1	1	1	–	–	–	–	–	–	–	6
Tumor of Breast	–	1	–	–	–	1	–	1	–	–	–	1	4
Goitre . . .	–	1	–	–	–	–	–	–	–	–	–	–	1
Adenitis . .	2	1	1	1	–	–	1	–	1	2	1	1	11
Scrofula . .	1	1	1	1	–	–	1	–	–	1	1	1	8
Morbus Coxarines . . .	–	–	–	–	–	–	–	–	1	–	–	–	1
Fatty Degeneration . . .	1	3	1	1	–	–	–	–	–	–	–	–	6
Lumbago . .	1	1	1	1	8	2	–	2	–	–	–	–	16
Sciatica . .	1	1	1	1	–	–	1	–	–	–	–	1	6
Pleurodynia .	–	–	–	–	1	–	–	–	–	–	–	–	1
Ephemeral Fever	–	–	–	–	1	1	–	–	–	–	–	–	2
Syphilis . .	–	–	–	1	–	1	–	–	–	–	–	–	2
Syphilis Secondary . .	–	–	–	1	1	–	1	–	–	–	–	–	3
Eczema . .	–	2	1	1	1	2	1	–	–	1	–	–	10
Herpes . . .	–	–	–	–	–	1	–	–	–	–	–	–	1
Porrigo . .	–	–	–	–	–	–	1	–	1	–	–	–	2
Total .	29	41	24	19	21	11	8	4	3	5	9	10	184

Male Patients, Classified	532	Deaths of Male Patients	22
Female Patients, Classified	328	Deaths of Female Patients	6
Patients, Unclassified by Sexes . . .	568	Deaths of Unclassified Patients . .	7
Total Patients, Sixty and over .	1,428	Total Deaths	35

Per cent. of deaths of Male Patients, of all ages 1.46

Per cent. of deaths of Female Patients, of all ages 1.08

Per cent. of deaths of Unclassified Patients, of all ages 0.25

Per cent. of whole number of deaths to whole number of Patients 0.92

TABULAR STATEMENT OF 26,549 VACCINATIONS AND REVACCINATIONS,

At Different Periods of Life, in which the Results were carefully observed and recorded by Physicians of the Relief and Aid Society, during the Winter of 1871 and 1872.

The number of cases of small-pox occurring after recent or remote successful vaccinations and revaccinations was 726. General average time of occurrence after a first successful vaccination seven years; second successful vaccination, eleven and five sixths years; third successful vaccination, fifteen and three fourths years. In addition to these figures, we have records of 4,197 cases which have been excluded, on the ground of incompleteness, from the general statement, and which, if added, would show a total of 30,746 vaccinations. The number of cases of small-pox occurring after recent or remote unsuccessful vaccinations and revaccinations was 658. The statistics of small-pox include cases that occurred previous to the winter of 1871-1872, and of which the evidence was satisfactory to the observers.

Nationality.	Successful. Under Five Years.								Successful. From Five to Ten Years.							
	Vaccinated and Revaccinated.			Small-pox.			Total Vaccinated and Revaccinated. Under Five.	Total Small-pox. Under Five.	Vaccinated and Revaccinated.			Small-pox.			Total Vaccinated and Revaccinated. From Five to Ten.	Total Small-pox. From Five to Ten.
	1.	2.	3.	1.	2.	3.			1.	2.	3.	1.	2.	3.		
Irish	1,098	337	111	7	2	4	1,546	13	298	783	189	3	4	4	1,270	11
Irish-American	225	153	2	1	2	-	380	3	42	306	22	1	9	-	370	10
German	457	182	71	3	-	2	710	5	142	416	68	6	3	1	626	10
German-American	386	191	13	4	-	2	590	6	63	366	29	2	16	1	458	19
American	320	76	18	3	-	2	414	5	72	148	29	2	1	-	249	3
English	101	20	7	1	1	-	128	2	32	55	5	-	-	-	92	-
Canadian	52	41	2	-	1	-	95	1	6	27	3	-	-	-	36	-
Norwegian	138	26	21	-	-	-	185	-	73	89	36	1	-	-	198	1
Swedish	218	73	33	3	-	-	324	3	87	117	40	3	2	-	244	5
Scotch	24	10	-	-	-	-	34	-	14	15	3	-	-	-	32	-
French	32	8	6	4	-	-	46	4	9	23	8	-	-	-	40	-
Miscellaneous Nationality	134	51	15	-	-	-	200	-	46	104	14	1	-	-	164	1
Total	3,185	1,168	299	26	6	10	4,652	42	884	2,449	446	19	35	6	3,779	60

TABULAR STATEMENT OF 26,549 VACCINATIONS AND REVACCINATIONS,

AT DIFFERENT PERIODS OF LIFE, IN WHICH THE RESULTS WERE CAREFULLY OBSERVED AND RECORDED BY PHYSICIANS OF THE RELIEF AND AID SOCIETY, DURING THE WINTER OF 1871 AND 1872. — *Continued.*

NATIONALITY.	SUCCESSFUL. FROM TEN TO TWENTY YEARS.								SUCCESSFUL. FROM TWENTY YEARS AND UPWARDS.								Total of each Nationality of Successful Vaccination and Revaccination.	Total Cases of Small-pox, in Nationality.
	Vaccinated and Revaccinated.			Small-pox.			Total Vaccinated and Revaccinated. From Ten to Twenty.	Total Small-pox. From Ten to Twenty.	Vaccinated and Revaccinated.			Small-pox.			Total Vaccinated and Revaccinated. From Twenty Years and upwards.	Total Small-pox. From 20 Years and upwards.		
	1.	2.	3.	1.	2.	3.			1.	2.	3.	1.	2.	3.				
Irish	207	919	353	8	19	12	1,479	39	347	1,607	452	84	150	42	2,406	276	6,701	339
Irish-American	14	395	66	5	26	4	475	35	5	39	11	4	9	1	55	14	1,280	62
German	97	485	127	2	3	2	709	7	190	1,030	395	18	41	18	1,615	77	3,660	99
German-American	40	377	41	10	30	2	458	42	3	26	5	1	1	1	34	3	1,540	70
American	95	208	63	3	7	1	366	11	107	303	135	13	5	3	545	21	1,574	40
English	7	68	21	–	3	1	96	4	35	97	44	9	13	2	176	24	492	30
Canadian	–	28	8	1	2	–	36	3	2	36	10	–	3	–	48	3	215	7
Norwegian	50	96	39	1	–	–	185	1	104	153	141	2	7	4	398	13	966	15
Swedish	48	147	40	4	2	1	235	7	126	283	155	9	12	2	564	23	1,367	38
Scotch	2	23	8	–	–	–	33	–	6	27	7	2	2	–	40	4	139	4
French	6	12	12	–	–	–	30	–	28	34	29	1	–	–	91	1	207	5
Miscellaneous Nationality	32	96	18	–	3	–	146	3	60	198	51	3	9	1	309	13	819	17
Total	598	2,854	796	34	95	23	4,248	152	1,013	3,833	1,435	146	252	74	6,281	472	18,960	726

TABULAR STATEMENT OF 26,549 VACCINATIONS AND REVACCINATIONS,

At Different Periods of Life, in which the Results were carefully observed and recorded by Physicians of the Relief and Aid Society, during the Winter of 1871 and 1872. — *Continued.*

Nationality.	Unsuccessful. Under Five Years.								Unsuccessful. From Five to Ten Years.							
	Vaccinated and Revaccinated.			Small-pox.			Total Vaccinated and Revaccinated. Under Five.	Total Small-pox. Under Five.	Vaccinated and Revaccinated.			Small-pox.			Total Vaccinated and Revaccinated. From Five to Ten.	Total Small-pox. From Five to Ten.
	1.	2.	3.	1.	2.	3.			1.	2.	3.	1.	2.	3.		
Irish	93	153	30	1	4	1	276	6	47	314	66	11	3	2	427	16
Irish-American	21	41	3	2	1	-	65	3	3	81	10	-	9	-	94	9
German	66	110	20	2	-	1	196	3	42	198	53	6	2	3	293	11
German-American	53	75	2	2	2	-	130	4	18	197	17	5	18	-	232	23
American	37	57	1	8	10	-	95	18	14	73	10	5	-	1	97	6
English	9	12	-	-	-	-	21	-	-	13	11	-	-	-	24	1
Canadian	1	2	-	-	1	-	3	1	-	3	2	-	1	-	5	-
Norwegian	25	7	5	-	-	-	37	-	11	28	5	-	-	-	44	-
Swedish	22	33	8	-	-	-	63	-	12	61	12	-	1	1	85	2
Scotch	4	6	-	-	-	-	10	-	1	9	1	1	-	-	11	1
French	4	4	-	-	-	-	8	-	4	7	-	-	-	-	11	-
Miscellaneous Nationality	16	42	8	-	-	-	66	-	5	40	2	-	-	-	47	-
Total	351	542	77	15	18	2	970	35	157	1,024	189	28	34	7	1,370	69

TABULAR STATEMENT OF 26,549 VACCINATIONS AND REVACCINATIONS,

At Different Periods of Life, in which the Results were carefully observed and recorded by Physicians of the Relief and Aid Society, during the Winter of 1871 and 1872. — *Continued.*

Nationality.	Unsuccessful. From Ten to Twenty Years.								Unsuccessful. From Twenty Years and Upwards.								Total of each Nationality of Unsuccessful Vaccination and Revaccination.	Total Cases of Small-pox in Nationality.
	Vaccinated and Revaccinated.			Small-pox.			Total Vaccinated and Revaccinated. From Ten to Twenty.	Total Small-pox. From Ten to Twenty.	Vaccinated and Revaccinated.			Small-pox.			Total Vaccinated and Revaccinated. From Twenty Years and Upwards.	Total Small-pox. From 20 Years and upwards.		
	1.	2.	3.	1.	2.	3.			1.	2.	3.	1.	2.	3.				
Irish	40	388	103	15	9	–	531	24	87	823	218	53	127	16	1,128	196	2,362	242
Irish-American	7	151	23	3	15	1	181	19	–	15	7	–	4	–	22	4	362	35
German	18	306	74	1	17	2	398	20	41	763	268	15	69	15	1,072	99	1,959	133
German-American	15	285	23	6	35	1	323	42	1	37	9	1	6	2	47	9	732	78
American	18	93	46	5	–	2	157	1	29	176	126	23	15	16	331	54	680	85
English	4	30	6	1	–	–	40	1	3	38	26	1	8	1	67	10	152	12
Canadian	–	–	1	–	–	–	1	–	–	6	5	–	1	–	11	1	20	2
Norwegian	2	22	9	1	–	–	33	1	7	87	31	–	3	–	125	3	239	4
Swedish	29	106	29	4	8	–	164	12	15	225	49	9	17	–	289	26	601	40
Scotch	–	3	2	–	1	–	5	1	5	21	10	4	3	–	36	7	62	9
French	6	17	5	–	–	–	28	–	3	23	13	–	3	1	39	4	86	4
Miscellaneous Nationality	8	49	27	–	2	–	84	2	11	100	26	3	6	3	137	12	334	14
Total	147	1,450	348	36	87	6	1,945	129	202	2,314	788	109	262	54	3,304	425	7,589	658

Remarks. Among the Swedes, in one case, there were three good scars on each arm; subsequently the patient had small-pox severely, in two other cases, after successful vaccination, small-pox occurred. Among the English, three cases had small-pox, and were afterward successfully vaccinated. Among the Norwegians, five cases of small-pox occurred after successful vaccination, of which, one case was fatal. Among the Irish, nineteen cases were successfully vaccinated after they had had small-pox, and fifty-five cases had small-pox after successful vaccination. Among the Germans, one case of small-pox after second unsuccessful vaccination, and twenty-three cases after successful vaccination. One case had small-pox twice. Among the German-Americans, one case had small-pox at seven years, and a successful vaccination occurred afterward between ten and twenty years. Among the Americans, one adult had been several times unsuccessfully vaccinated, and had small-pox. Another case, under five years, was successfully vaccinated, and at same time had small-pox.

CHICAGO RELIEF AND AID SOCIETY.

Requisition for Medical and Hospital Supplies.

From 187 *to* 187

Number of Beds in Hospital,

Articles.	On Hand.	Wanted.	Articles.	On Hand.	Wanted.
Apples			Rice		
Arrow-root			Salt		
Barley			Sago		
Beans			Soap		
Butter			Sugar		
Cabbages			Tea		
Cheese					
Carrots			Turnips		
Cod-fish			Vinegar		
Coffee					
Corn-starch					
Eggs					
Farina					
Flour					
Ginger					
Hams					
Lard					
Oat-meal					
Peaches (dried) . . .					
Pepper					
Potatoes					

187

Surgeon in Charge.

The indorsement on back of above was : —

Requisition for Medical and Hospital Supplies

For Hospital, Chicago, Illinois.

By *Surgeon in Charge.*

DAILY REPORT

OF HOSPITAL.

DATE.	Number of Beds in Hospital.	Number of Patients in Hospital at date of Last Report.	Number admitted since Last Report.	Discharged.	Deserted.	Died.	Number of Vacant Beds in Hospital	REMARKS.

I certify the above to be correct,

Surgeon in Charge.

The indorsement on back of above was: —

Daily Report

Of Hospital, Chicago, Illinois.

187

Surgeon in Charge.

CONSOLIDATED WEEKLY REPORT OF DISPENSARIES,

For Week ending 187 .

Dispensary.	Number of Patients Treated in Dispensary.	Number of Prescriptions put up.	Total Patients.	Total Visits.	Operations Performed.	Vaccinations.

The indorsement on back of above was: —
Consolidated Weekly Report
Of Dispensaries.
Week ending 187 .

RATION RETURN OF HOSPITAL, CHICAGO, ILLINOIS,

FROM THE DAY OF , 187 , TO THE DAY OF , 187 .

Number of Men.	Number of Women.	Number of Children.	Total.	Number of Days.	Number of Rations.	RATIONS OF																							REMARKS.

The Committee will issue on the above return.

Surgeon in Charge.

Chairman of Committee on Sick.

The indorsement on back of above was as follows: —

Ration Return of Hospital, Chicago, Illinois.

From , 187 , to , 187 .

Surgeon in Charge.

CERTIFICATE OF VACCINATION.

SANITARY DEPARTMENT,

DISTRICT NO. CHICAGO, 1872.

Name,

Residing at No. , Street.

Number in family,

Number vaccinated within three months,

All the members of this family must be vaccinated or revaccinated before receiving further aid.

Come to the office to be vaccinated. Always bring this ticket with you.

Superintendent of District.

All the members of the above family have been satisfactorily vaccinated.

M. D.

Physician to District, No.

DAILY REPORT

OF VISITING PHYSICIAN FOR DISTRICT.

DATE.	Name.	Age.	Nationality.	Sex.	Residence.	Diagnosis.	Result.	Number of Visits.

FORM OF RECORD BOOK.

Date.	Names.	Age.	Occupation.	Nativity.	Sexes.	Single.	Married.	Widow.	Widower.	Disease.	Duration of Sickness.	Residence Before the Fire.	Where Treated.	Ward of City Living in.	Result of Treatment.	Physician Attending the Patient.

CHAPTER XIV.

EMPLOYMENT BUREAU.

AT no time since the fire has there been lack of employment, particularly of unskilled labor; nevertheless it was thought prudent to establish an Employment Bureau in connection with the general work.

The usefulness of this department has increased almost daily from the time of its commencement, as will appear in the Tables indicating its work.

An Employment Committee, N. K. Fairbank, Chairman, was appointed and began systematically its labors on the 16th of October, 1871, with headquarters in a temporary building in the Court-house yard. This was a sort of labor exchange in the very heart of the burnt district, where those wanting mechanics or laborers could find them, and where those in need of work were provided with it. The Superintendents at all the points of distribution were instructed to send every able-bodied man or boy who applied to them for aid to the Bureau of the Employment Committee, and the ticket he took became a certificate of character. If labor was found for him — as was almost invariably the case — he surrendered the ticket and it was returned to the Superintendent who issued it. If the ticket was not presented at the Employment Bureau, and not returned, therefore, to the Superintendent, it was presumptive evidence that the bearer preferred to eat the bread of idleness rather than work for his own subsistence, and if he again presented himself at the distributing station, his claim for relief was rejected. If, having obtained work — of which the returned ticket was evidence — he asked again for relief, the proper inquiry decided whether his labor was not sufficient to sustain himself and his family, if he had one, or whether he had asked for bounty of which he was not in need. This check upon imposition served its purpose admirably, though it was no more than common justice to say that to shirk work and live upon charity by preference was the exception and not the rule among the laboring people of Chicago.

Most of the mechanics who applied at the Employment Bureau for work were in want of tools, without which they could do nothing at their trades. This want the Committee supplied, and by giving the applicant from ten to twenty dollars' worth of tools he was at once made self-supporting, and ceased to be dependent upon the Relief Society. A large number of carpenters were thus effectively and permanently helped, as the demand for their labor was greater than for that of any other class. Brick layers, gas fitters, shoemakers, and other mechanics were also aided in the same way. The Bureau did not undertake to find employment for women, but turned that class over to other organizations which have hitherto made its care their special business. Seamstresses were given abundant employment by the Ladies' Relief Society, the Ladies' Christian Union, the Womans' Aid Society, and other kindred institutions, and were otherwise cared for by the Bureau of Special Relief. Women seeking other kinds of employment were left under the direction of the societies above mentioned, which in this branch of the work were valuable coadjutors of the Relief and Aid Society.

The Bureau is still a useful branch of the Relief Society, and is conducted upon the same general principles as when first set in operation, though modified in the extent of its work.

RELIEF EMPLOYMENT BUREAU.

The number given employment from October 16, 1871, to January 1, 1872, was as follows: —

Laborers	2192	Steam Fitters	5
Teams	129	Teacher	1
Bakers	2	Plasterers	6
Shoemakers	4	Clerks	13
Teamsters	52	Plumbers	2
Engineer	1	Cabinet Makers	2
Upholsterers	2	Masons	108
Stone Cutters	3	Farm Hands	24
Bookbinders	6	Cook	1
Tailors	8	Painters	4
Machinists	8		
Carpenters	464	Total	3,038

The daily report of employment furnished for the month of January, 1872, was as follows: —

January 1.	Carpenters	19	
	Masons	3	
	Laborers	22	44
January 2.	Laborers	38	
	Farm Hand	1	
	Painter	1	
	Masons	2	
	Carpenters	13	
	Teamster	1	
	Clerks	2	58
January 3.	Tailors	4	
	Laborers	4	
	Clerk	1	
	Carpenters	33	42
January 4.	Laborers	19	
	Teamsters	2	
	Masons	12	
	Clerks	3	36
January 5.	Carpenters	21	
	Laborers	13	34

Date	Occupation	Number	Total
January 6.	Laborer	1	
	Carpenters	15	
	Machinist	1	
	Teamster	1	18
January 8.	Carpenters	20	
	Laborers	43	
	Machinists	5	
	Teamsters	2	
	Clerk	1	71
January 9.	Laborers	16	
	Machinists	4	
	Carpenters	5	25
January 10.	Carpenters	7	
	Laborers	6	
	Masons	3	
	Tailor	1	17
January 11.	Carpenters	3	
	Cabinet Makers	8	
	Laborer	1	
	Farm Hand	1	13
January 12.	Carpenters	6	
	Laborers	23	
	Cabinet Makers	4	
	Teamsters	2	
	Coachman	1	
	Engineer	1	
	Farmer	1	
	Brick Mason	1	39
January 13.	Laborers	25	
	Brick Masons	10	
	Carpenters	3	
	Shoemakers	2	40
January 15.	Laborers	9	
	Shoemakers	6	
	Carpenters	4	19

January 16.	Laborers	18	
	Masons	4	
	Teamsters	4	
	Shoemaker	1	27
January 17.	Laborers	10	
	Shoemakers	12	
	Blacksmiths	2	
	Gilder	1	
	Teamster	1	26
January 18.	Laborers	46	
	Packers	2	
	Chopper	1	
	Boys	2	51
January 19.	Carpenters	14	
	Laborers	6	
	Boys	3	
	Packer	1	
	Blacksmith	1	
	Machinist	1	
	Farmers	3	
	Tailor	1	30
January 20.	Laborers	4	
	Boys	4	
	Farmers	2	
	Carpenters	15	
	Teamster	1	
	Engineer	1	
	Gilders	2	
	Blacksmith	1	
	Coopers	2	32
January 22.	Teamsters	4	
	Farmers	3	
	Laborers	4	
	Quarrymen	6	
	Carpenters	2	
	Coopers	2	
	Boys	3	24

January 23.	Quarrymen	3	
	Coopers	2	
	Lather	1	
	Laborers	21	
	Cabinet Makers	3	
	Farm Hands	2	
	Drug Clerk	1	
	Teamster	1	
	Shoe Maker	1	
	Tailor	1	
	Teams	3	39
January 24.	Laborers	23	
	Teams	3	
	Cabinet Makers	7	
	Cooper	1	
	Turner	1	
	Trunk Maker	1	
	Clerk	1	37
January 25.	Carpenters	7	
	Laborers	5	
	Boys	2	
	Cabinet Makers	5	
	Finisher	1	
	Farmer	1	
	Turner	1	
	Teamsters	3	
	Cooper	1	26
January 26.	Laborers	26	
	Teamsters	5	
	Cabinet Makers	4	
	Carpenters	4	
	Cooper	1	
	Boy	1	
	Clerks	2	43
January 27.	Laborers	24	
	Cabinet Makers	2	
	Carpenter	1	
	Teamsters	2	
	Farmer	1	
	Turner	1	
	Trunk Makers	3	34

January 29.	Laborers	23	23
January 30.	Laborers	33	
	Carpenters	7	
	Cabinet Makers	4	
	Teamsters	4	48
January 31.	Laborers	19	
	Cabinet Makers	2	
	Boys	3	
	Shoe Maker	1	
	Carpenters	2	27
	Total		923

The following figures show the aggregate number furnished employment from February 1, 1872, to May 1, 1873:—

1872.

February	681	August	1,459
March	1,023	September	1,138
April	2,108	October	1,081
May	2,111	November	810
June	1,334	December	656
July	1,329		

1873.

January	604	March	577
February	449	April	841

Showing the entire number by occupation furnished employment from the organization of the Bureau, October 16, 1871, to May 1, 1873:—

Carpenters	2,710	Teams	370
Brick Masons	318	Finishers	4
Laborers	11,811	Turners	6
Teamsters	871	Trunk Makers	4
Farm Hands	869	Harness Makers	9
Clerks	110	Cooks	24
Painters	278	Cashiers	2
Tailors	13	Hostlers	194
Coopers	11	Watchmen	8
Quarrymen	94	Varnishers	3
Lathers	177	Stripper	1
Druggists	2	Canvassers	29

Blacksmiths	33	Jeweller	1
Waiters	103	Plainer	1
Gardeners	138	Collectors	4
Saddlers	2	Bell Hangers	3
Collar Maker	1	Steam Fitters	6
Plasterers	253	Circular Sawyers	6
Joiners	44	Scroll Sawyers	3
Stone Cutters	34	Porters	48
Firemen	6	Bill Poster	1
Foreman	8	Lumbermen	82
Brick Moulders	28	Carvers	2
Confectioner	1	Hair Pickers	4
Butcher	1	Nurserymen	44
Carriage Maker	1	Printers	8
Telegrapher	1	Bakers	10
Gas Fitter	1	Dairymen	18
Tanner	1	Mattress Makers	4
Stewards	3	Stone Masons	180
Bridge Builder	1	Stair Builders	2
Polisher	1	Slipper Maker	1
Tuck Pointer	1	Locksmiths	5
Tinners	2	Moulders	2
Book-keepers	2	Plumbers	5
Paper Hangers	3	Brick Setters	4
Wire Worker	1	Roofers	29
Salesmen	25	Nurses	25
Machinists	70	Furrier	1
Cabinet Makers	69	Photographer	2
Engineers	11	Upholsterers	9
Shoe Makers	38	Janitors	44
Gilders	3	Pipe Maker	1
Packers	5	Yard Men	12
Choppers	26	Teachers	4
Boys	846	Book Binders	6
Stickers	2	Soap Maker	1
Peddlers	2	Cheese Maker	1
Grainer	1	Calsominers	2
Coachmen	17		
Messengers	2	Total	20,232

NATIONALITIES.

Colored	227	Americans	3,443
Irish	4,247	Swedes	2,566
Germans	3,508	English	2,098

Norwegians	1,684	Poles	88
Danes	1,000	Swiss	41
Scotch	400	Welsh	40
Canadians	376	Nova Scotians	24
Dutch	114	Austrians	36
Egyptian	1	Russians	3
East Indian	1	Brazilians	2
Spaniard	1	Hungarians	8
Bohemians	97	Unknown	53
Italians	178		

AGES.

No. from 10 yrs. to 20 yrs.	3,131	No. from 50 yrs. to 60 yrs.	1,059
No. from 20 yrs. to 30 yrs.	8,909	No. from 60 yrs. to 70 yrs.	90
No. from 30 yrs. to 40 yrs.	4,772	No. from 70 yrs. to 80 yrs.	7
No. from 40 yrs. to 50 yrs.	2,113	Unknown	128

From November 1, 1871, to March 1, 1872, there were given out from this office to mechanics who had lost their tools by fire: —

Planes	840	Braces	152
Levels	164	Bits	606
Framing Chisels	321	Screw Drivers	120
Firmer Chisels	554	Gauges	103
Saws	1,009	Augers	96
Try Squares	120	Spoke Shaves	111
Steel Squares	527	Rules	58
Gimlets	157	Auger Handles	57
Hammers	571	Broad Axes	48
Hatchets	522	Gouges	258
Awls	282	Compasses	68
Chisel Handles	266	Bevels	49
Drawing Knives	50	Chopping Axes	12
Stone Sledges	2	Shovels	60
Picks	50		

The total amount expended for tools as above was $19,734.00.

[BLANK FORM.]

MR. J. M. HITCHCOCK, *Employment Bureau, Court House Square.*

Bearer, Mr.
Desires employment
Signed
Place of business

CHAPTER XV.

A. T. STEWART FUND.

New York, *October* 11, 1871.

Hon. R. B. Mason, *Mayor, Chicago, Ill.:* —

My dear Sir, — Last evening I sent you a telegram authorizing you to draw on me for fifty thousand dollars ($50,000) to be distributed by you, in conjunction with my much esteemed friends Messrs. Field and Leiter, and Mr. Jno. V. Farwell, among the needy sufferers by the late terrible conflagration which has visited your city.

I further stated that, if desired, I would expend the amount in purchasing and forwarding such articles of necessity as might be designated, should they, in your united opinion, be preferable to the money.

It is my desire that this fund shall be wholly under the joint charge of yourself and the friends I have named, believing that it will through your united action, be so distributed as to assist those needy sufferers whom you know to be worthy and entitled to help.

It is, however, my special wish that it shall be mainly devoted to the aiding of women who are dependent for support upon their own exertions, and also widows and children without means or protectors to provide for them.

Allow me through you, to express to the people of Chicago, my sincere and heartfelt sympathy in their great misfortune.

Sincerely your friend,
Alex. T. Stewart.

The Relief and Aid Society on the 20th of October, 1871, added to the gentlemen named in the communication of Mr. Stewart, Henry W. King and N. S. Bouton, who constituted the A. T. Stewart Fund Committee.

This Committee failed to find a person who would undertake the distribution of the Fund till about the 15th of November following, when N. S. Bouton consented to distribute the Fund according to the expressed wish of the generous donor.

The various records of the several distributing districts were examined, to ascertain approximately the number of applicants of the classes designated that might be reasonably expected to apply for aid from this Fund.

It was thus ascertained that the percentage of widows and single women dependent upon their own exertions for support who had been burned out was about thirty-four per cent.

The applications at first were laid before the Committee in order that some rule of limitation as to the amount to be given to the individual applicant might be established. Such applicants were required to give name, former and present residence, amount of losses by the fire, and what aid, if any, had been received from other sources.

The first action of the Committee fixed one hundred dollars ($100) as the maximum to be given in any one case, which amount was afterwards increased to two hundred dollars ($200).

In the month of March, 1872, the Executive Committee of the Relief and Aid Society directed the continuation of disbursements to the same classes and by the same Committee, till the total expenditures amounted to ninety-five thousand one hundred dollars ($95,100).

ABSTRACT OF
DISBURSEMENT OF THE A. T. STEWART FUND,
AND ADDITIONAL THROUGH SPECIAL RELIEF.

	A. T. Stewart Fund, $50,000.00	Additional, 45,100.00	Grand Total.
PERSONS AIDED.	Number.	Number.	Number.
Single Women	330	321	651
Widows	826	1,163	1,989
Children	1,295	1,920	3,215
Sewing Women	379	475	854
No other occupation	779	1,010	1,789
To whom money was given	739	487	1,220
Number Sewing Machines	228	302	530
APPLICATIONS.			
Approved	915	808	1,723
Rejected	159	540	699
Referred	23	23	46
No action taken	49	47	96
Not found	13	97	110
Approved, not called for	4		4
Paid on order A. T. Stewart	1		1
Number applications treated	1,164	1,515	2,679
NATIONALITIES.			
American	413	392	805
German	226	377	603
Irish	425	692	1,117
Scotch	7	1	8
English	21	2	23
Italian	2	1	3
French	5	6	11
Canadian	3	1	4
Scandinavian	9	2	11
APPROPRIATIONS.	Amount.	Amount.	Amount.
Sewing Machines	$5,494.55	$11,338.64	$16,833.19
Cash	44,505.45	33,761.36	78,266.81
	$50,000.00	$45,100.00	$95,100.00

CHAPTER XVI.

CHARITABLE INSTITUTIONS.

THE support which had hitherto been given to the permanent Charitable Institutions of the city, had been swallowed up in the greater calamity which had thrown fully one half of our people temporarily upon the charity of the world. But while their ordinary resources were thus taken away, the necessity for help for the particular classes under their care, was greater than ever.

The Relief Society would have failed in a complete discharge of the duties imposed upon it by the trust put into its hands if it had declined to recognize the claims of these special charities.

On the 20th of October, 1871, the following named persons were appointed a Committee on Charitable Institutions: N. S. Bouton, Henry W. King, R. B. Mason, Marshall Field, and J. V. Farwell.

To this Committee were afterwards added C. G. Hammond and Dr. H. A. Johnson.

In the distress of these Institutions they applied to this Society soon after the Fire, for such temporary aid as would enable them to continue their work. A large number were burned out, and all were cut off from their usual channels of support. The Society at once provided temporary shelter, beds, and blankets, for such as had their buildings destroyed, and for all such Institutions, supplies of food and fuel. Upon the organization of the Committee on Aid to Charitable and Benevolent Institutions, all these were visited, their condition carefully examined into, and excepting the hospitals, a monthly allowance of money was paid them in lieu of general supplies.

This allowance was made to all alike, based upon the number of inmates of each, and the expenses for the previous year. The Hospitals being filled mainly by those suffering directly from injuries and sicknesses as the result of the Fire, were under the especial charge of the Committee on Sick and Hospitals.

The Institutions receiving a monthly allowance which was continued for six months were as follows: —

St. Joseph's Orphan Asylum, $300 for six months.
Half Orphan Nursery and Asylum, $400 for six months.
Home for the Friendless, $200 for six months.
Protestant Orphan Asylum, $400 for six months.
House of the Good Shepherd, $150 for six months.
The Foundlings' Home, $150 for six months.
The Old Ladies' Home, $175 for six months.

An appropriation of $125 per month was made to Uhlich's Orphan Asylum for three months.

The Society felt it important early to take steps to place all of these Institutions, together with the Hospitals, upon a more permanent basis. This was plainly in the line of their duty, as most of these Institutions were heavy losers by the Fire, and for years to come their usual resources would be largely diminished and in instances their usefulness ended. It was also deemed the part of economy, by the Society, as these Institutions, if fostered thus promptly, would permanently relieve the Society of the direct care and responsibility of a large number of homeless and destitute, aged and infirm persons.

The Committee therefore issued a circular, addressed to these various Institutions, asking information as follows: —

CHICAGO RELIEF AND AID SOCIETY.

COMMITTEE ON CHARITABLE INSTITUTIONS.

Please make report upon the following questions, and answer at an early date and oblige Yours respectfully,

Where located?
How long established?
Whether chartered?
Object?
What means of support?
Whether any income?
What property, how held, and value?
Whether encumbered?
What debts, what amounts, when contracted, when due?
Amount of current expenses, exclusive of interest?
Number of inmates, exclusive of employés?
Number of employés, and amount of salaries?
Give detailed statement monthly, for last three months of receipts and expenses, number of inmates and employés.
State whether your institution is filled with inmates and whether your work could be enlarged if you had the means.
Names of officers, and other general information, including annual report.

On the 20th of March, 1872, the Executive Committee passed the following resolutions, which were made a condition to the giving of funds for the purposes herein indicated.

RESOLUTIONS OF THE EXECUTIVE COMMITTEE.

1. That any appropriation of money by this Society for the aid of Charitable Institutions be made upon condition that the managers of such Institutions, in the admission of applicants to the benefits of the same, shall not make any discrimination on account of race, nationality, or religious belief.

2. That in case of Hospitals it shall be agreed that every one thousand dollars given, shall be a perpetual endowment of one bed with necessary medical attendance and care for such patient as might in the future be sent to them by the Chicago Relief and Aid Society.

Upon the return of the circulars issued with the information asked, the Committee again visited all the Hospitals and Charitable Institutions, and made their recommendations to the Executive Committee for appropriations.

These recommendations were approved with little alteration, subject to the conditions embodied in the above resolutions.

The appropriations fixed upon by the Executive Committee, will appear in the subjoined abstract of appropriations by the Committee on Charitable Institutions. Appropriations have also been made to the Western

Seaman's Friend Society of $8,000.00
Chicago Seaman's Bethel Union, 15,000.00

Under an arrangement by which the above Societies provide annually stipulated assistance to transient, needy persons.

During the winter and spring application was made in behalf of a considerable number of aged and infirm persons, who prior to the Fire had been in comfortable circumstances; but who were now destitute and dependent, and who looked to the Society for aid. To meet the wants of this class a fund of $50,000 was set apart with which to provide a permanent home for aged people. The Old Ladies Home, a chartered Institution, of limited capacity and resources, surrendered its charter which restricted it to the care of women only, and organized anew, under the general laws of the State of Illinois.

The new Institution is known as The Old People's Home, and has entered into a contract with the Relief and Aid Society by which it will keep one inmate for every twenty-five hundred dollars paid to the Institution and further that it will make no discrimination in the admission of applicants to the benefit of the same, on account of sex, race, nationality, or religious belief. Other changes and provisions have been made in the management of the Institution, by which the objects of the Relief and Aid Society have been attained, namely: providing a home for old men and old women sixty years of age and upwards, who have not been public paupers, and who ought not to be treated as such, and who are pecuniarily unable to provide for themselves. This sum of fifty thousand dollars has been appropriated to this new Institution.

APPROPRIATIONS TO CHARITABLE INSTITUTIONS.

Chicago Nursery and Half Orphan Asylum.

1872.	March 22.	To Cash . .	$10,000.00	
	April 3.	To Cash . .	10,000.00	
	May 21.	To Cash . .	5,000.00	
1873.	March 20.	To Cash . .	2,000.00	$27,000.00

St. Joseph's Hospital.

1872.	March 23.	To Cash . .	$2,000.00	
	April 5.	To Cash . .	2,112.00	
	April 29.	To Cash . .	4,030.00	
	May 7.	To Cash . .	1,592.87	
	June 7.	To Cash . .	5,072.51	
	July 20.	To Cash . .	192.70	
	August 16.	To Cash . .	1,000.00	
	October 28.	To Cash . .	7,652.64	
	October 29.	To Cash . .	663.99	
1873.	February 3.	To Cash . .	345.00	
	March 5.	To Cash . .	6,474.22	$31,135.93

St. Luke's Hospital.

1872.	April 20.	To Cash . .	8,000.00	
	June 27.	To Cash . .	16,000.00	
1873.	March 3.	To Cash . .	4,000.00	$28,000.00

Chicago Protestant Orphan Asylum.

1872.	April 27.	To Cash . .	5,000.00	
	July 1.	To Cash . .	2,000.00	
	June 3.	To Cash . .	3,000.00	$10,000.00
				$96,135.93

Mercy Hospital.

1872.	April 30.	To Cash		$40,000.00

House of the Good Shepherd.

1872.	May 14.	To Cash . .	2,255.56	
	May 24.	To Cash . .	12,291.00	
	October 16.	To Cash . .	1,500.00	$16,046.56
		Appropriated . .		11,000.00

Scammon Hospital.

1872.	May 22.	To Cash . .	6,000.00	
1873.	April 1.	To Cash . .	9,000.00	$15,000.00

Western Seamen's Friend's Society.

1872.	September 23.	To Cash		$8,000.00
		Appropriated . .		10,000.00

Alexian Brothers' Hospital.

1872.	June 6.	To Cash . .	1,200.00	
	July 8.	To Cash . .	2,200.00	
	August 1.	To Cash . .	3,000.00	
	September 2.	To Cash . .	4,000.00	
	September 12.	To Cash . .	800.00	
	September 21.	To Cash . .	1,000.00	
	October 15.	To Cash . .	2,000.00	
	November 3.	To Cash . .	2,000.00	
	December 2.	To Cash . .	2,000.00	$18,200.00

St. Joseph's Orphan Asylum.

1872.	June 8.	To Cash . .	4,262.31	
	July 10.	To Cash . .	4,204.23	
	July 13.	To Cash . .	20,000.00	
	August 12.	To Cash . .	1,533.46	
1873.	January 25.	To Cash . .	1,428.14	$31,428.14

Newsboys' and Bootblacks' Home.

1872.	July 5.	To Cash . .	400.00	
	July 15.	To Cash . .	464.27	
	July 16.	To Cash . .	117.57	
	July 17.	To Cash . .	263.07	
	July 22.	To Cash . .	40.13	
	December 10.	To Cash . .	650.00	$1,935.04
		Appropriated . .		12,000.00

Home for the Friendless.

1872.	July 23.	To Cash . .	500.00	
	July 31.	To Cash . .	10,000.00	
	September 2.	To Cash . .	1,700.00	
	October 4.	To Cash . .	10,000.00	
	October 7.	To Cash . .	950.00	
	October 25.	To Cash . .	7,000.00	
	December 17.	To Cash . .	250.00	
1873.	March 12.	To Cash . .	6,000.00	$36,400.00

Deaconess Hospital.

1872.	August 1.	To Cash		$25,000.00

Chicago Foundlings' Home.

1872.	August 2,	To Cash . .	3,000.00	
	September 26.	To Cash . .	3,000.00	
	October 23.	To Cash . .	4,000.00	$10,000.00

Eye and Ear Infirmary.

1872.	August 5.	To Cash . .	18,000.00	
	September 27.	To Cash . .	2,000.00	$20,000.00

Women's and Children's Hospital.

1872.	September 10.	To Cash . .	25,000.00	
1873.	January 30.	To Cash . .	500.00	$25,500.00

Western Seamen's Bethel Union.

1872.	September 12.	To Cash . .	1,000.00	
	October 2.	To Cash . .	2,000.00	
	October 14.	To Cash . .	2,000.00	
	October 28.	To Cash . .	2,000.00	
	November 7.	To Cash . .	2,000.00	
	November 18.	To Cash . .	2,000.00	
	December 2.	To Cash . .	2,000.00	
	December 21.	To Cash . .	2,000.00	$15,000.00

Uhlich Orphan Asylum.

1872.	November 13.	To Cash . .	1,500.00
	November 14.	To Cash . .	1,500.00
	December 9.	To Cash . .	2,000.00
	December 13.	To Cash . .	2,000.00

1873.	January 22.	To Cash . .	2,000.00	
	February 17.	To Cash . .	1,500.00	
	March 18.	To Cash . .	500.00	
	March 24.	To Cash . .	2,823.12	
	April 9.	To Cash . .	600.00	
	April 29.	To Cash . .	1,275.00	
	May 7.	To Cash . .	500.00	
	May 14.	To Cash . .	3,801.88	$20,000.00

OLD PEOPLE'S HOME.

Appropriated $50,000.00

ST. JOSEPH'S ORPHAN ASYLUM.

$300 for six (6) months . . $1,800.00

CHICAGO NURSERY AND HALF ORPHAN ASYLUM.

$400 for six (6) months . . $2,400.00

UHLICH ORPHAN ASYLUM.

$125 for three (3) months . . $375.00

HOME FOR THE FRIENDLESS.

$200 for six (6) months . . $1,200.00

PROTESTANT ORPHAN ASYLUM.

$400 for six (6) months . . $2,400.00

HOUSE OF THE GOOD SHEPHERD.

$150 for six (6) months . . $900.00

THE FOUNDLINGS' HOME.

$150 for six (6) months . . $900.00

THE OLD LADIES' HOME.

$175 for six (6) months . . $1,050.00

$472,670,67

SUMMARY.

To Cash	$378,645.67	
Monthly Allowances . . .	11,025.00	
Appropriated	83,000.00	$472,670.67

Additional appropriations have been made as indicated in the following

STATEMENT OF WORK PERFORMED BY THE SOCIETY FROM MAY 1, 1873, TO MAY 1, 1874.

Articles Distributed.	Quantity.	Value.
Number of Men's Wear	664	
Number of Women's Wear	117	
Number of Children's Wear	923	
Pairs of Shoes	3,387	
Pairs of Blankets	1,156	
Pairs of Pillow Slips	23	
Number of Tons of Coal	8,103	$35,662.50
Number of Cords of Wood	58½	585.00
		$36,247.50
Number of Interments	133	
Number of Passes	1,081	8,885.14
Number of Patients in Hospitals	374	

STATISTICS OF VACCINATION DURING WINTER OF 1873–4.

Number Passed on Certificates	19,772
Number Passed on Examinations	6,991
Number of Persons Vaccinated	3,766
Number of Certificates Issued	7,708
Number of Persons Certificates call for . .	30,529

NATIONALITY AND NUMBER OF FAMILIES AIDED.

Nationality.	Families.	Children.
Irish	4,841	14,535
Scandinavian	1,417	4,165
German	3,512	10,480
American	2,537	6,365
English	949	2,790
French	247	724
Canadian	255	718
Scotch	306	897
Hollander	135	414
Bohemian	534	1,587
Negro	248	672
Belgian	28	67
Pole	326	892
Italian	48	113
Welsh	27	62
Russian	15	31
Swiss	29	46
Total	15,454	44,558

Cash Expenditures	$239,040.83
For Articles in Kind	45,132.64
Appropriations to Charitable Institutions	82,143.29
Total Disbursements, from May 1, 1873, to May 1, 1874	$366,316.76

CHAPTER XVII.

STATEMENT OF CONTRIBUTIONS AND DISBURSEMENTS.

CONTRIBUTIONS OF SUPPLIES.

STATE OF MAINE.

AUBURN.

Mrs. Samuel Pickard, one case goods.
John F. Cobb & Co., sixty pairs women's boots.

AUGUSTA.

John Dorr, for citizens, one box clothing.

BANGOR.

Citizens, five boxes of merchandise.

BATH.

Mary O. Robinson, citizens, one box clothing.
Emma E. Alvid, one box clothing.

GARDINER.

J. A. Andrew, personal contribution, lot of boots and shoes.

PORTLAND.

Portland Packing Co., two thousand four hundred cans preserved provisions.
G. W. Rich, one case clothing.
Deering, Milliken, & Co., one bale blankets, one case clothing.

STATE OF NEW HAMPSHIRE.

CONCORD.

B. F. Gale, six hundred boxes of burn salve.

LACONIA.

R. M. Appleton, citizens, one thousand two hundred and twelve pairs men and women's stockings.

LAKE VILLAGE.

John Pepper, two hundred and forty pairs misses' hose, two hundred and forty pairs ladies' hose, two hundred and forty pairs men's hose.

LEBANON.

Mrs. William Ela, ladies' contributions, three boxes and four barrels clothing.

MANCHESTER.

John Brugger, one box, containing three hundred and forty pairs woolen socks, three woolen jackets.
A. P. Olzendam, sixty-eight dozen pairs woolen hose.

NORTH LONDONDERRY.

John Haynes, one box goods.

PETERBOROUGH.

Charles Wilder, citizens, four feather beds, six quilts, two coats, one vest.

PORTSMOUTH.

Charles H. Rollins, one box.

STATE OF VERMONT.

BENNINGTON CENTRE.

C. R. Sanford, one box clothing, citizens.

NORTHFIELD.

O. D. Edgerton, citizens, two boxes clothing.

PROCTORSVILLE.

Miss S. Parker, one box clothing.

RUTLAND.

Mary E. Daniels, one box clothing.
Ladies of Rutland, two boxes clothing.

STATE OF MASSACHUSETTS.

AMHERST.

Charles S. Smith, one box clothing and shoes, and one box shoes.
Mrs. Mary H. Jones, ladies of Grace Church, three barrels clothing.

BARRE.

J. H. Goddard, citizens, one case of boots and shoes, and one case of clothing.

BOSTON.

Daymon, Thomas, & Lewis, large tent.
H. A. Hill, Secretary, one case rubber pouches.
C. T. Lee, three packages clothing.

W. & J. Wallace, one lot of merchandise.

Ewing, Wise, & Fuller, one case blankets.

James Lee, Middlesex Dying and Bleaching Co., one box clothing.

Hon. Alexander H. Rice, President Boston Relief Society, one box, twelve barrels, one bundle, one case, four barrels, eight boxes, two kegs, seventeen cases, one case, two crates crockery, one barrel supplies.

H. A. Hill, Secretary, lot of paper and paper bags.

Charles Merrill & Co. one box clothing.

H. Whitney, two trunks supplies.

Avery Plummer, five cases canned beef.

Portland Packing Co., one hundred cases canned goods.

Nonantum Knitting Mills, by George K. Snow, forty-eight cases clothing, and bedding.

Welch & Griffith, three hundred hand saws.

H. A. Hill, Secretary, contributions of the crockery and glass dealers, five crates crockery and glassware.

One box, one barrel merchandise.

From Boston Committee, by William Gray, one thousand dollars, to be made into ladies clothing by the Boston Sewing Circle.

C. Randolph, citizens, forty-nine packages sundries.

Boston Sewing Circle, through Mrs. H. G. Miller, Chicago, four boxes clothing.

BROOKFIELD.

Contributions of citizens, one package clothing.

Contributions of citizens, by H. Reed, four barrels clothing.

CAMBRIDGE.

E. Dresser & Co., contributions of employés, three boxes clothing.

Joseph Childs, Jr., one case clothing, contributions of ladies of Cambridgeport.

T. S. Hudson, citizens of East Cambridge, eleven cases clothing; two bundles clothing.

CHARLESTOWN.

Mary L. Gilmore, one cloak.

George L. Gilmore, contribution.

Hon. W. H. Kent, citizens, a number of packages of clothing to be delivered to parties mentioned in letter of advice.

CHERRY VALLEY.

Samuel May, citizens, one large case bedding and clothing.

FAIRHAVEN.

S. Chandler, one keg clothing.

FRAMINGHAM.

H. G. Spaulding, four boxes clothing, value $250.

GLOUCESTER.

E. F. Stacey & Co., one box supplies.

HADLEY.

E. Porter, donation of Russell Congregational Church, one barrel clothing and bedding.

LEICESTER.

A. M. Stone, citizens, one box clothing.
By Samuel May, one box clothing.
Citizens of Leicester, fifty-four cases clothing and bedding.
Relief Society of Leicester, one case clothing, etc.

LENOX.

Thomas Post, Treasurer, reports that clothing, etc., was forwarded by citizens immediately after the fire, and valued at $350.

LOWELL.

Charles Stott, contribution of Belvedere Woolen Manufactory, one bale flannel.
Members of St. Ann's Episcopal Society, two barrels clothing.

MARBLEHEAD.

K. V. Martin, three boxes clothing, one box boots and shoes.
Citizens, one case clothing.

MARLBOROUGH.

J. B. Brigham, one box boots and shoes.

MARSHFIELD.

James G. Day, six barrels produce.

MILTON.

T. W. K. Nye, thirty-eight boxes and barrels clothing.

NEW BEDFORD.

Union Boot and Shoe Co., three cases boots and shoes.
Rachel S. Howland, thirty-two barrels clothing (2,352 pieces), Ladies' Christian Association.
A. N. Libbey, one trunk clothing.

NEWBURYPORT.

Silas Marvle, one barrel clothing.
Carr, Brown, & Co., one box clothing.
Citizens, by Isaac H. Boardman, one box, one tierce, and four barrels clothing, etc.

NORTHAMPTON.

Mrs. Mary S. Clark, one barrel and one box clothing.

PEABODY.

E. W. Upton, thirteen cases clothing from citizens of Peabody.
Ladies of Peabody, one case clothing.

PITTSFIELD.

C. H. Kellogg, twenty-five boxes clothing, citizens.

PLYMOUTH.

B. A. Hathaway, contributions of First Universalist Sunday-school, one barrel clothing.
George H. Harton, contributions of First Universalist Church, one box clothing.

ROCHDALE.

E. G. Carleton, contributions of ladies, package flannel garments.

SALEM.

One family, eighty-two pieces clothing.
John R. Lakman, twenty cases clothing.

TAUNTON.

E. T. Jackson, citizens, five boxes clothing, bedding, etc.

WALTHAM.

Daniel French, thirty-one barrels, twenty-one cases clothing.

WARE.

Mrs. Charles Moore, four barrels clothing, contributions of children in Primary School.

WATERTOWN.

Per Daniel French, forty-four barrels, thirteen boxes, and eight cases clothing.
George K. Swan, fifty cases clothing and bedding.

WORCESTER.

William T. Brown, five boxes clothing from The People's Club.
Edward Earl, Mayor, fifty-two cases and two barrels merchandise.

STATE OF RHODE ISLAND.

BRISTOL.

C. M. Shepard, donation of First Congregational Church, $127.75 worth of clothing.

EAST GREENWICH.

Mrs. M. M. Baker, one barrel clothing.

PROVIDENCE.

St. Stephen's Church, six barrels clothing.

M. A. Blodgett, Secretary, a quantity of clothing.
Thomas A. Doyle, Mayor, citizens, fifty-five cases clothing.
Miss F. O. Bartlett, St. Stephen's Church, two barrels clothing.
Mrs. Whitehouse, one box clothing.
Ladies of Stewart Street Baptist Church, one box clothing.
Donations of citizens, fifty-four cases and twenty barrels of clothing and one stove.
Captain C. R. Dennis, contributions of First Light Infantry Company, several cases clothing, bedding, etc.

WARREN.

D. L. Turner, citizens, two cases clothing.

WOONSOCKET.

H. L. Ballou, citizens, three barrels clothing.

STATE OF CONNECTICUT.

ANSONIA.

Chas. H. Pine, citizens, three barrels clothing material, etc.

BRIDGEPORT.

Mrs. N. I. DeForest, one barrel clothing.
E. B. Goodsell, Esq., Treasurer, advises a quantity of supplies in barrels and boxes, sent soon after the fire; also, citizens sent two barrels clothing through Mrs. H. G. Miller.

BROOKLYN.

Miss Harriet White, citizens four boxes, and two barrels clothing.

DANBURY.

C. H. Merritt, one box clothing, boots and shoes.

FAIRHAVEN.

F. W. Fuller, four barrels bedding and clothing.

GOSHEN.

John W. Brooks, citizens, three boxes clothing and blankets.

HARTFORD.

J. M. Ney & Co., two boxes clothing.
G. S. Whiting, one box clothing.
S. Chandler, one keg clothing.

NORWALK.

A. H. Byington & Co., citizens, two boxes clothing.

NEW BRITAIN.

F. T. Stanley, Mayor, contributions of the operatives of the American Hosiery Company, one case woolen shirts, worth $300.

NEW HARTFORD.

H. W. Brown, donation of the ladies of the Congregational Church, one box clothing.

ROCKVILLE.

S. W. Johnson, citizens, one box and two barrels of supplies.

SHERMAN.

Lafayette Joyce, contribution of the Sherman Aid Society, three barrels clothing.

STAMFORD.

Mrs. Alexander McKenzie, ladies' contribution, one box clothing.

WINSTED.

Harvey L. Roberts, donations of ladies of St. James' Episcopal Church, one large box clothing.

WEST MERIDEN.

Isaac C. Lewis, Mayor, donations of citizens, one cask, one barrel, and two boxes of ladies' and children's clothing.

WESTPORT.

C. C. Alden, one box clothing.

STATE OF NEW YORK.

ALBANY.

Chapin & Foster, three boxes bread.
Burgess Corps, two hundred blankets.
J. V. Eswart, three hundred loaves bread.
E. J. Larabee & Co.'s employés, two thousand five hundred loaves bread.
John Rogers & Sons, eight barrels crackers.

ASTORIA.

Henry C. Johnson, one box clothing.

BATAVIA.

H. J. Glowacki, citizens, one box clothing.

BERGEN.

George H. Church, citizens, two boxes of clothing.

BINGHAMPTON.

Edward F. Jones, four platform scales.
Nellie Harkness and H. F. Lee, three barrels milk crackers.
Mrs. Mary Simms, citizens, one box clothing.
"A. V. S." donated six bed quilts.

BROCKPORT.

Mrs. Mary J. Homes, donations of ladies of St. Luke's Church, one box shoes, etc.

BROOKLYN.

William Wright, M. D., one box and one barrel clothing.

Public School, No. 15, seven cases clothing.

A. A. Wells, one box child's clothing.

C. Densmore, contributions of ladies of LaFayette Avenue Presbyterian Church, five boxes clothing and bedding.

Mrs. J. H. Gleeson, one box clothing.

Johnson Brothers, two cases clothing.

Wesley Methodist Church, one box and one barrel clothing.

Charles A. Homer, five barrels clothing, contributions of citizens.

Mrs. Benjamin Nelson, one barrel clothing.

L. W. Saltonstall, one box clothing from Adelphi Academy.

Park Congregational Church, one barrel clothing; one box boots and shoes.

Mrs. Vosburg, seven barrels clothing.

William Powell, contributions of the Memorial Presbyterian Church, four boxes clothing.

A. E. Silliman, two boxes blankets.

Public School No. 15, fourteen boxes clothing.

Martin Kalbfleisch, Mayor, five thousand pounds fresh bread.

John A. Fowle, contributions of Plymouth Church, three cases supplies; one case supplies, marked George F. Cram; two cases supplies, marked James P. Root, Hyde Park.

T. DeWitt Talmadge, donation of the Tabernacle Church, nine boxes and two bales merchandise.

Major John L. Broome, donation of Officers and Marines of Brooklyn Navy Yard, a quantity of provisions.

Mrs. B. Nelson, one barrel clothing.

C. E. Tuthill, contribution of Public School, No. 25, three boxes of clothing.

BUFFALO.

Alexander Brush, Mayor, two car loads bread and crackers.

Ninth Baptist Church, four boxes bedding and clothing and hospital supplies.

John A. Campbell, Chairman, sixteen car loads provisions and clothing.

Charles G. Irish, shipper, donations of citizens, fifteen barrels, five boxes, one bundle, two cases goods.

C. S. Stewart for Exhibitors of the Industrial Exhibition Fair, six thousand three hundred and ten loaves bread.

William T. Marcy, two cases blankets.

E. R. Newburg, one box, seventeen packages clothing.

St. James' Episcopal Church, five barrels clothing.

CANANDAIGUA.

Dr. John N. Potter, six barrels flour.

CANAJOHARIE.

A. Smith, six cases clothing and bedding.
H. X. Devandorf, ladies of Lutheran Church, three boxes clothing.

CATSKILL.

Citizens through E. L. Ingersoll, three boxes clothing.

CAZENOVIA.

A. P. Clark, contributions of citizens, one box clothing.

COHOES.

Clifton Co., two cases hosiery.
Citizens by Hon. C. H. Adams, Mayor, twelve cases knit goods.

CUBA.

Mrs. T. Lancaster, ladies, one box clothing.

DANSVILLE.

A. O. Burnell, citizens, one box clothing.

ELBA.

J. C. Long, one box clothing, citizens.

ELMIRA.

Marion Arnot, ladies' Relief Committee, twenty boxes clothing.
Marion Arnot, blankets, sheets, and drawers.

FLUSHING.

Mrs. W. T. Hemmingway, contributions of ladies, four boxes supplies.
Contributions of a few ladies and gentlemen, package of provisions and clothing.

FORT PLAINE.

Mrs. H. E. Williams, citizens, one box clothing and bedding.

FULTON.

H. S. Conde & Son, fourteen dozen knit drawers and shirts valued at $120.00.

GARRATTSVILLE.

Mrs. H. M. Deane, donation of ladies' Benevolent Association, two barrels clothing.

GOSHEN.

Merriam & Millspaugh, one box clothing.

GREENPOINT, L. I.

P. W. Paine, one bundle of clothing.
C. M. Ernesty, one bundle of clothing.

HAMPTON.

Mrs. A. B. Cook, one package clothing.

HIGHLAND MILLS.

Citizens, one box clothing.

HOMER.

S. McBarber, eight boxes blankets and clothing.
Charles O. Newton, eight boxes bed quilts, clothing, and underwear.

HOOSIC FALLS.

J. L. Lambert, contributions of citizens, three boxes clothing, and bedding.

HUDSON.

Cyrus Macy, two cases bedding and clothing.

IRVINGTON.

Mary C. Morgan, two boxes clothing.

KEYSTONE.

W. W. Brush, contributions of Reformed Church, two boxes bedding, boots and shoes.

KINDERHOOK.

Ladies of Kinderhook, contributions, three barrels clothing.

KINGSTON.

John L. Lee, contributions of citizens, one box clothing.

LANSINGBURG.

S. P. Welch, contributions of citizens, thirty barrels crackers.

LIVONIA.

Bowen & Stewart, four boxes clothing.

LOCKPORT.

Four boxes merchandise and one box clothing.

LONG ISLAND CITY, L. I.

Railroad employés, one box clothing.

MORRISANIA.

R. Garrigue, contributions of citizens, two cases clothing, two stoves.

NEWBURG.

Y. M. C. A., donation of ten pairs blankets.

NEW ROCHELLE.

E. A. Rubin, one package clothing.

NEW YORK CITY.

Freeman & Burr, one box clothing and one package ditto.
Hornthall, Whitehead, & Co., two cases clothing.
A. C. Leonard & H. L. Bushwell, three boxes clothing.

Wesley Smith, one trunk clothing.
B. W. Pierce, Saxonville Mills, fifty pairs blankets.
Ives Patent Lamp Co., by I. R. Marsh, Secretary, two casks, three barrels, and one box of lamp chimneys and burners.
Sweetzer, Pembroke, & Co., one case blankets.
Sonneborne & Co., two cases clothing.
Treadwell, Jarman, & Slote, one case clothing.
George G. Wolf, fifty pairs blankets.
G. & S. Heyman & Mack, one hundred mattresses, one hundred pillows, one hundred bolsters.
French & Ward, two cases clothing.
G. Schmidt & Co., two boxes clothing.
B. Atkinson, three cases, one bale flannel and woolens.
Seligman, May, & Isaacs, one case clothing.
George D. Pitkin, President, sixty-seven cases boots and shoes.
From Donors as follows: —
Nathaniel Fisher & Co., two cases.
Bay State Shoe and Leather Co., two cases.
Mellins, Trask, & Ripley, two cases.
Wallace & Elliott, two cases.
C. S. Parsons & Son, two cases.
East New York Boot and Shoe Co., two cases.
J. O. Whitehouse, one case.
Mabie, Murray, & Morgan, two cases.
Powell, Brother, & Co., three cases.
Dubois, McCovern, & Co., two cases.
Newell Brothers, three hundred pairs.
Porter, Day, & Co. one case.
Benedict, Hall, & Co., three cases.
W. A. Ransom & Co., three cases.
Howes, Hyatt, & Co., one case.
Hodge, Whitney, Cook, & Co., one case.
James Wiggins & Co., two cases.
Currier, Sherwood, & Co., one case.
L. E. Shoemaker & Co., one case.
William Neely & Co., one case.
Cummeyer & Mason, two cases.
Weil Brothers, one case.
Hedges, Powers, & Co., two cases.
Aaron, Claflin, & Co., four cases.
Studwell Brothers, two cases.
Aaron, Smith, & Co., one case.
Tucker & Mead, two cases.
Wheelock & Stark, one case.
F. & L. B. Reed, one case.
Westervelt & Barnes, one case.
J. R. Wells & Co., one case.

D. Torrence & Co., one case.
McKinney & Knox, two cases.
A. J. Bates & Co., one case.
H. G. Bell & Co., one case.
H. Tasker, one case.
W. W. Gilman, two cases.
J. & T. Cousins, one case.
S. Waterbury & Son, one case.
A. J. Bates & Co., employés, one case.
G. & D. Silver, one case.
Samuel Wilson, two cases.
M. & L. Stock, one case.

Stadler & Co., two cases clothing.
Acker, Merrill, & Condit, five dozen soap, one package clothing.
David, Gans, & Co., five and one half dozen gray woolen shirts.
A. Kemp, one trunk clothing.
Knapp & Co., one box clothing.
Andrew, Lester, & Co., one case clothing.
H. Kraus, three bundles clothing.
James Grant Wilson, one package clothing.
Felix Stoiber, one package clothing.
Newman Pulvermacher, one bundle clothing.
Newell Brothers, six cases shoes.
Rindskopf, Brothers, & Co., two cases clothing.
Burritt, Nephew, & Co., three bundles clothing.
Amidon, Lane, & Co., seven bales blankets.
Heman Vogel, one box clothing.
Mary McCloskey, sixteen cases clothing, from children of Grammar School No. 17.
John C. Draper, one box clothing.
F. H. Amidon & Son, one case hats and caps.
From a little girl, 52 University Place, a quantity of clothing.
Griessman, Brothers, & Hoffman, twenty-five seal skin overcoats.
John Ehlers, one box clothing, one bundle, two mattresses.
Seamless Clothing Manufacturing Co., fourteen dozen boys' and men's hats and caps.
J. F. Porter, Sylvan Grove Lodge, No. 275, of F. & A. M., quantity of ham, codfish, dried beef, etc.
J. H. Porter, one box clothing.
George B. Draper, contributions of St. Andrew's Church, eighteen boxes and three barrels bedding and clothing.
Brown & Bowers, one box clothing.
J. Cromieu, three barrels crackers.
P. Lynch, three barrels crackers.
James J. Condon, thirteen boxes cheese, three boxes meat.
James Cameron, one box clothing from DeSoto House.
New York Democrat, per F. Schwedler, three boxes clothing.

Ninth Ward German Relief Committee, one box underwear.

Griggs & Smith, eight barrels potatoes and one barrel onions.

J. C. Hoagland, Treasurer Royal Baking Powder Co., one thousand cans yeast powder.

Hotel keepers of New York City, by Samuel Hawks, one thousand dollars ($1,000) worth supplies.

Danl. Talmadge & Sons, ten bags rice.

Tift & Truesdale, fifty barrels flour through Adams & Wilcox, Joliet, Illinois.

Woodruff & Robinson, twenty-five boxes codfish.

John H. McKinley, eight barrels soda biscuit, four barrels pilot bread.

Wright, Gillies, & Brother, ten boxes coffee.

Keyser, Comstock, & Co., four boxes cheese.

A. Gunzburg, three bundles clothing.

J. B. Bechtold, two boxes wearing apparel.

Thomas H. Bates & Co., two thousand papers needles, worth $75.

Julian Allen, fifteen hundred rations Erbs fleischwurst.

David Dexter, one barrel of hickory stonecutters' mallets.

Charles Winans, contributions of First Precinct Police, two bales blankets.

Marvin, Brothers, & Co., two hundred and fifty pairs blankets.

Sarah J. Zabriski, contributions of Church of the Incarnation, two boxes clothing.

T. N. Jarrett, one package clothing.

H. G. Aspell, one box clothing.

Mrs. A. Mellon, one trunk and one box clothing.

A. Lester, one box clothing. .

Daniel Lowe, two hundred bushels potatoes and one hundred bushels corn ordered from Nebraska City.

J. T. Clayton, five barrels pickles.

H. & G. B. Farrington, through C. R. Bates, Kalamazoo, fifty barrels flour.

J. H. Diggles, ten barrels crackers.

Police of New York, two boxes clothing.

F. Schwedler, donation, three boxes clothing.

Mrs. R. F. Ware, contributions of citizens, one box clothing.

Simon A. Wolf, forty-eight shirts.

Grammar School No. 35, three cases clothing.

C. Schumaker, one box clothing.

NEW YORK MILLS.

W. D. Walcott, contributions of operatives of upper mill, one box clothing.

Walcott & Campbell, $2,000 worth of goods.

OGDENSBURG.

J. W. Judson, of Citizen's Committee, reports $782 worth of clothing, of which —

$350 worth was for general relief in Chicago.

$112 worth for private distribution in Chicago.

$320 worth for East Saginaw, Michigan.

Also a quantity of second-hand clothing for Chicago.

ONEIDA.

W. H. Dimmick, fifty hats, seventeen pairs shoes, seventeen pairs hose.

ONEONTA.

Citizens, one bag clothing and four barrels potatoes.

OSWEGO.

Delos DeWolf, contributions of citizens, one box knit shirts and six bedsteads.

PEEKSKILL.

John Worthington, contributions of the Peekskill Mutual Stove Works, twenty-five cook stoves.

PHELPS.

Alice R. Banta, contributions of ladies, three boxes bedding and clothing.

PIKE'S POND.

John W. Banta, one box clothing.

PORT BYRON.

H. B. Dutcher, a quantity of provisions and clothing.

PORT CHESTER.

John F. Mills, citizens, two cases of second-hand clothing.

PORT JERVIS.

M. V. Heller, eleven cases clothing, six barrels provisions.

POUGHKEEPSIE.

H. G. Eastman, Mayor, contributions of citizens, twenty-two boxes clothing.
W. A. Fanning, citizens, eight boxes clothing.

RIVERHEAD.

S. S. Terry, citizens, four boxes dry goods.

ROCHESTER.

Jacob Anderson, four boxes candles.
E. C. Jaquith, one car provisions, contributions of citizens.

SARATOGA SPRINGS.

S. E. Bushnell, contributions of ladies, one box clothing.
W. F. Redding, one barrel supplies.

SENECA FALLS.

George W. Mead, Treasurer Relief Fund, contributions of citizens, fourteen barrels potatoes, apples, and pork, nine packages, clothing, boots, and shoes.

SING SING.

J. J. R. Croes, citizens, four boxes and two barrels clothing.

SOUTHOLD, L. I.

Citizens, one bundle of clothing.
Miss A. M. Young, one garment.

STONE RIDGE.

W. W. Brent, two boxes bedding, boots, and shoes.

SYRACUSE.

D. & J. Leslie, five barrels smoked beef.
A. C. Yates & Co., one case clothing.
M. L. Burger, citizens, nine cases clothing.
Ladies of the Independent Church, one box new clothing.

TARRYTOWN.

Ladies' Relief Committee of Tarrytown, A. D. Reeves, Agent, ten boxes clothing, one barrel provisions, one trunk clothing.

TROY.

Mrs. Thatcher Clark, two boxes clothing and bedding.
N. B. Squires, nine boxes clothing, boots and shoes.
N. B. Squires, contributions of Board of Trade, one box and one trunk of clothing, seventeen boxes clothing and bedding..
N. B. Squires, citizens, two boxes and one barrel clothing.
Smith, House, & Co., one box clothing.
J. G. Ankam and employés, one case clothing and provisions.
L. E. Gurley, contributions of ladies of Fifth Baptist Church, seven barrels and one box clothing.
Roy, James, & Co., contributions of employés, two cases shawls.
A. Bills, one box clothing.
A. B. Elliott, one box clothing.
John B. Green, one box supplies.

UNADILLA.

W. H. Emery, citizens, one box sundries.

UTICA.

John F. Seymour, contributions of citizens, seventeen cases clothing and one of supplies, estimated by the Utica committee to be worth $4,620. Also, a quantity of clothing, etc., by ladies.

WARWICK.

Donation of Lodge No. 34, I. O. O. F., one box clothing.

WATERVILLE.

C. E. Harris, one box clothing.

WILLIAMSBURG.

A. Campbell, a Campbell Combination Printing Press, valued at $4,000.

STATE OF NEW JERSEY.

BELLEVILLE.

One barrel merchandise.

BELVIDERE.

J. Harris, box of merchandise, $200.

S. E. Harris, citizens, one box clothing.

BLOOMFIELD.

Citizens, one box clothing and bedding.

C. K. King, citizens, four boxes, twenty-seven bundles, and four barrels clothing.

BOUNDBROOK.

William R. Smith, three cases clothing.

BURLINGTON.

Richard F. Mott, seven boxes clothing, one stove, from citizens.

CAMDEN.

S. N. Gall, Mayor, four boxes clothing, twenty boxes coffee.

ELIZABETH.

J. O. Magie, eighteen cases merchandise.

E. P. Williams, one barrel merchandise.

Unknown, one package and one box merchandise.

FREEHOLD.

C. F. Richardson, citizens, three boxes clothing.

FREEMANS.

D. Garretson, one box merchandise.

HAMMONTON.

George F. Fay, citizens, seventy-eight barrels provisions and one bundle clothing.

JERSEY CITY.

Three cars relief goods, two boxes clothing, one barrel bread, four barrels crackers.

LONG BRANCH.

C. Vanderveer, citizens, two cases clothing.

Ladies' Aid Society, two cases clothing.

Citizens, one box clothing.

MADISON.

Mrs. L. T. Janes, a quantity of clothing.

S. D. Hunting, citizens, three boxes clothing.

MORRIS PLAINS.

Citizens, by Mrs. H. G. Miller, Chicago, one barrel clothing, etc.

NEWARK.

Miss Griffith, one bundle clothing.
A. B. Ely, one barrel clothing.
J. M. Hayes, one bag clothing.
J. M. Anderson, one bag clothing.
Mrs. C. A. Beach, one bale merchandise.
K. Little, one keg and one bale merchandise.
J. Winder, one case merchandise.
E. P. Williams, six cases merchandise.
Hibner and Peters, one case merchandise.
H. C. Baker, one case merchandise.
George Laurence, one bale clothing.
Rev. F. Girard, three boxes and five half barrels clothing; nine cases merchandise.
Unknown, one case clothing.
E. C. Hay, one bag clothing.
Mrs. Emma McCullum, one box and three barrels, donations of citizens.
Mrs. Hall, one case merchandise.
C. W. Pomroy, forty-two cases clothing, five bundles bedding, two kits mackerel, seven bundles clothing, six packages, seven thousand five hundred loaves bread. Citizens.
J. Major, four cases merchandise.
N. J. Belleville, one bundle merchandise.
George Mackintosh, three cases merchandise.
T. P. Lyon, one box merchandise.
N. L. Douglas, one case merchandise.
E. Vangieson, one barrel merchandise.
J. Henrey, two barrels bread.

NEW BRUNSWICK.

A. Provost, chairman, three large and one small cases of supplies.
Citizens, through R. B. Mason; two cases clothing.
George McIntosh, three cases merchandise.
Unknown, three cases supplies.

ORANGE.

Mrs. A. P. Halsey, contribution of ladies, four boxes clothing.
Mrs. M. M. Austin, citizens, one box clothing.

PERTH AMBOY.

A quantity of clothing and mattresses, by Marcus Spring.

RAHWAY.

E. H. Dunham, one case merchandise.
Unknown, one barrel and one box merchandise.

Rev. Mr. Wheeler, one case merchandise.

G. B. Marsh, one box supplies.

RUTHERFORD PARK.

Postmaster for citizens, one barrel clothing.

SOUTH ORANGE.

Rev. William L. Bostwick, citizens, one lot clothing.

J. W. Wilday, citizens, ten boxes and three packages clothing and bedding.

TOMS RIVER.

W. C. Abbe, one box supplies.

J. W. Perkins, one cot and mattress, one barrel bedding, etc.

TRENTON.

John C. Owens, donation of ladies Committee, four boxes clothing, and one box hats.

Henry Speeler's Sons, five packages crockery.

Millington & Astbury, three hogsheads of white earthenware, valued at $120.

Mrs. W. L. Dayton, ladies, two boxes clothing.

Yates, Bennett, & Allen, citizens, three packages stone-ware valued at $100.

WOODBURY.

Alexander Wentz, Mayor, nine boxes clothing.

STATE OF PENNSYLVANIA.

ALLEGHANY CITY.

Charles W. Cooper, Chairman, one car load supplies.

A. P. Callon, Mayor, contribution of Union Salt Manufacturing Company, one car load salt; contributions of citizens, two car loads provisions; two car loads cooking stoves.

Citizens of Alleghany City, six car loads coal; two cars of clothing, bedding, etc.; three boxes and one bag clothing, half barrel wine, and one barrel pickles.

ALLENTOWN.

Citizens, four cases clothing.

BRADDOCK'S FIELD.

Corey & Co., twenty car loads coal.

BROWNSVILLE.

S. S. Gorham, one box clothing, shoes, etc., from citizens.

BUTLER.

Seven small stoves.

CHESTER.

Miss E. R. Lea, two boxes clothing.

COATSVILLE.

Citizens, fourteen boxes clothing.

CORNWALL.

Donation of the ladies of the Cornwall Congregational Society, two barrels clothing.

EAGLEVILLE.

Rev. H. S. Rodenburg, contribution of Presbyterian Church, one box clothing.

EASTON.

E. H. Green, citizens, car coal, and one car load clothing.

ERIE.

W. A. Baldwin, contributions of the employés of the Erie R. R., at Renover, a quantity of provisions.

FAIR VIEW, P. O.

Mrs. Lynch, one quilt.

HANNERVILLE.

Three hundred and fourteen bushels potatoes, two hundred and eighty heads cabbage, three barrels apples, one box and one trunk clothing.

HARRISBURG.

A. L. R., two pairs blankets.

HOWELLVILLE.

C. Pennock, three packages clothing.

HYDE PARK.

Richards & Howell, four cases clothing, contributions of ladies.
Anna E. Steele, one box clothing, do do.

INDIANA.

James M. Stewart and wife, one barrel flour, two boxes clothing.

LANCASTER.

James Black, contributions of ladies, two cases clothing.

LATROBE STATION.

D. W. McConaugh, four boxes clothing.

LINWOOD.

A. B. Cummings, one box clothing.

MEADVILLE.

Meadville Woolen Mills, thirty woolen blankets.

MOSCOW.

N. L. Gage, citizens, eighty-eight barrels potatoes.

MOUNT JOY.

Mary E. Hoffer, two boxes bedding and clothing.

NEW MILLFORD.

Mrs. E. M. Burritt, donation of the ladies of New Millford and Sommersville, four boxes clothing and bedding, and one barrel potatoes.

NEWVILLE.

Mrs. T. McCandlish, donation of ladies, one box of clothing.

OIL CITY.

James McCarty, five boxes clothing.
Mrs. M. L. Hall and other ladies, one box clothing.

PHILADELPHIA.

William A. Fleet, contributions of German citizens, one car load of clothing.
S. Auerbach, one box clothing, two barrels peas.
M. Rosenbach & Co., two cases containing four hundred gray flannel shirts.
A. H. Franciscus & Co., three hundred cotton comforts (worth $525).
A. G. Cattell, one box clothing.
William Wood & Co., three cases shawls.
P. Lloyd, two boxes merchandise.
J. H. Weeks & Co., two boxes clothing, from ladies.
J. O. McHenry, one box, one lot clothing.
O. W. Gray, one bundle clothing.
J. Sibley, contributions of Central Presbyterian Church, one lot clothing.
John Harvey, four cases clothing, contributions of First Presbyterian Church.
J. Snell, three barrels merchandise.
Church of the Saviour, seven barrels merchandise.
Andrew Blair, three barrels clothing, ladies of the Princeton Presbyterian Church, Cohoksink.
H. Kellogg & Son, one case English biscuit.
Philadelphia Commercial Exchange, twenty barrels potatoes, two barrels lemons, one cheese, one firkin meat, one barrel hams, two stoves.
Elkins & Middleton, one car load breadstuffs.
L. G. Graff & Co., three boxes clothing.
E. Jaynes, one box clothing.
Macey & Delweller, one car load sweet potatoes, produce dealers.
American Stove and Hollow Ware Co., one lot stoves and hollow ware.
Armstrong & Winebreuner, forty-eight gallons syrup.
John Maguire, five boxes clothing.
Contribution of Mrs. Darcher, five boxes and two trunks clothing.
Mrs. A. R. McHenry, one lot clothing.
Mrs. S. A. Jones, contributions of citizens, one box clothing.
Frank H. Fouche, one box clothing.
N. & G. Taylor Company, twenty-five rolls roofing tin.
T. R. Garsed, donation of his children, one trunk clothing.

Thomas Hughes, 325 Chestnut Street, one case of hosiery.
Annie L. Archer, No. 637 10th Street, a trunk of clothing.

PIT HOLE.

Citizens, one box clothing, through Peter Schreiber.

PITTSBURGH.

J. M. Brush, Mayor, citizens, three car loads provisions and clothing; eighty-six stoves with full furniture; seventy-eight packages clothing.
Citizens, five cars coal.
John P. Pears, citizens, sixty boxes clothing.

PLEASANT UNITY.

George Chambers & Son, one box blankets.

POTTSTOWN.

E. C. Steele, four boxes clothing.

POTTSVILLE.

Ladies' donation, one box clothing.

READING.

J. P. Hammond, four boxes and three barrels clothing, contributions of Christ Church.
J. H. Sternberg, four boxes clothing, contributions of First Presbyterian Church.
Giles Bailey, three boxes clothing.

ROBESONIA.

Samuel Sherer, contributions of ladies, one box clothing and bedding.
Mrs. H. P. Robeson, citizens, a quantity of clothing.

ROXBURY.

A. W. Pomeroy, citizens, six barrels of potatoes, onions, dried fruit, etc.

SHICKSHINNY.

A. J. Cohen, ten gondolas coal, from Mocanaqua Coal Co.

ST. MARY'S.

Citizens, two boxes clothing.

STONEBOROUGH.

A. S. Throop, citizens, one car load potatoes.

TITUSVILLE.

J. C. Briggs, citizens, one car load provisions.

WEST CHESTER.

Mrs. W. M. Darlington, contributions of ladies, one box clothing.

WILLIAMSPORT.

J. O. Dutton, contribution of Y. M. C. A., one box bedding and clothing.

STATE OF DELAWARE.

DOVER.

J. M. Chamberlain, four cases canned fruit.

STATE OF MARYLAND.

BALTIMORE.

S. Hammerslough, seven cases bedding and clothing, donation of the Hebrew Ladies' Sewing Society.

Mrs. Dr. Arnold, citizens, seven cases wearing apparel.

Ladies of Baltimore, one box sundries.

STATE OF WEST VIRGINIA.

WHEELING.

R. H. Cummings, one barrel dried beef, two boxes clothing.

DISTRICT OF COLUMBIA.

WASHINGTON.

W. H. H. Terrell, one box clothing.

Sixth Auditor's Office, a quantity of clothing.

Charles Hallowell, one box clothing.

A Friend, one suit of clothes, one shirt.

One car load of clothing, reported by Mr. J. M. McNeill as having been sent here soon after the fire.

STATE OF NORTH CAROLINA.

WILMINGTON.

Mrs. Sue W. Cashwell, sixteen dozen Sheild's Eye Wash.

STATE OF GEORGIA.

SAUNDERSVILLE.

T. Herman, one box clothing.

STATE OF LOUISIANA.

NEW ORLEANS.

A. W. Brodhead, donation of First Congregational Sunday-school, one box clothing.

STATE OF TEXAS.

SAN ANTONIO.

E. D. L. Wicker offers the use of one hundred lots on Twelfth Street, Chicago, for sufferers, free of rent, for three years.

STATE OF OHIO.

AMHERST.

H. J. Jackson, citizens, two boxes clothing and bedding.

ASHLAND.

S. W. Beer, Y. M. C. A., seventeen barrels potatoes.

Bushnell & Wilson, citizens, seven boxes merchandise, two barrels potatoes and one barrel crackers.

BARNESVILLE.

Joseph Green, citizens, one box clothing.

CANTON.

J. C. Laverty, contributions of St. Paul's Church, three boxes clothing.

M. Ruhman, citizens, three boxes clothing.

CLEVELAND.

W. F. Pelton, Mayor, citizens, seven car loads supplies.

Citizens, two barrels potatoes.

Cleveland Non-explosive Lamp Co., two hundred and seventy lamps, complete, twenty-four half gallon oil cans, worth $500.00.

Two lamps, worth $2.20.

COLUMBUS.

Mrs. A. E. Denison, two boxes of A No. 1 clothing. Their committee report provisions have been sent worth $1,963.13, and clothing $739.35.

CRESTLINE.

Mrs. E. Blanchard, three barrels provisions.

CUYAHOGA FALLS.

Mrs. E. N. Sill, contributions of ladies, one box bedding.

Samuel Comstock, citizens, three boxes goods, one barrel dried apples.

DAYTON.

Robert W. Steele, contribution of ladies, four boxes and three cases clothing, shoes, etc.

Leonard Moore, contribution of First Presbyterian Church, five boxes clothing.

Mary E. Mitchell, citizens, four boxes clothing and blankets, one box goods.

Citizens, per statement R. W. Steele, Esq., provisions and clothing estimated at $3,500, distributed in this city by their own committees.

DAMASCOVILLE.

Two boxes clothing, from citizens, per W. Cattell.

DELAWARE.

Mrs. C. C. Chamberlain, seven boxes clothing and supplies from citizens.
W. P. Reed, seven boxes clothing.

DELPHOS.

J. W. Hunt, citizens, one car load supplies.

ELGIN.

Ladies' Benevolent Society, three boxes clothing.

ELYRIA.

Ladies' Benevolent Society, three boxes clothing.

GIRARD.

G. M. Schenck, one box clothing, citizens.
Samuel Moser, one box clothing.

GREENVILLE.

John Leckleder, Mayor, citizens, one car load provisions.

HANGING ROCK.

Hempstead & Co., centre pieces and lining for stove.

JEFFERSON.

A. S. Northway, citizens, nine boxes bedding and clothing.

KELLEY'S ISLAND.

William S. Webb, citizens, six boxes bedding and clothing ; one barrel apples, four barrels potatoes.
S. S. Dwellie, citizens, three barrels potatoes, and one barrel apples.

LEESBURG.

E. P. Johnson, citizens, a quantity of clothing and provisions.

MARIETTA.

W. F. Curtis, citizens of Marietta, Harman, and Warren townships, four boxes clothing, etc.

MASSILLON.

William A. Ronston, citizens, twenty-five cars coal.

MIDDLETOWN.

H. K. Thomas, citizens, sixteen boxes of merchandise.

MOUNT VERNON.

Citizens, two boxes bedding and clothing, and three boxes sundries.

NEW CARLISLE.

W. C. Catlin, Secretary, citizens, five boxes bedding, clothing, etc.

OBERLIN.

Mrs. H. Hulburd, five boxes clothing.

ORVILLE.

H. Walters sends one box containing clothing, etc.

PAINESVILLE.

W. W. Dingley, three boxes clothing, citizens.

RANDOLPH.

Citizens, thirty-two articles of clothing.
W. J. Dickinson, citizens, one box clothing and bedding.

SALEM.

Buckeye Engine Co., offer a five or ten-horse power press.

SANDUSKY.

Sandusky Tool Co., through Hibbard & Spencer, Chicago, seven cases double iron jacks.

SPRINGFIELD.

J. J. Hand, Mayor, citizens, one car load provisions.

TOLEDO.

J. K. Sibor, one car load provisions and supplies, and three crates of earthenware. Citizens.

URBANA.

L. H. Long, Mayor, citizens, one car load provisions, two boxes clothing.

WAUSEON.

C. W. Brown, four boxes clothing, citizens.
Mrs. G. Brown, one package clothing.

WEST LIBERTY.

Mrs. M. M. Taylor, one bucket supplies.

WILLOUGHBY.

H. G. Tryon, citizens, three hundred and fifty bags potatoes.

WOOSTER.

J. C. Plummer, Mayor, citizens, car load clothing and provisions.
D. Robinson, Jr., for citizens, one car supplies.

YOUNGSTOWN.

Mrs. W. J. Hitchcock, eleven boxes clothing. Citizens.

STATE OF INDIANA.

ANDERSON.

James Hazlett, citizens, four boxes bedding.

ATTICA.

P. S. Veeder, citizens, one car load supplies, worth about $1,000.

BRAZIL.

A. W. Knight, citizens, one box clothing and hats and caps.

William M. Morris, donation of Morris Coal Co., and miners, two cars of coal.

By J. Schrack, Secretary, one car block coal each, from —

Ormsby Coal Co.
Morris Coal Co.
Watson & Co.
Otter Creek Block Coal Co.
Niblock, Zimmerman, & Alexander.
J. W. McClelland & Sons.
Clay Coal Co.
Ashley Coal Co.
B. F. Maston.
Bartlett Coal and Mining Co.
Indiana Coal and Iron Co.
B. F. Veach & Co.
Hoosier Coal Co.

BRUNSON.

Citizens, two boxes provisions.

COVINGTON.

Citizens, one barrel flour, two barrels crackers, four sacks flour, one box cheese, one box meal, one box sundries.

C. F. King, citizens, one hundred and sixty-four bushels potatoes.

ELKHART.

M. F. Shuey, citizens, one box staple dry goods.

FORT WAYNE.

Citizens, per statement of Mr. F. S. Shurick — cash, $8,316.20; goods, clothing, etc., $5,925; total, $14,241.20: and distributed in this city by their own committee.

FRANKLIN.

H. H. Boyce, citizens, one car load clothing.

William H. Jennings, Mayor, citizens, one car load provisions.

GOSHEN.

Contributions of citizens, one car load sundries.

INDIANAPOLIS.

E. B. Martindale, contributions of citizens, car of provisions and clothing.
Scott & Steadman, six boxes cheese.

JEFFERSONVILLE.

L. Sparks, Mayor, contributions of ladies, one box clothing.

LA CROSSE.

Citizens, two barrels apples.

LAFAYETTE.

Ruger & Rogers, one thousand loaves bread.

LAPORTE.

Rev. J. P. Ash, contributions of ladies, one box clothing.

LAURENCEBURG.

John Ferris, citizens, twelve bureaus, nine stands, and nine bedsteads complete.

LIBERTY.

T. F. Huddlestone, small box bedding and clothing, from Oasis Society.

LOGANSPORT.

Citizens, two car loads provisions, clothing, bedding, etc., one car load potatoes and apples.

LOTUS.

T. F. Huddlestone, contributions of the Oasis Society, box of clothing, etc.

MADISON.

Haffslad & Thomas, eleven barrels bread.

NEW ALBANY.

H. O. Cannon, citizens, six heating stoves.

The following is a list of the goods bought and shipped (as per printed report) by the New Albany Committee to the sufferers at Chicago: —

One hundred and seven ladies' plaid flannel dresses, one hundred and fifteen ladies' calico dresses, one hundred and thirty-two misses' and children's plaid flannel dresses, ninety-seven ladies' chemises, one hundred and twenty-eight misses' chemises, one hundred and forty-seven misses' and children's calico dresses, eighty-one misses' drawers, one hundred and ninety-five ladies' flannel skirts, sixty-three ladies' canton flannel skirts, two hundred and seventy-four misses' and children's flannel skirts, one hundred and six misses' and children's canton flannel skirts, two hundred and eight boys' jackets, two hundred and seventy-six boys' pants, twenty-one boys' suits, one hundred and forty-six boys' drawers, two hundred and sixty-five boys' shirts, one hundred and eight bed-ticks, one hundred and nine sheets, four bolsters, twelve infants' knit jackets, fourteen boys' overcoats, one hundred and thirty dozen hosiery, twenty-four cooking stoves and ware, one cask tin-ware, two boxes tin-ware, fifty bedsteads, sixty pairs women's shoes, six pairs misses' shoes, one hundred and twenty pairs children's shoes, forty-four pairs youths' shoes. Total cost of above, about $6,500.

PARIS CITY.

W. D. Latsham, three boxes clothing, from ladies.

PERU.

H. E. & C. F. Stern & Co., twenty-five blankets.

W. A. McGregor, Mayor, one car load sundries.

ROCHESTER.

R. S. Clowry, citizens, car load provisions.

ROLLING PRAIRIE.

W. F. King, contributions of citizens, nine sacks potatoes, three sacks apples, three sacks beans, twelve sacks flour, three boxes provisions, one bundle bedding.

TERRE HAUTE.

L. A. Burnett & Co., one box clothing, one keg butter.

Citizens, one hundred barrels flour, one cask bacon, seventeen sacks meal.

L. A. Burnett & Co., twelve boxes clothing and four barrels potatoes, from citizens.

VINCENNES.

Laz. Noble, citizens, ten boxes clothing and provisions, one box coffee, nine boxes and barrels bacon.

M. D. Lacroix, two pairs blankets.

STATE OF ILLINOIS.

ASHLEY.

J. Monroe, citizens, thirty boxes cooked provisions.

ASTORIA.

W. H. Emerson, citizens, one car load provisions.

ATLANTA.

Seth Turner, Mayor, citizens, one car load supplies.

AURORA.

One box and one package second-hand clothing.

BARRY.

Citizens, six barrels provisions and clothing, per B. D. Brown.

BASCO.

G. W. Albert, citizens, one lot provisions.

BATAVIA.

D. Halliday, sundry goods, — flour, bedding, and beans, citizens.

BEARDSTOWN.

A. H. Tielsechott, Mayor, contribution of citizens, one car load provisions.

BELVILLE.

Citizens, five barrels and five boxes sundries ; one sack bacon.
F. H. Piper, forty packages clothing and provisions.
Russell & Hinkley, twenty-five barrels flour.
G. Koerner, citizens, one car provisions ; one car clothing and blankets.
Henry Abend, citizens, three boxes clothing.

BLANDINVILLE.

J. F. Coffman, contribution of Rebecca Lodge, two boxes green apples.

BLOOM.

C. L. Sweet, contributions of the farmers and citizens, one car load of supplies.

BLOOMINGTON.

R. H. Holden, citizens, two car loads provisions and supplies.

BUNKER HILL.

J. A. Delano, two boxes containing one hundred and fifty-six loaves bread, three sacks corn meal.

CAIRO.

Halliday & Brothers, eighty barrels flour.
J. M. Lunsden, Mayor, citizens, one car load provisions.
Harry Roadwright, one barrel potatoes, one barrel flour, two boxes supplies.

CAMBRIDGE.

D. A. Alfred, citizens, one car load provisions.

CANTON.

B. D. Brown, citizens, three boxes sundries, nine barrels flour, two barrels apples, three sacks dried apples.

CARTHAGE.

Little girls, mostly under eleven years old, forming " Golden Rule Society," send one box, containing forty-three articles female clothing.

CENTRALIA.

A. L. Barnes, Mayor, citizens, one car load provisions.

CHAMPAIGN CITY.

Citizens, through E. C. Larned, three boxes clothing and bedding.
Citizens, one car load provisions.

CHARLES CITY.

M. E. German Relief Society, citizens, one car load potatoes.

CHARLESTON.

J. W. Ogden, Mayor, citizens, one car load of provisions and clothing.

CHICAGO.

W. M. Reinhardt, 158 and 160 West Randolph Street, ten barrels beef.

Clement & Sayer, fifteen pairs Misses' shoes, two pairs boys' boots, twenty-two pairs youth's boots.

C. C. Merrick, one hundred tons soft coal.

Mrs. Randall, 124 South Morgan Street, one box clothing.

M. C. Spalding & Co., of "The Chicago Extra," donate the free use of five squares in their paper for advertising purposes.

Young Men's Christian Union, Chicago, fourteen cases clothing, first installment.

Hall & Frost donate $6.80 worth of lumber.

U. S. Government, through General Sheridan, ten thousand blankets, four thousand shirts, four thousand drawers, four thousand pairs stockings, one thousand five hundred pairs boots, one hundred and ninety-five tents complete.

CORDOVA.

D. Zimmerman reports citizens having contributed clothing, provisions, etc.

CRESTON.

H. C. Robbins, twenty-two boxes provisions, one box clothing. Citizens.

DANVILLE.

Citizens, one barrel of flour, and six hams.

Hon. J. C. Short, President, contribution of Moss Bank Coal Co., one hundred tons coal.

DECATUR.

L. Burrows, one bale bed comforts.

Citizens, four cars supplies.

Mrs. L. Burrows reports citizens as sending groceries valued at $50.00.

DELAVAN.

L. D. Lawton, twenty boxes provisions and clothing. Citizens.

DOWNER'S GROVE.

Citizens, through M. Foote, thirty-seven straw beds, and one car load of wood.

DU QUOIN.

Citizens, one car load provisions.

S. D. Goodale, one beef, dressed.

One car load coal from the miners.

DWIGHT.

W. H. Bradbury, citizens, twelve boxes provisions.

EARLVILLE.

Contributions of citizens, two barrels beef, one box bread.

EDGEWOOD.

Citizens, one box clothing; eight barrels flour, one barrel meal.

EDWARDSVILLE.

C. Nash, citizens, one box woolen clothing.

EFFINGHAM.

O. F. Libby, Mayor, citizens, $500.00 worth bacon and beans, and one box merchandise.

ELIZABETH.

Donations of two ladies, one box clothing.

ENFIELD.

Citizens, by R. C. Willis, two barrels flour, three boxes blankets and clothing.

FARMINGTON.

B. Fargo, seventeen barrels and four sacks flour.

FLORA.

J. S. Major, citizens, three boxes clothing; $200.00 worth of clothing and groceries.

FLORENCE STATION.

H. F. Milliken, seven boxes, three barrels, and three bags provisions.

FRANKLIN GROVE.

T. W. Scott, citizens, one box clothing.

GALENA.

Citizens, twelve bags potatoes; one carload supplies.
Thomas Foster, thirty bushels potatoes.
Thomas Foster, citizens, one box clothing, etc.

GENESEO.

Citizens, three boxes vegetables; one box clothing; one car provisions.

GENEVA.

Mrs. W. B. Plato, ten straw beds.
E. S. Plato, several straw beds.
Mrs. P. D. Hoyt, ladies, one box and one barrel wearing apparel.

GREENVILLE.

William S. Smith, citizens, one car load provisions.

HANOVER.

George Jeffers, contribution of first Presbyterian Church S. S., and others, of two barrels flour, one box butter, and one box blankets, clothing, etc.

HILLSBOROUGH.

Paul Walter, Mayor, citizens, one hundred barrels flour.
W. B. Robb, one box clothing.

IRVINGTON.

J. Harder, citizens, one barrel sweet potatoes, $10.00 worth of flour, two boxes merchandise.

JOLIET.

E. Washburn, contributions from Penitentiary, one thousand two hundred and ten loaves bread, eight barrels dried beef.

E. Porter, Mayor, citizens, two cars provisions.

KANKAKEE.

Citizens, provisions bought and furnished amounting to $450.30.

KANSAS.

F. W. Boyer, citizens, fourteen barrels flour, crackers, apples, beans, and potatoes.

Dr. Ringland, one box provisions.

LACON.

Citizens, two barrels hams, and sixty cords wood.

LAWNDALE.

Citizens, twenty sacks flour, six barrels potatoes, one box bedding and clothing.

LASALLE.

N. I. C. & I. Co., thirty car loads coal, estimated value $2,000.

LEE CENTRE.

Sewing Society sends one box supplies.

LENA.

S. Rising, one car load food and clothing from citizens.

LINCOLN.

Frank Fisk, one car load provisions, clothing, boots, shoes, and bedding, from citizens.

LOCKPORT.

From citizens, merchandise, worth $449.

LOMBARD.

Citizens, three barrels, two bundles, one box, seven bed ticks.

Mrs. F. E. Hull, citizens, one car load supplies.

Miss A. Hull, contributions of ladies of the Church of Christ, one box bedding and clothing.

LOMAX.

Citizens, one car provisions, by R. L. Pepper.

MANCHESTER.

Citizens, five boxes boots, shoes, and clothing.

MATTOON.

J. H. Richmond, two boxes, one bundle clothing, one car, two boxes supplies, from citizens.

METAMORA.

William Sampson, citizens, one car load provisions, eighty-eight bags corn meal.

MINIER.

J. M. Edmiston, citizens, one car load provisions.

MOLINE.

E. Wheelock, Treasurer, citizens, bread, crackers, and meat, worth $592.34, also a large quantity of clothing.

MOMENCE.

H. Worcester, citizens, one car load provisions, two barrels sweet milk.

MONMOUTH.

Citizens, three car loads supplies.

MORRIS.

Citizens, one car load provisions and supplies, shipped immediately after the fire.

MOUNT CARROLL.

A. H. Mills, donations of citizens, sundry barrels clothing.

Donation of ladies, one box clothing.

A lady, through G. Blake, Secretary, sends a box, containing two comforters, one overcoat, and scarfs.

MOUNT CARMEL.

J. Zimmerman, Masonic fraternity, one box clothing.

A. C. Edgar, one barrel clothing.

MOUNT VERNON.

Mrs. Lyon, contributions of ladies, four boxes clothing, one box provisions.

NASHVILLE.

George S. Anderson, Secretary, citizens, three hundred pounds bacon and ham, one box bedding and clothing.

OLNEY.

C. D. Johnson, Mayor, citizens, part of car load flour and provisions.

ORCHARD COAL MINES, Peoria Co.

Miners, two car loads coal.

ORION.

George O. Nelson, citizens, a quantity of provisions.

PALATINE.

Citizens, two barrels of onions, one box beans, and sixty cords wood.

August Schneidermann reported that he collected from citizens a quantity of flour, meat, and provisions, which were sent on immediately after the fire.

PARIS.

W. A. Wozencrants, citizens, one car provisions; three boxes blankets; two boxes clothing.

The total worth about $1,000.

PEKIN.

E. Hudson, citizens, two car loads provisions.

Citizens, four car loads provisions and clothing.

PEORIA.

Mark M. Aiken, citizens, fourteen car loads supplies.

George Puterbaugh, citizens, two car loads supplies.

G. H. McIlvane, citizens, one car load supplies.

Robert C. Grier, Treasurer, expended for provisions forwarded, $2,112.77.

PETERSBURG.

J. M. Robbins, citizens, one box clothing, one barrel dried fruit, one box butter.

PLEASANT HILL.

S. R. Cannon & Co., twenty-four barrels flour, citizens.

PITTSFIELD.

N. A. Wells, for the Hon. Scott Wike, one hundred barrels flour.

PONTIAC.

W. B. Fyfe, citizens, $52.62 worth of bread, etc., and sixteen cases provisions.

PRINCETON.

Mrs. C. J. Richardson reports citizens sending two dry goods boxes, supplies for "Good Samaritan Society," sent February 8, 1872.

Mrs. C. J. Richardson, citizens, two boxes clothing.

QUINCY.

J. H. Rowland, Mayor, citizens, one train of provisions and supplies, including a thousand pairs of shoes.

RIDOTT.

S. C. Buckley, citizens, two car loads provisions, supplies, etc.

ROCKFORD.

Scholars of South Rockford School, twelve bed comforters.

ROCK ISLAND.

W. Payne, citizens, one car load provisions, three boxes clothing, two quarters beef, and one dressed hog.

RUSHVILLE.

W. A. Ray, citizens, fifty-one tons coal, one bag meal, one thousand pounds clear side bacon, three bags beans, forty-three sacks flour, one bag sundries, one barrel flour, six barrels apples and potatoes, one box blankets and comforts, one sack bacon, one tub dried apples, one box clothing, one jar apple butter.

SANDWICH.

A. P. Crapsey, contributions of ladies, one car load straw beds and pillows.

SHELBYVILLE.

Citizens, one box clothing and blankets, and five hundred pounds flour, in sacks, through M. W. Wright, Chairman, etc.

SPRINGFIELD.

Contributions of citizens, through Hon. John M. Palmer, nine car loads supplies, and five cars of coal.

A. J. Bean, contribution of the Western Coal Mining Co., one hundred tons coal.

STERLING.

Citizens, per J. G. Manahan, one car load provisions and clothing; one hundred barrels and twelve sacks flour.

SYCAMORE.

R. A. Smith, Mayor, citizens, twenty-seven boxes and barrels provisions.

TALLULA.

Citizens, Menard & Co., one case fresh beef, five boxes provisions, two barrels potatoes.

TISKILWA.

Charles M. Stevens, two cases clothing.

TONICA.

J. C. Meyers, one box clothing. Citizens. Methodist Episcopal Church, one box clothing.

TOWER HILL.

Citizens, two boxes provisions.

TRIVOLI.

J. Linck, citizens, ninety-eight bushels potatoes and one sack beans.

VIRDEN.

B. Cowan, six boxes goods, five boxes clothing. Citizens.

U. Lindley, citizens, one box clothing.

WASHBURN.

T. J. Houston, citizens, one car load supplies.

WASHINGTON.

Citizens, one car supplies.

WAVERLY.

S. H. Curtis, citizens, one car load supplies.

Citizens, fifty-three barrels potatoes, three barrels crackers, one barrel molasses, one bag beans, seventeen sacks flour, one firkin butter, one box potatoes.

WILMINGTON.

Bowe, Gregg, & Co., four cases clothing.

WINNEBAGO.

William A. Grey, contribution of the Presbyterian Church, one box clothing.

WOODWORTH STATION.

J. C. Roberts, one box provisions, one barrel flour.

YATES CITY.

Citizens sent fifty-three sacks corn meal, weighing five thousand and eighty-eight pounds.

STATE OF KENTUCKY.

LOUISVILLE.

Jacob Schmidt, three boxes socks.
J. L. Singer, six cars supplies, citizens.
J. G. Baxter, five cars supplies, citizens.
Citizens, eight bags rice, fifty-nine barrels syrup.
B. F. Woodward, one box merchandise.
Citizens, four cars supplies, and other goods which were purchased from the relief fund in Louisville, and cost as per following recapitulation of statement of the "Executive Committee of Louisville for the Chicago sufferers": —

Paid for general merchandise	$45,421.20
Paid for transportation, freight, and parties in Louisville	3,656.65
Discrepancy in bills	.45
Total disbursements	$49,078.30
Sundry vouchers, per order F. P. Schmitt, Chairman . .	359.50
Total cost	$49,437.80

PADUCAH.

Citizens, one box merchandise.

STATE OF TENNESSEE.

MEMPHIS.

Southworth & Thayer, one case women's boots.

STATE OF MICHIGAN.

ADRIAN.

Citizens, twenty-four boxes supplies.

BUCHANAN.

L. P. P. Alexandre, citizens, one car provisions.

COLDWATER.

Citizens, six boxes, four barrels, pail, and one sack supplies.

DETROIT.

A. Sanderson, two car loads shawls and blankets, donation of Board of Trade.
Fred. Carlisle, ten thousand dollars ($10,000) worth of lumber.

HOLLAND CITY.

From J. L. Lee, New York, two boxes supplies.

SALZBURG.

Brooks & Adams, nine car loads lumber and three car loads scantling.

WHITE PIGEON.

Citizens, two boxes provisions.

STATE OF WISCONSIN.

ARENA.

H. Reed, five boxes and one barrel provisions. Citizens.

BARABOO.

Citizens, two car loads supplies.

BELOIT.

David S. Foster, Mayor, citizens, forty-eight packages clothing and provisions.

KENOSHA.

A. Farr, Mayor, citizens, one car load provisions.

MADISON.

J. M. Bowman, citizens, one car load provisions.

MANITOWOC.

P. Johnson, Mayor, fifty barrels flour, one barrel pork, one firkin and one crock butter, one barrel crackers. Citizens.

MILWAUKEE.

Citizens, four car loads provisions, two car loads potatoes.

PORTAGE CITY.

S. S. Brown, Mayor, citizens, five thousand pounds cooked provisions.

PRAIRIE DU CHIEN.

Citizens, car potatoes.

RACINE.

J. H. Kelley, citizens, one car load provisions, blankets, and clothing.

RIPON.

A. Eberhart, Mayor, citizens, twenty-five boxes provisions.

ROLLING PRAIRIE.

J. Smith, citizens, one car provisions.

SHARON.

Mrs. Harrington, one box provisions.

SHEBOYGAN.

Citizens, three barrels and one sack potatoes, one jar butter, four boxes sundries, one box bread, one sack clothing, one box fish, two bags peas.

STATE OF MINNESOTA.

MANKATO.

William Frisbie, citizens, one hundred bushels potatoes, sixty-six barrels flour.

NEW ULM.

Dr. Muller, citizens, two hundred sacks flour.

NORTHFIELD.

Mrs. C. A. Wheaton, donations of ladies, one box ladies' and children's clothing,

RED WING.

F. R. Sterretts, one car potatoes, eighty-five barrels flour, six barrels pork, five barrels onions.

ROCHESTER.

Lake & Humanson, by J. D. Blake, five barrels flour.
S. J. Barlow, citizens, two cars potatoes, seven hundred bushels.

ST. PAUL.

Citizens, lot of provisions.

WINONA.

Citizens, one car load potatoes, five barrels flour, one hundred and ninety-two sacks flour.
J. H. Woodruff, one pair felt boots.

STATE OF IOWA.

BEACON STATION.

W. W. Wallace, citizens, one car load potatoes.

BELLE PLAINE.

Citizens, one and one half car loads provisions.

BELLEVIEW.

J. Kelso, Mayor, citizens, $250.00 worth provisions; three barrels potatoes, eight sacks beans and potatoes.

BONAPARTE.

Citizens, Thomas Christy, one car load provisions and clothing.

BRIGHTON.

W. G. Israel, flour, provisions, clothing, etc., from citizens.

BROOKLYN.

C. H. Libbey, one car potatoes and flour.

Thomas J. Holmes & Sons, six boxes and one barrel bread and cakes, from citizens.

Citizens, one car supplies.

BURLINGTON.

James Putnam, citizens, twelve thousand pounds corn meal, ten barrels and five boxes crackers, three barrels pork, one bag beans, one crock butter, two bundles merchandise, one car containing onions. Three car loads provisions.

Ladies' Aid Society sent three thousand six hundred articles of clothing, etc., valued by them at $3,000.

CEDAR RAPIDS.

C. Rawley, citizens, one car load provisions.

CORDOVA.

D. Zimmerman, citizens, one lot of provisions.

CRESCO.

M. B. Doolittle, one car potatoes, for citizens.

DAVENPORT.

Citizens, one car load clothing; one car load provisions; four car loads supplies.

Nicholas Fejervary, citizens, one car supplies.

DENMARK.

G. B. Bracket, two boxes merchandise, from citizens.

DES MOINES.

Tuttle Martin, Mayor, citizens, two car loads provisions and clothing.

DEWITT.

D. Whitney, citizens, fourteen boxes provisions.

DUBUQUE.

Citizens, two car loads provisions and supplies.

J. Chapman, twenty-five packages provisions, from citizens.

Citizens, eighteen sacks flour, two boxes bacon, thirty three sacks and one barrel potatoes, one barrel sauerkraut.

A. Fuller, one barrel provisions.

Joseph Herod, two car loads of supplies (by citizens).

NOTE. — Citizens' contributions of provisions, etc., worth about $5,000, as per statement of the Dubuque Committee.

DUNLAP.

Mrs. C. M. Eaton, citizens, two boxes clothing.

FAIRFAX.

J. Dick, ten barrels and six boxes provisions, two boxes clothing.

IOWA CITY.

Citizens, two boxes goods; one car load supplies.

KEOKUK.

Citizens, one car load provisions; nine boxes supplies.

LYONS.

J. N. Cross, Mayor, citizens, one hundred barrels and boxes of cooked provisions, and many boxes clothing.

MAQUOKETA.

B. A. Spencer, citizens, one box clothing.

J. M. Hoag, citizens, forty bushels beans.

MASON CITY.

J. V. W. Montague, citizens, three boxes bedding and clothing.

MOUNT PLEASANT.

Rev. E. Crane, president, ladies and citizens, two boxes goods; a quantity of clothing, provisions, and bedding.

Rev. E. Crane, one box containing seven bed comforts and four sheets, twelve sacks flour, two sacks dried fruit, one sack beans; one hundred and seventy-three sacks white winter wheat flour.

MOUNT VERNON.

Citizens, thirteen boxes supplies.

MUSCATINE.

Citizens, by H. W. Moore, one car load potatoes; one hundred and fifty packages clothing and provisions.

Mrs. W. B. Clapp, contributions of Young Ladies' Mission Circle of First Congregational Church, one box clothing.

NEW SHARON.

B. Stanton, citizens, one car of clothing and provisions.

OSKALOOSA.

Isaiah Frankel, two cars provisions, clothing, etc.

OTTUMWA.

C. F. Blake, Esq., Treasurer, advises of one car load of provisions being sent immediately after the fire, valued by them at $600.

PRAIRIE CITY.

H. M. Howard, citizens, three hundred and fifty bushels potatoes.

SHELLSBURG.

Citizens, one car load provisions.

SIOUX CITY.

Citizens, three boxes merchandise, one car load supplies and one car load potatoes.

STUART.

Charles Stuart, personal contribution, three hundred bushels potatoes.

TIPTON.

William Elliott, citizens, three boxes bedding and clothing.

TOLEDO.

A. J. Tree, for citizens, one car load goods.

WAPELLO.

Citizens, twenty-one boxes provisions, and one box clothing.

WASHINGTON.

Citizens, one lot clothing.

Citizens, by M. C. Parker, thirteen boxes clothing and sundries.

WAVERLEY.

James Stevenson, Mayor, citizens, fifty-six barrels flour, twenty-five sacks flour, one barrel meal, seventy-one barrels potatoes, one barrel molasses, one bag beans, one firkin butter, one box potatoes, three barrels crackers.

J. D. Benton, donation one trunk clothes.

WEST LIBERTY.

James Morgan, citizens, two hundred and forty bushels potatoes, one barrel and two sacks flour, a quantity of bread.

Citizens, one car vegetables and one car load corn; thirteen sacks potatoes, one sack beans, three barrels apples.

WILTON.

D. A. W. Perkins, Mayor, citizens, one car provisions and clothing.

STATE OF MISSOURI.

CHILLICOTHE.

L. S. Pearce, citizens, one car load provisions and blankets.

HANNIBAL.

Citizens, one car load provisions.

HERMANN.

Poeschel & Scherer, three half barrels wine, twenty-one gallons Concord wine, twenty-one gallons Catawba wine, twenty-one gallons Norton's Virginia wine.

HIGH HILL.

Mrs. R. D. Bresco, contributions of ladies, one lot of clothing.

HOPKINS.

George W. Oles, citizens, one car potatoes.

KANSAS CITY.

Citizens, two car loads of supplies, one barrel apples, one box sundries.

MARYVILLE.

Citizens, one car potatoes.

ST. JOSEPH.

Citizens, one car load of provisions.

R. E. Turner, President Board of Trade, estimates the donations of supplies forwarded from St. Joseph, and disbursed by Citizens' Committee, at about $8,000 in value.

ST. LOUIS.

Citizens, one box clothing; three half barrels of wine.

T. Dorris, five bales blankets.

G. Gorin, Esq., one box flannels.

STATE OF KANSAS.

ATCHISON.

W. F. Downs, ten barrels flour.

FORT SCOTT.

Citizens, through C. W. Goodlander, seventeen cars coal, one car potatoes.

Chapin & Cleary, one box boots and shoes.

JUNCTION CITY.

R. O. Rizer, Mayor, citizens, one hundred and twenty sacks and one hundred and sixty half-sacks flour.

LAWRENCE.

Citizens, one car provisions.

LEAVENWORTH.

Durfee & Peck, four cars supplies, citizens.

M. S. Grant, one box goods.

Durfee & Peck, one box clothing.

Hon. P. G. Lowe, two hundred sacks flour, one hundred and five sacks flour and meat, twenty barrels apples, fifty-nine sacks bacon, thirteen sacks sweet potatoes, fourteen sacks Irish potatoes, nine sacks onions.

J. W. Pierce, agent, seven boxes supplies.

Citizens, twelve boxes bedding and clothing.

W. P. Lobenstein, personal contribution, five bales buffalo robes.

E. H. Durfee & Co., one box blankets.

Hon. P. G. Lowe, citizens, eight boxes clothing, two barrels pork.

OTTAWA.

J. W. McGee, contributions of ladies, five boxes clothing and one barrel onions. Contributions of citizens, five sacks flour, four boxes groceries.

WYANDOTTE.

Rev. S. P. Jacobs, citizens, $300 worth clothing and blankets.

STATE OF NEBRASKA.

GRAND ISLAND.

W. H. Platt, citizens, one car load potatoes.

NEBRASKA CITY.

Donations of citizens, eighteen barrels potatoes, one box of clothing, one sack of beans, and two hundred bushels of potatoes.

Citizens, one car load potatoes.

T. Ashton, one car load corn, citizens.

B. Davenport, citizens, car load of flour and bacon.

OMAHA.

Mrs. F. Drake, and another lady, one box clothing.

W. H. Dimmick, fifty hats, seventeen pairs shoes, seventeen pairs boys' socks.

Omaha National Bank, one hundred and thirty-six packages corn meal, five sacks flour, one package blankets.

Citizens, through F. Drake, one box clothing, three cars potatoes, and five cases merchandise.

PLATTSMOUTH.

Citizens, three boxes clothing.

SCHUYLER STATION.

W. P. P. St. Clair, twenty sacks flour, five sacks potatoes.

COLORADO TERRITORY.

CENTRAL CITY.

N. Young & Co., citizens, several boxes clothing.

DENVER.

J. J. T. Ball, ten packages clothing.

GREELEY.

Citizens send thirty sacks flour.

DAKOTA TERRITORY.

FORT SULLY.

Officers and soldiers, U. S. Army, report having disbursed, through General Sheridan, Mrs. Rucker, etc., $343.30.

STATE OF CALIFORNIA.

GEORGETOWN.

W. H. Cushman, citizens, 2 boxes clothing.

SACRAMENTO.

Mrs. J. H. Carroll, citizens, five boxes clothing.

SAN FRANCISCO.

M. Morganthorn, fifty pairs blankets.
Mrs. McBein, citizens, one box clothing.
H. Y. Luddington, citizens, four cases and three bales clothing.

STOCKTON.

E. S. Holden, one box clothing, citizens.

MISCELLANEOUS.

Unknown, three boxes of cloth, marked "R. W.," and No. 1 and No. 2.
"P. D. C.," from "A. T. & S.," one case clothing.
From "Col.," two boxes merchandise.
"P. D. C.," one box provisions, one car coal.
Unknown, through Rumsey Bros. & Co., a package of lard.
E. B. Lewis, a little boy, a bag of marbles.
Mrs. L. L. Hyatt, one box merchandise.
Messrs. Whitwell & Sons, England, one package clothing.
George H. Lee and George H. Lee, Jr., one box clothing.

CANADA.

BRANTFORD.

W. E. Welding, citizens, thirteen cases blankets, boots, shoes, etc., eighty-two stoves, fifty-seven iron kettles, several packages and bundles.

BURLING.

G. D. Bowman, $1,000 worth of provisions.

GODERICH.

Julia McKid, three packages clothing, from ladies.

GUELPH.

Armstrong, McCrue, & Co., eighteen dozen articles of ladies' and children's underwear.

HAMILTON.

Citizens, six boxes and thirty packages clothing.

W. E. Lanford, nine cases clothing.

A. T. Wood, two cases housekeeping supplies.

Citizens' donation of clothing, tools, blankets, boots, shoes, etc., worth $2,282.97.

LONDON, ONTARIO.

Charles P. Smith, citizens, clothing, blankets, etc., worth, as per statement of their committee, $3,420.18.

MEADFORD.

Joseph Stovel, one box goods.

MONTREAL.

George Winks & Co., four bales blankets.

James McClure & Co., large lot of dry goods and clothing.

Hugh McLennan, nine cases and one bag clothing from citizens, and his personal contribution, one case clothing.

J. T. Clayton, five barrels Nabob pickles.

Brown & Childs, citizens, large lot clothing, and boots and shoes.

S. H. & J. Morse, citizens, boots, shoes, and clothing.

H. Beaudry, lot of woolen hose, clothing.

J. C. Brydges, citizens, two car loads clothing and blankets.

G. Michon, citizens, one package clothing.

E. B. Carmichael, two trunks clothing.

S. H. May, one parcel clothing.

M. P. O. Johnson & Co., one box flannels.

Mrs. Heckson, one box clothing.

Mrs. Dowe, one box clothing.

Robertson, Stevenson, & Co., one box clothing.

Frothingham & Workman, two dozen hand saws, five and a half dozen steel hammers.

J. G. McKenzie & Co., advise of five hundred and seventy-four men's lambs' wool shirts.

Alexander Walker, one bale blankets.

J. Atkin, one case clothing.

Private contributions of merchandise not mentioned in Montreal Committee's Report (as advised by Hugh McLennan, worth $2,196).

NEWCASTLE.

Citizens, two hundred and sixty and three-fourths yards tweed, worth $253.15.

W. H. Warner, citizens, one case cloth.

QUEBEC.

Col. Martindale, donation of British Government, six thousand seven hundred and twenty blankets.

SHERBROOK.

R. N. Hall, citizens, four cases blankets and clothing.

Richard Smith, one box clothing.

ST. CATHERINES.

R. Norton, four cases clothing.

ST. JOHN, N. B.

Miss Baldwin, one box clothing and one box books.

TORONTO.

John McDonald & Co., one hundred and twenty-three pairs blankets, ten pieces linsey.

William Hessin, one hundred boxes biscuit.

Queen's Hotel, fifty boxes biscuit, six boxes cheese.

Lyman Brothers & Co., one case medical stores.

ENGLAND.

BRADFORD.

Firth, Booth, & Co., citizens, one case clothing; from a neighbor, one case clothing.

BRISTOL.

Eighteen packages blankets, from citizens, through E. E. Morgan's Sons, New York.

Samuel Butter, one package clothing.

A few drapers' assistants, one bundle of clothing.

Payne & Thompson, ten pairs blankets and forty-eight pairs hose.

CLIFTON.

Mr. and Mrs. William Sturge, one package clothing.

EXETER.

One bale new clothing from citizens, per R. P. Culley, and bundles for sundry persons, which are all delivered.

GRANTHAM.

W. D. Cowle (New York), citizens, one box clothing.

H. Wilson (Liverpool), citizens, one box clothing.

HUDDERSFIELD.

C. H. Jones, Mayor, citizens, twenty-six bales blankets, worth £1,199 16s. sterling.

LEEDS.

L. T. Newell, citizens, three bales blankets, worth £172 10s.

John Barran, Mayor, contributions of citizens, nineteen bales merchandise, worth £451 19s. 2d; five bales blankets, worth £262 4s. 1d.

LIVERPOOL.

J. Davidson, contributions of the Scotch resident Drapery Trade, five packages woolen and cotton goods.

Hughes & Dixon, one box clothing.

Joseph Donnell, one bale cloths.

MANCHESTER.

Mrs. Robert Whitworth, one dozen boxes shirts.

Our society have received up till this time, through A. T. Stewart & Co., of New York, invoices of purchases made in Manchester, amounting to £17,227 11s. 10d. sterling.

MILNROW.

Contribution of John Alsworth and James Heap, a bale of flannels, valued at £17 sterling.

NOTTINGHAM.

Citizens, one box of clothing.

STOW MARKET.

L. Webb, one box clothing.

Congregational Church, Rev. Jonah Reeve, Pastor, one box clothing.

IRELAND.

WATERFORD.

Twenty bales blankets (510 pairs), valued at £300 sterling, through Hon. Henry F. Slattery, Mayor.

SCOTLAND.

ABERDEEN.

Matthew McDougall (of Dundee), donation of a lady, one box clothing.

GERMANY.

BERLIN.

Donation of Capt. H. J. Sweeney, one case clothing.

HAMBURG.

One case clothing, from J. R. McDonald & Co.

AUSTRIA.

VIENNA.

Twenty-four dozen pairs shoes, through P. S. Post, U. S. Consul, valued at $337, gold.

ITALY.

ROME.

Oil painting, from Charles Caryl Coleman, Artist, of Buffalo, N. Y.

CONTRIBUTIONS OF MONEY.

STATE OF MAINE.

AUBURN.

Oct. 24, 1871.	J. C. Haskell	$2.00	
31.	Hattie Haskell	3.00	$5.00

BANGOR.

Dec. 11.	Henry McLaughlin	50.00	50.00

BIDDEFORD.

Oct. 27.	E. W. Wedgwood, Mayor, for citizens .	1,000.00	
March 15, 1872.	Citizens, E. W. Wedgwood, Mayor	719.85	1,719.85

BUCKSPORT.

Nov. 6, 1871.	Congregational Church, per E. Swasey	155.00	155.00

CASTINE.

Oct. 25.	Trinitarian Society, per S. Adams .	50.00	
Nov. 21.	Unitarian Church, George H. Witherle, Treasurer	65.50	
	Methodist Church	10.25	125.75

EASTPORT.

Oct. 31.	General S. K. Dawson, U. S. A. . .	50.00	50.00

HOLDEN.

Feb. 5, 1872.	Congregational Church, Rev. J. S. Cogswell	19.00	19.00

LEWISTON.

Dec. 19, 1871.	Howard B. Abbott	5.00	5.00

PORTLAND.

Oct. 15.	Emery, Waterhouse, & Co.	200.00	
24.	Twitchell, Champlin, & Co.	100.00	
27.	Samuel G. Spring, for citizens, . .	10,000.00	
Dec. 1.	Metropolitan Theatre Co., for Dramatic profession	100.00	
19.	Citizens, S. E. Spring, Treasurer . .	8,407.61	18,807.61

RUMFORD.

Date	Contributor	Amount	Total
Oct. 30.	H. A. Libbey	1.00	1.00

WINTHROP.

Date	Contributor	Amount	Total
Nov. 8.	Public School Children	15.26	
27.	Congregational Church, C. A. Wing .	50.00	65.26

YORK.

Date	Contributor	Amount	Total
Nov. 8.	M. E. Church, by Rev. D. Halloran .	40.00	40.00
			$21,043.47

STATE OF NEW HAMPSHIRE.

CONCORD.

Date	Contributor	Amount	Total
Oct. 31, 1871.	First Congregational Church . .	$150.00	$150.00

DOVER.

Date	Contributor	Amount	Total
Oct. 20.	St. Thomas's Episcopal Church, . .	76.00	
25.	Joseph Hayes	10.00	86.00

EPPING.

Date	Contributor	Amount	Total
Oct. 28.	Mill operatives	50.00	50.00

HAMPSTEAD.

Date	Contributor	Amount	Total
Oct. 30.	Citizens	187.75	
Nov. 11.	W. E. Ballard	2.00	189.75

KEENE.

Date	Contributor	Amount	Total
Oct. 14.	Charles S. Faulkner	100.00	100.00

LACONIA.

Date	Contributor	Amount	Total
Jan. 13, 1872.	Freewill Baptist Society, S. R. Wiggins	50.00	50.00

LEBANON.

Date	Contributor	Amount	Total
Dec. 5, 1871.	Citizens, W. S. Ela and others .	770.40	770.40

MANCHESTER.

Date	Contributor	Amount	Total
Nov. 14.	City appropriation, by J. E. Bennett .	15,000.00	15,000.00

NEW IPSWICH.

Date	Contributor	Amount	Total
Oct. 27.	Citizens, by W. A. Preston	110.50	110.50

NEW LONDON.

Date	Contributor	Amount	Total
Oct. 21.	Pupils of New London Institute . .	122.15	122.15

NORTH CONWAY.

Date	Contributor	Amount	Total
Oct. 21.	——	28.85	28.85

PORTSMOUTH.

Oct. 19.	Contribution of U. S. Navy Yard . .	314,00	
23.	First National Bank (naval officers) .	86.00	
Nov. 6.	Citizens, by W. R. Preston . . .	4,500.00	
	Mechanics U. S. Navy Yard . . .	896.00	5,796.00

RINDGE.

Oct. 20.	Mite	2.00	2.00

SOUTH NEWMARKET.

Oct. 21.	Citizens	84.00	84.00

SOUTH NEWBURY.

Oct. 23.	Citizens, by J. Morse, P. M. . . .	9.50	9.50

WARNER.

Oct. 24.	Citizens, by W. K. Bartlett . . .	106.00	106.00

WINCHESTER.

Nov. 20.	Methodist Church, Rev. J. W. Adams .	57.00	
	Citizens, Rev. J. W. Adams . . .	15.00	72.00
			$22.727.15

STATE OF VERMONT.

Jan. 5, 1872.	National Life Insurance Co. of Vermont, C. T. Langford, General Agent	$50.00	$50.00

BENNINGTON.

Oct. 27, 1871.	Church collection, per W. S. Southworth	160.00	160.00

BETHEL.

Nov. 9.	Drummer	.20	.20

BRATTLEBOROUGH.

Jan. 10, 1872.	Central Congregational Church, C. F. Thompson, Treasurer	100.00	
10.	Methodist Church, C. F. Thompson .	24.00	124.00

BURLINGTON.

Oct. 27, 1871.	Citizens, per N. C. Dodge, Mayor	3,000.00	
Dec. 15.	" " " .	432.23	3,432.23

EAST HARDWICK.

Dec. 6.	Congregational Church, J. D. Bell . .	61.00	61.00

MIDDLEBURY.

Oct. 19.	Citizens	410.00	410.00

PROCTORSVILLE.

Nov. 2. Ladies, per A. S. Parker . . . 2.00—— 2.00

RUTLAND.

Nov. 29. Citizens, L. Daniels, Chairman . . 1,400.00—— 1,400.00

WEST BRATTLEBOROUGH.

Jan. 10, 1872. Ladies of Glenwood Seminary, by C. F. Thompson . . . . . . 30.00—— 30.00

WOODSTOCK.

Oct. 26, 1871. Dramatic Club . . . . . 120.00—— 120.00

$5,789.43

STATE OF MASSACHUSETTS.

AMHERST.

Jan. 5, 1872. Citizens, C. S. Smith, Chairman $831.50—— $831.50

ATHOL DEPOT.

Nov. 18, 1871. Citizens, per A. L. Newman . . 173.04—— 173.04

ANDOVER.

Oct. 21. Citizens . . . . 5,443.10—— 5,443.10

BALDWINSVILLE.

Oct. 20, 1871. Sunday-school . . . . . 27.87—— 27.87

BARRE.

Jan. 6. Citizens, J. H. Goddard, Treasurer . . 300.00—— 300.00

BEVERLY.

Nov. 4. Citizens, per R. G. Bennett . . . 3,000.00—— 3,000.00

BOSTON.

Oct. 15. E. A. Davis, small boy 1.00
16. Citizens, per Hon. W. Gray, Chairman 25,000.00
18. George Warren, of Liverpool . . 5,000.00
Sympathizer 1.00
Mite 25
George H. Cutter 10.00
20. St. James Theatre Benefit . . . 438.55
21. A. Hardy, and schoolmates . . . 10.00
Joseph Burnett & Co. 1,000.00
City of Boston, per Kidder, Peabody, & Co. 100,000.00
Macullar, Williams, & Parker . . 500.00
25. Church of Disciples, per Otis Inman . 596.46

Nov. 2.	Miss Sarah, of Hyde Park . . .	1.00	
Jan. 31, 1872.	Rich & Stetson, proprietors of "Howard Athenæum," . . .	300.00	
Feb. 15.	Citizens, Hon. Wm. Gray, Chairman	200,000.00	
May 14, 1873.	" " "	82,776.93	415,635.19

BROOKFIELD.

Jan. 6, 1872.	M. E. Church, Rev. R. H. Howard	424.00	424.00

CAMBRIDGE.

Nov. 11, 1871.	Citizens, per H. R. Harding, Mayor	8,000.00	
Dec. 22.	" " "	2,500.00	10,500.00

CHARLESTOWN.

Oct. 27.	U. S. Navy Yard	3,658.84	
	City of Charlestown, per W. H. Kent, Mayor	8,000.00	
	State Prison contribution, G. Haynes, Warden	617.32	
Nov. 27.	Children Primary School No. 1, H. G. Turner, Teacher	10.00	12,286.16

CHELSEA.

Oct. 16.	A poor widow	1.00	
Dec. 2.	Citizens, E. C. Fitz, Treasurer . .	3,215.03	3,216.03

CHICOPEE.

Oct. 27.	Employés Ames Manufacturing Company	630.79	
Jan. 20, 1872.	Citizens, Dexter Dickinson, Treasurer	2,472.80	3,103.59

CLINTON.

Oct. 18, 1871.	Employês of S. Harris & Son, Comb Manufactory	30.00	30.00

CONCORD.

Dec. 16, 1872.	Balance citizens' subscriptions, by John L. Keeps, chairman . . .	950.00	950.00

DALTON.

Oct. 30, 1871.	Citizens	350.00	350.00

EDGARTOWN.

Nov. 20.	Citizens, J. W. Coffin, Treasurer . .	407.00	407.00

EAST LONGMEADOW.

Oct. 20.	Congregational Church	20.00	20.00

EASTHAMPTON.

Oct. 24.	Employés Nashawannock Manufacturing Company	320.00	320.00

FAIRHAVEN.

Nov. 4, 1871.	Citizens, per J. C. Tripp	488.00	488.00

FALL RIVER.

Oct. 17.	Second Class Morgan Street Grammar School	26.00	
20.	St. Paul's M. E. Church	86.68	
	Nantasket Lodge of Good Templars	20.00	
27.	City Treasurer	20,000.00	
28.	Sunday-school class, per Lyman W. Dean	10.00	20,142.68

FITCHBURG.

Oct. 16.	B. F. & C. R. R. employés	500 00	
	Whitman & Myers Manufacturing Co.	500.00	1,000.00

FLORENCE.

Oct. 27.	Florence Sewing Machine Company employés, S. Strong, Treasurer	718.00	718.00

GREENFIELD.

Oct. 21.	Citizens	1,000.00	
Nov. 9.	Master Bertie Tyler, result of molasses taffy	.25	1,000.25

HADLEY.

Nov. 4.	Russell Congregational Church	46.27	46.27

HAVERHILL.

Oct. 21.	Citizens, per D. B. Tenny	10,000.00	
Dec. 9.	Contributions of Working men, J. V. Smiley, Chairman	1,000.00	11.000.00

HOLYOKE.

Oct. 16.	Citizens, per A. Heywood	2,767.00	
Dec. 19.	Citizens, A. Higginbottom, Chairman	988.45	3,755.45

HOUSATONIC.

Oct. 27.	Citizens, per I. M. Seeley	373.50	373.50

JAMAICA PLAINS.

Oct. 20.	A. L. Murdoch	15.00	15.00

LAWRENCE.

Oct. 27.	City of Lawrence, per R. H. Tewksbury	10,000.00	
	Citizens, per J. C. Hoadley, Chairman	3,300.00	

Nov. 29.	Citizens, per J. C. Hoadley, Chairman .	6,552.80	
April 10, 1872.	Employés of L. W. Wilder, by J. C. Hoadley, Treasurer . .	22.00	19,874.80

LEICESTER.

Nov. 2, 1871.	Citzens, per H. E. Sargent, Chicago	1,388.00	1,388.00

LENOX.

Jan. 20, 1872.	Citizens, per Thomas Post, Treasurer	468.25	
20.	Employés Lenox Glass Co.	201.00	669.25

LEXINGTON.

Nov. 6, 1871.	Charles Hudson and others . .	478.05	478.05

LOWELL.

Oct. 17.	George J. Carney	25.00	
18.	Citizens, per J. Rogers, Treasurer . .	9,218.77	
Nov. 27.	" " " . .	25,51	
Jan. 2.	" " " . .	20.00	9,289.28

LYNN.

Oct. 21.	Citizens, per Doggett, Bassett, & Hills .	10,000.00	
Nov. 2.	Police department	117.70	10,117.70

MARBLEHEAD.

Nov. 14.	Citizens, per W. B. Brown, Treasurer .	1,000.00	1,000.00

MARLBOROUGH.

Oct. 18.	Hook and Ladder Co. No. 1	21.00	21.00

MIDDLEBOROUGH.

Oct. 18.	C. F. Vaughn	2.00	2.00

NEW BEDFORD.

Oct. 18.	German Citizens	100.00	
30.	Citizens, J. A. Beauvais, Treasurer .	4,000.00	
Jan. 19, 1872.	" " " .	3,000.00	7,100.00

NEWBURYPORT.

Oct. 16, 1871.	Carr, Brown, & Co.	100.00	
18.	Employés of Carr, Brown, & Co. . .	63.00	
27.	Citizens, per I. S. Boardman . . .	2,000.00	2,163.00

NORTH CHELMSFORD.

Oct. 23.	Citizens, per N. B. Edwards	160.00	160.00

NORTHAMPTON.

Nov. 17.	Employés North Cutlery Co.	205.00	
Dec. 20.	Employés Williams Manufacturing Co., H. F. Williams, Treasurer . . .	180.50	385.50

PEABODY.

Date	Contributor	Amount	Total
Oct. 26.	Mrs. C. T. Southwick	25.00	25.00

PERU.

Date	Contributor	Amount	Total
Oct. 25.	Congregational Church, per H. W. Gilbert	27.10	27.10

PITTSFIELD.

Date	Contributor	Amount	Total
Oct. 16.	Citizens, per J. C. West, Chairman .	5,000.00	
	E. Learned	500.00	
Dec. 29.	Citizens, balance, E. H. Kellogg, Chairman	127.50	5,627.50

PLYMOUTH.

Date	Contributor	Amount	Total
Dec. 29.	Citizens, Albert Mason, Chairman . .	1,127.57	1,127.57

ROCHDALE.

Date	Contributor	Amount	Total
Dec. 27.	Greenville Church, E. G. Carlton . .	28.00	28.00

ROCKPORT.

Date	Contributor	Amount	Total
Oct. 24.	North Village Sunday-school . . .	15.00	15.00

SALEM.

Date	Contributor	Amount	Total
Oct. 21.	Citizens, per N. Weston	750.00	
	N. Weston	200.00	
27.	City of Salem, per W. G. Webb, Treasurer	15,000.00	
April 30, 1872.	A lady, per J. R. Lakeman . .	10.00	15,960.00

SPRINGFIELD.

Date	Contributor	Amount	Total
Oct. 30, 1871.	Citizens, per A. T. Folsom, City Treasurer	15,171.00	
Dec. 19.	Citizens, per City Treasurer . . .	440.00	
April 15, 1872.	Citizens, balance, A. T. Folsom, Treasurer	250.00	15,861.00

STOCKBRIDGE.

Date	Contributor	Amount	Total
Nov. 27, 1871.	Citizens, D. A. Kimball, Cashier .	1,066.95	1,066.95

TAUNTON.

Date	Contributor	Amount	Total
Oct. 18.	Bay State Screw Co.	123.25	123.25

WALTHAM.

Date	Contributor	Amount	Total
Oct. 23.	Emmet Literary Association . . .	100.00	
28.	Citizens, per D. French	4,076.00	4,176.00

WARE.

Date	Contributor	Amount	Total
Oct. 21.	Children's Primary School . . .	5.00	5.00

WATERTOWN.

Oct. 15. Citizens, per G. K. Snow . . . 1,000.00
Feb. 28, 1872. Citizens' additional subscriptions, per Joseph K. Stickney . . 1,700.00 —— 2,700.00

WESTBOROUGH.

Nov. 2. Citizens, per G. O. Brigham, Treasurer 1,110.00 —— 1,110.00

WESTFIELD.

Nov. 13. Jessup & Laflin 500.00
18. Citizens, by Fletcher & Norton . . 2,574.33
23. J. R. Rand . . . . 25.00 —— 3,099.33

WOBURN.

Nov. 23. Citizens, W. H. Baldwin . . . 815.50 —— 815.50

WORCESTER.

Nov. 10. Citizens, per C. B. Whiting, Treasurer . 10,000.00
28. " " " . 10,000.00
Dec. 30. " " " . 9,700.00 —— 29,700.00

$629,672.41

STATE OF RHODE ISLAND.

BRISTOL.

Oct. 23, 1871. Avails concert, L. Herreshoff . $112.27
Nov. 3. Contributions of churches . . . 312.52 —— $424.79

CAROLINA MILLS.

Oct. 23. Citizens, by Tinkham & Metcalf . . 122.50 —— 122.50

MIDDLETOWN.

Nov. 13. Proceeds lecture, by B. A. Chase . . 30.00 —— 30.00

NEWPORT.

Oct. 18. Citizens, by James Atkinson . . . 3,000.00
Torpedo Corps, E. O. Matthews, U. S. N. Com. 205.00
Jan. 2, 1872. Citizens, W. C. Cozzens, Chairman 7,000.00
April 30, 1873. Citizens, balance, W. C. Cozzens, Chairman . . . . 910.12 —— 11,115.12

PAWTUCKET.

Oct. 27, 1871. Congregational Church, by T. P. Barnefield 143.91
Jan. 6, 1872. Green & Daniels, with their employés 1,000.00

Jan. 10. Citizens, by Thomas Moies, Treasurer . 1,000.00
Feb. 5. Citizens, by Thomas Moies, Treasurer, balance . . . . 709.80——— 2,853.71

PORTSMOUTH.

Oct. 18, 1871. Employés Copper Works . . 30.00——— 30.00

PROVIDENCE.

Oct. 16. Mite 1.63
Olive Branch Temple of Honor . . 100.00
29. Citizens, by Thomas A. Doyle, Mayor 12,000.00
31. " " " 28,000.00
Jan. 4, 1872. First Light Infantry Company, Captain C. R. Dennis . . . 100.00
6. Citizens, balance, H. Lippitt, Treasurer 3,607.71——— 43,809.34

WARREN.

Nov. 6, 1871. Citizens, by George Williams 571.87——— 571.87

WOONSOCKET.

Oct. 16. Temple of Honor 50.00
Nov. 2. Citizens, by H. S. Ballou . . . 500.00——— 550.00

$59,507.33

STATE OF CONNECTICUT.

BRIDGEPORT.

Oct. 18, 1871. Churches (Trinity and Grace) . $16.00
19. Citizens, by W. E. Goodell, Mayor 10,000.00
17. Burlock Manufacturing Company . . 236.00
Feb. 6, 1872. Citizens, per W. E. Goodell, Mayor 2,451.53——— $12,703.53

DAYSVILLE.

Dec. 16, 1871. Citizens, J. L. Greene, Mayor . 90.00——— 90.00

DEEP RIVER.

Nov. 7. Congregational Church . . . . . 100.00——— 100.00

FAIRHAVEN.

Oct. 20. First Congregational Church . . . 121.56——— 121.56

HAMPDEN.

Dec. 5. George O. Catlin . . . . . . 25.00——— 25.00

HAMPTON.

Nov. 6. Citizens, by H. G. Tainter . . . 70.84——— 70.84

HARTFORD.

Oct. 16. Smith, Northam, & Robinson . . . 300.00

Oct. 28.	Phenix Mutual Life Insurance Company, by R. Swift.	5,000.00	
	Cheney Brothers	3,000.00	
	Citizens	5,000.00	
27.	Citizens	15,000.00	
Nov. 3.	Citizens	3,872.50	
7.	Congregation Beth Israel	200.00	32,372.50

LIBERTY HILL.

Nov. 13.	Citizens, by W. A. Fuller	21.00	21.00

MIDDLE HADDAM.

Feb. 12, 1872.	Henry W. Clark	20.00	20.00

MIDDLETOWN.

Oct. 18, 1871.	William S. Camp	100.00	100.00

MYSTIC BRIDGE.

Dec. 4.	Congregational Church, E. P. Randall, Treasurer	171.83	171.83

NAUGATUCK.

Nov. 24.	Tuttle Manufacturing Company, and employés	25 00	25.00

NEW BRITAIN.

Oct. 28.	Citizens, by F. T. Stanley . . .	4,659.73	4,659.73

NEW HAVEN.

Oct. 16.	Henry Farnham	5,000.00	
17.	George and Mary K. Gibbs . . .	10.00	
28.	Employés N. Y. & N. H. R. R. Co. .	125.00	
Jan. 6, 1872.	Citizens, by H'y G. Lewis, Chairman	25,304.98	30,439.98

NEW HARTFORD.

Dec. 14, 1871.	Ladies of Congregational Church, for freight on box	2.00	2.00

NEW LONDON.

Oct. 23.	Wilson Manufacturing Company . .	100.00	
	Citizens, by H. P. Haven . . .	2,000.00	2,100.00

NORWALK.

Feb. 13, 1872.	Citizens, George E. Miller, Treasurer	1,450.00	
Feb. 19.	Citizens, George E. Miller, Treasurer, balance	41.78	1,491.78

NORWICH.

Nov. 19, 1871.	Citizens, by James Lloyd Green	10,000.00	10,000.00

PORTLAND.

Oct. 23.	Middlesex Quarrying Company . .	500.00	500.00

PUTNAM.

Nov. 6.	Second Congregational Church . .	161.50	161.50

SEYMOUR.

Nov. 4.	Congregational Church and Sunday-school	57.00	57.00

SOUTH WOODSTOCK.

Oct. 28.	Second Baptist Church	31.00	31.00

SOUTH NORWALK.

Oct. 27.	D. P. Ely	100.00	100.00

STONINGTON.

Nov. 8.	Mrs. Waldron	10.00	10.00

STAMFORD.

Nov. 1.	Citizens, by H. M. Humphrey . .	2,000.00	
17.	" " . .	50.00	2,050.00

STRATFORD.

Nov. 16.	Citizens, by F. Sedgwick	239.00	239.00

THOMPSONVILLE.

Nov. 22.	Hartford Carpet Company's employés, J. D. Houston, Treasurer	779.91	779.91

WALLINGFORD.

Nov. 11.	Congregational Church	55.00	55.00

WATERBURY.

March 9, 1872.	Citizens, per Chas. Benedict, Chairman	7,206.91	7,206.91

WEST CORNWALL.

Oct. 27, 1871.	J. C. Sherwood, Treasurer . .	61.50	61.50

WEST HAVEN.

Oct. 24.	Congregational Church	137.00	137.00

WEST MERIDEN.

Jan. 31, 1872.	Citizens, B. H. Catlin, Treasurer .	100.00	
March 27.	Citizens, Isaac C. Lewis, Treasurer .	568.30	668.30

45

WESTMINSTER.

Nov. 2, 1871.	Citizens.	12.50	12.50

WILLIMANTIC.

Oct. 28.	Episcopal Mission Church	5.00	5.00

WINDHAM.

Oct. 28.	St. Paul's Episcopal Church	33.55	33.55

WINDSOR LOCKS.

Oct. 28.	Citizens, by A. W. Converse	560.00	560.00

WINSTED.

Dec. 1.	A poor German woman	1.00	1.00
			$107,183.92

STATE OF NEW YORK.

ALBANY.

Oct. 19, 1871.	Pupils of Free Academy	$313.65	
	W. P. Halpin	20.00	
23.	Employés Taylor's Brewery	150.00	
27.	Citizens, by G. H. Thatcher, Mayor	10,000.00	
	Burgess Corps, by B. W. Whimple, Treasurer	1,000.00	
	Board of Lumber Dealers	10,000.00	
	Working Men's Relief Association of West Albany	100.00	
Jan. 18, 1872.	Citizens, by George H. Thatcher, Mayor	16,000.00	$37,583.65

AMENIA.

Nov. 4, 1871.	Church of the Immaculate Conception	100.00	100.00

AMSTERDAM.

Oct. 18.	Citizens, by H. VanBrokelin	859.00	859.00

ASTORIA.

Oct. 15.	E. I. Woolsey	2,000.00	2,000.00

AUBURN.

Feb. 5, 1872.	Citizens, by S. Willard, Treasurer	2,456.41	2,456.41

BALDWINSVILLE.

Oct. 16, 1871.	Mohegan Lodge I. O. O. F. No. 29	100.00	100.00

BELMONT, ALLEGHANY CO.

Nov. 28.	St. Peters Church	30.00	30.00

BINGHAMPTON.

Oct. 18.	Excelsior Hook and Ladder Company .	100.00	
26.	Citizens, by W. Dwight, Mayor .	5,000.00	
Nov. 9.	" " " . .	191.00	5,291.00

BROCKPORT.

Oct. 17.	Citizens	50.00	
Nov. 17.	Ladies of St. Luke's Church . . .	1.00	51.00

BROOKLYN, L. I.

Oct. 16.	E. Neville	10.00	
18.	Public School No. 15	162.52	
21.	Mechanics' and Traders' Exchange .	1,000.00	
26.	Tabernacle Church, by Rev. T. DeW. Talmadge	1,116.36	
27.	Rev. R. Meredith	1,150.63	
	J. E. Eldridge, for employés U. S. Navy Yard	5,550.00	
30.	Westminster Presbyterian Church . .	59.50	
Nov. 15.	Boys' Club, by H. S. Gray . . .	10.00	
20.	Brooklyn Eagle office subscriptions, F. M. Mooers, cashier	1,022.75	
29.	City appropriation	100,000.00	
	Citizens, by M. Kalbfleish, Mayor .	25,000.00	
Jan. 19, 1872.	Reformed Church, S. Brooklyn, by G. C. Adams	90.75	
25.	Second Street M. E. Church, A. C. Harrison, Treasurer	480.00	
April 27.	Citizens, balance subscriptions, per M. Kalbfleish, Treasurer	1,657.97	
Oct. 21.	Students of Polytechnic Institute, by Rev. C. D. Helmer, Chicago . .	687.25	137,997.73

BUFFALO.

Oct. 16, 1871.	Queen City Lodge of Crispins, No. 54	180.00	
17.	Neptune Hose Co. No. 5 . . .	500.00	
	C. E. Walbridge	30.00	
23.	German Insurance Company, through Alex. Martin, Secretary . . .	2,000.00	
Nov. 3.	Captain G. H. Clark	10.00	2,720.00

BUTTERNUTS.

Dec. 13.	Presbyterian Church, F. Shaw . .	116.00	116.00

CANAJOHARIE.

Nov. 6.	A lady, by H. X. Devendorf, Secretary	2.00	2.00

CANANDAIGUA.

Oct. 16. Citizens, by Thomas B. Beal, Treasurer 3,965.00—— 3,965.00

CANDOR.

January 23, 1872. Congregational Church, per J. Thompson . . . . 54.13—— 54.13

CAIRO.

Feb. 21. Dr. Levi King . . . . . . 5.00—— 5.00

CARMANSVILLE.

Oct. 30, 1871. Presbyterian Church . . . 24.62—— 24.62

CATSKILL.

Nov. 8. Citizens, by O. Day . . . . 1,370.90—— 1,370.90

CAZENOVIA.

Oct. 27. Citizens, E. B. Crandall, Treasurer . 400.00
Jan. 27, 1872. " " " 55.26—— 455.26

CHAMPLAIN.

Nov. 6, 1871. M. V. B. Stetson, cashier Presbyterian Church . . . . . . 155.00—— 155.00

CLEVELAND.

Jan. 12, 1872. Dramatic Association, per J. F. Warren & Co. . . . . 50.00—— 50.00

CLIFTON PARK.

Nov. 17, 1871. Union Sunday-school . . . 8.00—— 8.00

CLIFTON SPRINGS.

Nov. 1. Sanitarium . . . . 618.65—— 618.65

CLYDE.

Oct. 30. Citizens, by A. Griswold . . . 931.00—— 931.00

COHOES.

Oct. 16. Citizens, by M. Hubbard, Treasurer . 2,500.00—— 2,500.00

COOPERSTOWN.

Feb. 12, 1872. Friends, by Frederick Palmer . 36.91—— 36.91

COXSACKIE.

Oct. 17, 1871. J. L. B. & P. H. Sylvester . . 35.00—— 35.00

CUBA.

Dec. 4. Baptist Church, Rev. J. C. Seely . . 20.00—— 20.00

DEERFIELD, ONEIDA CO.

Oct. 21.	Citizens	153.00	153.00

DOVER.

Jan. 13, 1872.	Citizens, per A. J. Ketchum, Cashier.	64.00	64.00

EAST BLOOMFIELD.

Feb. 7.	Citizens, per Theodore Perkins, Treasurer	175.60	175.60

ELLINGTON, CHATAUQUA CO.

March 25.	Citizens, by A. D. Olds.	12.00	12.00

ELMIRA.

Oct. 27, 1871.	Citizens, by J. Arnott, Jr. . . .	8,700.00	8,700.00

ELIZABETHTOWN, ESSEX CO.

Oct. 21.	A. C. Hand and others	132.00	132.00

ELYRIA.

Oct. 16.	Lodge 103, I. O. O. F.	50.00	50.00

FISHKILL.

Nov. 22.	Citizens, S. A. Hoyt, Treasurer . . .	34.00	34.00

FORT EDWARD.

Oct. 17.	C. Barber	50.00	50.00

GENEVA.

Nov. 1.	Citizens, S. H. Verplanck	1,119.50	
6.	McLaren Sisters	4.95	1,124.45

GLENN'S FALLS.

Oct. 20.	Citizens, by E. T. Johnson	1,000.00	1,000.00

GLOVERSVILLE.

Oct. 21.	Rev. George Harkness	175.00	
27.	Citizens, by National Fulton Co. Bank .	1,500.00	1,675.00

GOSHEN, ORANGE CO.

Dec. 27.	Citizens, by A. S. Murray	2,171.00	2,171.00

GREENE.

Oct. 18.	Amateur Dramatic Association . . .	69.00	69.00

GREENPOINT, L. I.

March 8, 1872.	Citizens, per E. F. Williams, Treasurer	650.00	650.00

HAMILTON.

Oct. 20, 1871.	Madison University . . .	6.00	6.00

HASTINGS.

Oct. 21.	Fraser Free School	57.07	57.07

HAVANA.

Oct. 18.	Havana Lodge, I. O. O. F. . . .	50.00	50.00

HIGHLAND FALLS.

Dec. 26.	Citizens, H. G. Parry	30.00	30.00

HOMER.

Feb. 19, 1872.	F. B. Carpenter	25.00	
19.	Citizens, balance, per S. McC. Barber, Treasurer	70.00	95.00

HOOSIC FALLS.

Oct. 21, 1871.	Presbyterian Sunday-school . .	52.28	
Dec. 6.	E. B. Kenyon, Treasurer . . .	12.00	64.28

HUDSON.

Oct. 16.	Citizens	3,000.00	
Nov. 1.	Citizens, by George H. Powers, Mayor .	3,000.00	6,000.00

HYDE PARK, DUTCHESS Co.

Oct. 23.	Citizens, by J. L. Rosevelt . . .	1,000.00	
Jan. 24, 1872.	Friend of Public Library . .	45.00	1.045.00

ITHACA.

Oct. 17, 1871.	S. A. Foster	5.00	5.00

JAMESTOWN.

Oct. 18.	Citizens, R. E. Fenton	1,350.00	1,350.00

JAMAICA, L. I.

Nov. 2.	Roman Catholic Church, by John Fleming	100.00	
3.	First Presbyterian Church . . .	526.00	
Oct. 17.	Lodge 166, Sons of Temperance . .	12.00	638.00

KINDERHOOK.

Oct. 27.	Citizens, by W. R. Mesick . . .	550.00	550.00

KINGSTON.

Oct. 18, 1871.	Kosciusko Lodge, No. 86, I. O. O. F.	50.00	
23.	D. B. Judson	100.00	
Nov. 1.	Citizens, by C. H. VanGassbeck, Treasurer	1,485.25	1,635.25

LANSINGBURG.

Oct. 21.	Citizens, F. B. Leonard	1,262.34	1,262.34

LIMA.

Nov. 4.	Citizens, by A. McCune . . .	155.60	155.60

LIVONIA.

Oct. 18.	Ira Patchin	10.00	10.00

LODI, Seneca Co.

Dec. 19.	Village Churches, C. C. Covert, Treasurer	125.00	125.00

LOCKPORT.

Nov. 6.	Citizens, by O. Storrs, Mayor . .	3,000.00	
Dec. 15.	" " " . .	237.50	3,237.50

LONG ISLAND CITY.

Nov. 2.	L. I. R. R. employés, by J. D. Barton, Superintendent	225.00	225.00

MALONE.

Dec. 30.	Citizens, by W. W. Paddock . . .	100.00	100.00

MIDDLETOWN.

Jan. 2.	Citizens, by E. P. Wheeler, Treasurer .	2,500.00	2,500.00

MORRISANIA.

Nov. 9.	Citizens, by R. Garrigue	999.68	
	German Citizens, by R. Garrigue, for German Aid and Relief Society . .	28.50	
Jan. 23, 1872.	W. Reynolds Brown . . .	10.00	1,038.18

NEWBURG.

Oct. 27, 1871.	Citizens, by Quassaic National Bank	5,000.00	
Nov. 11.	N. W. Richardson, agent Erie Railway .	12.50	
Feb. 27, 1872.	Balance Citizens, J. N. Weed, Treasurer	18.75	5,031.25

NEW HAMBURG.

Nov. 8, 1871.	Scholars of Union School . .	10.00	10.00

NEW ROCHELLE.

Oct. 18.	Little Girl	1.00	1.00

NEW YORK CITY.

Oct. 15.	Generals Winslow and Wilson, through General Sheridan	100.00	
	O. Smedbury	250.00	

Oct. 16.	Mite	2.00
	New York Times, subscription at their office	2,545.77
	Dan Rice, proceeds of a benefit	601.65
	New York Journal of Commerce,	
	First installment	3,000.00
	Second installment	5,000.00
	Third installment	3,000.00
	J. P. & George M. Thomas, 937 Broadway	442.00
	New York Bank Clerk, for self and others, for suffering bank clerks	75.00
	Barbers' and Hair Dressers' Association	100.00
	Catlin, Brundell, & Co.	1,000.00
	Ellen F. Vought	1.00
	Abigail W. Lyman	2.00
	George Cecil, 38 Broad Street	100.00
	James Cameron, 351 Broadway	30.80
	A. Belmont & Co., Bankers	5,000.00
	Duncan, Sherman, & Co.	5,000.00
	Brown Brothers & Co.	5,000.00
	John Franz, 435 Sixth Avenue	120.00
	F. Copcutt	100.00
	Adams Express Co.	10,000.00
	Produce Exchange	15,000.00
	E. & G. Muller	2.63
	Cataract Lodge	100.00
	Ogden & Co.	100.00
17.	G. H. Watson	.35
	G. C. McEwen	5.00
	Frankie Moulton	200.00
	School of Miss Haines and Mlle. De Janon	356.00
	Company C., 22d Infantry, N. G.	50.00
	Hebrew Orphan Asylum	300.00
	James Lee	100.00
	Stamford Manufacturing Co.	500.00
	Two Little Sisters	5.00
	H. Krauss	1.00
	Bank Clerks Association	1,500.00
	Naval Officer's employés	80.00
18.	Druggists, by A. V. Blake, Treasurer	150.00
	John F. Tracy	1,000.00
	W. B. Humbert	20.00
	N. Y. Demokrat, employés	258.50
	Mary B. Drysdale	25.00
	Davis, Clark, & Co.	25.00
	Mike Halm, butcher boy	1.00
	Hyatt & Spencer	250.00

Oct. 18.	Brennan Society	500.00
	Sheldon, Collins, & Co., for Printers	100.00
	Charles Phaff	100.00
	A Shipmaster	10.00
	New York Standard	182.00
	Knickerbocker Life Insurance Co.	1,500.00
	Sunday-school of the Church of the Epiphany	69.65
	Smith, Crosby, & Co.	100.00
	F. Heppenheimer & Co.	125.00
	D. M. Griffin	5.00
	Edward Schaff and neighbors, Division Street	208.00
	Fr. Beck & Co.'s employés	100.25
	James Gregory, 112 Cannon Street	25.00
	Felix Stobier, 132 Essex Street	100.00
	Rodman & Hepburn	50.00
	Germania Lodge, No. 182	200.00
	William D. Smith, Bedloe's Island	1.00
	John F. Henry's employés	101.00
19.	Frederick Myles, Copake Iron Works	100.00
	Citizens, by New York Herald	10,523.66
20.	L. H. King, Pastor of 43d Street M. E. Church	175.00
	Degener & Weiler, for employés	220.75
	Allertons & Moore	300.00
	Dauchy & Co., 75 Fulton Street	100.00
21.	New Post-office and Court House officials and employés	300.00
	R. A. Olmstead, employés	23.00
	C. C. Cranmer, 2 Grove Street	2.00
	Progressive Spiritual Society	141.55
	Mrs. A. T. Bower, Gilsey House	50.00
	North British and Mercantile Insurance Co.	5,000.00
	Continental Life Insurance Co.	2,000.00
	Merchants' Life Insurance Co.	1,000.00
	Guardian Life Insurance Co.	1,000.00
	Robinson, Chase, & Co.	5,000.00
	Standard Fire Insurance Co.	1,000.00
23.	Davidson & Jones	57.00
	Mrs. Keep and daughter	2,000.00
	Cornucopia Lodge No. 16, I. O. O. F.	200.00
	H. C. Houghton, M. D.	363.70
	Employés 8th Avenue R. R. Co.	513.00
	Fanwood Literary Association of Deaf and Dumb Institution	200.00
24.	Catlin, Brundell, & Co.'s clerks	100.00

46

Date	Contributor	Amount
Oct. 24.	I. M. C. Association, M. J. Schnabl .	50.00
	New York Stock Exchange . . .	20,000.00
26.	Subscriptions at Times Office . .	1,066.36
	Leggett & Storms, hotel keepers' donation	100.00
	Otis Brothers & Co.	500.00
	Standard Office, balance of contributions	33.25
27.	Bank Clerks M. B. Association . .	1,606.25
	7th Street M. E. Church . . .	143.01
	Saron Lodge, No. 3, I. O. B. B. . .	100.00
	Manufacturers' and Builders' Insurance Company	500.00
	Employés of "American Agriculturist" and "Hearth and Home" through Orange Judd & Co.	650.00
	Grammar School No. 17 . . .	533.42
	Rev. C. F. Deems, Church of Strangers	300.00
	I. W. England, Sun Office . . .	1,055.08
	E. R. Smith, Treasurer, 461 Broadway .	354.00
	Darling, Griswold, & Co. . . .	5,000.00
	J. R. Elsey, Treasurer of Lodge 330 .	1,030.50
28.	M. E. Church, by Rev. N. B. Thompson	21.46
	Employés of Peck and Bogart's Planing Mill	31.00
	Humanitat Ladies' Benevolent Society of New York	80.00
	Mutual Musical Protective Union . .	1,000.00
30.	Atlantic Garden Orchestra . . .	27.00
	New York Journal of Commerce Relief Fund	1,679.50
	Mechanics' and Traders' Exchange .	1,500.00
	James Fisk, Jr., for employés of Erie Railway Offices	2,558.00
31.	A poor boy	50
Nov. 1.	Orange Judd & Co., for E. Eggleston .	27.00
	New York Stock Exchange . . .	12,649.00
	New York Cotton Exchange . .	16,275.00
3.	Lexington Avenue M. E. Church . .	143.00
4.	New York Lodge, No. 330, J. R. Elsey	43.00
	Contributed by New York Herald .	3,076.34
8.	Contribution of Washington Markets .	1,380.84
	New York Stock Exchange . . .	4,325.00
11.	Mrs. H. L. King, 1 Cottage Place .	100.00
14.	New York City Gold Exchange . .	15,690.00
	A. Gross & Co.'s employés . . .	40.00
	M. E. Churches, per C. C. North, Treasurer	1,952.38

Date	Contributor	Amount
Nov. 14.	New York Chamber of Commerce Fund, after deducting foreign subscriptions paid into the same	21,452.89
16.	New York Herald Office Fund . .	8,000.00
17.	L. H. Holmes, proceeds of concert .	300.00
	Drexel, Morgan, & Co.	5,000.00
20.	J. L. Libby	500.00
	New York Times Office, subscriptions .	35.00
22.	New York Journal of Commerce, subscriptions	520.00
	Ivison, Blakeman, Taylor, & Co. . .	1,000.00
	Commissioners New York Fire Department, W. Hitchman, President . .	2,629.50
Dec. 4.	"Swiss Residents" by Henry Enderis, Consul at Chicago	679.90
	"Hudson River Sheep Yards," West 48th Street	150.00
8.	New York Herald Office, subscriptions .	775.00
16.	Narragansett S. S. Co. employés, James Fisk, Jr., President	760.00
26.	New York Produce Exchange, balance of subscription, B. C. Bogert, Treasurer	20,692.00
29.	Employés of A. T. Stewart & Co., wholesale embroidery department, D. T. Ackerman, Treasurer . . .	170.00
Jan. 6, 1872.	A. Campbell, Sun Building, proceeds from sale of printing press .	1,600.00
8.	New York Lodge No. 330, F. & A. Masons, J. R. Elsey, Treasurer . .	5.00
11.	"Manager's Aid Fund," of New York, Philadelphia, Boston, and St. Louis, per J. H. McVicker, Esq., Chicago .	1,976.55
12.	M. C. B., by John P. Crosby . .	100.00
20.	Balance subscriptions at office of "New York Journal of Commerce," per D. M. Stone	152.50
27.	"Managers' Aid Fund," J. H. Magonigle, Treasurer	3,960.00
29.	Collections by Fowler & Wilson, 26 Broad Street	225.00
Feb. 1.	Laflin & Rand Powder Co. . . .	1,000.00
2.	Church unknown, by A. H. McPherson .	30.00
13.	Employés of Otis, Bross, & Co., Hoisting Machine Manufactory . . .	48.50
15.	New York Life Insurance Co. . .	5,000.00
21.	Balance "Sun" Office subscriptions, per J. W. England	137.00

Feb. 26.	Mrs. A. N. Gunn		15.00	
March 1.	New York Chamber of Commerce, J. C. Green, Assistant Treasurer .		500,000.00	
April 27.	Balance subscriptions, "New York Herald" Office, W. T. Henry, Treasurer .		150.00	
June 7.	Charles W. Bance, 74 William Street .		5.00	
July 24.	New York Chamber of Commerce, by A. A. Low, Treasurer of Committee		199,049.73	
Oct. 1871.	New York Hotel Keepers: —			
	A. French, French's Hotel .	1,000.00		
	S. Hawkes, St. Nicholas Hotel	2,000.00		
	C. A. Stetson & Sons, Astor House	250.00		
	Simmons & Co., Hoffman House	1,000.00		
	C. H. Reed, Hoffman House .	500.00		
	Tweed & Garfield, Metropolitan Hotel	250.00		
	H. H. & F. A. Brockway, Ashland House	75.00		
	W. G. Schenck, Merchants' Hotel	250.00		
	C. B. Ferrin, Westminster Hotel	75.00		
	Elias Hotchkiss, St. James Hotel	100.00		
	H. M. Smith, Grand Hotel .	250.00		
	H. L. Powers, Central Hotel .	250.00		
	Rand Brothers, St. Cloud Hotel	100.00		
	D. Sweeney, Sweeney's Hotel .	500.00		
	Officers and employés St. Nicholas Hotel	352.75		
	Guests, St. Nicholas Hotel . . .	50.00		
	Officers and employés French's Hotel	117.00		
	Friend, French's Hotel . .	25.00		
	Wm. Wilkinson, superintendent Metropolitan Hotel . . .	50.00		
	Earle Brothers, Earle's Hotel	500.00		
	M. M. VanDyke, VanDyke's Hotel and Dining Saloon .	50.00		
	Clarendon and Everett Hotels .	500.00		
	Thos. D. Winchester, Western Hotel	100.00		
		$8,344.75		
	Less amount expended by donors	1,150.00		
			7,194.75	$974,280.47

NIAGARA FALLS.

Oct. 16.	Rescue Hook and Ladder Co. . .	100.00	
23.	Citizens, by N. K. Van Leusen . .	1,700.00	1,800.00

NORWICH.

Oct. 18. D. Maydole & Co. . . . . . . 200.00——— 200.00

NYACK.

Oct. 28. Sunday-school Teachers' Association . 140.50——— 140.50

OGDENSBURG.

Oct. 30, 1871. Members of the Maple City and Pastime B. B. Club 125.00
Nov. 6. Citizens, by J. W. Judson . . . 744.00——— 869.00

ONEIDA, Madison Co.

Oct. 16. L. F. Bentley 50.00
21. B. N. Dyer, Foreman . . . . . 50.00——— 100.00

ONEONTA.

Dec. 9. Citizens, E. M. Carver, Cashier . . 101.29——— 101.29

OSWEGO.

Oct. 26. Board of Trade, by B. Hageman . . 2,000.00
Nov. 16. Citizens, by Delos DeWolf . . . 6,796.91——— 8,796.91

OWEGO.

Nov. 28. Tioga Circuit, M. E. Church, by D. G. Taylor 26.00
Jan. 5, 1872. Dr. Ransom Walker . . . 5.00——— 31.00

PALMYRA.

Oct. 20, 1871. Teachers' Institute 78.60
Citizens, per First National Bank . . 300.00——— 378.60

PAWLING.

Oct. 18. M. J. M. . . . . 2.00——— 2.00

PEEKSKILL.

Nov. 6. Citizens, by P. Stewart . . . . . 259.25——— 259.25

PETERBOROUGH.

Nov. 4. Hon. Gerritt Smith . . . . . 500.00——— 500.00

PIKE POND.

Oct. 25. J. W. Banta 5.25
Nov. 3. " " . . . . 2.00——— 7.25

PORT BYRON.

Oct. 21. A. N. Green . . . . 250.00——— 250.00

PORT JERVIS, Orange Co.

Oct. 20.	Church Street School	6.50	
28.	Citizens, by J. Conkling	833.05	
May 6, 1872.	Balance subscriptions, by J. Conkling	6.25	845.80

PORT MORRIS.

Oct. 23, 1871.	Gouverneur Morris	200.00	200.00

POUGHKEEPSIE.

Oct. 18.	W. W. Smith	10.00	
19.	W. A. Fanning, Treasurer, citizens .	4,000.00	
March 20, 1872.	" " "	1,919.44	5,929.44

PULASKI.

Dec. 6, 1871.	Charles A. Gurley	50.00	50.00

RIVERHEAD.

Dec. 16.	Citizens, S. S. Terry	395.91	395.91

ROCHESTER.

Oct. 16.	Erie R. R. employés	70.50	
18.	Independent Literary Union . . .	100.00	
19.	Printers' contributions, by W. S. Falls	202.25	
26.	A. S. Mann	500.00	
Jan. 5, 1872.	City appropriation, C. W. Briggs, Mayor	35,000.00	35,872.75

ROME.

Oct. 16.	Citizens, by George Merrill, Mayor .	2,061.50	2,061.50

RONDOUT.

Oct. 21.	Relief Committee	2,000.00	
Dec. 29.	Relief Committee, T. Cornell, Treasurer	1,239.00	3,239.00

RURAL GROVE.

Oct. 20.	M. E. Church	34.50	34.50

SAG HARBOR, L. I.

Oct. 25.	First Presbyterian Church	50.00	50.00

SANDY HILL.

Oct. 27.	M. E. Church, by J. K. Pixley . .	100.00	100.00

SARATOGA SPRINGS.

Oct. 16.	C. E. Durkee	100.00	
	Walworth Hose Association . . .	125.00	

Oct. 16.	Citizens	1,000.00	
17.	Citizens, by J. Hurlbut, Chairman	575.00	
Jan. 29, 1872.	Citizens, balance, by J. Hurlbut, Chairman	239.67	2,039.67

SAUGERTIES.

Oct. 27, 1871.	Citizens, by B. M. Freleigh	2,000.00	2,000.00

SAUQUOIT.

Oct. 30.	Citizens	30.00	30.00

SCHENECTADY.

Feb. 16, 1872.	Citizens, W. J. Van Horn, Mayor	3,240.00	3,240.00

SENECA FALLS.

Oct. 16, 1871.	Citizens, by G. B. Daniels	2,659.75	2,659.75

SHERBURNE.

Feb. 1, 1872.	Citizens, by Walter Elsbre, Treasurer	27.00	27.00

SING SING.

Oct. 19, 1871.	Citizens, by J. B. Hoxon, President	1,000.00	
Nov. 4.	Corporation, by J. B. Hoxon, President	500.00	1,500.00

SKANEATALES.

Dec. 30.	Citizens, Smith & Lawrence	1,000.00	1,000.00

STANLEY CORNERS.

Oct. 20.	Presbyterian Church, Seneca No. 9	152.00	152.00

SUSPENSION BRIDGE.

Oct. 27.	Citizens, by O. W. Cutler	450.00	450.00

SYRACUSE.

Oct. 16.	Euchre Club, Howlett, President	150.00	
	M. B. Society of employés N. Y. C. & H. R. R. R.	200.00	
	Mrs. H. M. Hardy	.50	
23.	Citizens, by F. A. Carroll, Mayor	25,000.00	
Nov. 25.	Employés of S. B. & N. Y. R. R. Co., P. E. Sloane, Superintendent	350.00	
Dec. 15.	Citizens, balance, by H. L. Duguid, Treasurer	7,198.76	32,899.26

TROY.

Oct. 16.	R. B. Rankin, Apollo Lodge No. 13	100.00	
17.	Schagticoke Woolen Mills	159.00	

Date	Contributor	Amount	Total
Oct. 18.	Wash. Volunteer Steamer Company .	100.00	
	Troy Academy	30.00	
19.	N. B. Squires, chairman, contribution Board of Trade	10,000.00	
26.	Lane, Gale, & Co.	250.00	
28.	Employés of Wood, Prentice, & Co. .	153.00	
Nov. 2.	Children, Clara and Lizzie Holmes .	3.40	
	Presbyterian Church	85.00	
Dec. 1.	Employés Littlefield Stove Manufactory .	10.00	
June 12, 1872.	Balance citizens' fund, Thomas Tillinghast, Treasurer . . .	11,528.22	22,418.62

UNADILLA.

Date	Contributor	Amount	Total
Oct. 31, 1871.	W. H. Emery . . .	.25	.25

UTICA.

Date	Contributor	Amount	Total
Oct. 16.	W. Niblack	2.00	
	T. S. Faxon, President Second National Bank	500.00	
	D. & D. N. Crouse	250.00	
18.	Utica Typographical Union to Chicago Typographical Union	159.00	
Jan. 5, 1872.	Citizens, R. S. Williams, Treasurer	6,602.94	
April 24.	Balance citizens' subscriptions, R. S. Williams, Treasurer . . .	150.00	7,663.94

WALTON.

Date	Contributor	Amount	Total
Oct. 16, 1871.	T. & W. Bishop	35.00	35.00

WAPPINGERS FALLS.

Date	Contributor	Amount	Total
Nov. 1.	Citizens, by J. Faulkner	611.46	611.46

WATERFORD.

Date	Contributor	Amount	Total
Nov. 8.	J. C. House	25.00	
	Mrs. Hugh White	100.00	125.00

WATERTOWN.

Date	Contributor	Amount	Total
Oct. 18.	J. L. Hooker	5.00	
Nov. 17.	Employés Davis Sewing Machine Company	300.75	305.75

WATERVLIET.

Date	Contributor	Amount	Total
Nov. 4.	W. Lodge No. 23, C. D. Slingerland .	10.00	10.00

WATKINS.

Date	Contributor	Amount	Total
Oct. 20.	Fallbrook Coal Company	1,000.00	1,000.00

WAVERLY.

Date	Contributor	Amount	Total
Oct. 23.	Telegraph Operator	5.00	5.00

WEISSEIC, DUTCHESS CO.

Oct. 20. N. Gridley . . . . 50.00—— 50.00

WELLSVILLE.

Oct. 16. Talmud Lodge, by J. N. Stoddard . 50.00—— 50.00

WEST CHARLTON, SARATOGA CO.

Dec. 12. United Presbyterian Congregation, Geo. Bell . . . . 182.00—— 182.00

WEST POINT.

Oct. 27. United States Military Academy, officers and cadets . . . . 203.50—— 203.50

WEST TROY.

Nov. 1. Citizens, by J. F. Phelps . . . 1,000.00
Dec. 27. J. M. Jones & Co., Carbuilders . . 100.00—— 1,100.00

WHITEHALL.

Dec. 6. Citizens, W. H. Cooke, President . . 623.10—— 623.10

WHITE PLAINS.

Nov. 4. Citizens, by Rev. R. Wheatley . . 129.50—— 129.50

WILLIAMSBURG.

Oct. 16. Council No. 14, A. O. U. 31.25
17. B. E. D. Butchers 165.50
18. Employés of Campbell's Press Works . 230.00
" Sangerbund " 100.00
21. Deutchen Cigarren Arbeiter . . . 100.00—— 626.75

WILLIAMSON.

Oct. 17. Mite . . . . 1.00—— 1.00

$1,358,451.50

STATE OF NEW JERSEY.

BAYONNE.

Oct. 23, 1871. Citizens, per J. Conner Smith . $1,000.00—— $1,000.00

BELVIDERE.

Oct. 21. Israel Harris . . . . 111.00—— 111.00

BERGEN.

Dec. 1. St. Paul's Church 100.00
Jan. 13, 1872. Bergen Institute, by Amos M. Kellogg . . . . 27.33—— 127.33

BLOOMFIELD.

Nov. 14, 1871.	J. C. Beach, for citizens . .	779.60	779.60

BRANCHVILLE:

Nov. 8.	Citizens, by E. A. Dunning . . .	64.50	64.50

BRICKSBURG.

Oct. 28.	Presbyterian Church	16·50	16.50

BRIDGETON.

Nov. 27.	Commerce St. M. E. Church . . .	120.00	
Dec. 11.	Collections of Churches, by R. C. Nichols	631.84	751.84

BURLINGTON.

Nov. 6.	Citizens, by F. Woolman . . .	2.333.00	2,333.00

CAMDEN.

Nov. 25.	Citizens, Samuel M. Gaul, Mayor .	5,500.00	
Nov. 9, 1872.	Citizens' balance, S. M. Gaul, Mayor	267.00	5,767.00

CLINTON.

Nov. 20, 1871.	Citizens, by W. W. Voorhees .	134.50	134.50

CRAWFORD.

Oct. 19.	Security Bank, for citizens . . .	275.00	275.00

ELIZABETH.

Oct. 16.	Citizens, per A. Dutcher, Jr. . .	500.00	
17.	James Moore	100,00	
20.	Kranken Verein No. 1	50.00	
Nov. 14.	Citizens, by D. J. Mecker . . .	157.75	807.75

FRANKLIN FURNACE.

Oct. 23.	J. C. Platt	5.00	5.00

FREEHOLD.

Oct. 26.	Cash	34.00	34.00

GREENVILLE.

Dec. 4.	Peabody Lodge, J. Backus, Secretary .	20.00	20.00

HAMMONTOWN.

Oct. 26.	Miss M. E. Gregory	35.00	35.00

HIGHTSTOWN.

Oct. 27	Charles Keeler	100.00	
Jan. 9, 1872.	Charles Keeler, Treasurer . .	50.25	150.25

HOBOKEN.

Dec. 1, 1871.	City, by F. C. Schmersahl, Mayor	977.45	
	Harmonic Club, proceeds of concert .	200.00	
Feb. 7, 1872.	William P. Mabor, by Gov. Randolph	50.00	
7.	N. Goetz, by Gov. Randolph	100.00	
29.	Public School No. 2, Pupils . . .	3.90	1,331.35

JERSEY CITY.

Oct. 15, 1871.	G. B. Hogeland	5.00	
16.	Mechanics' Lodge, No. 66, I. O. O. F. .	101.30	
	Erie Railway employés, Treasurer's Department	75.00	
20.	Citizens, through Jersey City National Bank	35,000.00	
27.	New York and Philadelphia Railway employés	1,829.32	
Dec. 19.	Citizens, C. H. O'Neil, Mayor . .	5,454.09	42,464.71

LAMBERTSVILLE.

Oct. 26.	Citizens, per J. A. Anderson . .	1,103.22	1,103.22

LODI, Bergen Co.

Feb. 2, 1872.	Citizens, by William Greig, Treasurer	68.50	68.50

LONG BRANCH.

Oct. 30, 1871.	Cornelius Vanderveer, for Citizens	107.00	107.00

MADISON.

Nov. 18.	Presbyterian Church, per J. Baker, Treasurer	400.00	
	Miss Hattie Hathaway	1.00	401.00

MORRISTOWN.

Oct. 27.	Citizens, per M. Mitchell	3,000.00	3,000.00

MOUNT HOPE.

Dec. 12.	Citizens, by P. A. Hiller	435.45	435.45

NEW BRUNSWICK.

Oct. 16, 1871.	H. N. Marsh	25.00	
21.	Sympathizer	1.00	
23.	W. S. Lighthall, eight years old . .	3.00	
27.	City Treasurer, for Council . . .	5,000.00	
Nov. 14.	Citizens, by G. Conover, Mayor . .	70.00	
Dec. 30.	Citizens	1,979.77	7,078.77

NEW HAMPTON.

Nov. 20.	Musconetong Valley, Presbyterian Church	79.70	79.70

NEWARK.

Oct. 16.	W. V. Snyder	50.00	
18.	E. Simon & Brothers, employés . .	178.75	
19.	Rev. Prentiss de Veuve . . .	10.00	
27.	Republic Trust Co.	400.00	
28.	City appropriation. . . .	10,000.00	
Nov. 8.	Republic Trust Co.	347.50	
14.	Citizens, per Beach Vanderpool, Treasurer	32,000.00	
18.	St. Albans Lodge.	50.00	
Jan. 22, 1872.	Citizens, balance by Beach Vanderpool, Treasurer . . .	400.00	43,436.25

NEWTON.

Feb. 7.	Levi Shepherd, by Gov. Randolph .	323.74	323.74

OCEAN GROVE.

Oct. 30, 1871.	H. B. Beegle	5.00	5.00

ORANGE.

Feb. 19, 1872.	Citizens, balance by John L. Blake	1,219.70	1,219.70

PATERSON.

Oct. 16, 1871.	Citizens, per S. Tuttle, Mayor .	7,000.00	
27.	Employés of Grant Locomotive Works	1,600.00	
Nov. 11.	Vanderberg, Wells, & Co., for printers of Chicago	50.00	
Jan. 2, 1872.	Citizens, by A. S. Allen . .	5,000.00	
Feb. 16.	Citizens, by John J. Brown, Treasurer .	5,975.00	19,625.00

PEMBERTON.

Oct. 28, 1871.	Baptist Church, per J. W. Wilmarth	123.77	123.77

PERTH AMBOY.

Dec. 14.	Citizens, by Charles Kean, Treasurer .	441.70	441.70

PHILLIPSBURG.

Oct. 23.	Central Railroad of New Jersey Railroad Shop employés	78.65	
Nov. 29.	Warren Foundry and Machine Co. employés	1,000.00	
Nov. 21.	Presbyterian Church, L. M. Teel, Treasurer	112.00	1,190.65

PLAINFIELD.

Nov. 3.	C. H. Stillman	50.00	
20.	Citizens, J. H. Evans, Mayor . .	950.00	1,000.00

PRINCETON.

Feb. 7, 1872.	G. T. Olmstead, Cashier, by Gov. T. F. Randolph . . .	622.21	622.21

RAHWAY.

Oct. 16, 1871.	The Owl Club, per T. J. Rayner .	100.00	
17.	Rahway Woodworks' employés . .	25.00	
26.	St. Paul's Episcopal Church, per J. M. Tufts	113.00	238.00

RED BANK.

Oct. 27.	Citizens, per First National Bank . .	350.00	
Nov. 2.	Citizens, per A. S. Parker . . .	22.00	372.00

SALEM.

Nov. 16.	Citizens, per Samuel D. Githers, Mayor	285.27	285.27

SAMPTOWN.

Oct. 28.	Baptist Church Sunday-school . .	25.50	25.50

SUMMERVILLE.

Oct. 23.	Board of Commissioners . . .	500.00	500.00

TOM'S RIVER.

Oct. 25.	Charles A. Gilmore	100.00	100.00

TRENTON.

Oct. 16.	City appropriation	1,000.00	
17.	Employés of New Jersey Steel and Iron Co.	700.00	
19.	Citizens, per R. C. Bellville . .	17,000.00	
April 3, 1872.	Citizens, by R. C. Bellville, Treasurer	1,284.15	
Feb. 7.	Paul Tulane, by Gov. T. F. Randolph .	200.00	
	Ainwell Sunday-school, by Gov. T. F. Randolph	7.00	20,191.15

WAWAYANDA.

Oct. 31.	George Hunt	10.00	10.00

WEST HOBOKEN.

Oct. 31, 1871.	Citizens, per H. E. Courvoisier .	204.34	204.34

WOODHAVEN.

Dec. 4.	A poor man and two boys . . .	1.50	1.50
			$158,397.75

STATE OF PENNSYLVANIA.

ALLENTOWN.

Oct. 27, 1871.	City, J. H. Good, Mayor .	$3,000.00	
Jan. 27, 1872.	Citizens, by J. H. Good, Mayor .	135.76	$3,135.76

BALDWINSVILLE.

Oct. 27, 1871.	Pennsylvania Steel Works, by Joseph Potts	229.75	229.75

BELLEFONTE.

Oct. 21.	Citizens, by J. A. Beaver, Treasurer .	1,000.00	1,000.00

BETHLEHEM.

Dec. 8.	Bethlehem Iron Company . . .	1,000.00	
21.	Citizens, C. A. Luekenback, Treasurer .	1,472.39	2,472.39

BIRDSBOROUGH, Berks Co.

Oct. 18.	Birdsborough Lodge No. 141, K. of P. .	10.00	10.00

BIRMINGHAM, Huntington Co.

Nov. 6.	A. G. Morris, for citizens . . .	107.00	
March 4, 1872.	A. G. Morris	5.00	112.00

BRISTOL.

Oct. 28, 1871.	Livingston Brass Band . . .	50.00	50.00

BROWNSVILLE.

Oct. 21.	Citizens, by H. W. Robinson . . .	1,000.00	1,000.00

BUTLER.

Jan. 27, 1872.	Citizens, William Campbell, Treasurer	384.81	384.81

CANONSBURG.

Nov. 4, 1871.	Y. M. C. A., W. B. Stewart . .	16.00	
March 9, 1872.	Mt. Zion M. E. Church, balance, by W. W. Smith, Treasurer . .	7.00	
	W. Cameron, W. W. Smith, Treasurer .	2.50	25.50

CARLISLE.

Jan. 26.	Citizens, by Joseph W. Patton, Treasurer	304.00	304.00

CATASAUQUA.

Nov. 15, 1871. Oliver Williams, for contribution of citizens . . . , . . . 415.60——— 415.60

CHAMBERSBURG.

Oct. 18. T. B. Kennedy 250.00
28. Citizens, by J. Hoke 350.00
Nov. 29. " " . . . . . 50.00——— 650.00

CHESTER.

Nov. 14. Citizens, per J. Irving, Treasurer . . 3,000.00
April 5, 1872. Citizens, balance by James Irving, Treasurer . . . . 2,139.96——— 5,139.96

COMLY.

Oct. 20, 1871. T. J. Galbraith . . . . . 1.00——— 1.00

CORNWALL.

Nov. 1. A. Wilhelm . . . . 1,250.00——— 1,250.00

DOYLESTOWN.

Jan. 3, 1872. John J. Brick, for citizens of Bucks County . . . . 408.58——— 408.58

EASTON.

Oct. 18, 1871. Citizens, by B. R. Swift . . 100.00
19. Town Council, by E. H. Greene . . 2,000.00
26. A. B. Shepperson 21.57
Dec. 26. Citizens, balance, E. H. Greene . . 408.85——— 2,530.42

EPHRATA.

Oct. 21. Albert Bowman . . . . . . 3.00——— 3.00

ERIE.

Oct. 19. Citizens, by Mayor Camphausen . 15,000.00——— 15,000.00

FACTORYVILLE.

June 24, 1872. Per C. G. Hammond . . . 24.50——— 24.50

GLENDON.

Oct. 27, 1871. J. Bacon, Treasurer Glendon Iron Company and employés . . . . 350.00——— 350.00

GREENCASTLE AND ANTRIM TOWNSHIP, FRANKLIN CO.

Feb. 12, 1872. Citizens, by J. C. McLanahan . 100.00——— 100.00

HARRISBURG.

Oct. 21, 1871. E. L. DuBarry, N. C. Railroad, telegraph department 900.00

Oct. 30.	Citizens, J. W. Weir, Treasurer	3,500.00	
Nov. 23.	" " "	500.00	
27.	Harrisburg Car Manufacturing Company, W. T. Hildrup, Treasurer	1,250.00	
Jan. 20, 1872.	Citizens, balance, by J. W. Weir, Treasurer	69.64	6,219.64

HARRIS TOWNSHIP.

Oct. 26, 1871.	Citizens, per John Hamilton	385.01	385.01

HICKORY RUN, CARBON Co.

Nov. 25.	M. E. Church, per William Buckalew	28.50	28.50

HONESDALE.

Nov. 22.	Edwin F. Torrey	110.77	110.77

HUMMELSTOWN, DAUPHIN Co.

Feb. 16, 1872.	Citizens, by J. W. Weir, Treasurer	22.00	22.00

HUNTINGTON.

Nov. 16, 1871.	J. George Miles	500.00	500.00

INDIANA.

Dec. 1.	Citizens, John Sutton, Treasurer	547.30	547.30

JOHNSTOWN.

Oct. 30.	Forepaugh's Menagerie	46.00	46.00

KITTANING.

Oct. 23.	Citizens, J. P. Brown, Treasurer	230.00	
Nov. 8.	Concord Presbyterian Church	10.00	
16.	Citizens	1,132.00	
22.	Citizens, J. P. Brown, Treasurer	60.00	1,432.00

LANCASTER.

Nov. 11.	Lancaster Male Grammar School	40.00	
29.	Citizens, W. A. Attle, Mayor	115.50	155.50

LEHIGHTON.

Oct. 30.	M. E. Church	13.75	13.75

LYKENS.

Nov. 1.	W. E. Ray, Superintendent, employés of Summit Branch R. R.	202.00	202.00

MANHEIM.

Jan. 22, 1872.	Citizens, by Nathan Morley	59.00	59.00

MARIETTA.

Nov. 4, 1871. Lieut. E. S. Houston, United States Navy . . . . 5.00—— 5.00

MAUCH CHUNK.

Oct. 30. Citizens, per J. H. Salkeld . . . . 341.26—— 341.26

McKEESPORT.

Nov. 11. Citizens, per W. E. Harrison 696.80
Citizens, per R. S. Riggs, Treasurer . 100.25—— 797.05

MEADVILLE.

Oct. 21. Citizens, by A. S. Dickson, Mayor . 2,000.00
Dec. 11. " " " . 181.68—— 2,181.68

MIFFLINBURG.

Oct. 28. Reform Church . . . . . . 40.62—— 40.62

MILLERSVILLE.

Oct. 23. State Normal School . . . . 170.00—— 170.00

MINERSVILLE.

Oct. 20. English Lutheran Church . . . 27.00—— 27.00

MONTROSE.

Nov. 10. Joseph D. Drinker . . . . 20.00—— 20.00

MOUNT HOLLY SPRINGS.

Nov. 18. Samuel G. Given . . . . . . 28.25—— 28.25

MOUNT JOY.

Oct. 30. Citizens, per Mary E. Hoffer . . . 171.85—— 171.85

MT. JACKSON, LAWRENCE CO.

Nov. 27. Westfield Congregational Church, Dement Clark, Treasurer . . . . 50.00—— 50.00

NEW BRIGHTON.

Oct. 20. Kenwood Boarding School . . . 70.00—— 70.00

NORRISTOWN.

Nov. 14. Citizens, per George Shannon, Treasurer 742.68
Feb. 5, 1872. N. M. Society of Montgomery Co., George Shannon, Treasurer . . 28.50—— 771.18

OIL CITY.

Nov. 6, 1871. Colored ladies . . . . . 20.00—— 20.00

48

PALO ALTO.

Date	Contributor	Amount	Total
Oct. 21.	Railroad employés	154.00	154.00

PARNASSUS.

Date	Contributor	Amount	Total
Oct. 23.	Citizens, by D. Alter	127.00	127.00

PHILADELPHIA.

Date	Contributor	Amount	Total
Oct. 16.	Morris, Tasker, & Co.	1,000.00	
17.	F. D. Howells & Brothers	20.00	
	Diligent Steam Fire Company, G. Gardom, Treasurer	250.00	
	Nellie Brown	1.00	
18.	W. A. Warner	5.00	
	J. N. Hughes, Ridgeway House	10.00	
	R. Kirkpatrick & Co.	52.00	
21.	A. J. Drexel, Treasurer, City of Philadelphia	100,000.00	
30.	William Sellers & Co., by Allen & Mansell	1,000.00	
	Parepa Rosa Opera Company	1,400.00	
Nov. 2.	Mrs. L. A. Garnett	50.00	
29.	Commercial Exchange Relief Committee, R. Gray, Treasurer	40,000.00	
Dec. 19.	Commercial Traveller	50.00	
23.	Pennsylvania Railroad Company's employés, A. J. Cassatt, General Manager	3,054.62	
Jan. 17, 1872.	Contributions of Episcopal Churches, B. G. Godfrey, Treasurer of Diocese	5,000.00	
Feb. 24.	Citizens' Committee, A. J. Drexel, Treasurer	157,436.40	
26.	Widow's mite, per W. Stewart	.25	
March 7.	Union League, J. G. Fell and others	4,678.00	
April 20.	Balance Contributions Epis. Churches, B. G. Godfrey, Treasurer of Diocese	679.87	314,687.14

PHILLIPSBURG.

Date	Contributor	Amount	Total
Oct. 23, 1871.	Red Warrior Tribe, Lodge 109	50.00	
26.	M. E. Church, per J. R. Lovell	60.60	110.60

PHŒNIXVILLE.

Date	Contributor	Amount	Total
Nov. 25.	Citizens, N. M. Ellis, Treasurer	650.00	650.00

PINE GROVE CENTRE.

Date	Contributor	Amount	Total
Nov. 13.	Rev. R. C. Bryson	78.00	78.00

PITTSBURGH.

Date	Contributor	Amount	Total
Oct. 25.	William Thaw	5,000.00	
	R. C. Loomis	100.00	
	Relief Committee, J. P. Pears, Treasurer	45,000.00	
	W. H. Brown, Kansas City Bond $1,000 proceeds	969.13	
Dec. 6.	Relief Committee, J. P. Pears, Treasurer	35,000.00	86,069.13

POTTSVILLE.

Date	Contributor	Amount	Total
Oct. 31.	A. J. Derr, Quartermaster . . .	55.00	
Nov. 4.	Bannon & Ramsay	1,000.00	1,055.00

READING.

Date	Contributor	Amount	Total
Oct. 18.	Giles Bailey, pastor	67.07	
19.	J. H. Sternberg and employés . .	100.00	
Feb. 21, 1872.	C. C. J. and H. Maltzberger . .	100.00	267.07

ROUSEVILLE, Oil Creek.

Date	Contributor	Amount	Total
Jan. 4.	Citizens, C. W. Castle, Treasurer . .	605.00	605.00

SCRANTON.

Date	Contributor	Amount	Total
Oct. 27, 1871.	Concert at Opera House . .	598.00	
	Citizens, per G. Coray, Treasurer . .	1,500.00	
	" " " . .	2,500.00	
Dec. 28.	W. R. Storrs	50.00	
Feb. 28, 1872.	Citizens, balance, George Coray, Treasurer	1,513.14	6,161.14

SHAMBURG.

Date	Contributor	Amount	Total
Oct. 26, 1871.	Citizens	343.00	343.00

SHARON.

Date	Contributor	Amount	Total
Nov. 8.	Emp's Westerman Iron and Coal Co. .	639.24	
28.	Westerman Iron Co.	84.60	
	Brookfield Coal Co.	123.00	846.84

SHARPSBURG.

Date	Contributor	Amount	Total
Nov. 9.	Citizens, by H. E. Campe . . .	400.00	400.00

SLATINGTON.

Date	Contributor	Amount	Total
Oct. 24.	Presbyterian Church, by R. McDowell .	50.00	50.00

ST. MARY'S, Elk Co.

Date	Contributor	Amount	Total
Nov. 13.	Citizens	157.85	
	Miners	66.00	
Dec. 26.	Citizens, balance, J. S. Bates, Treasurer	13.00	236.85

STRASBURG.

Nov. 20.	Citizens, E. M. Eberman, Treasurer	96.00	96.00

SUSQUEHANNA DEPOT.

Nov. 9.	M. L. Hawley, Treasurer for citizens	611.70	
	W. Emrey, Treasurer for citizens, additional	10.00	621.70

SUSQUEHANNA SHOPS.

Nov. 2.	Erie Railroad employés	620.20	
9.	Sunday-school	6.00	626.20

THORNDALE.

Oct. 20.	Employés of W. L. Bailey & Co.	66.25	66.25

TIDIOUTE.

Oct. 16.	E. W. Pascall, Chairman for citizens	100.00	
Nov. 6.	E. M. Curtis, Cashier, for citizens	1,072.75	1,172.75

TITUSVILLE.

Oct. 14.	W. H. Abbott, for citizens	11,400.00	
27.	German Sangerbund	173.50	11,573.50

TOWANDA.

Nov. 6.	Lodge 290, Knights of Pythias	50.00	50.00

WARRINGTON.

Nov. 4.	Citizens, per J. E. Wells & Co.	72.85	72.85

WASHINGTON.

Oct. 16.	Citizens	1,154.85	
Nov. 13.	Citizens, additional	152.00	1,306.85

WEST CHESTER.

Nov. 11, 1871.	Citizens, G. M. Rupert, Treasurer	500.00	
29.	" " "	1,500.00	
Jan. 30, 1872.	" " "	1,615.00	3,615.00

WEST FAIRVIEW.

Nov. 3, 1871.	Literary Association, J. T. Journey, Secretary	14.00	14.00

WILKESBARRE.

Oct. 18.	George F. Bamberger	20.00	
27.	Citizens, per Fraser & Smith	970.22	990.22

YORK.

Oct. 21.	Meyer & Small, for employés . .	500.00	
	Citizens, Samuel Small, Treasurer .	1,400.00	
Nov. 23.	York Co. Academy pupils . . .	18.00	1,918.00
			$482,976.72

STATE OF DELAWARE.

MIDDLETOWN.

Nov. 7, 1871.	M. E. Church, by Rev. V. Smith	$125.00	$125.00

WILMINGTON.

Oct. 27.	Citizens, per Union Bank . . .	100.00	
Nov. 13.	Citizens, per William Canby . . .	7,845.70	7,945.70
			$8,070.70

STATE OF MARYLAND.

ANNAPOLIS.

Oct. 24, 1871.	Crew U. S. Steamer Santee . .	$14.00	
	Officers and Attaches Naval Academy .	524.28	
Jan. 25, 1872.	Citizens, by James Monroe, Mayor	105.00	$643.28

BALTIMORE.

Oct. 16, 1871.	General Convention Episcopal Church, W. S. Perry, Treasurer	1,900.89	
17.	P. C. F..	1.00	
18.	Citizens, by McKim Brothers .	10,000.00	
Nov. 8.	" " " . .	32,850.00	
Oct. 20.	General Convention Episcopal Church, balance . . . . , . .	290.05	
20.	City Registrar, J. A. Robb . .	100,000.00	
21.	C. C. Fulton & Son, Baltimore American	9,500.00	
24.	Front Street Theatre Comique . .	300.00	
	Equitable Society, by T. Kelso, President	1,000.00	
	Flour Exchange, by J. M. Parr .	14,224.00	
	C. C. Fulton & Son, Baltimore American	5,200.00	
	New York Tea Co., Gustav Frank. .	96.00	
Nov. 1.	Citizens, by J. M. Parr	513.30	
	Baltimore Liderkranz, by F. Raine .	750.00	
Jan. 6, 1872.	Baltimore Gazette, Glenn & Co. .	200.00	176,825.24

BARTON.

Nov. 21, 1871.	Citizens, by Robert Shriver . .	39.25	
Dec. 6.	Employés of Potomac Coal Co., by Robert Shriver	13.00	52.25

CUMBERLAND.

Nov. 1.	Citizens, by Robert Shriver . . .	1,612.85	
21.	" " . . .	132.50	1,745.35

HAGERSTOWN.

Oct. 19.	St. John's Parish	51.47	
Nov. 4.	Reformed Church	30.00	81.47

LONAWING.

Nov. 1.	Citizens	170.09	170.09

MOUNT SAVAGE.

Nov. 8.	Citizens, by H. J. Kenah . . .	300.00	300.00
Jan. 16, 1872.	Masonic Fraternity of State of Maryland, J. H. B. Latrobe, Grand Master	2,304.62	2,304.62
			$182,122.30

STATE OF VIRGINIA.

ALEXANDRIA.

Oct. 18.	J. M. Stewart	$50.00	$50.00

CHARLEMAGNE.

Oct. 19.	Donation	2.50	2.50

DANVILLE.

Oct. 21.	G. D. Smith	5.00	5.00

HAMPTON.

Nov. 3.	St. John's Church	10.50	10.50

HARTFORD CITY.

Oct. 21.	Liberty Lodge No. 121, I. O. O. F. .	100.00	100.00

LEESBURG.

Oct. 20.	St. James Episcopal Church . . .	35.81	
Dec. 9.	Episcopal Congregation, per Matthew Harrison	18.00	53.81

NORFOLK.

Nov. 10.	U. S. Navy Yard, Admiral C. H. Davis	234.00	234.00

PETERSBURG.

Oct. 24.	St. Paul's Church	37.19	37.19

RICHMOND.

Oct. 21.	Tredegar Iron Works, by A. M. Keiley, Mayor	500.00	
	Police Force, by A. M. Keiley, Mayor	121.00	
24.	Manchester Presbyterian Church	5.80	
25.	St. Mark's Church	6.61	
27.	Citizens, by P. H. Stark	10,000.00	
30.	Citizens, by J. Davenport, Treasurer	135.87	
Nov. 10.	Leigh St. Baptist Church	41.66	
	Third St. Methodist Church	12.47	
15.	B. W. Haxall	25.00	
Dec. 26.	Balance citizens, J. Davenport, Treasurer	6.25	10,854.66

WARM SPRINGS.

Oct. 25.	Christ Church	15.00	15.00
			$11,362.66

STATE OF WEST VIRGINIA.

PARKERSBURG.

Oct. 17.	4,000 citizens	$3,013.75	
Nov. 14.	Pupils Washington School	4.55	$3,018.30

WESTON.

Nov. 20.	Citizens, by A. H. Kunst	70.00	70.00

WHEELING.

Oct. 16.	Citizens, by G. W. Jeffers, Mayor	5,000.00	
19.	Employés Penitentiary	87.60	
Nov. 16.	Citizens, by R. H. Cummings	7,420.50	12,508.10
			$15,596.40

DISTRICT OF COLUMBIA.

WASHINGTON.

Oct. 15, 1871.	Contribution, Paymaster General's Office, per Gen. P. H. Sheridan	$75.50
	Clerks Interior Department, by White & Thompson	4,000.00
	Iowa Republican Association, by Gen. Sheridan	172.00
16.	Officers and Clerks Office Comptroller Currency	375.00
	N. H. Barrett	100.00
	O. S. Buxton, Doorkeeper's Department, House of Representatives	273.00

	Illinois Republican State Association, by E. C. Ingersoll, Chairman . .	785.00	
	Bureau of Printing and Engraving .	1,500.00	
	Citizens, by Hon. R. T. Merrick .	15,000.00	
Oct. 17.	Washington Shutzen Verein . .	500.00	
	Officers U. S. Jail	63.57	
18.	Hon. E. C. Ingersoll, Chairman . .	200.00	
	Page, House of Representatives . .	2.00	
	Board Supervisors and Inspectors . .	220.00	
	Clerks, Treasury Department . .	2,942.00	
19.	Israelites, by S. Wolf	424.20	
20.	Architects and employés, Capitol Building	151.50	
	G. A. R., Department Potomac . .	400.00	
	Treasury Department	873.00	
	Clerks, War Department . . .	1,103.10	
21.	Hon. E. C. Ingersoll, Chairman . .	174.25	
	Employés Congressional Printing Office	2,750.00	
23.	Metropolitan Police	600.00	
25.	Officers and employés U. S. Navy Yard	532.63	
26.	Hackman's Association, by J. W. Plant	155.00	
30.	Unknown Donor, by Hon. Lyman Trumbull	100.00	
Nov. 4.	Olympic B. B. Club	154.00	
6.	Choral Society, by D. S. Burnett . .	439.90	
25.	G. Trumbull, for J. Randolph . .	4.00	
Dec. 18.	Washington L. I. Battalion and President's Mounted Guard, Capt. W. J. Moore, proceeds of concert . .	267.40	
May 10, 1872.	Citizens, by Fitz Hugh Coyle, Treasurer C. R. Fund . .	60,000.00	
Nov. 25.	Balance Citizens' Subscription, R. T. Merrick, Chairman	133.43	94,470.48
			$94,470.48

STATE OF NORTH CAROLINA.

CHARLOTTE.

Nov. 7, 1871.	G. B. Hannah	$10.00	$10.00

NEWBERN.

Oct. 23.	Julius Ash	5.00	5.00

WILMINGTON.

Oct. 23.	DeRossett & Co.	100.00	100.00
			$115.00

STATE OF SOUTH CAROLINA.

BEAUFORT.

Nov. 14.	Citizens, by G. W. Johnson . .	$60.00	$60.00

CHARLESTON.

Oct. 26.	Citizens, per Riorden, Dawson, & Co. .	821.50	
Nov. 27.	A sympathizer, per Riorden, Dawson, & Co.	5.00	
Dec. 7.	Officers and crew of the U. S. Lighthouse Buoy Tender, "Alanthus," H. Brown, Master	71.00	
Jan. 23, 1872.	Colored Baptist Churches, by W. Dart	40.05	937.55

COLUMBIA.

Nov. 1, 1871.	F. S. Jacobs and others . .	70.00	70.00

ORANGEBURG.

Oct. 28.	Geo. H. Cornelson	50.00	50.00
			$1,117.55

STATE OF GEORGIA.

AMERICUS.

Nov. 5.	Rev. Geo. F. Cooper	$5.00	$5.00

ATLANTA.

Oct. 19.	Madison Bell	25.00	25.00

AUGUSTA.

Oct. 27.	Branch, Sons, & Co.	1,000.00	1,000.00

CARTERSVILLE.

Oct. 18.	Six citizens	25.50	25.50

COCKSPUR ISLAND.

Nov. 9.	Pat. Eagan, Lighthouse Keeper . .	5.00	5.00

SAVANNAH.

Oct. 24.	Geo. W. Schaffer	5.00	
31.	City Appropriation	1,000.00	1,005.00

SPARTA.

Oct. 25.	A sympathizer	.25	.25
			$2,065.75

STATE OF FLORIDA.

PENSACOLA.

Oct. 26.	Officers and crew of U. S. S. Ship Nipsic	$381.00	
	Geo. E. Wentworth	20.00	
	Officers and men U. S. Navy Yard, Edward Middleton, Commandant . .	648.23	1,049.23
			$1,049.23

STATE OF ALABAMA.

SELMA.

Oct. 25.	Widow's mite	$5.00	5.00
			$5.00

STATE OF MISSISSIPPI.

GRENADA.

Nov. 4.	Colored Sunday-school, Miss Anna Harwood	$16.50	$16.50

VICKSBURG.

Oct. 23.	Christ Church, by W. T. Balfour . .	10.50	
	Church of the Holy Trinity . . .	18.00	28.50

YAZOO CITY.

Oct 21.	Citizens, by F. E. Bidwell, P. M. . .	20.00	20.00
			$65.00

STATE OF LOUISIANA.

NEW ORLEANS.

Oct. 16.	Bank of America	$1,000.00	
24.	Proceeds Benefit at Academy of Music	104.80	
	Citizens' subscriptions, I. N. Marks, Chairman, ...	10,000.00	
Nov. 4.	Louisiana National Bank . . .	500.00	
Dec. 23.	Citizens' subscription balance, by I. N. Marks, Chairman	17,329.16	28,933.96
			$28,933.96

STATE OF TEXAS.

AUSTIN.

Nov. 17.	Miss Ella Wren's Theatrical Co. .	$165.94	$165.94

FORT STOCKTON.

Nov. 22.	Army officers and citizens, by W. E. Friedlander & Co.	280.00	
Dec. 22.	Company K, 25th U. S. Infantry, Capt. J. S. Tompkins	88.85	368.85

GALVESTON.

Oct. 23.	Starr S. Jones	39.50	
25.	Citizens, by F. R. Lubbock	4,626.15	4,665.65

HOUSTON.

Oct. 21.	Citizens, by Gen. R. Avery	1,000.00	
Nov. 6.	H. & T. C. R. R. employés	275.00	1,275.00

MONTGOMERY COUNTY.

Nov. 3.	C. B. Stewart	30.00	30.00

SAN ANTONIO.

Nov. 17.	Citizens, by Mayor	1,604.67	1,604.67
			$8,110.11

STATE OF OHIO.

AKRON.

Oct. 18, 1871.	Citizens, by Lewis Miller	$1,838.25	$1,838.25

ALLIANCE.

April 15, 1872.	Welsh Congregational Churches, by Daniel Davies	20.00	20.00

BARNESVILLE.

Oct. 16, 1871.	Citizens, by A. Plumly	300.00	
Nov. 6.	Citizens, by 1st National Bank	200.00	500.00

BELLAIRE.

Oct. 21.	Bellaire Nail Works employés	106.25	106.25

BELLEVUE.

Oct. 27.	Citizens, by J. W. Goodson	1,000.00	1,000.00

BELMONT COUNTY.

Oct. 25.	Jacob Maule	39.00	39.00

BEREA.

Jan. 24, 1872.	Ladies' Relief Society, Mrs. A. H. Goodman	100.00	100.00

BUCYRUS.

Oct. 27, 1871.	Citizens, by J. A. Gormly	180.00	180.00

CADIZ, HARRISON CO.

Nov. 11.	Citizens, donation, through C. P. Dewey	610.00	
Dec. 19.	Residents of Harrison County, per C. P. Dewey, Treasurer	218.17	
30.	Citizens, per C. P. Dewey, Treasurer .	43.00	871.17

CANTON.

Oct. 18.	Citizens, Geo. D. Saxton, Treasurer .	203.35	203.35

CARDINGTON.

Oct. 16.	Citizens, by A. Kerr, Mayor . . .	217.00	217.00

CHAGRIN FALLS.

Oct. 23.	J. W. Williams, Mayor	255.92	255.92

CHILLICOTHE.

Oct. 27.	Citizens, by A. S. Waddle, Mayor .	3,000.00	3,000.00

CINCINNATI.

Dec. 4.	W. Sayres	3.50	3.50

CIRCLEVILLE.

Nov. 17.	Poor man's mite	2.00	2.00

CLARKSVILLE.

Oct. 18.	Eli Hadley	17.00	17.00

CLEVELAND.

Oct. 16.	M. Converse, Union Iron Works employés	244.00	
Nov. 16.	H. Garretson, Treasurer, collection of citizens to pay freight on coal . .	4,324.75	
Dec. 12.	Cleveland Heights Cong'l Church, by T. K. Noble	121.08	
Jan. 6, 1872.	Citizens, by H. Garretson, Treasurer, expended for coal . . .	15,049.59	
19.	Citizens, H. Garretson, Treasurer . .	3,535.42	23,274.84

COLUMBUS.

Oct. 16, 1871.	City appropriation, through W. G. Deshler, Treasurer	10,000.00	
Jan. 13, 1872.	Citizens, by Treasurer . . .	2,969.10	
Feb. 24.	Citizens, by Treasurer, balance . .	105.00	13,074.10

CRESTLINE.

Nov. 2, 1871.	Lodge No. 237 I. O. O. F. . .	50.00	50.00

DAMASCOVILLE.

March 21, 1872.	Citizens, by William Cattell .	105.58	105.58

DAYTON.

Feb. 12. Citizens, John Powell, Treasurer . 2,600.00——— 2,600.00

DELAWARE.

Oct. 27, 1871. S. Moore, for citizens 650.00
Nov. 23. " " . . . . 41.95——— 691.95

EATON.

Oct. 16. J. H. Foos, Mayor, for citizens . . 317.25——— 317.25

ELYRIA.

Nov. 3. Proceeds Lecture, by N. B. Gates . 51.25
Feb. 8, 1872. Amateur Musicians, proceeds of concert, J. W. Bullock, Treasurer . 152.00——— 203.25

GALLIPOLIS.

Oct. 27, 1871. A. S. Langley, Ariel Lodge No. 156, I. O. O. F. 250.00
City appropriation . . . 1,000.00——— 1,250.00

HANGING ROCK.

Oct. 18. Contribution, Presbyterian Church . 48.50
J. N. Hempstead and family . . . 50.00
Nov. 14. Mrs. R. R. Hamilton . . . 1,000.00——— 1,098.50

HOMER.

Nov. 11. Tobias H. Wisler . . . . . 1.00——— 1.00

HUBBARD, Trumbull Co.

Nov. 24. Rev. George S. Rice . . . . . 5.00——— 5.00

IRONTON.

Oct. 27. Iron Lodge No. 198 . . . . . 200.00
Iron City Lodge No. 452 . . . . 100.00
Board of Trade 300.00
Employés, Stockholders, etc., through 1st National Bank 1,568.00
Nov. 6. Employés, Stockholders, etc., through 2d National Bank . . . . . . 706.75——— 2,874.75

JEFFERSON.

Oct. 18. S. A. Northway . . . . 16.00——— 16.00

KELLEY'S ISLAND.

Oct. 18. Citizens, by W. S. Webb . . . . 130.00——— 130.00

LANCASTER.

Oct. 21. John Wagenhals . . . . . . 5.00——— 5.00

LARUE.

Oct. 23.	Five citizens, by H. S. Lucas . .	40.00———	40.00

LEESBURG.

Oct. 25.	Citizens, by C. E. Johnson . . .	118.25———	118.25

MANSFIELD.

Dec. 12.	C. J. L.	1.00———	1.00

MARIETTA.

Oct. 21.	Marietta Iron Works	100.00	
	1st National Bank	100.00	
	Marietta National Bank	100.00	
	Union Bank	100.00	
	Bosworth Mills	50.00	
	C. K. Leonard	25.00	
	Shipman, Holden, & Co. . . .	25.00———	500.00

MARION.

Oct. 18.	Citizens, by J. F. McNeil, Mayor . .	196.00	
Nov. 7.	Presbyterian Church	27.15	
	Episcopal Church	13.10———	236.25

MIAMISBURG.

Oct. 21.	Adam Arend	10.00———	10.00

MIDDLETOWN.

Oct. 28.	Proceeds of concert, J. K. Thomas .	40.00———	40.00

MORRISTOWN.

Oct. 25.	Citizens, by J. V. Fisher . . .	29.05———	29.05

MOUNT PLEASANT.

Feb. 12, 1872.	J. K. Ratcliff, Treasurer . .	91.80———	91.80

MOUNT UNION.

Oct. 30, 1871.	Contribution, Mt. Union College	31.75———	31.75

NILES.

Oct. 27.	E. Thomas, for citizens	500.00———	500.00

NORWALK.

Oct. 27.	Mayor, for citizens	1,100.00———	1,100.00

OBERON.

Oct. 16.	W. H. Backus, Mayor, for citizens .	394.25	
	David Kinnester	5.00———	399.25

OXFORD.

Oct. 23. Children District School, J. Frye . . 27.20 —— 27.20

PORTSMOUTH.

Nov. 13. German Glee Club, by A. Brunner . 30.00 —— 30.00

RAVENNA.

Oct. 30. "Poet" . . . . .20 —— .20

RIPLEY.

Oct. 16. Citizens, by 1st National Bank . . 159.25 —— 159.25

ST. CLAIRSVILLE.

Oct. 23. Joseph Daniel . . . . . . 5.00 —— 5.00

SHELBY.

Feb. 17, 1872. John Kahl . . . . . . 15.25 —— 15.25

STEUBENVILLE

Oct. 28, 1871. Citizens 2d Ward 453.00
Citizens, by J. G. Morris, Treasurer 2,123.84
28. Exhibition by Grand Army of the Republic, "Drummer Boy of Shiloh" 192.90 —— 2,769.74

TIFFIN.

Oct. 15. Lodge Good Templars, by E. Lefner 25.00
16. Citizens, J. G. Gross, Chairman [1] . 2,300.00 —— 2,325.00

TOLEDO.

Oct. 18. Citizens . . . . 4,000.00 —— 4,000.00

UHRICHSVILLE.

Feb. 13, 1872. Unknown . . . . .10 —— .10

VERSAILLES.

Nov. 8, 1871. Citizens, by F. Kusnick . . 100.00 —— 100.00

WAUSEON.

Oct. 25. E. L Barber . . . . 100.00 —— 100.00

WOOSTER.

Oct. 27. Citizens, by J. C. Plummer, Mayor . 1,000.00 —— 1,000.00

YOUNGSTOWN.

Oct. 17. Citizens . . . . 5,000.00 —— 5,000.00

ZANESVILLE.

Oct. 16. City Council appropriation . . 2,000.00
Nov. 6. Citizens, by W. S. Harlan . . 260.50

[1] This donation of citizens was returned to J. G. Gross, Chairman, for relief of sufferers by fire in Tiffin, April 17, 1872.

Nov. 9.	Citizens, by C. W. Potwin, as follows: Proceeds Concert by Zanesville Dramatic Association	84.50	
	Contributions Citizens 1st Ward . .	827.50	
	Contribution of J. A. Armstrong . .	10.00	
	Contribution Salt Creek Sons of Temperance	5.00	
	Contribution Salt Creek Sons of Temperance Concert	15.00	3,202.50
			$75,882.25

STATE OF INDIANA.

ANDERSON.

Nov. 21, 1871.	James Hazlitt . . .	$166.00	$166.00

ATTICA.

Oct. 21.	Children Attica Public School . .	60.00	60.00

BROOKVILLE.

Oct. 18.	W. A. Lindsay	10.00	10.00

CONNERSVILLE.

Oct. 31.	N. W. Wright	64.25	
	W. H. Wherrett	25.00	89.25

COVINGTON.

Oct. 15.	Citizens, by J. L. Cherry . . .	235.00	235.00

CRAWFORDSVILLE.

Oct. 31.	Citizens, by W. F. Ellston . . .	525.00	525.00

DANVILLE.

Nov. 14.	Citizens, by Allan Hess . . .	285.00	285.00

DERBY.

Oct. 26.	W. O'Neil	12.00	12.00

EVANSVILLE.

Oct. 16.	Citizens, by M. Henning . . .	2,000.00	2,000.00

GOSHEN.

Oct. 18.	Citizens, by E. W. H. Ellis	200.00	
24.	Citizens, N. P. Jacobs	50.00	250.00

GREENCASTLE.

Oct. 21.	First National Bank	200.00	
	Citizens	400.00	
Nov. 20.	Citizens, W. A. Brown, Mayor, . .	674.56	1,274.56

GREENFIELD.

April 19, 1872.	Proceeds of Reading Entertainment by Nelson Bradley	16.85	16.85

HARMONY.

Oct. 18, 1871.	Citizens, by J. B. Harris	72.50	72.50

INDIANAPOLIS.

Nov. 11.	Citizens, by J. D. Howland	10,000.00	
Dec. 8.	" " "	5,000.00	
Jan. 19, 1872.	Citizens, balance, by J. D. Howland, Treasurer	7,396.32	
Feb. 20.	Employés of Ind. & St. L. R. R., S. E. Frazee, P. M.	2,129.00	24,525.32

JEFFERSONVILLE.

Oct. 18, 1871.	Tell Lodge No. 272	50.00	
21.	Citizens, by L. Sparks, Mayor	1,000.00	
27.	Employés Ohio Falls Car Co.	2,140.65	
Dec. 21.	Citizens, by L. Sparks, Mayor	1,304.80	4,495.45

KOKOMO.

Oct. 24.	Proceeds Young Ladies' Festival, Miss Fanny Murray	94.15	94.15

LAPORTE.

Dec. 2.	Employés of L. S. & M. S. R. R. Co. by Charles Paine	2,507.50	
April 16, 1873.	Citizens, E. L. Adams, Treasurer	237.25	2,744.75

LIGONIER.

Oct. 25.	Citizens	30.00	30.00

LOGANSPORT.

Oct. 20.	Citizens, by A. C. Hall, Mayor	156.50	
24.	" " "	21.65	178.15

LOTUS.

Dec. 2.	"Oasis Society" of Ladies	30.00	30.00

MONTGOMERY.

Dec. 8.	Rev. B. Preis	5.50	5.50

NORTH VERNON.

Oct. 27.	Citizens, by H. Tripp	94.25	94.25

PERU.

Oct. 18.	R. P. Effinger	10.00	10.00

50

ROCHESTER.

Feb. 29, 1872.	Balance, by E. P. Cowgill . .	60.00	60.00

ROLLING PRAIRIE.

Oct. 20, 1871.	Citizens	30.00	30.00

SHELBYVILLE.

Oct. 15.	City Council, per S. Allen . .	1,000.00	1,000.00

SOUTH BEND.

Oct. 18.	C. M. Heaton	8.84	
Feb. 24, 1872.	Citizens, balance, by Wm. Miller, Treasurer	500.00	508.84

TERRE HAUTE.

Nov. 1, 1871.	Citizens, by L. A. Burnett . .	5,558.00	
14.	Citizens, McKean & Minchall . .	172.55	
25.	Citizens, J. O'Meara, Treasurer . .	250.00	5980.55

TIPTON.

Oct. 11.	Julius Meyer	5.00	5.00

VEVAY.

Nov. 10.	Julius Dufour	10.00	10.00

VINCENNES.

Dec. 6.	City appropriation, W. B. Robinson, Mayor	1,000.00	
Feb. 26, 1872.	Citizens, Lazarus Noble, Chairman	497.50	1,497.50

WASHINGTON.

Nov. 14, 1871.	Citizens, by Exchange Bank .	360.00	360.00

WILLIAMSPORT.

Oct. 16.	C. R. Boyer	75.00	75.00

YORK TOWNSHIP.

Nov. 14.	Citizens, by R. F. Graves . . .	21.00	21.00
			$46,751.62

STATE OF ILLINOIS.

ALBANY.

Oct. 18, 1871.	Unknown	$10.00	
Nov. 2.	Citizens, by F. M. Rockwell . . .	33.00	$43.00

ALTON.

Jan. 11, 1872.	Citizens, by Isaac Scarrett, Treasurer	2,000.00	2,000.00

ASHLEY.

Oct. 18, 1871.	Citizens, by J. Monroe . .	33.25	33.25

BARNESVILLE.

Jan. 20, 1872.	Citizens, balance, by A. Plumly, Chairman	35.15	35.15

BASCO.

Oct. 20, 1871.	Citizens	7.50	7.50

BATAVIA.

Oct. 10.	Congregational Church, per W. Coffin .	47.52	
	Methodist Church, " " . . .	13.48	
Dec. 7.	New Church S. S., per W. Coffin, Treas.	21.74	
	Citizens, " " .	3.00	85.74

BLOOMINGTON.

Oct. 27.	Citizens, by McClure, Holden, & Co.	13,820.77	
Feb. 3, 1872.	Unknown	.50	13,821.27

BRIGHTON.

March 12.	Congregational Church, Edwin Amass, Clerk	26.50	26.50

BUNKER HILL.

Oct. 18, 1871.	Friend, by J. A. Beech . .	10.00	
March 13, 1872.	Citizens, per S. N. Sanford, Town Clerk	96.00	106.00

CAIRO.

Oct. 21.	Citizens, per J. N. Lansden . . .	500.00	
27.	Employés of Southern Insane Asylum, Hon. J. Wood, Commissioner . .	159.50	659.50

CAMBRIDGE.

Dec. 18.	Citizens, balance, S. D. Alfred, Treasurer	34.30	34.30

CANTON.

Nov. 8.	Citizens, by I. W. Ingersoll . . .	268.63	268.63

CARLYLE.

Oct. 26.	Citizens, by R. N. Ramsey . . .	500.00	500.00

CARROLTON.

Oct. 18.	Citizens	1,018.25	1,018.25

CHARLESTON.

Date	Donor	Amount	Total
Oct. 20.	Dr. H. Rutherford, of Oakland	25.00	
	J. W. True	5.00	30.00

CHICAGO.

Date	Donor	Amount	Total
Oct. 16.	D. M. Osborne & Co.	1,000.00	
	George Phillips	50.00	
23.	Merrill & Skeele	125.00	
	G. R. Douglas, A. P. M.	5.00	
28.	Batcheller & Benton	200.00	
Nov. 4.	Miss Jane Coombs	50.00	
	John H. Ross	50.00	
7.	W. B. Haughton	20.00	
11.	T. J. Driggs, Treasurer	20.00	
	A. T. King & Co.	500.00	
14.	Mabley & Hull, 10 per cent. for sales for the day	150.00	
15.	Ludington, Wells, & Van Schaack	1,500.00	
18.	Charles Reitz & Brother	500.00	
	Hughes' Dry Goods Store	10.00	
20.	Charles Wilson, proprietor "Evening Journal"	100.00	
21.	B. L. Anderson & Co.	250.00	
27.	Goodspeed & Co.	100.00	
29.	J. D. Gardner & Co.	1,000.00	
	Julius White	100.00	
Dec. 12.	A. E. Morley, 748 Michigan Avenue	20.00	
26.	W. S. Babcock & Co.	750.00	
	Richard Schulenburg	100.00	
	R. A. Loveland	1,000.00	
Jan. 16, 1872.	I. P. Sunderland, Board of Trade Provision Inspector	11.85	
Feb. 14.	S. D. Twining, for a friend	13.50	
June 8.	George R. Granger (little boy)	1.00	
Jan. 17, 1873.	J. B. Galloway	5.00	7,631.35

COLLINSVILLE, Madison Co.

Date	Donor	Amount	Total
Jan. 6.	German Citizens, by Hon. R. B. Mason	250.00	250.00

DANVILLE.

Date	Donor	Amount	Total
Oct. 16, 1871.	Citizens	1,753.00	
Feb. 14, 1872.	Master Chester W. Forbes (a lad)	5.00	
March 11.	Per Third National Bank	2.00	1,760.00

DECATUR.

Date	Donor	Amount	Total
Oct. 27, 1871.	Contribution of Ladies of M. E. Church	71.00	
Jan. 6, 1872.	Citizens, L. W. Burrows, Treasurer	2,479.50	2,550.50

DEKALB.

Dec. 4. F. W. Smith . . . . . . 10.00——— 10.00

DELAVAN.

Oct. 21. Citizens, per L. D. Lawton . . . 160.00
Antioch Church . . . . . . 21.00——— 181.00

DUNTON.

Jan. 31, 1872. Methodist and Presbyterian Churches, by Rev. N. Barrett . . 25.00——— 25.00

DURAND.

Oct. 16, 1871. Citizens 108.35
27. E. C. Stevens . . . . . . 6.00——— 114.35

DWIGHT.

Nov. 17. Citizens, by W. H. Bradbury . . 159.46——— 159.46

EARL.

March 5, 1872. Citizens, by C. C. Warren . 8.00——— 8.00

EDWARDSVILLE.

Nov. 7, 1871. Citizens, by H. C. Barnsbach . 775.00——— 775.00

ELGIN.

Nov. 29. National Watch Co.'s employés, G. P. Lord, Manager . . . . . 1,591.50——— 1,591.50

EL PASO.

Jan. 23, 1872. Jer. P. Parkhurst . . . . 5.00——— 5.00

ENFIELD.

Oct. 31, 1871. Citizens, by R. C. Willis . . 39.50——— 39.50

EUREKA.

Nov. 25. Citizens, by J. A. Davis . . . 10.00——— 10.00

FARMINGTON.

Oct. 26. Citizens, proceeds of car load of hogs . 523.80——— 523.80

FLORA.

Dec. 29. Citizens, J. S. Major, Treasurer . . 130.90——— 130.90

FLORENCE STATION.

Oct. 16. Citizens 5.00
Nov. 23. Citizens, by Edwin Strevill . . . 153.75——— 158.75

FORREST.

Feb. 15, 1873. Subscriptions, per E. H. Denison, 242 So. Water St., Chicago . . 11.00——— 11.00

FRANKLIN GROVE.

Oct. 26.	Citizens, by B. W. Scott . . .	5.00	5.00

FREEPORT.

Oct. 31.	Ladies' Aid Society	168.00	168.00

GALENA.

Oct. 24.	Thomas Foster, drayage on goods sent .	1.00	
Dec. 8.	Dr. George O. Howard . . .	3.70	4.70

GALESBURG.

Oct. 16.	Society of Engineers C. B. & Q. R. R. .	112.00	
Jan. 20, 1872.	Citizens, A. Knowles, Treasurer .	800.00	912.00

GENESEO.

Nov. 24, 1871.	J. F. Dresser, Cashier . .	7.50	
Jan. 4, 1872.	George H. Breed . . .	5.00	12.50

GOOD HOPE.

Oct. 16.	Citizens	23.50	23.50

GRAND TOWER.

Oct. 16.	Citizens, per J. Stevens, Jr., Cashier .	79.50	79.50

GREENFIELD.

Nov. 1.	Citizens, per W. H. Haven . . .	200.00	200.00

HALE, Ogle Co.

Jan. 10, 1872.	Mrs. Lydia Youngs . . .	1.00	1.00

HILLSBOROUGH.

Oct. 27, 1871.	W. Seymour	10.00	10.00

HUNTLEY.

Feb. 27, 1872.	Balance, citizens, T. L. Parsons, Treasurer	1.25	1.25

IRVINGTON.

Oct. 16, 1871.	Citizens, by J. Hardee. . .	70.50	70.50

JACKSONVILLE.

Oct. 28.	William Rankin, Mayor . . .	4,690.00	4,690.00

JERSEY COUNTY.

Dec. 2.	Citizens, W. H. Pogue, Chairman, Jerseyville	963.00	963.00

JOLIET.

Oct. 24.	Employés State Penitentiary. . . .	319.00	
Nov. 22.	" " " Jas. Miller.	3.25	322.25

KANE COUNTY.

Nov. 21.	Burlington Circuit M. E. Churches, Rev. L. Clifford	20.00	20.00

KANKAKEE.

Oct. 25, 1871.	Proceeds Excursion, by J. H. Smith	259.50	
27.	Citizens, by Chas. Holt, balance . .	113.82	373.32

KNOXVILLE.

Oct. 25.	Citizens, per John Babington . . .	231.65	
	First National Bank	600.00	831.65

LEBANON.

Oct. 20.	J. M. Chamberlin, for citizens . . .	300.00	300.00

LEE CENTRE.

Jan. 26, 1872.	Ladies' Sewing Society, by Martin Wright	1.25	1.25

LENA.

Oct. 30, 1871.	Citizens, by S. Rising . . .	300.00	300.00

LINCOLN.

Nov. 27.	Citizens, F. Fisk, Treasurer . . .	329.90	329.90

LITCHFIELD.

Oct. 27.	City appropriation	250.00	
Nov. 11.	Citizens, by H. H. Hood	21.35	271.35

LOCKPORT.

Nov. 22.	Citizens, by John Heck	670.72	
Jan. 23, 1872.	" "	10.00	680.72

LOUNDALE.

Oct. 16, 1871.	G. B. Roberts and A. Esten .	61.75	61.75

MAGNOLIA.

Feb. 12, 1872.	Relief Associations of Magnolia and Hope Townships, of Putnam and La Salle Counties, by John Swaney	126.28	126.28

MARENGO.

Dec. 7, 1871.	Citizens, G. V. Wells . . .	172.86	
April 10, 1872.	" " "	88.00	260.86

McLEAN.

Feb. 14.	Citizens, by C. C. Aldrich . . .	52.50	52.50

MARSHALL.

Oct. 24, 1871.	Citizens, by J. Wheelock . .	20.00	20.00

MASON CITY.

Oct. 16.	Citizens, ...	261.00	261.00

MATTOON.

Oct. 18.	Citizens, by H. S. Clark, Treasurer . .	87.41	87.41

MENDON, ADAMS CO.

Oct. 27.	Citizens, by C. H. Hoffman	47.50	47.50

MILAN.

Feb. 8, 1872.	A. McConnell	10.00	10.00

MINIER.

Oct. 16, 1871.	Citizens, per J. N. Edmiston . .	71.10	71.10

MISSION, LA SALLE CO.

Dec. 30.	W. J. Terry	5.00	
Feb. 22, 1872.	Elias D. Terry	5.00	10.00

MOLINE.

Jan. 8.	Citizens, per Mary L. Deere . .	1,000.00	
Feb. 16.	Citizens, balance, W. G. Morris, Treasurer	532.35	1,532.35

MOMENCE.

Oct, 18, 1871.	Citizens	40.00	
26.	Mrs. E. Worcester	5.00	45.00

MONMOUTH.

Dec. 8.	John M. Turnbull	220.00	220.00

MORGAN COUNTY.

Nov. 7.	Pisgah Presbyterian Church	377.20	377.20

MORRIS.

Jan. 16, 1872.	Citizens, by Levi Pierce . .	128.00	128.00

MOUND CITY.

Nov. 13, 1871.	Citizens, by Geo. E. Freeman .	314.25	314.25

MT. CARROLL.

Nov. 8.	Citizens, per H. A. Mills	200.00	
18.	" " "	100.00	
Feb. 27, 1872.	Citizens, additional, H. A. Mills, Chairman	107.14	407.14

MOUNT VERNON.

Oct. 16, 1871.	Citizens, by Carlin, Cross, & Co.	225.00	225.00

NAPERVILLE.

Dec. 27.	E. G. Shumway	12.00	12.00

NASHVILLE.

Oct. 15.	Citizens, by J. Garvin, Chairman . .	250.00	250.00

NEW BEDFORD.

Nov. 20.	W. L. Hay, per J. H. Harris . . .	10.00	10.00

NORMAL.

Dec. 9.	Rev. W. H. Webster	51.90	51.90

ODELL.

Jan. 28, 1872.	Citizens, F. M. Hotchkiss, Treasurer	195.00	195.00

OLNEY.

Oct. 27, 1871.	C. D. Johnson, Mayor . .	501.10	
	German Reform Sunday-school . .	4.55	505.65

ONION, Henry Co.

Dec. 7.	Good Templars, H. H. Parks . .	27.25	27.25

PEKIN.

Nov. 4.	Citizens, by D. C. Smith . . .	193.03	193.03

PEORIA.

Oct. 16.	Citizens, by R. C. Grier . . .	4,750.00	4,750.00

PERU.

Nov. 17.	Citizens, by T. D. Brewster . . .	394.18	394.18

PETERSBURG.

Oct. 30.	Citizens, by J. M. Robbins . . .	584.00	584.00

PITTSFIELD.

Nov. 9.	Congregational Church, per Rev. W. W. Rose	20.75	20.75

PONTIAC.

Dec. 1.	Citizens, balance, W. B. Fyfe . .	185.70	185.70

PORT BYRON.

Nov. 7.	Citizens, by H. B. Dutcher . . .	40.10	40.10

PRINCETON.

March 30, 1872.	Citizens, balance, by W. H. Winter, Chairman	97.00	97.00

RIDOTT.

Dec. 7, 1871.	Citizens, J. A. Kerr, Secretary .	39.25	39.25

ROCKFORD.

Dec. 1. Pupils of South Rockford School . . 5.00——— 5.00

ROCK ISLAND.

Dec. 23. Citizens, Elijah Carter . . . . 1,305.34——— 1,305.34

RUSHVILLE.

Nov. 27. Citizens, W. H. Ray, Chairman . . 131.83
Sept. 11, 1872. Citizens, balance, by W. H. Ray, Chairman . . . . . . 9.15——— 140.98

SAVANNA.

Oct. 23, 1871. Citizens, per L. H. Bowen . . 104.77——— 104.77

SHAWNEETOWN.

Nov. 9. Citizens, by M. M. Poole . . . 500.00
Jan. 25, 1872. Citizens, per George Beck . . 148.00——— 648.00

SHEFFIELD.

Oct. 16, 1871. N. R. Hawkins . . . . . 25.50——— 25.50

SHELBYVILLE.

Jan. 11, 1872. Citizens, by W. M. Wright, Chairman . . . . 164.20——— 164.20

SPARTA.

Nov. 16, 1871. Citizens, by H. Gardener, Mayor 381.40——— 381.40

SPRINGFIELD.

Oct. 16. State of Illinois Contingent Fund, per J. H. Wines 2,000.00
18. Metropolitan Theatrical Troupe . . 39.00
26. Musical Union, by W. P. Emery, Treasurer 154.50
Nov. 2. African M. E. Church 27.05
20. State of Illinois Contingent Fund . . 3,000.00——— 5,220.55

SYCAMORE.

Dec. 29. Citizens, Moses Dean, Treasurer . 47.45——— 47.45

TOULON.

Oct. 16. Citizens, per R. Nolan . . . . 100.00——— 100.00

URBANA.

Dec. 16. First Presbyterian Church . . . 32.35——— 32.35

UTAH, Warren Co.

Nov. 14. R. J. Adcock . . . . 5.00——— 5.00

VICTORIA.

Nov. 29. H. Davison . . . . 3.00——— 3.00

VIRDEN.

Oct. 26.	Citizens, by W. L. Heaton	897.05	
Nov. 17.	" " "	14.00	
Dec. 6.	Thanksgiving collection, "	14.00	925.05

WARSAW.

Oct. 20.	Citizens	44.75	44.75

WESTFIELD.

Dec. 23.	Thanksgiving collection, Rev. H. Elwell	15.75	15.75

WHITEHALL.

Nov. 11, 1871.	Citizens, by Pearson, Gregory, & Co.	557.00	557.00

WOOSUNG.

Oct. 16.	J. H. Anderson	2.00	2.00

WYANET.

Dec. 7.	Citizens, Geo. Field, Treasurer . .	10.35	10.35
			$66,527.18

STATE OF KENTUCKY.

CASEYVILLE.

Nov. 2, 1871.	St. Paul's Church	$10.40	$10.40

CYNTHIANA.

Oct. 16.	Citizens, by J. Q. Ward . .	112.50	
30.	" " "	24.00	136.50

GLASGOW.

Oct. 21.	Citizens, by J. G. Rogers	82.00	82.00

HARRODSBURG.

Nov. 20.	Hon. B. Magoffin	300.00	300.00

HENDERSON.

Jan. 19, 1872.	Subscriptions Masonic Fraternity, by E. W. Worsham, Treasurer	100.00	
19.	Strangers, Rent, I. O. O. F. No. 13, by E. W. Worsham, Treasurer . .	100.00	
	Citizens, " " " . . .	550.35	750.35

LANCASTER.

Nov. 24, 1871.	Citizens, by W. H. Kinnaird .	76.50	76.50

LEXINGTON.

Oct. 27.	Citizens, by J. B. Wilgus . . .	1,000.00	1,000.00

LOUISVILLE.

Nov. 6.	Employés L. & N. R. R. shops . .	1,044.20	
Dec. 29.	Citizens, J. M. Duncan, Treasurer .	5,000.00	
Jan. 5, 1872.	" " " .	5,000.00	
19.	" " " .	5,000.00	
27.	" " " .	5,000.00	
Feb. 20.	" " " .	1,533.45	22,577.65

MAYSVILLE.

Oct. 18, 1871.	Citizens, by M. C. Hutchins, Mayor	1,000.00	
26.	Unknown	3.50	1,003.50

MOUNT STERLING.

Nov. 15.	Citizens, by W. Mitchell . . .	55.15	55.15

OWENSBOROUGH.

Oct. 27.	Citizens, by S. D. Kennedy, Mayor .	400.00	400.00

PADUCAH.

Oct. 24.	Citizens, by M. Weil, Mayor . .	868.10	868.10

PARIS.

Oct. 18.	Citizens, by B. F. Pollen . . .	500.00	500.00

UNIONTOWN.

Nov. 2.	St. John's Church	9.05	9.05
			$27,769.20

STATE OF TENNESSEE.

CHATTANOOGA.

Oct. 24, 1871.	Hebrew Benevolent Association	$300.00	
24.	St. Paul's Episcopal Church . .	21.55	$321.55

FLINTVILLE.

Nov. 18.	Rev. J. W. Waite	7.00	7.00

KNOXVILLE.

Oct. 30.	Philharmonic Society	152.00	
	St. John's Episcopal Church . .	111.25	
Dec. 22.	Masonic Lodge No. 244, L. C. Shepard, Treasurer	71.50	
Jan. 16, 1872.	Swiss Residents, by Emile Buffat	5.00	339.75

MEMPHIS.

Oct. 20, 1871.	Citizens, by F. S. Davis . .	15,000.00	
30.	" " " . .	521.05	
Nov. 10.	Citizens, by J. Johnson, Mayor . .	5,000.00	20,521.05

NASHVILLE.

Nov. 10.	St. Peter's Mission	1.80	
16.	Citizens, by A. G. Adams, Treasurer .	2,439.30	
Jan. 4, 1872.	" " " . .	25.00	
	Joel A. Battle, Battle House . .	100.00	2,566.10

SPRINGFIELD.

Oct. 18, 1861.	Robertson Lodge, No. 87, I. O. of O. F.	100.00	100.00

WINCHESTER.

Oct. 19.	Protestant Episcopal Church . .	1.25	1.25
			$23,856.70

STATE OF MICHIGAN.

CASSOPOLIS.

Oct. 16, 1871.	Citizens.	$173.00	$173.00

CHELSEA.

Oct. 16.	Citizens, ...	264.00	264.00

DETROIT.

Oct. 16.	Invalid child	1.00	
25.	C. A. Mann	5.00	
28.	Mrs. Commodore Rogers . . .	10.00	
Nov. 25.	Relief Committee, G. F. Bagley, Treasurer	5,883.50	
Dec. 30.	E. B. Ward	659.19	
Jan. 6, 1872.	Relief Committee, G. F. Bagley, Treasurer	30,910.20	37,468.89

HUDSON.

Oct. 20.	Common Council	38.00	38.00

PAW PAW.

Oct. 23.	Citizens, per A. Sherman . . .	100.00	100.00

QUINCY.

Oct. 16.	Citizens and Thespian Club . . .	141.25	141.25

ST. JOSEPH.

Feb. 21, 1872.	" Association," J. H. Hatch, Sec.	229.50	229.50
			$38,414.64

STATE OF WISCONSIN.

ARENA.

Oct. 16, 1871.	Mites	$1.00	$1.00

JEWETT MILLS.

Dec. 18.	Employés S. A. Jewett	62.50	62.50

KENOSHA.

Oct. 17.	American Eye Salve Co.	50.00	
25.	A Friend in Conn.	5.00	55.00

MILWAUKEE.

Jan. 15, 1872.	Club, by Edward Kron	4.40	4.40

VIROQUA.

Oct. 14, 1871.	J. M. Rush, for citizens	300.00	300.00
			$422.90

STATE OF MINNESOTA.

CANNON FALLS.

Nov. 9, 1871.	Two Citizens	$5.40	$5.40

CHATFIELD.

Nov. 7.	Milo White and others	80.00	
20.	St. Matthew's Church Sunday-school, C. G. Ripley	6.75	86.75

HASTINGS.

Feb. 6, 1872.	Citizens, D. E. Eyre, Treasurer	300.00	300.00

LEROY.

Oct. 30, 1871.	First Presbyterian Church . .	7.00	7.00

STILLWATER.

Oct. 27.	Citizens, per City Treasurer	500.00	500.00

ST. PAUL.

Oct. 15.	City appropriation, per W. Lee, Mayor	20,000.00	
	J. Lewis, for a brother O. F. . . .	5.00	
23.	Strong & Anderson	71.00	
	Citizens, per W. Lee, Mayor . . .	375.00	
Nov. 1.	" " " " . . .	65.00	
Dec. 13.	Dr. Bevan	2.00	20,518.00

WINONA.

Oct. 16.	Citizens' Donation	3,000.00	
Dec. 2.	For freight on box	75	3,000.75
			$24,417.90

STATE OF IOWA.

BELLEPLAIN, Benton Co.

Jan. 22, 1872.	Citizens, S. S. Sweet, Treasurer	$75.40	$75.40

BELLEVIEW.

March 11.	Citizens, J. Kiles, Mayor . . .	95.60	95.60

BLAIRSTOWN.

Oct. 21, 1871.	Presbyterian Church . . .	11.00	11.00

BONAPARTE.

Oct. 27.	Citizens, by F. Cristy	58.25	58.25

BOONSBOROUGH.

Dec. 6.	Thanksgiving collection in united meeting of churches	10.15	10.15

BRIGHTON.

Feb. 29, 1872.	W. G. Israel	9.57	9.57

BROOKLYN.

Nov. 29, 1871.	C. H. Libby	45.25	45.25

BUCKINGHAM.

Nov. 18.	Citizens, per D. Connell	117.85	117.85

BURLINGTON.

Jan. 6, 1872.	Citizens, James Putnam, Treasurer	3,595.47	
Feb. 12.	" " "	1,099.03	
12.	Ladies' Relief Society, Mrs. B. M. Gay, Treasurer	83.05	4,777.55

CASEY.

Oct. 30, 1871.	Sunday-school	11.00	11.00

CEDAR RAPIDS.

Jan. 26, 1872.	Citizens, by Mayor Medill of Chicago	35.00	35.00

CHARITON.

Nov. 18, 1871.	Citizens, per G. W. Blake . .	265.00	265.00

CORYDON.

Dec. 21.	Corydon Aid Society, Ocobock Brothers	40.00	40.00

DAVENPORT.

Nov. 6. Citizens, per N. Fejervary, Chairman 2,000.00
20. " " " 1,000.00
27. Citizens, by B. B. Woodward, Cashier 595.00—— 3,595.00

DECORAH.

Jan. 15, 1872. Charlotte C. Baker, Secretary Relief Committee . . . . . . 29.05—— 29.05

DENMARK, Lee Co.

Dec. 1, 1871. Citizens, by G. B. Brackett . . 129.15—— 129.15

DUBUQUE.

Nov. 30. Citizens, per Joseph Herod, Secretary 745.50—— 745.50

FORT MADISON.

Oct. 27. Ladies' Aid Society. . . . . . 17.00—— 17.00

FREDERICKSBURG.

Nov. 11. J. W. Sharpe . . . . 5.00—— 5.00

GRANDVIEW.

Jan. 13, 1872. German Congregational Church, Rev. F. W. Judieth . . . . 11.50—— 11.50

GRUNDY CENTRE.

Dec. 13, 1871. Church collections, E. H. Beekman, Treasurer . . . . 41.00—— 41.00

ILLYRIA.

Nov. 6. Citizens, by R. A. Richardson . . 10.25—— 10.25

KEOKUK.

Oct. 16. Citizens, ... 635.50
Contributions of citizens, collected by Miss Reiter 66.75
Dec. 30. Citizens, balance, S. Hamill . . . 76.83—— 779.08

LECLAIR.

Nov. 14. Citizens, per James Gamble . . . 113.00—— 113.00

LYONS.

Oct. 26. Citizens, by J. N. Cross, Mayor . . 170.60—— 170.60

MANCHESTER.

Nov. 18. Citizens, ... 500.00—— 500.00

MOUNT VERNON.

Oct. 21. Presbyterian Church 41.50
26. M. E. Church . . . . . . 108.00—— 149.50

MUSCATINE.

Oct. 16.	Citizens, per W. H. Moore	1,500.00	
18.	No Name	1.00	
Nov. 25.	Citizens, by W. H. Moore.	182.10	
Jan. 6, 1872.	Citizens, by W. H. Moore	50.00	1,733.10

NEW SHARON.

Oct. 30.	Citizens, by B. Stanton.	59.70	59.70

NORA SPRINGS.

Oct. 18.	Citizens	72.00	72.00

ONOWA.

Nov. 6.	Citizens, by I. P. Holmes	116.50	116.50

ONSLOW.

Nov. 22.	William Litten	15.00	15.00

OSAGE.

Dec. 13.	M. E. Church, by J. H. Brush	8.50	8.50

OSKALOOSA.

Oct. 30.	St. James Parish	3.50	
Nov. 16.	Citizens, per I. Frankel	371.30	374.80

OTTUMWA.

Jan. 20, 1872.	Citizens, Charles F. Blake, Treasurer	1,003.29	1,003.29

SCHELSBURG.

Nov. 22, 1871.	Proceeds 128.44 bushels ear corn, by F. E. Rue, Chicago	51.54	51.54

SIOUX CITY.

Oct. 31.	W. J. H.	2.00	
Feb. 7, 1872.	Citizens, J. P. Allison, Treasurer	824.83	
	City appropriation, Warrant No. 937 650		
	Less dis. on sale, 30 per cent . 195	455.00	1,281.83

STUART, Guthrie Co.

Nov. 9, 1871.	Stuart Quadrille Club	32.00	32.00

TIPTON.

Nov. 18.	Citizens, by W. H. Tuthill	540.00	540.00

TOLEDO.

Oct. 28.	Citizens, by A. J. Free.	11.45	11.45

VICTOR.

Oct. 26.	Citizens, by E. P. Hall, Mayor	26.00	26.00

WASHINGTON.

March 6, 1872.	3 cars corn, sold by Murry Nelson & Co.	425.64	425.64

WILTON.

Oct. 21, 1871.	Andrew Kaufman	10.00	10.00

WINTERSET.

Oct. 21.	1st Presbyterian Church	40.00	40.00
			$17,648.60

STATE OF MISSOURI.

CAMERON.

Oct. 23, 1871.	E. M. Shaw	$20.00	$20.00

CANTON.

Dec. 11.	Christian Church and Sunday-school, by D. P. Henderson	23.00	23.00

CLINTON.

Oct. 23.	Citizens, by J. B. Gantt	916.25	916.25

HANNIBAL.

Oct. 23.	Citizens, by J. Hunt, Treasurer	1,000.00	
Jan. 11, 1872.	" " "	630.65	1,630.65

HARRISONVILLE.

Oct. 18, 1871.	Citizens, by D. Dale	112.75	112.75

KANSAS CITY.

Oct. 21.	Citizens, by City Treasurer	10,000.00	
27.	J. D. Smith	110.00	
	Citizens, by W. Warner, Mayor	3,000.00	
Dec. 5.	Jour. tailors	50.00	
22.	Citizens, balance	43.43	13,203.43

KIRKSVILLE.

Oct. 20.	Cumberland Presbyterian Church	29.00	
Nov. 8.	Cumberland Presbyterian Sunday-school	7.35	36.35

LIBERTY.

Oct. 25.	Citizens, by A. P. Morse	193.20	193.20

MACON.

Dec. 2.	Citizens, W. F. Williams	500.90	500.90

MOBERLY.

Oct. 16.	Citizens, B. G. N. Clarkson, Mayor	213.90	213.90

PALMYRA.

Oct. 17.	Second Presbyterian Church . . .	10.00	
27.	Employés H. & St. Jo. R. R. . . .	144.00	154.00

ROCHEPORT, BOONE CO.

Dec. 27.	Mechanic, by Postmaster . . .	2.50	2.50

SPRINGFIELD.

Oct. 27.	Citizens, by W. J. Teed . . .	440.00	440.00

ST. JAMES.

Oct. 16.	Employés Dunmoor Mills . . .	29.50	
	Citizens	10.50	40.00

ST. JOSEPH.

Dec. 18.	Citizens, Abram Nave, Treasurer .	12,917.50	12,917.50

ST. LOUIS.

Oct. 18.	A poor man	.25	
	W. Baird	23.00	
	Bartholow, Lewis, & Co.	700.00	
Dec. 8.	Citizens' Committee, Geo. H. Morgan, Secretary	25,716.27	
Jan. 6, 1872.	" " " .	10,635.30	37,074.82

TIPTON.

Oct. 16, 1871.	Maclay & Co.	25.00	25.00
			$67,504.25

STATE OF ARKANSAS.

LITTLE ROCK.

Oct. 18, 1871.	Citizens, by D. E. Jones, Treas'r	$1,500.00	
18.	Eliza S. Edwards	536.55	
31.	Citizens, by D. E. Jones, Treasurer .	500.00	
Dec. 1.	" " " .	174.30	$2,710.85

EVENING SHADE, SHARP CO.

Feb. 24, 1872.	John Cook	15.00	15.00
			$2,725.85

STATE OF KANSAS.

ABELINE.

Oct. 30, 1871.	Augustine & Seibold . . .	$41.50	$41.50

FAIRVIEW.

Nov. 6.	Citizens, by G. Gates	5.10	5.10

HOPKINTON.

Oct. 25.	Citizens, by C. E. Merriam . . .	90.35	90.35

LAWRENCE.

Oct. 21.	Citizens, by G. Grosvenor, Mayor .	5,000.00	5,000.00

LEAVENWORTH.

Oct. 16.	Citizens, ...	9,581.15	
18.	Opera House Theatrical Performance	257.00	
	Iron Moulders	50.00	
27.	Workingmen's Association, by Thos. Jones	266.75	
Feb. 26, 1872.	Major Taylor	5.00	10,159,90

OSWEGO.

Oct. 23, 1871.	Hobert & Langwell . . .	34.00	34.00

PAOLA.

Oct. 23.	St. James Church	5.00	5.00

TOPEKA.

Oct. 16.	Citizens	5,400.00	5,400.00

WHITE CLOUD.

Oct. 24.	Citizens, by O. Bailey	100.00	100.00

WYANDOTTE.

Nov. 8.	Citizens, by P. Connolly . . .	396.00	396.00
			$21,231.85

STATE OF NEBRASKA.

FREMONT.

Oct. 19, 1871.	St. James Episcopal Church .	$25.00	$25.00

LINCOLN.

Oct. 27.	Jno. Eaton	100.00	100.00

NEBRASKA CITY.

Dec. 12.	Citizens, W. W. Bell, Treasurer .	826.37	826.37

OMAHA.

Oct. 16.	Citizens, ...	7,000.00	
18.	"	5,000.00	
Nov. 21.	Citizens, C. W. Mead, Treasurer .	2,000.00	
Dec. 1.	" " " .	314.55	
Jan. 11, 1872.	Contributions Employés U. P. R. R. Co., by Charles S. Stebbins .	1,481.90	
27.	Balance " " " .	153.50	15,949.95

PLATTSMOUTH.

Oct. 18, 1871.	Citizens, by T. A. Riorden .	569.00	569.00
			$17,470.32

COLORADO TERRITORY.

CENTRAL CITY.

Oct. 28, 1871.	Citizens, by H. Butler. .	$2,100.00	$2,100.00

DENVER.

Oct. 17.	Citizens, by J. Harper, Mayor . .	7,220.73	
21.	St. John's Church	61.00	
23.	Citizens, additional	1,432.00	
Jan. 20, 1872.	Citizens, balance, John Harper, Mayor	182.07	8,895.80

GEORGETOWN.

Oct. 25, 1871.	Children	3.80	
Nov. 1.	Citizens, by W. H. Cushman . .	1,200.00	1,203.80

GOLDEN CITY.

Oct. 18.	Citizens, ...	341.00	341.00

GREELY.

Oct. 18.	Citizens, by F. W. West	225.00	
Nov. 17.	" "	69.50	
Dec. 4.	Two boys	.75	295.25
			$12,835.85

NEVADA TERRITORY.

MOUNTAIN CITY.

Oct. 26, 1871.	Citizens, by J. P. Cross (gold) .	$177.00	
Nov. 2.	Premium thereon	20.80	$197.80

VIRGINIA CITY.

Oct. 26.	Proceeds Concert by Miss Belle Taussig (gold)	406.00	
	Employés Crown Point Gold and Silver Mining Co. (gold)	764.50	
Nov. 2.	Premium thereon	137.53	1,308.03
			$1,505.83

STATE OF CALIFORNIA.

BENICIA.

Oct. 27, 1871.	Miss H. M. Field, Ladies' Seminary	$22.72	$22.72

CACHEVILLE.

Nov. 1.	Misses Elsie Babcock and Emma Bonham	69.00	69.00

CHICO, BUTTE Co.

Nov. 4.	Citizens, by J. Bidwell (gold)	500.00	
	Premium on gold	56.25	556.25

EUREKA.

Nov. 15.	Citizens, by Weeks & Vance	337.28	337.28

GILROY.

Nov. 4.	St. Stephen's Episcopal Church	7.00	7.00

HAYWOOD.

Nov. 3.	Congregational Church	35.00	35.00

MOKELUMNE HILL.

Oct. 25.	Citizens, of Calaveras County	17.63	17.63

NEVADA COUNTY.

Nov. 7.	Citizens, by A. H. Parker (gold)	750.55	
	Premium on gold	69.64	820.19

NEW ALMADEN.

Nov. 10.	Quicksilver Mines	97.22	97.22

OAKLAND.

Oct. 26.	Additional subscription, N. W. Spaulding, Mayor	15.00	
Oct. 26.	Citizens, by 9th National Bank of New York (gold)	10,000.00	
30.	Premium on gold	1,200.00	11,215.00

PETALUMA.

Oct. 30.	Brass Band	46.90	46.90

RENO.

Jan. 12, 1872.	Citizens, L. H. Dyer, Treasurer	176.75	176.75

SACRAMENTO.

Oct. 23, 1871.	Sacramento Savings Bank (gold)	1,000.00	
30.	Premium on gold ($1,000.00)	117.50	

	Citizens, C. H. Swift, Mayor.	20,000.00	
Feb. 23, 1872.	Employés C. P. R. R. (5,182 in number), by A. N. Towne, Gen. Sup't	9,002.87	30,120.37

SALINAS CITY.

Nov. 2, 1871.	Citizens, by R. L. Porter (gold)	135.60	
	Premium on above	15.80	151.40

SAN FRANCISCO.

Oct. 27.	Members California Theatres (gold)	1,442.75	
	Board of Brokers (gold)	8,000.00	
	Mrs. Lapige (gold)	100.00	
	Premium on $8,100 gold	1,002.38	
30.	Premium on gold ($1,442.75)	173.13	
Nov. 9.	Citizens, by T. H. Selby, Mayor	100,000.00	
Dec. 1.	Citizens, balance, by T. H. Selby, Mayor	10,038.62	120,756.88

SAN JOSE.

Oct. 27.	Citizens	2,500.00	2,500.00

STOCKTON.

Oct. 27.	Fire Department	111.75	
	City appropriation	1,101.67	1,213.42

U. S. NAVY YARD, MARE ISLAND.

Jan. 9, 1871.	Officers and Employés, E. C. Doran, Pay Director	369.42	369.42
			$168,512.43

STATE OF OREGON.

PORTLAND.

Oct. 24, 1871.	Citizens, by Henry Failing, President	10,000.00	
Dec. 14.	Citizens, by P. Wasserman, Mayor	3,000.00	
March 5, 1872.	Citizens, balance, per P. Wasserman, Mayor	883.52	13,883.52
			$13,883.52

DACOTAH TERRITORY.

DACOTAH.

Oct. 16, 1871.	Headquarters U. S. Army, by officers	$90.00	90.00
			$90.00

WASHINGTON TERRITORY.

LA CONNOR, Whatcom Co.

Feb. 17, 1872.	Citizens, by Roger S. Greene, Treasurer	$60.00	$60.00

OLYMPIA.

Oct. 25, 1871.	Citizens, by Marshall Blinn . .	100.00	
Feb. 17, 1872.	Citizens, by Roger S. Greene, Treasurer	505.49	605.49

PORT DISCOVERY.

Feb. 17.	Citizens, by Roger S. Greene, Treasurer	166.66	166.66

SEABECK.

Feb. 17.	Citizens, by Roger S. Greene, Treasurer	138.88	138.88

UTSALADY.

March 18.	Citizens, by Roger S. Greene, Treasurer	38.80	38.80

VANCOUVER.

Oct. 24, 1871.	Citizens, by Henry Failing, President	450.00	
Nov. 13.	Citizens, per H. W. Janes, Treasurer .	50.00	500.00
			$1,509.83

UTAH TERRITORY.

OGDEN CITY.

Nov. 14, 1871.	Citizens, by L. J. Herrick, Mayor	$604.65	$604.65

SALT LAKE CITY.

Oct. 18.	Citizens, by D. H. Wells, Mayor . .	12,000.00	
Nov. 4.	Citizens, additional " " . .	2,776.46	14,776.46
			$15,381.11

WYOMING TERRITORY.

LARAMIE.

Dec. 14, 1871.	Employés Western Division U. P. R. R., L. Fillmore, D. S. . . .	$800.00	800.00
			$800.00

NEW MEXICO.

ALBUQUERQUE.

Nov. 13.	Citizens, W. M. Guinness . . .	$65.00———	$65.00

FORT UNION.

Oct. 20.	Citizens, by A. S. Kimball . . .	311.00———	311.00

GRAND ARMY OF THE REPUBLIC.

Nov. 8.	Post No. 2, by General Rucker, U. S. A.	40.00———	40.00

LOS VEGAS.

Oct. 23.	Citizens, by John Dold	400.00———	400.00

MORENO MINES, COLFAX CO.

Nov. 1.	Citizens, by Thomas Lowthear. . .	255.50———	255.50

SANTA FÉ.

Oct. 20.	Citizens, by M. Kayser, Chairman . .	424.00———	424.00
			$1,495.50

MISCELLANEOUS.

Oct. 15, 1871.	Widow's mite	$1.00
	Two poor men, $1 each	2.00
	Charity	10.00
16.	Charity, per C. C. P. Holden . . .	2.55
17.	Charity, unknown	5.00
	A friend	5.00
	Unknown, to impoverished . . .	5.00
	Unknown poor man's mite . . .	1.00
	Unknown contributor	1.00
18.	Unknown, ...	1.00
	Unknown	20.00
	No name	1.00
20.	Unknown, mite	2.00
21.	An Englishman	15.00
23.	R.	10.00
	Friend	5.00
26.	Unknown	1.00
28.	Unknown	1.00
	Unknown, per C. B. & Q. R. R. 361.24 bushels corn	180.70
Nov. 4.	Contents of wallet	.25
2.	Child's contribution	1.00
15.	Unknown, from Tribune office . . .	5.00
16.	Englishmen, per S. M. Moore . . .	26.40

	James Twiggs, orphan	.50	
	No name	.50	
17.	Friend of the needy	5.00	
24.	Unknown, per C. B. & Q. R. R., 181.34 bushels corn	79.91	
28.	" " 301.20 bushels corn	135.55	
Dec. 1.	Unknown	10.00	
6.	Unknown, proceeds sale car load apples and potatoes	26.85	
Jan. 8, 1872.	Unknown	1.00	
	A poor blind man	.35	561.56
			$561.56

CANADA.

AURORA.

Oct. 19, 1871.	D. W. Doane, P. M.	$41.00	$41.00

BARRIE, Ont.

Oct. 18.	C. H. Clark	25.00	25.00

BELLEVILLE.

Oct. 27.	Citizens, by Thomas Hilden, Mayor, gold *	500.00	
Nov. 24.	Officers of Deaf and Dumb Institute, gold *	31.00	531.00

BRADFORD, Ont.

Nov. 21.	A friend of some poor widow	5.00	5.00

BRANTFORD, Ont.

Nov. 20.	Citizens, by W. E.	23.26	23.26

CLIFTON.

Oct. 31.	Citizens, by F. J. Preston	468.73	
	Premium on Canada currency.	9.69	478.42

COLLINGWOOD.

Oct. 19.	Citizens, by D. Watson, Mayor	500.00	
	Premium on Canada currency	55.00	555.00

GODERICH.

Oct. 27.	Town appropriation, gold *	500.00	500.00

GUELPH.

Oct. 19.	Swiss Bell Ringers, gold.	60.00	
	Premium on gold	7.17	67.17

* These donations were collected by the "Bank of Montreal," and premiums thereon are included in its statement of sale of gold, January 15, 1872.

HAMILTON.

Oct. 21.	Citizens, by E. B. Chisholm, Mayor, gold *	2,000.00	
Dec. 29.	" " " " "	3,400.00	
March 22, 1872.	Premium on gold ($3,400), per E. B. Chisholm, Mayor	322.59	5,722.59

KESWICK, ONT.

Nov. 18, 1871.	A. G. P. Dodge	1,000.00	1,000.00

KINGSTON.

Oct. 18.	Citizens, by J. Carruthers & Co. . .	2,000.00	
27.	Citizens, by A. Livingston, Mayor . .	2,000.00	
Nov. 4.	" " " balance	145.88	4,145.88

LYNEDOCH.

Nov. 8.	Citizens, by W. A. Charlton	111.00	111.00

MADOC.

Oct. 21.	Citizens, by A. F. Wood, gold * . .	500.00	500.00

MONTREAL.

Oct. 27.	City appropriation, gold * . .	50,000.00
	Citizens, C. J. Brydges, Chairman, U. S. Currency	10,000.00
Dec. 26.	Grand Trunk Railway employés, gold *	2,529.23
	and U. S. currency	760.50
	Proceeds Amateur Concert, by F. Boscovitz, gold *	431.00
	Donations of —	
	R. B. Angus, gold *	100.00
	W. E. Logan, gold *	100.00
	Bank of British N. America, gold * .	15.00
	A Friend, gold *	5.00
	C. D. Proctor, gold *	20.00
	P. S. Ross & Brother, gold * . .	20.00
	W. J. Anderson, gold *	10.00
	W. H. Brimacombe, gold * . .	5.00
	G. A. Farmer, gold *	2.00
	J. Carr Griffin, gold *	5.00
	W. S. Smith, gold *	5.00
	H. Benjamin, gold *	5.00
	D. McArthur, gold *	2.50
	R. A. & Control Department, gold *	75.00
30.	Citizens' fund, C. J. Brydges, Chairman, gold *	48,610.25

Of this amount $37,133.13 was expended in purchases by Citizens' Committee, and balance paid Treasurer in gold, $11,477.12.

* See note on page 418.

Jan. 15, 1872.	Premium in New York, on gold received by Bank of Montreal, by Richard Bell & C. F. Smithers, 8 11-16 per cent. on $86,205.89	7,489.13	120,189.61

NAPANEE, ONT.

Nov. 22, 1871.	Citizens, at Bank of Montreal, gold *	400.00	400.00

ONSLOW.

Jan. 12, 1872.	Municipality, by Bank of Montreal, gold	100.00	
March 14.	Premium on gold	10.00	110.00

OTTAWA, PR. QUEBEC.

Dec. 27, 1871.	H. O. Burritt, Esq., check	50.00	50.00

QUEBEC.

Dec. 6.	City contribution, P. Gaineau, Mayor, gold *	3,164.95	3,164.95

SAINT ANDREW'S, QUEBEC.

Oct. 18.	The Jones family	112.30	112.30

SHERBROOKE.

Oct. 21.	Citizens, by W. Griffith	1,000.00	
27.	Citizens, by R. N. Hall, gold *	764.40	
Nov. 9.	Citizens, " " balance, gold *	38.69	1,803.09

SIMCOE, ONT.

Oct. 18.	D. B. Wallace	5.00	5.00

ST. ARMAND, P. Q.

Oct. 21.	Citizens, by Mayor Montreal	48.65	48.65

STAYNER, ONT.

Oct. 21.	Citizens	74.30	74.30

ST. CATHERINE'S.

Oct. 27.	Citizens, by W. A. Miltenberger, gold *	2,000.00	2,000.00

TORONTO.

Oct. 19.	Employés "Globe"	177.85	
Nov. 2.	City contribution, gold *	10,000.00	
11.	William Blakie, proceeds $10 gold	11.11	
Nov. 14.	Employés St. Lawrence Foundry, gold *	500.00	10,688.96

COUNTY OF WATERLOO, ONT.

Dec. 26.	Per Bank of Montreal, gold *	1,000.00	1,000.00

* See note on page 418.

WINNIPEG, MANITOBA, AND PARISH OF KILDONAN.

Jan. 27, 1872.	Citizens, by John Sutherland, M. P. P., £21 proceeds	110.60	110.60
			$153.462.78

NOVA SCOTIA.

HALIFAX.

Oct. 20, 1871.	Hon. M. M. Jackson, U. S. Consul	$50.00	
Dec. 15.	Citizens, John Doull, Treasurer, proceeds $6,007 gold	6,547.63	
March 5, 1872.	A. N. Heatherington, Esq.	55.00	
21.	Citizens, balance, by John Doull, Treasurer, gold	50.00	
30.	Premium on same	5.00	$6,707.63
			$6,707.63

NEWFOUNDLAND.

ST. JOHN'S.

Dec. 13, 1871.	James Lyons Norman, Government Secretary	$1,090.00	$1,090.00
			$1,090.00

NEW BRUNSWICK.

ST. JOHN'S.

Feb. 6, 1872.	Citizens, per W. Richardson, Treasurer, Chicago, $8,634.55 gold at 109½	$9,411.64	$9,411.64
			$9,411.64

BRITISH COLUMBIA.

VICTORIA.

Dec. 4, 1871.	Residents, D. Eckstein, U. S. Consul	$535.70	$535.70

BARKERSVILLE AND LOWHEE, CARIBOO.

Feb. 1, 1872.	Wesleyan Congregations, by David Eckstein, U. S. Consul at Victoria, British Columbia	105.00	105.00
			$640.70

ISLAND OF CUBA.

HAVANA.

Nov. 6, 1871.	Merchants and others by S. De Visser, New York . . .	$10,000.00	$10,000.00

MATANZAS, CARDENAS, CIENFUEGOS, CAIBARIEN.

Dec. 1.	Citizens, by H. C. Hall, U. S. Consul at Havana	6,393.37	6,393.37
			$16,393.37

MEXICO.

CITY OF MEXICO.

Jan. 11, 1872.	German citizens, through U. S. Department, Washington (gold) .	$557.00	
11.	Citizens' subscriptions " "	1,449.40	
August 20.	Premium on gold	265.85	$2,272.25
			$2,272.25

CENTRAL AMERICA.

ASPINWALL.

Nov. 22, 1871.	C. E. Perry, U. S. Consul . .	$25.00	$25.00

COSTA RICA.

Dec. 21.	Hon. C. N. Riotte, U. S. Minister . .	27.25	27.25

PANAMA.

Jan. 5, 1872.	Citizens, O. M. Long, U. S. Consul	350.00	350.00
			$402.25

SOUTH AMERICA.

VENEZUELA.

CARACAS.

Jan. 27, 1872.	Contributions at U. S. Legation, by W. A. Pile, gold	$269.48	
Feb. 6.	Premium on gold	26.15	$295.63
			$295.63

BRAZIL.

RIO JANEIRO.

Date	Description	Amount		Total
Dec. 28, 1871.	Citizens' subscription, Hon. J. R. Partridge, U. S. Envoy, Chairman, £1,566 2s. 11d.	$8,250.00		
Jan. 13, 1872.	Commander-in-chief, officers and crew of U. S. Flagship "Lancaster," £60	317.33		
26.	Contributions at U. S. Consulate, Francis M. Cordeira, Vice Consul, £57 14s. 7d. proceeds	305.97		
April 20.	Contributions at U. S. Consulate . .	223.00	———	$9,096.30

SANTOS.

Date	Description	Amount		Total
Jan. 26.	Contributions by W. T. Wright, U. S. Consul, £278 12s. 11d. . . .	1,467.53		
March 6.	Additional contributions, by the same, £21 8s. 9d.	113.38	———	1,580.91
				$10,677.21

ARGENTINE REPUBLIC.

BUENOS AYRES.

Date	Description	Amount		Total
Jan. 27.	Citizens, by John C. Zimmerman, Treasurer, gold	$711.12		
	Premium on same	69.33		
March 1.	Don Domingo F. Sarmiento, President, 2,000 mil Reas	80.00		
14.	Premium on same, gold	8.00	———	868.45
				$868.45

URUGUAY.

MONTE VIDEO.

Date	Description	Amount		Total
Feb. 29.	Subscriptions, by John S. Stevens, U. S. Consul	$1,316.33		
March 25.	Premium on same, less exchange . .	124.72	———	1,441.05
				$1,441.05

PERU.

CALLAO.

Date	Description	Amount		Total
Dec. 27, 1871.	Citizens, by D. J. Williamson, U. S. Consul	$10,000.00		

March 4, 1872.	Contributions by U. S. Ship "Ossippee," George W. Beaman, paymaster, gold	125.00	
15.	Premium on same	12.50	$10,137.50

SAN JOSE DE LAMBAYEQUE.

April 10.	Subscriptions, by William B. Fry, U. S. Consular Agent, £32 16s. 3d. . .	173.91	173.91
			$10,311.41

SANDWICH ISLANDS.

HONOLULU.

Dec. 13, 1871.	Contributions, by A. J. Cartwright, Chairman	$1,635.00	1,635.00
			$1,635.00

CHINA.

CANTON.

April 12, 1872.	Per R. G. W. Jewell, U. S. Consul, £263 16s., proceeds, .	$1,409.86	$1,409.86
	Being contributions of foreign residents, silver dollars $655.00		
	Of Chinese residents, do. 546.74		
	Silver $1,201.74		

HONG KONG.

Jan. 6, 1872.	Proceeds of concert by "German Leidestafel," Amateur Society, by D. H. Bailey, U. S. Consul	$894.89	
Feb. 8.	"German Leidestafel," balance proceeds concert, by D. H. Bailey, U. S. Consul, gold	150.00	
	William Dolan and Captain Theabaud, Americans, at H. K.	33.00	
14.	Premiums on above	18.98	
April 26.	Choral Society, James K. Houghtrie, Secretary	344.09	
May 6.	Premium on same	46.88	1,487.84
			$2,897.70

INDIA.

BOMBAY.

March 1.	Master of "Lodge Cyrus," of Bombay, by B. F. Farnham, U. S. Consul, 50 rupees	$26.58	$26.58

EGUTPOORA (near Bombay.)

Feb. 1.	Lodge "Friendship and Harmony," per B. F. Farnham, U. S. Consul, at Bombay, £4 19s.	26.34	26.34

JUBBULPORE.

Feb. 24.	"Lodge Alexandra," for the craft or Blue Lodge, by B. F. Farnham, U. S. Consul, Bombay	26.64	26.64

SATTARA.

Feb. 24.	R. F. Mactior, 100 reals, by B. F. Farnham, U. S. Consul, Bombay . .	53.29	53.29

SEEBSAGOR, Assam.

May 7.	Subscriptions of Tea-planters, etc., by W. Kitts, Esq., 254 Rupees, 8 an. . .	127.25	127.25

SINGAPORE.

March 16.	Subscriptions by A. G. Studer, U. S. Consul, £384 0s. 7d.	2,065.22	2,065.22
			$2,325.32

GREAT BRITAIN.

ENGLAND.

ASHTON-UNDER-LYNE.

Feb. 19, 1872.	Inhabitants, James Buckley, Chairman, £868 17s. 10d., by A. T. Stewart & Co.	$4,678.00	$4,678.00

BIRMINGHAM.

Oct. 18, 1871.	Citizens, Hon. George B. Lloyd, £2,000	10,978.83
Nov. 13.	The same, £1,500	8,157.22
18.	Citizens, by J. S. Gould, U. S. Consul	163.00
Dec. 12.	" " " .	50.75
Jan. 19, 1872.	Contributions, by J. S. Gould, U. S. Consul, in gold and Canada currency	485.75

Date	Description	Amount	Total
	Premiums thereon	40.50	
	In American currency	6.00	
Dec. 10.	Proceeds £64 11s. 11d., per J. S. Morgan & Co., London	352.75	20,234.80

BRADFORD.

Date	Description	Amount	Total
Oct. 30, 1871.	Joint remittance from Bradford, England, and Greenock, Scotland, £2,800	15,270.40	
Nov. 2.	Citizens, £2,000	10,895.03	
15.	Citizens, £1,000	5,416.95	
Jan. 28, 1871.	Citizens, through London American Committee, by Drexel, Morgan, & Co.	4,296.75	35,879.13

BRIGHTON.

Date	Description	Amount	Total
Dec. 27, 1871.	Citizens, by London and Westminster Bank, £300	1,614.99	1,614.99

BRISTOL.

Date	Description	Amount	Total
Nov. 21.	Citizens, by Baring Bros. & Co. £1,000 .	5,401.91	
May 6, 1872.	Donation of City, per advice H. T. Parker, Honorary Secretary C. R. Fund, £1,182 2s. 10d. . . .	6,342.85	
16.	Balance citizens' subscriptions, G. B. Floyd, ex-mayor, £588 12s. 3d. . .	3,165.43	14,910.19

CHESHIRE.

Date	Description	Amount	Total
Nov. 8, 1871.	Ambrose Sutton, Esq.	500.00	500.00

EXETER.

Date	Description	Amount	Total
April 3, 1872.	Citizens, by Josh. Harding, Mayor, £63	334.64	334.64

GASTON VILLAGE, NEAR LIVERPOOL.

Date	Description	Amount	Total
Dec. 19, 1871.	Citizens, by Robert Trimble, £16 .	84.98	84.98

HALIFAX.

Date	Description	Amount	Total
April 12, 1872.	Mr. John Lewis, per Field, Leiter, & Co., £25	134.17	134.17

HULL.

Date	Description	Amount	Total
Nov. 27, 1871.	Citizens, by London and Westminster Bank, £300	1,614.99	
Jan. 10, 1872.	Additional contributions, H. F. Atkinson, U. S. Consular agent, £90 1s. 6d.	471.06	
May 10.	From same, £21	116.10	2,202.15

JERSEY.

March 6.	Subscriptions, by Thomas Renouf, U. S. Consular agent, £52 9s. 4d. . . .	280.99	280.99

KIDDERMINSTER.

Nov. 21, 1871.	Citizens, by Morgan & Co., London, £500	2,700.95	2,700.95

LINCOLN.

Jan. 27, 1872.	Citizens, by Hon. Charles Pratt, Treasurer, £120 8s. 9d. . . .	637.87	637.87

LONDON.

Through Drexel, Morgan, & Co., New York.

Oct. 14, 1871.	American Committee,	£3,300	18,252.36	
23.	" "	3,600	19,597.35	
Nov. 7.	" "	2,000	10,888.21	
Oct. 14.	Guinness Corporation	1,000	5,811.20	
17.	Mansion House Committee	7,000	38,527.25	
23.	" "	15,000	81,564.97	
25.	" "	8,000	43,815.15	
	J. S. Morgan & Co., bankers . .		5,000.00	
31.	Mansion House Committee	1,500	8,161.05	
Nov. 7.	" "	4,000	21,776.41	
17.	" "	£7,730 2s. 6d.	41,903.09	
	Total		$295,297.04	
Oct. 23.	Jay Cooke, McCulloch, & Co.. . .		5,000.00	
Nov. 9.	London "Corn Trade," by J. H. Reed, New York		3,549.26	
15.	Lieutenant-general Howden, £50 . .		270.09	
20.	Stevens & Haynes, law publishers, No. 13 Bellyard, Temple Bar, £10 . .		53.95	
Jan. 13, 1872.	American Committee, London, through Drexel, Morgan & Co., £1,000, proceeds		5,304.09	
Dec. 10.	Balance funds received by late Lord Mayor, per J. S. Morgan & Co., London, £1,213 0s. 9d. . . .		6,624.50	316,098.93

MILNROW.

Dec. 27, 1871.	Citizens, by London and Westminster Bank, £298 8s. 4d. . . .	1,606.47	1,606.47

NEWCASTLE-ON-TYNE.

Nov. 7.	Citizens, £1,000	5,444.10	
Jan. 26, 1872.	Subscriptions £600, per American Committee, London	3,178.83	

Jan. 17, 1873. Balance citizens' subscriptions, by B. Plummer, Jr., Secretary, £200 sterling . . . . 1,093.33 —— 9,716.26

NOTTINGHAM.

Nov. 23, 1871. Citizens, by Glynn, Mills, Currie, & Co., London, £1,000 . . . . 5,388.65

Jan. 23, 1872. Fleirsheim, Feilmann, & Co., £25, proceeds, by Carson, Pirie, & Co. . 133.75

25. Collection, by Samuel George Johnson, Town Clerk, £918, proceeds . . 4,845.11 —— 10,367.51

PETERBOROUGH.

Dec. 20, 1871. Citizens, by London and Westminster Bank, £40 1s. 10d. . . . 213.16 —— 213.16

ROCHDALE.

Dec. 9. Citizens, by Drexel, Morgan, & Co., £500 2,673.48

Jan. 25, 1872. Rochester Eq. P. Society, by J. R. Shepherd, President, £20 . . . 105.99 —— 2,779.47

ST. HELENS.

Jan. 11. Citizens, U. S. Consulate, J. Hammell, Secretary, gold 547.72

August 20. Premium on gold . . . . . 72.57 —— 620.29

SOUTHAMPTON.

Dec. 10, 1872. Citizens, proceeds £93 2s. 6d. by J. S. Morgan & Co., London . . . 508.61 —— 508.61

SOUTHPORT, near Liverpool.

Jan. 2, 1872. W. H. Newett, Esq., proceeds of Concert, £10 5s. . . . . . 54.44 —— 54.44

STAFFORDSHIRE POTTERIES.

Nov. 18, 1871. By Chamber of Commerce, £500 2,688.80

Feb. 10, 1872. Chamber of Commerce, £600, by E. M. Archibald, Br. Consul-general, N. Y. . . . . 3,226.65 —— 5,915.45

SUNDERLAND.

May 10. Citizens, by W. Nicholson, Mayor, £181 17s. 6d. . . . . 1,008.40 —— 1,008.40

SUNDRY SMALL TOWNS.

March 6. By advice of H. T. Parker, Hon. Secretary C. R. Fund, London, Feb. 9, £317 17s. 2d. . . . . . . 1,705.49 —— 1,705.49

WALSALL, Staffordshire.

Dec. 12, 1871. Citizens, by Drexel, Morgan, & Co., £250 . . . . 1,329.17 —— 1,329.17

$435,023.18

WALES.

CARDIFF.

Dec. 23, 1871. Citizens, by Drexel, Morgan, & Co., £555 18s. 9d. . . . $2,954.28 —— $2,954.28

NEWPORT.

Dec. 23. Citizens, by Drexel, Morgan, & Co., £28 3s. $148.78

Oct. 10, 1872. Citizens, by Col. H. H. Davies, U. S. Consul, Cardiff, £11 0s. 4d. . . . 60.40 —— 209.18

$3,163.46

IRELAND.

BANBRIDGE.

Dec. 1, 1871. Citizens, by Robert McClelland, Chairman, £400 . . . $2,151.11 —— $2,151,11

BELFAST.

Through Drexel, Morgan, & Co.

Oct. 31.	Citizens, £4,000	21,762.80		
Nov. 7.	" 100	544.41		
13.	" 900	4,894.32		
Dec. 12.	" 1,370	7,316.99	——	34,518.52

CARRICK ON SHANNON.

Dec. 30. Collection of Mrs. William Peyton, of "Castle Carrow" £70 13s. 6d. . . . 373.79 —— 373.79

CORK.

Dec. 12, 1871. Citizens, by Lord Mayor, £500 . 2,666.67

Feb. 10, 1872. Additional subscriptions, by Right Hon. John Daly, Lord Mayor, £469 2,509.15 —— 5,175.82

DUBLIN.

Oct. 19, 1871.	Citizens, by Ranney & Inglis, Chicago,	£500	2,764.30
Nov. 6.	Citizens, by J. Campbell, Mayor	1,000	5,401.80
20.	" "	1,000	5,395.84
28.	" "	1,000	5,383.68
Dec. 21.	" "	1,000	5,286.41

Feb. 12, 1872. Citizens, by John Campbell, ex-mayor, £157 2s.	841.36	25,073.39

LIMERICK.

Nov. 15, 1871. Citizens, by Mayor, £300 . .	1,620.55	
June 6, 1872. Citizens' subscriptions, second installment of £50, by Archibald Murray, Hon. Secretary	267.35	1,887.90

LONDONDERRY.

Feb. 6. Citizens, by Pitt Skipton, Mayor, £216	1,156.80	
March 16. Same, £10	53.78	1,210.58

NEWRY.

Nov. 21, 1871. Citizens, by Mayor, £200 . .	1,080.38	
Jan. 10, 1872. Additional subscriptions of £131 12s. 9d., from Francis Horner, Treasurer	698.41	1,778.79

TUAM.

Nov. 25, 1871. Archbishop John of Tuam, £50	267.34	
April 22, 1872. By the same, citizens' additional subscriptions, £110	591.50	
June 3. By the same, citizens' third contribution, £55 6s. 2d	306.15	1,164.99

WATERFORD.

Nov. 21, 1871. Citizens, by Mayor, £150 . .	810.29	
April 15, 1872. Citizens, by E. W. Kenney, Mayor's Secretary, £3	16.18	826.47
		$74,161.36

SCOTLAND.

ABERDEEN.

Nov. 17, 1871. Citizens, by James Warrack, Chicago, £1,000	$5,406.11	
Feb. 27, 1872. Citizens, additional, by R. Lumsden, Hon. Treasurer, £659 14s. 9d. .	3,547.92	$8,954.03

AYR.

Jan. 12. Citizens, by Henderson Bros., Glasgow	381.18	381.18

CATRINE, AYRSHIRE.

Feb. 14. Collections by Rev. J. M. Copland, £8 2s. 8d., by Henderson Bros. . .	42.95	42.95

CUMNOCK.

Jan. 8.	Workmen in Ayrshire Nurseries, by Henderson Bros.	18.85	18.85

DUMBARTON.

Dec. 12, 1871.	Citizens, by Henderson Bros., Glasgow, £295	1,565.20	1,565.20

DUNDEE.

Nov. 21.	Citizens, by Provost, £1,000	5,401.91	
25.	" " 600	3,226.56	
Feb. 22, 1872.	Citizens, by Robert Stewart, Hon. Treasurer, £201 12s. 6d.	1,082.06	9.710.53

DUNFERMLINE.

Feb. 13.	Second installment, per P. Donald & Co. (1st paid to N. Y. Chamb. Commerce),	553.90	
29.	Additional, £2 16s.	15.00	568.90

GALASHIELS.

Nov. 21, 1871.	Citizens, by Robert Stewart, Town Clerk, £140	756.27	756.27

GLASGOW.

Nov. 19.	Citizens, by Henderson Brothers, £5,000 proceeds	26,934.00	
Dec. 6.	2,000 "	10,656.00	
Jan. 17, 1872.	1,000 "	5,233.34	
Feb. 2.	500 "	2,616.67	45,440.01

KILMARNOCK.

Feb. 2, 1872.	Citizens, by Henderson Brothers, Glasgow, £100	523.33	523.33

KIRCALDY.

Nov. 21, 1871.	Citizens, by Commercial Bank of Scotland, £100	540.19	
Dec. 12	The same, £100	533.33	1,073.52

LANARK.

Jan. 18, 1872.	Citizens, by W. Brown, Provost, £72	381.20	381.20

PAISLEY.

Nov. 21, 1871.	Citizens, by Provost, £600	3,241.14	
March 25, 1872.	Citizens, per David Murray, Provost, £157 10s.	850.50	4,091.64

PERTH AND PERTHSHIRE.

Date	Description	Amount	Total
Nov. 21, 1871.	Citizens, by Provost, £300 . .	1,620.57	
April 3, 1872.	Balance subscriptions, per D. Morton, City Treasurer of Perth, £35 .	187.44	1,808.01
			$75,315.62

THE CONTINENT.

FRANCE.

DUNKIRK.

Date	Description	Amount	Total
April 1, 1872.	Citizens, by E. B. Washburne, U. S. Minister at Paris, gold, 375 fr., proceeds	$84.66	$84.66

HAVRE.

Date	Description	Amount	Total
April 1.	Citizens, by E. B. Washburne, U. S. Minister at Paris, 4,625 fr. proceeds .	1,044.08	
15.	Subscription, Chamber Commerce, by E. B. Washburne, U. S. Minister to France, gold	446.15	
23.	Premium on same	49.63	1,539.86

PARIS.

Date	Description	Amount	Total
Oct. 27, 1871.	American residents, by John Monroe & Co.	30,000.00	
Nov. 1.	" " "	12,000.00	
2.	Frederick T. Palmer and sister, per E. B. Washburne, U. S. Minister . .	200.00	
Dec. 18.	August Seydoux, Lieber, & Co. . .	1,086.25	
23.	American residents, balance subscription, by John Monroe & Co. . . .	10,595.47	
26.	Subscriptions, through H. L. Hoguet, New York	3,500.00	
Feb. 28, 1872.	G. Delahante, 1,000 fr. per H. W. Derby, New York	1,050.42	
Oct. 26.	Balance subscriptions by Americans in Paris, 12,675 fr. by J. Monroe & Co.	2,726.14	61,158.18
			$62,782 80

BELGIUM.

ANTWERP.

Date	Description	Amount	Total
Dec. 14, 1871.	American and English Church, Rev. Mr. Byron	$121.00	
Jan. 2, 1872.	Unknown, by George Schneider, Esq., Chicago, 45 fr	10.00	$131.00
			$131.00

HOLLAND.

ARNHEM.

Jan. 18, 1872.	Publishers of "Arnhemske Courant," by Rev. E. Van Norden . .	$6.65	$6.65

THE HAGUE.

Dec. 27, 1871.	Contributions at U. S. Legation, C. T. Gorham	72.66	
Feb. 2, 1872.	Donation, Basch & Son, of "Utrecht Dagblad," by C. T. Gorham, U. S. Legation at Hague	34.14	
12.	Premium on same	3.58	110.38

ROTTERDAM.

Nov. 9, 1871.	American residents, by F. Schultz, Consul	124.32	124.32
			$241.35

GERMANY.

AIX LA CHAPELLE.

March 1, 1872.	Citizens, by James Park, U. S. Consul, gold	$495.40	
	Premium thereon	49.54	$544.94

BADEN-BADEN.

Nov. 22, 1871.	Citizens, by W. H. Young, U. S. Consul	173.37	
Jan. 19, 1872.	Citizens of Baden-Baden, by W. H. Young, U. S. Consul, 155 fl. 15 krs. per H. Claussenius & Co.	67.35	240.72

BARMEN AND ELDERFELD.

Nov. 7.	Citizens, by Hon. Emil Hoechester, U. S. Consul	2,220.00	
11.	" " " .	2,212.50	
18.	" " " .	601.70	5,034.20

BERLIN.

Oct. 21.	Hardt & Co., citizens' subscription	15,000.00	
Nov. 4.	" " "	10,000.00	
9.	Hon. N. Fish, Secretary U. S. Legation	20.00	25,020.20

CASSELL.

Jan. 30.	Citizens, by W. P. Webster, U. S. Consul-general, gold	1,325.00	
	Premium on same	132.50	1,457.50

CHEMNITZ.

Date	Description			
Dec. 18, 1871.	Citizens, by Vietor & Achellis, New York		3,282.86	3,282.86

CREFELD.

Date	Description			
Nov. 22.	Citizens, J. Magnus, U. S. Consular Agent (gold)	$2,045.00	2,249.50	
27.	" " "	1,164.75	1,272.48	
Dec. 23.	" " "	797.36	865.14	4,387.12

DRESDEN.

Date	Description		
Nov. 16.	American residents, by O. H. Irish, U. S. Consul	1,315.00	
Dec. 5.	S. S. Marvin	150.00	
7.	Citizens, by O. H. Irish, U. S. Consul	1,116.40	
March 19, 1873.	Balance subscriptions of citizens, by Robert Thode & Co., $60.80 at 115½	70.22	2,651.62

FRANKFORT-ON-THE-MAIN.

Date	Description		
Nov. 24.	Merchants and others, by J. & W. Seligman & Co., N. Y., $12,500 U. S. Bonds, proceeds	13,875.00	
Jan. 30, 1872.	Citizens, by W. P. Webster, U. S. Consul-general, gold	4,000.00	
Feb. 8.	Premium on same	400.00	18,275.00

HAMBURG.

Date	Description		
Nov. 22, 1871.	Mrs. M. M. Harbleicher, 10 thalers	7.70	
Dec. 20.	Citizens, by Kunhardt & Co., New York	4,645.39	4,653.09

HEIDELBERG.

Date	Description		
Jan. 22, 1872.	Neckarguemend & Dossenheim, in Baden, Germany, by Thomas Hilgard, Sr., of Heidelberg, per Thomas J. Kraft, Belleville, Illinois	471.00	471.00

HANAU.

Date	Description		
Jan. 30.	Citizens, by W. P. Webster, U. S. Consul-general, gold	500.00	
	Premium on same	50.00	550.00

LAHR AND FREIBURG.

Date	Description		
Feb. 2.	John Schneider, Mannheim, R.R. and U.S. Coupons, and premium, less U. S. tax	125.90	125.90

LUBEC.

Date	Description		
Feb. 6.	Citizens, by J. Meyer, Jr., U. S. Consular Agent, gold	463.66	
	Premium on same	46.36	510.02

MANHEIM, FREIBURG, LORRACH, LAHR, EMMINDINGEN, AND CONSTANZ.

Nov. 18, 1871.	Citizens, by Emil Hirsch, $4,000, gold		4,430.00	
Jan. 18, 1872.	14,089fl., gold .	5,800.00		
	Less first remittance, by Emil Hirsch, Secretary, Mannheim	4,000.00		
	Balance gold . . .	1,800.00		
	proceeds		1,953.00	
Feb. 21.	Balance of Mannheim, gold $55.00, proceeds		60.77	6,443.77

MAYENCE.

Dec. 4, 1871.	Citizens, by Mayor Carl Racke .	3,113.63	3,113.63

MEININGEN.

Feb. 5, 1872.	Coburg & Sonneberg Com., per H. J. Winser, U. S. Consul at Sonneberg, gold	1,015.46	
	Premium on same	106.62	1,122.08

MUNICH, BAVARIA.

Dec. 9, 1871.	Subscriptions at "Bayerische Vereinsbank," £145 11s. 7d. . . .	782.89	
Jan. 20, 1872.	Additional subscriptions through "Bayerische Vereinsbank," £7 19s. 4d. proceeds	42.18	
Feb. 9.	Additional subscriptions through "Bayerische Vereinsbank," gold . .	62.24	
14.	Premium on same	6.46	893.77

OFFENBACH.

Dec. 4, 1871.	Citizens, by Mayor Carl Racke .	500.00	500.00

PLAUEN.

March 7, 1872.	Contributions, by H. B. Ryder, U. S. Consul, Chemnitz . . .	176.00	176.00

RASTATT.

Jan. 18.	From Simon Meyer, sight draft on New York, gold	32.85	
	Premium on same	2.96	35.81

SINSHEIM, NEAR HEIDELBERG.

Dec. 28, 1871.	Citizens, by George A. Sidler .	50.83	50.83

SONNEBERG.

Nov. 16.	Contributions from his Consular District by H. J. Winser, U. S. Consul	1,333.50	

July 8, 1872.	Balance of same, gold, $25.73, proceeds	29.33	1,362.83

STRASBURG.

Jan. 6, 1872.	Citizens, by C. E. Ehrman, 2,340.55 fr. proceeds	490.60	490.06
			$81,393.29

AUSTRIA.

VIENNA.

Nov. 7, 1871.	George Griswold, by Hon. J. Jay	$500.00	
	C. G. Dinsmore, "	250.00	
	W. K. Marvin, "	200.00	
11.	Hon. John Jay, U. S. Minister	222.00	
	Augustine Heard	111.13	
	J. F. Delaplaine	166.50	
20.	Adolph Verdereau, 200 fr., proceeds	42.12	
March 4, 1872.	Kirsch Bros., agents Wheeler & Wilson Manufacturing Co., $100 gold, proceeds	110.00	
14.	Subscriptions, by P. S. Post, U. S. Consul	1,690.68	
June 3.	Balance of same, £91 7s. 2d. proceeds	509.07	3,801.50
			$3,801.50

SWITZERLAND.*

BASLE.

Nov. 22, 1871.	Citizens, proceeds 16,000 fr., by A. Goettel & Co.	$3,395.66	
Dec. 29.	" " additional	583,89	
1.	Contributions through U. S. Legation at Berne, from Geneva, Brugg, and other places (gold) $1,761.13, proceeds	1,933.06	
Feb. 17, 1872.	Citizens, additional, 102 fr. per A. Goettel & Co., New York.	21.47	
April 30.	Contributions in Alsace, 320 fr., by H. Erni, U. S. Consul, Basle, gold, proceeds	64.71	
Oct. 17.	Balance subscriptions of citizens, per Hon. J. Medill	7.44	$6,006.23

* NOTE. — From these donations, in accordance with wishes of donors, the Treasurer has paid to Henry Enderis, Swiss Consul at Chicago, $1,500.00.

BERNE AND CHAUX DE FONDS.

Jan. 15.	Citizens, proceeds of two Concerts, Horace Rublee, U. S. Legation, gold .	190.94	
Feb. 3.	Premium on same	16.67	207.61

ST. GALL.

Dec. 28, 1871.	Citizens, by S. H. M. Byers, U. S. Consul	1,121.22	1,121.22

ZURICH.

Nov. 21.	Citizens, by S. H. M. Byers, U. S. Consul	6,396.63	
Dec. 28.	" " " "	2,009.26	8,405.89
			$15,740.95

RUSSIA.

ST. PETERSBURG.

Feb. 17, 1872.	Contributions, by Eugene Schuyler, Sec. U. S. Legation, £27 3s. 9d., proceeds	$145.91	$145.91
			$145.91

ITALY.

GENOA.

Nov. 9, 1871.	Citizens per Granet, Brown, & Co., £50, proceeds	$271.38	
18.	The same, £25 15s. 9d., proceeds .	136.48	
April 30, 1872.	Contributions, by O. M. Spencer, U. S. Consul	15.00	$422.86

NICE.

Dec. 8, 1871.	Officers and crew of U. S. ship "Guerriere," by J. B. Creighton, Captain commanding, 891 fr., proceeds	182.56	182.56

TURIN.

Aug. 20, 1872.	Protestant Inhabitants of Italian Vaudois Vallies, by Rev. M. Meille, through Hon. G. P. Marsh, U. S. Minister at Rome, £44 5s. 6d., proceeds	242.29	242.29
			$847.71

PORTUGAL.

LISBON.

Dec. 21, 1871.	Countess of Edla, £60, proceeds of	$317.28	$317.28
			$317.28

ADDENDA.

RICHMOND, VIRGINIA.

July 9, 1873.	Manchester Presbyterian Church	$8.00	$8.00

CHICAGO, ILLINOIS.

Dec. 8, 1873.	First Presbyterian Church, Thanksgiving collection	142.40	
22.	A stranger	10.00	
	Hugh Gormley	25.00	
	E. E. Ryan	5.00	
Jan. 15, 1874.	C. A. Spring	25.00	
	Sundry	1.25	
16.	J. Luckman, Cinn., O.	1.00	209.65
			$217.65

RECAPITULATION.

UNITED STATES.

Maine	$21,043.47	Illinois	$66,527.18
New Hampshire	22,727.15	Kentucky	27,769.20
Vermont	5,789.43	Tennessee	23,856.70
Massachusetts	629,672.41	Michigan	38,414.64
Rhode Island	59,507.33	Wisconsin	422.90
Connecticut	107,183.92	Minnesota	24,417.90
New York	1,358,451.50	Iowa	17,648.60
New Jersey	158,397.75	Missouri	67,504.25
Pennsylvania	482,976.72	Arkansas	2,725.85
Delaware	8,070.70	Kansas	21,231.85
Maryland	182,122.30	Nebraska	17,470.32
Virginia	11,362.66	Colorado Territory	12,835.85
West Virginia	15,596.40	Nevada Territory	1,505.83
District of Columbia	94,470.48	California	168,512.43
North Carolina	115.00	Oregon	13,883.52
South Carolina	1,117.55	Dacotah Territory	90.00
Georgia	2,065.75	Washington Territory	1,509.83
Florida	1,049.23	Utah Territory	15,381.11
Alabama	5.00	Wyoming Territory	800.00
Mississippi	65.00	New Mexico	1,495.50
Louisiana	28,933.96	Miscellaneous	561.56
Texas	8,110.11		
Ohio	75,882.25	Total, United States	$3,846,032.71
Indiana	46,751.62		

FOREIGN.

Canada	$153,462.78	England	$435,023.18
Nova Scotia	6,707.63	Wales	3,163.46
Newfoundland	1,090.00	Ireland	74,161.36
New Brunswick	9,411.64	Scotland	75,315.62
British Columbia	640.70	France	62,782.80
Island of Cuba	16,393.37	Belgium	131.00
Mexico	2,272.25	Holland	241.35
Central America	402.25	Germany	81,393.29
Venezuela	295.63	Austria	3,801.50
Brazil	10,677.21	Switzerland	15,740.95
Argentine Republic	868.45	Russia	145.91
Uruguay	1,441.05	Italy	847.71
Peru	10,311.41	Portugal	317.28
Sandwich Islands	1,635.00		
China	2,897.70	Total, Foreign	$973,897.80
India	2,325.32		

Total, United States	$3,846,032.71
Total, Foreign	973,897.80
Addenda	217.65
Total Sum	$4,820,148.16

FINANCIAL STATEMENT.

FROM OCTOBER 15, 1871, TO APRIL 30, 1874.

Total amount, foregoing donations, ...		$4,820,148.16
Amount collected from Banks for interest on deposits, . .		126,634.58
Amount of Mr. A. T. Stewart's donation to be specially expended,		50,000.00
		$4,996,782.74
Amounts expended:—		
Paid orders of and returned to donors .	41,590.60	
by Shelter Committee in erection of houses, barracks, and for furniture, .	919,680.89	
by Hospital Committee for care of sick and infirm	74,358.18	
by Bureau of Special Relief . . .	376,346.97	
for the "A. T. Stewart" special relief .	50,000.00	
in cash distributions	478,902.44	
for purchases of supplies . . .	1,171,564.42	
for fuel distributed	303,897.71	
for rents of various premises occupied by the Society	21,116.33	
for office furniture	5,587.34	
for printing and stationery . . .	21,893.27	
for expenses (pay rolls, insurance, transportation, postages, etc.) . . .	490,222.67	
for night lodging-houses, and for erection of a small-pox hospital . . .	3,706.18	
paid to sundry charitable institutions on account of appropriations . . .	456,587.08	
		$4,415,454.08
Balançe		$581,328.66

CHICAGO, 1*st May*, 1874.

In regard to the fund in hand, the Society wish to say that with prudent management they believe it will be found sufficient to complete engagements already entered into with different charitable Institutions, and to provide for those who are thrown as a permanent burden upon the Society as the direct result of the fire.

www.ingramcontent.com/pod-product-compliance
Lightning Source LLC
LaVergne TN
LVHW021129110826
845150LV00005B/971

* 9 7 8 1 4 2 5 5 5 0 6 0 8 *